2604

MORALITY'S PROGRESS

MORALITY'S PROGRESS

Essays on Humans,
Other Animals,
and the Rest of Nature

DALE JAMIESON

CLARENDON PRESS · OXFORD

OXFORD
UNIVERSITY PRESS

Great Clarendon Street, Oxford OX2 6DP

Oxford University Press is a department of the University of Oxford.
It furthers the University's objective of excellence in research, scholarship,
and education by publishing worldwide in

Oxford New York

Auckland Bangkok Buenos Aires Cape Town Chennai
Dar es Salaam Delhi Hong Kong Istanbul Karachi Kolkata
Kuala Lumpur Madrid Melbourne Mexico City Mumbai Nairobi
São Paulo Shanghai Taipei Tokyo Toronto

Oxford is a registered trade mark of Oxford University Press
in the UK and in certain other countries

Published in the United States
by Oxford University Press Inc., New York

British Library Cataloguing in Publication Data

Data available

Library of Congress Cataloging in Publication Data
Jamieson, Dale.
Morality's progress : essays on humans, other animals, and the rest of
nature / Dale Jamieson.
p. cm.
Includes bibliographical references and index.
1. Animal welfare—Moral and ethical aspects. 2. Human-animal relationships
—Moral and ethical aspects. 3. Environmental ethics. I. Title.
HV4711 .J36 2002   179'.3—dc21   2002070220

ISBN 0–19–925144–4 (hbk.: alk. paper)
ISBN 0–19–925145–2 (pbk.: alk. paper)

1 3 5 7 9 10 8 6 4 2

Typeset by SNP Best-set Typesetter Ltd., Hong Kong
Printed in Great Britain
on acid-free paper by
Biddles Ltd.,
Guildford & Kings Lynn

*In memory
of my father
Dale Walter Jamieson*

*and
for my mother
Betty Jo Jamieson*

PREFACE

This volume is a selection of the essays on animals and nature that I have written over the past twenty-five years. In the largest sense, I think of this book as an attempt to draw out the moral consequences of a thoroughgoing Darwinian Naturalism. Broadly speaking, the perspective that informs this work is philosophically naturalist, morally consequentialist, and metaethically constructivist. While some may find these commitments controversial, I find them virtually irresistible when seriously thinking through the issues I address here. Despite the influence of these commitments on my work, they are not systematically articulated and defended in this book. As my teacher Paul Ziff used to say, "sufficient to the day are the problems thereof", and many of the problems I discuss here are as difficult as any in philosophy. If this book does nothing else, I hope it convinces some sceptical readers that thinking about our moral relations to animals and nature is every bit as intellectually challenging as analysing theories of reference or contemplating nuclear strategy. In light of the difficulty and under-researched nature of the problems I address, this work should be regarded not as a final statement, but as an initial attempt to assess the progress that has been made and to reach some tentative conclusions.

In rereading these essays I have been struck by how consistent in tone, temperament, and substance my work has been over an extended period of time. The papers collected here tell a more or less unified story about various aspects of the morality of our relationships to animals and nature. The volume begins by addressing the possibility of moral progress and the value of practical ethics. It then moves on to discuss the nature of animal minds and our moral duties with respect to animals. It concludes with essays that address larger environmental questions. I have only included essays that are mutually reinforcing and, in my opinion, still contribute to ongoing discussions. I have excluded minor or redundant pieces on animals and nature, as well as most of my work on other topics, including the foundations of ethics and global environmental change. I hope to publish systematic treatments of these topics in the future.

Most of the pieces collected here were written as responses to particular events, invitations, or provocations. A few have been multiply anthologized, but many have appeared in rather obscure places. Almost no one will have read all of them. Of the twenty-two papers collected here, all but the title essay have previously been published or are in press. Despite the generally unified perspective that informs these essays, there are inconsistencies in tone, substance, and style. I have not tried to resolve these inconsistencies, nor bring all the thoughts expressed into alignment with my current views. The revisions that I have made have been guided by the concern to make this book easier to use and more approachable by a wider audience. Generally I have resisted the temptation to make myself appear wiser or nicer than I was when I wrote the original papers. If I said something then that was ignorant or insensitive, I have generally let it stand—not because I endorse such beliefs and attitudes now, but because they reflect my sensibility and thought as it was then. This is, after all, a book about progress.

The notes to particular chapters acknowledge many debts. While this goes some way towards revealing how much I owe to various people, it understates how much I have been helped by so many. While I cannot provide a full accounting here, there are some people and institutions whose help I would especially like to acknowledge.

First things first. This book owes its existence to Peter Momtchiloff, who first suggested such a volume many years ago, and whose gentle intervention improved the book at every stage; it is hard to imagine a better or more supportive editor. I am also grateful to Rebecca Bryant, Rupert Cousens, Hilary Walford, and Virginia Williams for guiding the book through the press, and to my research assistant, Katie Renshaw, for creating the index.

I would like to thank three institutions, extraordinary in their generosity and in the degree to which they support intellectual curiosity: Carleton College, which has been supportive of my endeavours in ways both professionally essential and profoundly personal; the Henry R. Luce Foundation which funds my professorship at Carleton, and is one of the few institutions that provides long-term support for scholars whose intellectual passions sometimes lead them to transgress disciplinary boundaries; and the University Center for Human Values at Princeton University, which supported this project in its final stages.

I owe an enormous amount to Tom Regan and Marc Bekoff, who co-authored some of the essays included here. Tom and I were colleagues at North Carolina State University from 1975 to 1978, and our non-stop conversations during those years contributed greatly to my philosophical development. I especially admire Tom for his courage in pioneering unfashionable topics and defending unpopular views in a thorough and careful way, in a philosophical environment that was often, at best, unsupportive. Before meeting Marc in the mid-1980s I had an amateur's interest in, and knowledge of, animal behaviour, ecology, and evolutionary theory. After working with Marc for nearly twenty years I'm still an amateur in these fields, but now I know where to go to for expert opinions. The depth of Marc's learning is exceeded only by his energy and enthusiasm; his encouragement over the years has been vital to my work.

On the cover of this book is a photograph taken by Pavo Urban, a native of Dubrovnik, who was studying film and photography in Zagreb when the Serbs attacked his native city. He hurried home to document these events. The haze that partially obscures the ancient buildings is from exploding shells, one of which killed the photographer. Pavo Urban died on 6 December 1991, at the age of 23, only seconds after taking this picture. Fifteen months before I had been in Dubrovnik, on the invitation of Onora O'Neill, to take part in an institute on the "Survival of the Planet: Human Needs and Human Communication". As the institute unfolded, I developed a great deal of affection for the old city. I also forged close bonds with my colleagues, a small group of scholars, mostly from Eastern Europe and the Soviet Union, who were bravely working to realize the possibilities that were opening up with the collapse of communism and the end of Reaganism. When I look at this photograph it reminds me of the opportunities that have been squandered and the hopes that have been dashed; but the bravery and optimism of the young man who took this picture is also inspiring. Giving one's life to document an act of barbarism expresses enormous faith in the future.

This book is dedicated to my parents, Dale and Betty Jo Jamieson, whose financial and emotional sacrifices made my education possible. For their generosity I will always be grateful. Their love and devotion have enabled me to live a much more privileged life than was ever possible for them; I can only hope that I have made good use of these advantages.

Finally over the twenty-five years in which these essays were written, many friends were the source of joy and affection in my life. While I cannot thank them all by name, I would like to express my gratitude to Béatrice Longueness for her love and companionship while this project was being brought to completion.

Dale Jamieson

San Diego, California
New Year's Day, 2002

CONTENTS

ACKNOWLEDGEMENTS

"Is Applied Ethics Worth Doing?", in D. Rosenthal and F. Shehadi (eds.), *Applied Ethics and Ethical Theory* (Salt Lake City: University of Utah Press, 1988): 116–38.

"Great Apes and the Human Resistance to Equality", in P. Cavalieri and P. Singer (eds.), *The Great Ape Project* (London: Fourth Estate, 1993): 223–7.

"Science, Knowledge, and Animal Minds", *Proceedings of the Aristotelian Society*, 98 (1998): 79–102.

"On Aims and Methods of Cognitive Ethology", in M. Forbes, D. Hull, and K. Okruhlik (eds.), *PSA, 2* (Lansing, Mich.: Philosophy of Science Association, 1994): 110–24.

"Cognitive Ethology at the End of Neuroscience", forthcoming in C. Allen, M. Bekoff, and G. Burghardt, *The Cognitive Animal* (Cambridge, Mass.: The MIT Press).

"Pain and the Evolution of Behaviour", *Vlaams Diergeneeskundig Tijdschrift*, 70 (2001): 22–4.

"On the Ethics of the Use of Animals in Science", in T. Regan and D. VanDeVeer (eds.), *and Justice For All: New Introductory Essays in Ethics and Public Policy* (Totowa, NJ: Rowman and Littlefield, 1982): 169–96.

"Experimenting on Animals: A Reconsideration", *Between the Species*, 1 (summer 1985): 4–11.

"Ethics and the Study of Animal Cognition", in M. Bekoff and D. Jamieson (eds.), *Readings in Animal Cognition* (Cambridge, Mass.: The MIT Press, 1996): 359–71.

"Against Zoos", in Peter Singer (ed.) *In Defence of Animals* (Oxford: Basil Blackwell, 1985): 108–17.

"Zoos Revisited", in B. Norton, M. Hutchins, E. Stevens, and T. Mapel (eds.), *Ethics on the Ark: Zoos, Animal Welfare, and Wildlife Conservation* (Washington: Smithsonian Institution Press, 1995): 52–66.

"Wild/Captive and Other Suspect Dualisms", in Andrew N. Rowan (ed.), *Wildlife Conservation, Zoos and Animal Protection: A Strategic Analysis*, a workshop held at the White Oak Conservation Center, Yulee, Florida, April 21–24, 1994 (Grafton, Mass.: Tufts Center for Animals and Public Policy, 1995): 31–8.

"Animal Liberation is an Environmental Ethic", *Environmental Values*, 7/1 (1998): 41–57.

"Ecosystem Health: Some Preventive Medicine", *Environmental Values*, 4 (1995): 333–44.

"Values in Nature", forthcoming in C. Wellman and R. Frey, *Companion to Applied Ethics* (Oxford: Blackwell Publishers).

"The City around Us", in T. Regan (ed.), *Earthbound: New Introductory Essays in Environmental Ethics* (New York: Random House, 1984): 38–73.

"Ethics, Public Policy, and Global Warming", *Science, Technology, and Human Values*, 17/2 (spring 1992): 139–53.

"Global Environmental Justice", in R. Attfield and A. Belsey (eds.), *Philosophy and the Natural Environment* (Cambridge: Cambridge University Press, 1994): 199–210.

"Discourse and Moral Responsibility in Biotechnical Communication" (with addendum), *Politeia*, 15/54 (1999): 29–37; *Science and Engineering Ethics* 6/2 (2000): 285–7.

"Sustainability and Beyond", *Ecological Economics*, 24 (1998): 183–92.

"Child of the Sixties", published as "Figlio degli anni Sessanta", in the Italian journal, *Etica and Animali*, 2 (autunno 1989): 99–103.

Morality's Progress

Recently I attended a family reunion. The site was a park near the homestead that had been farmed by my great grandfather, August ("Augie") Kienast, who in 1872 had immigrated to the United States from a village near what was then Königsberg in East Prussia, and is now Kaliningrad in Russia. After lumberjacking in Michigan and travelling throughout the West, Augie settled in an isolated immigrant farming community near Atlantic, Iowa. This community was defined by its pietistic Protestantism, and was intensely loyal to German language and culture. German remained the language of the community until the 1950s, even for public education, despite periodic attempts to suppress it.

I attended the reunion with my mother, the daughter of an Irish Catholic and the granddaughter of Margaret Ryan, about whom it is said that she could not utter the word 'Protestant' without prefixing the phrase, 'Goddamned', which she was said to have meant literally. Many in Augie's community probably would have returned the compliment. By 1947 these sentiments had subsided sufficiently so that when my parents married, although their religious differences mattered (my mother converted to Lutheranism), they did not engender serious conflict. Now, surrounded by several generations of Augie's progeny, I could not help but reflect on how much more accepting of religious differences Americans had become. Intermarriage between Catholics and Protestants, which would have been intolerable to many of Augie's contemporaries, barely raises an eyebrow, much less an objection, among his descendants. As I watched several generations of Kienasts playing with the newest member of the family, Bradley, an African-American child adopted by one of my cousins, I wondered whether the contemporary American obsession with racial differences will come to be viewed as dangerously atavistic as a fixation on religious differences appears to us now. From the perspective of the Kienast family reunion anyway, moral progress seems palpable.

From another perspective, however, it is easy to be sceptical. In the twentieth century more people died in wars, famines, and preventable disasters than in the rest of history combined.[1] For the first time we have developed technology that allows us to threaten the very existence of our own species as well as much of the rest of the biosphere. Even today, religious differences are implicated in mass killings and atrocities, as the attack on the World Trade Center made vivid to many Americans. While there is a rising tide of concern about human rights, the treatment of animals, and the state of the environment, this may simply reflect the hope for something better rather than marking real progress towards achieving it.

And yet, I cannot help but believe in moral progress. Without such a possibility, what would be the point of doing moral philosophy? I began my career as a philosopher of language, but emigrated to moral philosophy in part because I wanted to make a difference in the world. How cruel it would be to discover, a quarter of a century later, that I might as well have continued the battle against possible world semantics as devoting myself to protecting the interests of animals and nature.

When reflection leads to such dark thoughts it is usually helpful to make distinctions. A number of different questions arise in thinking about moral progress. The question of its possibility is different from the question of its actuality, and some account of its meaning is prior to asking either question.

Let us begin with a simple, abstract account of what moral progress consists in. This account is rough, but refinements can be introduced as needed. Call this simple account, the Naïve Conception:

> Moral progress occurs when a subsequent state of affairs is better than a preceding one, or when right acts become increasingly prevalent.[2]

While it might be admitted that this account would be acceptable to a broad range of philosophers, it might be thought that it is more congenial to some normative views than to others. Consequentialists, for example, will be comfortable with the idea that states of affairs can be ordered according to their goodness, and many deontologists will be satisfied by an account of

---

[1] But see Keeley (1996) for an argument that the casualty rates of twentieth-century wars were generally lower than in wars fought by non-state societies.

[2] A cautionary note: the Naïve Conception does not imply that claims about moral progress require a complete ordering of states of affairs within a universe of discourse; a partial ordering can be sufficient. For example, we may know that A is better than B, but be clueless about C's relation to either A or B, yet we could claim that moral progress had occurred in the transition from B to A.

moral progress in terms of the prevalence of right acts.[3] But what about Kantians and virtue theorists? Their favoured objects of evaluation—the will and agents, respectively—do not directly figure in the Naïve Conception.[4]

Virtue theory can, I think, be accommodated by the Naïve Conception. This would involve seeing moral progress as consisting in the moral improvement of humanity, and information about the prevalence of right acts at particular times as proxy for how this project of improvement is faring. Another approach would be to count the occurrence of various virtues as part of what gives value to a state of affairs.

Kant's writings on moral progress are extremely rich but sometimes sketchy, often obscure, and deeply entangled with various parts of his systematic philosophy. In his philosophy of religion Kant is concerned with individual moral progress, especially as it is viewed in the eyes of God. For Kant, this concern is closely connected to the question of immortality. In his writings on philosophy of history, Kant is concerned with the moral progress of societies and nations. Here his focus is much more political and empirical than in his philosophy of religion. In such writings as "Perpetual Peace" he makes concrete proposals for improving the human condition that are very much in the spirit of the contemporary human rights movement. Kant was explicit that moral progress in this sense did not necessarily constitute moral progress in the deeper sense of moral worthiness, explicated in his moral philosophy. In addressing the question of "what profit will progress toward the better yield humanity?", he wrote:

Not an ever-growing quantity of morality with regard to intention, but an increase of the products of legality in dutiful actions whatever their motive. That is, the profit (result) of man's striving toward the better can be assumed to reside alone in the good deeds of men, which will become better and better and more and more numerous . . . we have only empirical data (experiences) upon which we are founding this prediction, namely, the physical cause of our actions as these actually occur as phenomena; and not the moral cause—the only one which can be established purely a priori—which contains the concept of duty with respect to what ought to happen.[5]

Since our focus here is on "the good deeds of men" rather than on Kant's deeper notion of moral worthiness, so long as we recognize that this does not exhaust Kant's view of our duties, we can assimilate his views to the Naïve

---

[3] For introductions to Consequentialism, see Pettit (1991) and Jamieson (forthcoming a); for deontology, see Davis (1991).

[4] For an introduction to Kantian ethics see O'Neill (1991); for virtue theory see Pence (1991).

[5] Kant (1798/1963: 151).

Conception by treating him as a kind of deontologist who holds that moral progress occurs when right acts become more prevalent.[6]

In the end it seems to me that the Naïve Conception can provide a notion of moral progress consistent with most normative views in moral philosophy. However, another challenge can be raised. It might be suggested that the Naïve Conception is more at home with some metaethical views than with others.[7] Moral realism, for example, would seem to provide a natural explanation for how states of affairs can be ranked according to their goodness.[8] On this view, the point of moral language is to correspond to the moral order, and the role of moral action is to exemplify or conform to it. Moral progress is assessed on the basis of how adequately our moral thought and action reflect this objective order in temporally successive stages. Alternative metaethical views, which may be plausible in their own right, may turn out to be implausible when conjoined with the Naïve Conception; and this, it might be thought, counts against the Naïve Conception rather than against these alternative views.

Moral realism might be contrasted with a view that sees morality as a human construction grounded in evolutionary history.[9] On such a view morality is a behavioural system, with an attendant psychology, that has evolved among some social animals for the purposes of regulating their interactions. From this perspective moral progress might be thought to consist in better-regulated social interactions. But what does it mean for social interactions to be better regulated? It might be thought that on an evolutionary account moral thought and action would ultimately have to answer to the primary currency of evolutionary theory: biological fitness.[10] From here it may seem a short step to the view that moral progress would consist in a behavioural system becoming ever more conducive to promoting the biological fitness of those who participate in it.

The Naïve Conception is a nice instrument for contrasting these two views of moral progress. According to the Naïve Conception, moral progress occurs when a subsequent state of affairs is better than the preceding one. Moral

---

[6] See Herman (1993, ch. 10) for some reminders that Kant is not, in the deepest sense, a deontologist.

[7] "Metaethics is concerned with the status and nature of the ethical claims we make" (O'Neill 2001: 163).

[8] See Essay 16 for further discussion of moral realism. For an introduction to the topic, see Smith (1991).

[9] See Essays 14–16; and also Singer (1981), Gibbard (1990), and Nozick (2001).

[10] A fairly standard definition of 'fitness' can be found in Mayr (1991: 189): "[t]he relative ability of an organism to survive and transmit its genes to the gene pool of the next generation" (some would omit the words 'survive and').

realism understands 'better than' as something like 'more adequately reflects moral reality', while the evolutionary view understands 'better than' as something like 'is more conducive to biological fitness'.

Moral realism is rejected by many philosophers because of the thought that it must rely on either supernatural or "queer" properties in order to explain why we are motivated to pursue the good. Normally, objective properties such as length, and perhaps color and taste,[11] are not intrinsically motivating; whether or not we seek to realize them depends on our desires. Yet we do seem intrinsically motivated to seek what we regard as good. Perhaps goodness is "queer" among properties in being both objective and intrinsically motivating; or perhaps we are motivated to seek goodness because doing so has some external warrant (e.g. God requires it). But to many philosophers, the most plausible explanation for why we seek the good is that the idea of goodness is our own construction, and we only count as good what we are motivated to seek.[12] A further consideration that inclines some towards the evolutionary view is that any respectable theory will have to find some place for evolutionary considerations (even if only to push them aside), and evolutionary accounts of morality discharge this obligation in a big way.[13]

While the evolutionary conception of morality may appear plausible in other respects, it is doubtful that our intuitive idea of moral progress can be understood in terms of promoting biological fitness. Whatever exactly moral progress consists in, it is plausible (for reasons I will explain later) to suppose that it involves at least the following: the abolition of war and slavery, the reduction of poverty and class privilege, the extension of liberty, the empowerment of marginalized groups, and respect for animals and nature. But there is no reason to believe that a society that is morally progressive in these terms is on the way to greater biological fitness of its members than one that is not. Nor is it plausible to suppose that a society whose members' genes are better represented in the next generation is one that we would regard as morally progressive (it may be, for example, a society that is characterized by a high incidence of rape).

The problem appears to be this. Moral realism may respect our intuitions about moral progress but it violates our metaphysical sensibilities. The

---

[11] There is a debate about just how objective "secondary" properties such as colour and taste really are. For an introduction to the literature, see Byrne and Hilbert (1997).

[12] This argument roughly follows Mackie (1977). Of course, not everyone is persuaded. For an introduction to the literature, see McCord (1988).

[13] There are interesting ways of trying to link evolutionary epistemology to realism, but the practical nature of our assessments of value appears to present a special obstacle to providing such an account for the moral domain.

evolutionary perspective, on the other hand, provides metaphysical comfort but at the cost of our views about moral progress. How do we get out of this jam?

One approach would be to find some additional room within the idea that morality is directed towards producing organisms that are biologically fit. Perhaps there are multiple paths to fitness, each of which encompasses a different morality. Moral progress would consist in moving towards adopting that morality whose substantive values are best. Being conducive to biological fitness would, on this view, be a constraint on acceptable moralities, but would not uniquely identify the one we should adopt.

I don't think that such a strategy can ultimately succeed. The most plausible way of reconciling the evolutionary account of morality with the intuitive idea of moral progress is not to look for space that the technical notion of biological fitness might make available, but rather to interpret more flexibly the evolutionary account of morality.

In my characterization of the evolutionary account of morality, I slipped into describing it as another version of realism. In this case the objective reality which morality is supposed to mirror is that expressed by evolutionary biology, with the ultimate value being evolutionary fitness. But to reject realism is to reject altogether the idea that the function of morality is to mirror an external reality, and that progress is to be assessed by its success in so mirroring. In so far as the evolutionary story provides an alternative to the first conception, it must provide the makings of an account in which morality is autonomous, not a shadow of something external to itself. This requires a different understanding of the evolutionary account than the one expressed earlier.

We can begin to formulate this different understanding by distinguishing the project of explaining a phenomenon from characterizing its content, and both of these from the project of justification. The evolutionary account should be understood as explaining why morality evolved and persists among creatures like us, but it should not be construed as providing a characterization of the content of morality. The explanation of why morality exists will surely refer to biological fitness, but, once called into existence, morality has the power to issue its own imperatives. This is because the twin motors of morality, reason and sentiment, each has the power to be the source of moral prescriptions and to project our concern beyond ourselves. Both embody, in different ways, impulses towards ever greater abstraction and impartiality.

Peter Singer (1981) emphasizes the role of reason in ethics. He suggests that reason evolved and has been sustained in creatures like us because of the advantages it confers in finding food and avoiding danger. But once a creature begins to reason, the results are unpredictable. "Beginning to reason is like stepping onto an escalator that leads upward and out of sight. Once we take the first step, the distance to be traveled is independent of our will and we cannot know in advance where we shall end."[14] The reasoner may adopt new beliefs when they come to be seen as consequences of beliefs already held, or give up familiar beliefs that come to be viewed as resting on shaky grounds. The demands for coherence, consistency, and the other features characteristic of reason can take the reasoner to surprising and unanticipated destinations.

According to Singer, morality develops because of the role that reason plays in our social lives. "In a dispute between members of a cohesive group of reasoning beings, the demand for a reason is a demand for a justification that can be accepted by the group as a whole."[15] Once we begin to respond to the demand for impersonal justifications of our behaviour, this can lead to moral change. This is exactly what Singer thinks has occurred from the time of the Hebrews and Greeks to the present. "The idea of a disinterested defense of one's conduct emerges because of the social nature of human beings and the requirements of group living, but in the thought of reasoning beings, it takes on a logic of its own which leads to its extensions beyond the bounds of the group."[16] The result is an expanding circle of moral concern that progressively broadens "from the family and tribe to the nation and race, and we are beginning to recognize that our obligations extend to all human beings".[17] Eventually, Singer believes, this mechanism leads to encompassing all sentient beings in the circle of moral concern.[18]

However we should be cautious about what conclusions we draw from these observations. If what I have said is correct, then the evolutionary view of morality does not exclude the possibility of moral progress but neither does it ensure it. To suppose otherwise is to deny the autonomy of morality. In this case it would be to fall into the old trap of thinking that evolution itself is inevitably progressive, taking life from the simpler and less valuable, to the

[14] Singer (1981: 88).

[15] Singer (1981: 93). The idea that the demand for reasons is a demand for a justification that can be accepted by others is surprisingly similar to Scanlon's (1982) formulation of contractualism. In that paper Scanlon cites other writings of Singer's, and suggests that utilitarians have no account of distinctively moral reasons, but he does not cite Singer (1981).

[16] Singer (1981: 114).

[17] Singer (1981: 120). Singer's story (told in 1975/2001) of the way reason brought him to his animal liberationist position is an instance of this narrative.

[18] A similar story, derived from Hume, can be told about what Baier (1991) calls "a progress of sentiments", and what Rorty (1993/1998) calls "sentimental education". See Essays 14 and 15.

grander and more complex.[19] Evolution may have brought morality into existence and established the parameters of what may constitute possible moralities for creatures like us, but the particular moral ideals that emerge can be quite various. Biology does not dictate the content of morality because morality is both an evolutionary phenomenon and a human construction. Even if "selfish" genes construct us in order to further their own "interests", once constructed, we often act in ways that are contrary to the "interests" of our genes.[20] Indeed, one moral ideal that I share with many environmentalists is voluntary childlessness (or that, at most, people should have only one child).[21] It seems clear that acting on this principle is to act against one's own biological fitness.[22]

It might be wondered how evolution could have produced creatures with such views, or why they would not be extinguished in favour of those whose moralities support the pursuit of their own biological fitness. The obvious point to make first is that it is one thing to espouse a principle and it is another to act upon it; some of the most militant members of such groups as Zero Population Growth stand condemned by their own principles. Still, it is true that many people not only espouse fitness-denying moralities but act upon them as well. How is this possible?

Particular moralities are largely cultural phenomena subserved by various capacities and dispositions, which are themselves complex products of development and genetics. Morality has its own imperatives, in part, because it is constructed from multi-purpose devices that play various other roles in our lives. Flack and de Waal (2000) identify the capacities for empathy and sympathy, and behaviours such as reciprocity, food-sharing, reconciliation, consolation, conflict intervention, and mediation as some of the building blocks of morality. Even without full-blown moralities, there is reason for such capacities and behaviours to evolve and persist.

While this may go some way towards explaining how the evolution of morality may be possible, it does not explain how fitness-denying moralities

---

[19] See Ruse (1991) for discussion of this fallacy.

[20] The idea of the "selfish gene" was popularized by Dawkins (1976/1989). I place 'selfish' and 'interests' in scare quotes because it is a *façon de parler* at best to suppose that genes have interests and are selfish. For discussion, see Singer (1981: 126–33).

[21] For a defence of this principle see McKibben (1998).

[22] There are cases, some of which are predicted by Hamilton's (1964) theory of inclusive fitness, in which reducing fertility can increase biological fitness. Among humans this can occur when it enables parents to invest more heavily in fewer offspring, increasing the chances of each successfully reproducing, thus increasing the overall likelihood that the parents' genes will be represented in future generations. Despite these cases, it is clear that many instances of voluntary fertility reduction diminish agents' biological fitness.

can persist. While the answer to this question is not fully settled, a picture is beginning to come into focus. The key, as Darwin understood, is group selection. This picture was largely obscured for much of the last generation by a single-minded focus on the gene as the unit of selection, and the relative neglect of development, culture, and the importance of both the physical and social environments.[23]

Let us call those who sometimes act in such a way as to increase the fitness of others while decreasing their own fitness, "altruists", and those who always act so as to increase their own fitness, "the selfish". While it is true that altruists do badly in communities dominated by the selfish, they will often do better in altruistic communities than the selfish will do in selfish communities. But since selfish individuals in altruistic communities will do best of all, community policing (of which morality is a part) and recruitment of altruistic individuals (the expanding circle) become vitally important if the benefits of group selection are to be realized. How and whether any of this works in practice is highly sensitive to specific traits and features of the environment, but generally we can say this: autonomous moralities evolve and survive because they may, under some conditions, confer fitness advantages; and their complexity in construction, inter-group and intra-group relationships makes it difficult to eliminate them.

A great deal more would have to be said to develop this picture, but if it is at all plausible in conception, then we can see how autonomous moralities could evolve and persist. It is thus open to us to endorse an evolutionary understanding of morality and still hold out the possibility of moral progress understood in the way that I have suggested: as involving the abolition of war and slavery, the reduction of poverty and class privilege, the extension of liberty, the empowerment of marginalized groups, and respect for animals and nature.

This, however, invites the next challenge. It is one thing to say that an evolutionary account of morality does not exclude this conception of moral progress, but it is another to say that this is the account that we should accept. Why should we think that moral progress can be assessed in the terms that I suggest?

One audacious idea is that moral progress consists in the increasing dominance of objective, impersonal, or agent-neutral reasons for action over subjective, personal, or agent-relative reasons.[24] Seen from this perspective, the

---

[23] There are many researchers responsible for developing the picture that I sketch below, but see especially Sober and Wilson (1998) and Boehm (1999).

[24] There is a point to distinguishing between the terms on each side of the contrast but for present purposes we can be fairly relaxed in our usage without causing much trouble.

values that appear on my index of moral progress are landmarks on the road to objectivity, since they demand a relatively large universe of moral concern (including, e.g., animals and nature) and specify a relatively high degree of other-regarding behaviour (e.g. the reduction of poverty and class privilege, and the empowerment of marginalized groups). This accords nicely with Singer's view of reason as an escalator that leads one to expand the circle of moral concern. From this perspective moral progress involves moving from a tribal morality, for example, to a more universal one, and this can be seen as a move towards greater objectivity, impersonality, and so forth. On such a view moral progress would come to an end only with the complete conquest of personal reasons by impersonal ones.[25]

Many, however, would resist this conclusion because they see impersonal morality as desiccated, lacking the substantive commitments and values that make life worth living. Thomas Nagel (1986: 186) goes further when he writes that "[o]bjectivity needs subjective material to work on" and there is a limit on "[h]ow far outside ourselves we can go without losing contact with this essential material". Yet Nagel generally sees moral progress as moving away from personal concerns, towards greater objectivity and impersonality. He appears to think that the moralities that have historically prevailed have given too much privilege to the personal point of view, but that the best morality would be one that "harmonizes" these perspectives.[26] Demonstrating this would require showing that, at each point along some region of a continuum, the impersonal point of view should prevail, but that at some point we would enter another region in which the impersonal point of view should no longer win. Having given so much credence to the impersonal point of view, it would be difficult to show convincingly why its power should flag at any particular point.[27]

It seems clear that a fully impersonal perspective would endorse values that are at least as universal and demanding as those that appear on my index. However, various other moral perspectives could also endorse this index. In

---

[25] Perhaps this is analogous to the idea that science will come to an end with the completion of the true picture of the universe. See Horgan (1996).

[26] The metaphor of harmony is different from the metaphor of balance. While balancing might involve one perspective outweighing another, harmonizing occurs when "the claims of objectivity . . . come to form a . . . part of each individual's conception of himself" (1986: 187).

[27] One argument for why morality can never be completely impersonal would appeal to the evolutionary conditions required for the survival of morality. If what I suggested earlier is correct, then morality survives because of group selection. Group selection requires distinctions between groups, and a completely impersonal morality would effectively efface these distinctions, thus leading to the extinction of morality.

order to see this, it would be helpful to consider what it means to be an index of moral progress, and this requires elaborating the idea of a theory of value, which in turn requires some filling out of the notion of a normative theory.

A plausible normative theory includes both a value theory and a set of deontic principles.[28] The value theory specifies what matters, and the deontic principles determine how we should act in choice situations in which various alternatives would have different effects on the prevalence or distribution of what matters.[29] A value theory can be represented as an abstract structure that specifies a set of fundamental values that, when conjoined with propositions about particular people, societies, and so forth, implies a nested hierarchy of less fundamental values. I will call more fundamental values "deep values", and less fundamental values "shallow values". Values can stand in relations of "deeper" and "shallower" with respect to each other.[30]

An index can be related to a particular value theory in a number of different ways. The items on an index could directly specify deep values, or they could specify shallower values implied by deeper values in conjunction with other premises. Different items on an index could occur at different levels in a value theory. For example, a particular value theory might demand both the extension of liberty and the reduction of poverty, but find one of these values deeper than the other. Another value theory might reverse this relation. A theory could also fail to acknowledge an item as a value, yet treat it as a key indicator as to whether or not a particular value is expressed in some state of the world. For example, a theory may for its own reasons refuse to acknowledge the abolition of slavery as a value, instead taking it as an indicator of whether what is acknowledged as a value, say respect for persons, prevails in the world at a particular time. Some theories may refuse to acknowledge some of the items on the index at all. Other theories may include values that do not

---

[28] Thus I reject as plausible, normative theories such as absolute deontology which have no place for value theory, since they hold that morality consists entirely in conformity to exceptionless rules. For discussion, see Davis (1991).

[29] For those who think that the class of normative theories is a superset of the class of moral theories, it should be clear from the context that the normative theories I am concerned with here are moral theories. I refrain from saying this in the main body of the text since, on my view, a normative theory is only part of a moral theory. But these are pedantic points, not worth pursuing for present purposes. However, before abandoning pedantry, I want to add that prevalence and distribution may be only two of the relevant dimensions which distinguish actions in choice situations.

[30] While my rhetoric here may sound foundationalist I think that this way of representing a theory of value is consistent with alternative models, such as coherentist ones. I could just as well speak of "central" and "peripheral" values as deep and shallow ones, though it would be stylistically awkward to do so. For more on foundationalism in ethics, see Jamieson (1991a).

occur on the index. Since there is a great deal of variation in the ways in which the items in my index might be taken up in various theories of value, it is plausible to suppose that a wide range of value theories would find a place for the items on my index. This is just a fancy way of saying that it is hard to imagine a plausible theory of value that does not acknowledge the importance of abolishing war, slavery, reducing poverty, and so on. This is important because it explains why my proposed index could be endorsed by a wide range of those who have dramatically different views about the foundations of value (i.e. those who restrict it to desirable consciousness, preference-satisfaction, welfare, the realization of capacities, or some other feature(s)). Each theory could endorse the index, but see it (or some of its elements) as standing in different relations to what they regard as fundamental values. Understood in this way, from the perspective of different theories of value, improvement with respect to the index could be constitutive of, provide necessary or sufficient conditions for, or provide a strong criterion of, moral progress. Different theories could endorse this index, yet see it standing in different relations to moral progress.

Consider the first clause of the index: the abolition of war and slavery. Any theory that is committed to the importance of basic rights or goods, the presumption that people's preferences should be satisfied, or that asserts the importance of human happiness, ought to be willing to find a place for these aspirations somewhere in their value theory. The same is true of the items specified in the second clause of the index: the reduction of poverty and class privilege. The third clause focuses on the extension of liberty, a good that has been appealed to by virtually every moral and political theory. The fourth clause focuses on participatory values: empowering marginalized groups. Anyone who believes that participation matters, either in itself or as a means to realizing the goods specified in the other clauses, should be willing to accept these items as part of an index of moral progress. The fifth clause which concerns respect for animals and nature may be the most controversial because it challenges conventional views about the boundaries of the moral domain. This is not a reason to reject it, however, since the expansion of the moral domain has historically been one of the central features of what we count as moral progress.[31] The classical utilitarians are paradigm moral progressives because of their insistence on taking seriously the interests of all who are affected by an action or policy, not only the rich and powerful. This led them

---

[31] This view has been endorsed by such thinkers as Leopold (1949: 201–3), Singer (1981: 111–24), Rorty (1993/1998: 177 ff.), Nozick (2001: 278–80).

to advocate the rights of women, the abolition of slavery, and even to consider the rights of animals. I can't help but believe that the air of controversy that hangs over this fifth clause stems from the fact that many people (including most philosophers) have either dismissed these concerns with little thought, or ignored them altogether. One of the themes of this book is that someone who approaches these questions in an intellectually honest and morally serious way will see that strong cases have been made from a variety of moral perspectives for respecting animals and nature. And although it is sometimes suggested that we have to apportion our concern between humans on the one hand and animals on the other, a moment's reflection shows that accepting the value of animals and nature is quite consistent with endorsing the humanitarian values articulated in the first four clauses of my index. Indeed, a strong case could be made for the view that the five clauses of the index are mutually reinforcing.

I have argued that a wide variety of theorists would be able to endorse the elements of the index of moral progress that I have announced.[32] However, it is clear that the index would not be acceptable to everyone. It would be rejected by some who believe that moral values are constituted by religious values, and that moral progress consists in the spread of Christianity or Buddhism, or increasing fidelity to the Koran or Torah.[33] Others might loftily object that the index is ethnocentric. War, slavery, hierarchy, paternalism, and the domination of nature are central to the ways of life of various cultures around the world. Who am I to denounce them?

A full answer to this objection would be a large undertaking. I will confine myself to only two brief observations. First, most cultures are not simple, unbreakable units, whose participants are single-minded in their support of prevailing practices. Intra-cultural diversity is as ubiquitous among humans as inter-cultural diversity. Every slave culture has had its dissenters. There were abolitionists, anti-racists, and proletarian revolutionaries even among the soldiers who imposed European domination on the New World.[34] Secondly, the goods that appear on my index are both extremely important and general, and a variety of reasons for valuing them become manifest as soon as one begins to think impartially about them. Perhaps there is something

[32] Some theorists would accept this list and add some elements. Although the index can be characterized as broadly egalitarian, it is quite unspecific about various distributive concerns that are the sites of some of the most fractious differences among normative theorists. For an introduction to these disputes see Temkin (1993).

[33] For an amusing attack on this view see Blackburn (2001).

[34] For a fascinating discussion see Linebaugh and Rediker (2001).

ethnocentric about impartiality, but without taking up some such perspective it is difficult see how a serious moral charge of ethnocentrism could be mounted. From the perspective of a thoroughgoing relativism, my ethnocentric philosophizing should be seen as simply expressing the attitudes of my culture thus immune from universalist moral denunciation.[35]

In addition to those who would object to my index on these grounds, there are those within the Western philosophical tradition who would reject it as well; for example, a certain kind of Perfectionist. Perfectionism can be characterized as the moral view that directs us to "maximize the achievement of human excellence in art, science, and culture".[36] A perfectionist might take the heights of human intellectual and artistic achievement as the index of moral progress, rather than the concerns about war, poverty, and so on that appear on my index. Such a theorist might see morality regressing since the time of the Renaissance, while a hedonistic utilitarian who values the maximization of pleasure might see it as progressing.

There are different versions of perfectionism. Perfectionism has been an unpopular doctrine in recent philosophy in part because it has often been identified with what we might call brutal perfectionism. Brutal perfectionism is indifferent to suffering, or perhaps even attaches positive value to it.[37] From this perspective, increases or reductions in suffering would not bear on the question of moral progress, or would affect it paradoxically.[38] However, an alternative version of perfectionism, which we might call soft perfectionism, might be seen as more plausible. This theory could be viewed as simply advocating the inclusion of perfectionist values in the index of moral progress, along with the other items that I have identified.

While soft perfectionism is a tempting view, the realization of perfectionist values has historically often been in conflict with the more egalitarian values that are included on the index. It is simply not plausible to suppose that the heights of Greek civilization could have been achieved without such

---

[35] Cf. the discussion of the post-modern mullah in Jamieson (1991*b*).

[36] Rawls (1971: 325); see Hurka (1993) for a slightly different characterization of Perfectionism and for a recent discussion of this view.

[37] Although there is intense scholarly debate about how to interpret Nietzsche, he sometimes seems to embrace brutal perfectionism, for example, when he writes that "the wretchedness of struggling men must grow still greater in order to make possible the production of a world of art for a small number of Olympian men". For discussion of Nietzsche's views in this regard, and relevant citations, see Glover (1999/2000, ch. 2).

[38] By 'affecting paradoxically' I mean that contrary to what most of us believe, increases in suffering would indicate moral progress rather than regression.

hierarchical institutions as slavery.[39] The connection between the realization of perfectionist ideals and human exploitation is quite direct in the Baroque churches of Italy. Il Gesù, the mother church of the Jesuit order, is the most ornate church in Christendom with the exception of St Peter's, and an aesthetic marvel of the highest order. It is rumoured that much of the gold and silver with which Il Gesù is decorated was brought directly from the New World. Las Casas, the Dominican priest who travelled on some of the early Spanish missions of conquest, described his countrymen's methods of obtaining gold. "[The Spaniards] slew many Indians by hanging, burning, and being torn to pieces by savage dogs, also by cutting the hands and feet and heads and tongues, and for no other reason than to spread terror and induce the Indians to give them gold."[40] Other, equally horrifying, methods of extracting wealth were used as well. By the end of the sixteenth century, between 60 and 80 million native inhabitants of Spanish America had been killed, worked to death, or had died from introduced diseases.[41]

Despite the difficulties involved in soft perfectionism, the idea that moral progress consists in the marriage of egalitarian and perfectionist ideas is a powerful one, and indeed it is at the heart of the social vision of John Stuart Mill.[42] Mill, a self-proclaimed hedonistic utilitarian, thought that the realization of perfectionist values would be part of a pleasure-maximizing regime. This suggests that it is at least worth trying to take up perfectionist concerns within the range of theories that endorse my index of moral progress. A full discussion of how this might be done would take us too far afield, however. For present purposes, I will stick with my index in the hope that it succeeds in taking up perfectionist values where it is plausible to do so.

In the end I see no way to fully defend an index of moral progress short of defending the range of normative theories which find a place for the values it expresses. About all one can do in defending a normative theory, in my opinion, is to appeal to its intrinsic plausibility, and then demonstrate that it suffers from fewer and less severe infirmities and failures than alternative views. The late coach Vince Lombardi may have been right about football

---

[39] Or more strongly still, "Without slavery, no Greek state, no Greek art and science; without slavery, no Roman Empire. Without Hellenism and the Roman Empire at the base, also no modern Europe" (Engels, as quoted in Williams 1993: 171).

[40] Las Casas (1974: 78).

[41] Stannard (1992: 95). The demography of the Americas prior to European contact is a highly contested and politically charged subject. Stannard is not an extreme voice in the discussion, but even if his numbers are too high by an order of magnitude, they are still horrifying. For recent discussions of some of these issues see Krech III (1999) and Raudzens (2001).

[42] See Mill (1863/1993).

when he said that the best offence is a good defence, but the reverse is true when defending a particular normative point of view.

Judgements about moral progress are comparative judgements about the value of states of affairs or the prevalence of right actions, but not all such comparative judgements are judgements about moral progress. It would make little sense to compare Classical Athens and the Inca Empire with respect to moral progress. Claims about moral progress presuppose some significant relations between the states of affairs that are being compared. While I will not attempt to provide a full and specific account of the nature of these relations, at least this much is clear: there must be close causal, cultural, and temporal connections for the language of progress to take hold. State of affairs A may be better than state of affairs B, but if there is no causal connection between A and B, then the move from B to A cannot be said to constitute progress.[43] The states of affairs must also in some sense exist in a common cultural milieu in order for a judgement about moral progress to have traction. Even though there were causal relations between Europe and Africa there would be little point to making claims about moral progress (or the lack of it) on the basis of comparing sixteenth-century Lisbon with twentieth-century Maputo. Finally, even if we suppose that there is a common cultural tradition that runs from Athens to Washington, it still may not be possible to assess in a meaningful way whether or not moral progress has occurred from fourth-century BCE Athens to twentieth-century CE Washington. Here the problem is that there are too many distinct dimensions on which such a judgement might be made. States of affairs must be relevantly similar for judgements of progress to be meaningfully made about them.[44]

As Nelson Goodman (1970/1972) pointed out years ago, it is difficult to say anything of general interest about what constitutes relevant similarity. Indeed, a great deal of practical argument about moral progress turns on whether states of affairs are similar enough for judgements about moral progress to be meaningful. This similarity is not given to us by the formal features of what is being compared, but is deeply affected by our interests, and what we

[43] Nor will any old causal relation do, as I am grateful to Marsha Mason for reminding me. Suppose that all the same people exist at the same levels of happiness in state of affairs A and its consequent, state of affairs B, but that there is an additional slightly happy person who also exists in B. This would not be sufficient for supposing that the transition from A to B constitutes moral progress. The moral of the story is that we cannot simply breed our way to moral progress.

[44] One set of complications that I will not consider in detail concerns the temporal structure of states of affairs. Suppose, for example, that the world is getting very bad, very fast, but at one point it improves slightly, but that this improvement is a necessary condition for the world becoming so bad, so fast. I doubt that we would say that this brief bump up constitutes moral progress.

consider to be similar (or not), and this can shift from moment to moment. Consider again my claim about comparing sixteenth-century Lisbon with twentieth-century Maputo. If the comparisons are meant to apply specifically to the moralities that prevailed in these places, then they are without much point. But suppose that someone conceives of humanity as a single community. He is concerned about whether there has been moral progress from the sixteenth to the twentieth century. He focuses on Lisbon and Maputo, let us assume, only because they provide easily researchable samples of the human moral condition. He might just as well have focused on sixteenth-century Königsberg and twentieth-century Atlantic, Iowa. We might still think that his project is misconceived and call into question the idea of aggregating and comparing morality on a global basis, but this would no longer be a matter of committing the simple error of evaluating moral progress by comparing states of affairs from different cultural traditions. What would be in question now is whether or not there is a common cultural tradition that prevails over humanity. The same argument can occur at much smaller scales. Suppose that I notice that the incidence of murder was vastly greater in Kansas in 1930 than in Oklahoma in 1920, and from this infer that there had been a decline in morality in the American Great Plains, with respect to murder, anyway, during this period. It is still open to someone to argue against this claim on the grounds that Kansas and Oklahoma did not form a common community during that period.[45]

The upshot is that judgements about moral progress must, in some sense, be local. Often what will be worth comparing are particular practices within communities over time. Questions about moral progress are pragmatic. They do not come out of a vacuum. We want to know whether or not moral progress has occurred for specific reasons that serve particular purposes. This should not surprise us. In my opinion, many important judgements are local and contrastive despite philosophers' penchant for seeing them as universal and unconditioned.[46] The pragmatic and local nature of claims about moral progress also may help to put to rest a nagging suspicion that those who make

[45] But couldn't we say that morality had advanced to a higher level in fifth-century BCE Athens than in fifteenth-century Peru? Such general claims about comparative moral development escape some of the difficulties that attach to similar claims about moral progress, but also invite some new objections. While the idea of moral progress with respect to a dimension can be made reasonably clear, those who speak in metaphors of "higher" and "lower" moralities "advancing" and "receding" have got some explaining to do.

[46] In one of his movies Woody Allen complains that life seems meaningless since the Earth will someday fall into the sun. The humour arises from the character's failure to contextualize these facts. A lot of philosophy is funny in just this way.

such claims on behalf of themselves or their societies are arrogant because they imply that they are morally better than those who have come before. Putting aside complications involved in moving from claims about states of affairs and right actions to claims about agents, the most that could be said about such people is that they are claiming that they are better on some dimensions by their own lights than those who have come before. This is a suitably modest claim. The view that I am urging may disappoint those who lust for a grand narrative about moral progress, one that would sweep through time, space, and society, leaving a vision of clarified humanity in its wake. But of course, such grand narratives are themselves often the source of staggering amounts of human misery.[47]

Western societies have not always been centrally concerned with the idea of progress.[48] There is scholarly debate about whether the ancients and medievals had the idea of progress (as opposed to the idea of degeneration), and if so how influential it was, but there is a high level of consensus that this notion moved to centre stage with the work of such thinkers as Descartes, Fontenelle, Perrault, and St Pierre. Scholars typically date the centrality of the concern with progress to the late seventeenth or early eighteenth century.[49] Nisbet (1980: 171) writes that between 1750 and 1900 the idea of progress was "the dominant idea [in the West], even when one takes into account the rising importance of other ideas such as equality, social justice, and popular sovereignty". According to Brinton (1959/1990: 414), in the eighteenth and nineteenth centuries "most Westerners were confident that human beings everywhere were getting morally better as well as materially better off". The Reign of Terror in the last stages of the French Revolution may have led to some doubts, but these events were confined to a ten-month period and claimed only about 20,000 lives in a population of 22 million.[50] Brinton acknowledges that there was persistent underground opposition to the idea of progress from disgruntled intellectuals (e.g. Ruskin, Arnold, and Dostoevsky) who seemed to think that material progress necessarily implied moral decline. Still, it is reasonable to think of the period from the signing of the Declaration of the Rights of Man in 1789 to the outbreak of World War I in 1914, as

[47] See Glover (1999/2000, part 5). Of course, excessive "localism" is not itself without risk. What is wanted (as usual) is something "just right".

[48] In what follows I will limit my remarks to the idea of progress in Western societies. For some suggestive remarks about this notion in non-Western societies, see Tuan (1989).

[49] e.g. Bury (1920/1932), Brinton (1959/1990), Hildebrand (1949).

[50] The use of the word 'only' may seem callous but compare the death toll of the Terror with that of the Vietnam war which claimed about two million lives in a population of about fifty million.

the great age of belief in moral progress. This came to an end on Flanders' fields.

Still, the question of moral progress remains deep in the European psyche. At the dawn of a new century, the horrors that Europeans inflicted on each during the first half of the previous century seem like ancient history. Yet the intensity of the European horror of American callousness about inflicting death, both as a form of punishment and as an instrument of foreign policy, suggests the anxiety of suppressed recognition. This sense of guilty familiarity may also help to explain European compassion for the developing world compared to American indifference. The brutalities of colonial history were so extreme that in some cases they amounted to what has been described as a holocaust.[51] Without fully acknowledging their responsibility, many Europeans now express a sincere willingness to aid developing countries. Americans, without a colonial legacy of the same extent and explicitness, are more likely to view the developing world as completely irrelevant to their concerns, except when terrorists emerge to "attack freedom".[52] This attitude is dangerous for many reasons, not least because it feeds a tendency to say "a plague on both your houses" when confronted by wars and atrocities in the developing world.

The case for the European Union is to a great extent a moral case; it is seen by some as a way of preventing another world war precipitated by rivalries between France and Germany. Indeed, Europe is now the centre of thought and action forwarding a vision of the world in which universal human rights prevail, and nations are governed by international norms that keep the peace, guarantee environmental protection, and prevent global hunger.

The idea of moral progress is also deeply embedded in American culture.[53] American exceptionalism is founded on the idea that America is "the city on the hill" whose mission is to bring light to the nations of the world. Occasionally American leaders and opinion-makers admit to well-intentioned "mistakes" or "failures", but the language is almost always one of self-correction and constant improvement. I can't think of an American president in my lifetime who was re-elected (thus excluding Carter) for whom the mantra "our best days are yet to come" did not figure centrally in his political

[51] By Davis (2001).

[52] I owe this point to Norman Vig. This explanation would not bear (at least very directly) on the behaviour of the Scandinavian states, which lead the world in concern for global poverty and inequality. Of course they have their own histories of colonialism, but they are far more limited than those of many other European states, and then only marginally related to what are now the poorest countries in the world.

[53] See Ekirch Jr. (1944), and Lasch (1991).

rhetoric. While America may appear to the world as a bastion of materialism and greed,[54] the sense of optimism that these political leaders convey is not just confidence in the economic future of the nation, but also faith in its moral mission (though of course in America economic growth is often seen as a sign of moral virtue, or even as part-constitutive of it).

In light of this history, it is surprising how much disagreement there is among thoughtful people about the prospects for moral progress. Reflecting on his fifty years in journalism, retiring *New York Times* columnist, Anthony Lewis, recently said: "I have lost my faith in the idea of progress . . . in the sense . . . that mankind is getting wiser and better . . . how can you think that after Rwanda and Bosnia and a dozen other places where these horrors have occurred?"[55] Yet Richard Rorty seems to take moral progress for granted, and even thinks that its pace has increased over the last two centuries: "the nineteenth and twentieth centuries saw, among Europeans and Americans, an extraordinary increase in wealth, literacy, and leisure. This increase made possible an unprecedented acceleration of the rate of moral progress."[56] Christopher Lasch's 1991 book, *The True and Only Heaven*, reads as if it is directly addressed to Rorty. "This inquiry began with a deceptively simple question. How does it happen that serious people continue to believe in progress, in the face of massive evidence that might have been expected to refute the idea of progress once and for all?"[57]

The historical record is undeniably equivocal and tragically ironic. The French Revolution produced both the Declaration of the Rights of Man and the Terror. World War I, which was the war to end all wars, led to the bloodiest war in human history. A generation later, in their attempts to stop one of the most inhumane regimes in human history, the English-speaking democracies unleashed a total war against civilians and ushered in the nuclear age.

Piling up such anecdotes proves little. Still it is hard to read the historical record and not form some impressions. One impression I have is that language has changed. The rhetoric that promotes peace, human rights, and respect for nature is better entrenched today than it was in most previous

---

[54] Salman Rushdie writes, "[n]ight after night, I have found myself listening to Londoners' diatribes against the sheer weirdness of the American citizenry . . . American patriotism, obesity, emotionality, self-centeredness: these are the crucial issues" (*New York Times*, Op-Ed, 4 Feb. 2002).

[55] *New York Times*, Sunday, 16 Dec. 2001, WK 9.

[56] Rorty (1993/1998: 175). This remark seems to suggest that just as Europeans and Americans are leaving the world in the dust when it comes to economic progress, so they dominate with respect to moral progress as well.

[57] Lasch (1991: 13).

periods in human history. Rather than being the language only of reformers and radicals on the margins of society, these sentiments are now voiced by some of the most powerful people in the world. The cynic will say that what this shows is not the progress of morality, but the growth of hypocrisy.[58] The same old corrupt behaviour is described in ever prettier terms. Still, there is a case to be made for the idea that language matters. What people do is important, but it also matters how they justify their actions and what ends they claim to seek. But again the cynic will point out that while on the whole softer language may have become more prevalent, this kinder, gentler vocabulary has been available for a very long time. One only has to be reminded that the Golden Rule in its various formulations occurs in a great many ancient traditions to see that the language of moral progress was in place long before people had even begun to perform their greatest horrors.[59] Still, moral and political change in the last several centuries does seem to be away from hierarchy, towards greater egalitarianism.[60] The differences between people that were enforced in Europe and America well into the twentieth century would be intolerable today. The idea that a government could exclude most of its citizens from voting and still be representative sounds to us like a joke. It also appears that there has been a softening in human cruelty. Until the eighteenth century, the atrocities that occur today in ethnic and tribal wars were the norm rather than the exception. The cruel forms of public execution and the merriment that they evoked occur nowhere in the world today. Even the common forms of amusement in early modern Europe—bear-baiting, cock-fighting, and so on—continue only in attenuated and atavistic forms. Perhaps we have become better in face-to-face encounters. Yet technology has given us the power to engage in remote destruction on a scale that is unprecedented. The amount of killing of humans, animals, and the rest of the biosphere that we have engaged in over the last century would have been unthinkable by even the greatest of ancient tyrants. And although our kind of killing is often represented as precise, targeted, even "antiseptic", anyone who has really tried to understand what goes on in modern slaughterhouses or contemporary warfare will come face to face with the same old horrors: people and animals burned alive, flayed, left to die in abject misery with little or no comfort, and so on. I am inclined to agree with Brinton, when he writes that "[w]e may

[58] Cf. La Rochefoucauld (*Maximes*, No. 218; as quoted in Brinton 1959/1990: 26): "[h]ypocrisy is the tribute vice pays to virtue".

[59] See Singer (1991, part 2) on the ubiquity of the Golden Rule.

[60] Of course if egalitarianism were the only criterion on which moral progress were assessed, then we might think that it has been a downhill slide since humans lived as hunter-gatherers.

indeed be no worse morally than our ancestors, and we may even be on the average a bit less cruel, less brutal, but grouped in nation-states we can do a lot more evil more quickly and more efficiently than they could".[61]

Still, the Enlightenment ideology of *fraternité, égalité,* and *liberté* remains deep in our bones and rhetoric. We look back at institutions of slavery and sexual subordination that were the norm only a heartbeat ago, by historical time, and it is hard not to feel smug about the progress that has occurred. But on the other hand the horrors of the twentieth century seem to impel a kind of post-modern cynicism. Language changes, but life goes on; and life in society is fundamentally about power, difference, and oppression. Americans are horrified by the Chinese eating dogs, while the Chinese don't understand how Americans can eat pigs but not dogs. The Romans were horrified by the human sacrifice practised by the Celtic tribes in Gaul, but the carnage of the Roman games did not seem to cause a flicker of conscience. Or so it is said.

These arguments are worth having because they remind us of how much is in play when we consider the question of moral progress, and how different the question looks depending on our focus. But ultimately, nothing very satisfying can be said at this level. We are back to the importance of thinking locally about moral progress, and that is what I will do in concluding this chapter.

In my lifetime, in America, there are two examples that seem to me to provide clear cases of moral progress. One is the struggle against apartheid in America, which came to a head in the 1960s; and the other is the animal rights movement, reinvigorated in the 1970s.[62] In different ways, and with various degrees of focus and clarity, both of these movements are still in motion.

About the time that I was born, an unelected President from a border state that was traditionally aligned with the old Confederacy, took a major political risk under pressure from civil rights leader A. Philip Randolph: he issued an executive order outlawing racial segregation in the nation's military. It is difficult today to recapture the importance and courageousness of Truman's action. Although they were forced to serve in segregated units under the command of white officers, African-Americans had fought bravely in World War II. It might seem that such a demonstration of loyalty and courage would

---

[61] Brinton (1959/1990: 443).

[62] Some would disagree with the choice of these examples or my interpretations of them; or would offer different examples of moral progress. I have no interest in arguing these points here. I simply assert that the examples I give are in fact cases of moral progress. I present these examples because they involve movements that I have experienced and participated in to some degree.

have been enough to convince even confirmed racists that blacks should be granted equality in this limited domain. For that matter, it might seem that integrating the military was a very small step towards justice in a society that was still lynching young black men. Yet this decision almost cost Truman the 1948 election, and had far-reaching consequences. Six years after Truman's order, the United States Supreme Court declared that segregated schools were inherently unequal, thus effectively requiring school integration throughout the nation. In the wake of this decision a new generation of black leaders came to prominence, leading demonstrations, boycotts, and campaigns of civil disobedience in the fight against racial discrimination in public accommodations, voting, and housing. In 1964, another unelected president, this one from one of the states of the old Confederacy, persuaded Congress to pass the most sweeping civil rights law since Reconstruction. This was followed by a battery of other laws, and in 1967 by the appointment of Thurgood Marshall to the United States Supreme Court. Marshall, the first African-American to serve on the Court, had argued the school desegregation case before the Court thirteen years earlier. By 1970 the legal structure of apartheid had been abolished, affirmative action programmes were being instituted, and the national consciousness regarding race had been radically altered. Although racism had not been abolished, it was now shunned and outlawed in its most overt and blatant forms.

Consider another story. Several years after the first Earth Day in 1970, books such as Peter Singer's *Animal Liberation* and articles like Tom Regan's "The Moral Basis of Vegetarianism" began to appear.[63] Many people who thought of themselves as politically progressive began to see the abuse of animals and nature as part of the same structure of oppression that produces racism, sexism, and class domination.[64] Some, inspired by the non-violence of the civil rights and anti-war movements, saw vegetarianism as a natural extension. What had been sleepy animal welfare organizations, staffed mainly by people with sentimental attachments to animals, almost overnight became animal rights or animal liberation groups, sometimes militantly directed towards changing the moral and legal status of animals. This movement has gained some victories, but on the whole it remains very much a work in progress.[65] What has changed is the consciousness about animals, at least in many sectors of society. Many people now find themselves sharing meals with

---

[63] Singer (1975/2001), Regan (1975).

[64] Henry Spira was an example. His story is recounted in Singer (1998), and in the video, *Henry: One Man's Way*, available from Bullfrog Films, PO Box 149, Oley PA 19547.

[65] See Salem and Rowan (2001).

moral vegetarians, perhaps for the first time having to acknowledge in some way or other that using animals for food at least stands in need of justification. To some degree what happens in laboratories and slaughterhouses has been brought to light. Those who retain "Old Macdonald" fantasies of how farm animals are treated now border on denial or culpable ignorance. Behaviour change lags this growth in awareness and various contradictions in our treatment of animals are painfully obvious. But even the recognition of contradiction is itself a sign of moral progress, at least compared to the moral complacency that governed our treatment of animals prior to the 1970s. While widespread legal reforms have yet to occur in the United States, the European Union is in the process of transforming the conditions under which hundreds of millions of farm animals live.

In light of these stories, it seems plausible to suppose, as a first approximation, that moral progress with respect to a subordinated group has four stages. The first stage involves recognizing the practices of subordination as presenting a moral issue, as opposed to presenting questions of taste, etiquette, or personal preference.[66] Having got this far we might take a paternalistic interest in defending those who are being badly treated; we come to see them as objects of morally admirable charity. The next stage is to recognize that rather than being only the objects of charity, those who have been subordinated have rights not to be harmed. Finally, we may come to see them as bearers of "positive rights", entitled to what they need in order to realize their ends.[67]

How do these changes occur? This is an important and under-researched area of inquiry, and what I have to say here will be quite tentative.[68] As a beginning, it is helpful to distinguish between appeals that are launched from within the conceptual frameworks of those whose practices are the target of change, and those that originate from without.

Martin Luther King Jr. often appealed to principles that were taken to be foundational in America, such as "all men are created equal". When protesters were arrested for sitting in at "whites only" lunch counters, he argued that it was they who were acting in the spirit of America, not the racist sheriffs

---

[66] I am reminded of a girl in my high school who was morally outraged by air pollution when most of us had never even heard the term. We were living in what we regarded as paradise: Northern California in the early 1960s. We had to strain to see the decrements of visibility that so outraged her. Finally, under her tutelage, we began to see what she was seeing, then to see it as a bad, then as a harm, and then as a moral problem. Thank you Claudia Winckleman.

[67] It should be obvious that this fourth stage has not been reached with respect to our attitudes towards most humans.

[68] See also Glover (1999/2000); Williams (1993); Moody-Adams (1997, 1999); and Jamieson and VanderWerf (1993, 1995).

who arrested and beat them. The problem was not that some young black people wanted to be served at a lunch counter, it was that American law and morality did not prevail in the states of the old South where service was being denied. In a more abstract way both Singer and Regan argue that broadly accepted moral principles have much wider application than is often realized. Singer (1975/2001) claims that the principle of equal consideration of interests applies to all who have interests: it is inconsistent to apply this principle to the interests of humans but not to the interests of non-humans. The point of the principle is that it is interests that matter, not whose interests they happen to be. Regan (1983) argues that whatever plausible criteria we have for attributing rights to all humans apply also to many non-humans; thus many non-human animals should be seen as having the same fundamental rights as human animals. Once one accepts that it is arbitrary to limit the application of general moral principles on the basis of skin colour or merely biological characteristics, then inconsistencies become apparent. Why are millions spent to keep alive a severely brain-damaged human whose interests are not as urgent or expansive as those of the dog who is being used for practice surgery? Why, for that matter, are some dogs honorary persons while others are disposable entertainments or even food?

External assaults on conceptual frameworks that support subordination are often motivated by the failure of internal appeals. For example, frustrated by the failure to move the supporters of slavery by rational argument or appeals to human decency, nineteenth-century abolitionist literature often aimed at something like a religious conversion—this was often seen as the only hope for changing people who had been corrupted by slavery.[69] Similarly, animal rights activists often try to bring people to see animals in a new light—as complex, intelligent creatures, rather than as defective humans, governed only by instinct.[70] Environmentalists try to bring us to see swamps as wetlands, and "nature red in tooth in claw" as Darwin's entangled bank.[71] This can be a risky business. As Rorty (1994/1998: 204) points out, those who pursue this strategy often sound "crazy"—until (and unless) they succeed.

These strategies are often employed in tandem. Often inconsistencies become clearer and arguments for extending principles become stronger if questions are reframed and reconceptualized. At the same time there is no reason to think that every case of moral change proceeds in the same way, or that I have even begun to catalogue the strategies that are available.

---

[69] Smith (1998) tells this story quite convincingly.   [70] See Essays 4–6.
[71] See Essays 14 and 16.

This essay will end where moral change begins. What I have tried to do is to characterize moral progress, and provide a brief account of two cases in which it has occurred. In both of these cases philosophers have had some role in bringing it about.[72] Professional philosophers have been quite important in the animal liberation movement, and both Martin Luther King Jr. and Malcolm X were, in their own way, philosophers.[73] In the background and in the rhetoric of both movements, we can hear the voices of Kant, Bentham, and Mill. Thinking about these movements in such terms is important because identifying with the aspirations and ideals that underlie them can inspire us to feel part of a struggle directed towards world-historical changes. Still in the end it is difficult to live at a level as general and abstract even as the American fight for civil rights and animal rights. Ultimately, most of us live short lives compared to human history, and in small neighbourhoods compared to the global community. It is from this point of view that our lives are lived and our motivation is gathered. Small moments of success should be savoured. Thus I return to where I began. The moral progress that is palpable in the Kienast family over several generations is real and important. This, as much as anything, makes me feel that it is worth devoting one's life to the pursuit of moral progress, even in the tortured, precious way of a moral philosopher.[74]

[72] For a more detailed discussion of the role of philosophers in moral change see Jamieson (1999a).

[73] A fuller treatment of the twentieth-century civil rights movement in America would explicitly discuss the work of such black philosophers and intellectuals as Alain Locke Jr. and W. E. B. DuBois.

[74] I thank the members of 4M (Minnesota Monthly Moralphilosophy Meeting), especially Valerie Tiberius, for discussing an earlier draft of this essay; and Simon Keller, Peter Singer, Elliott Sober, and David Sloan Wilson for their comments on the penultimate draft. Some of the ideas expressed in this essay are further developed in Jamieson (forthcoming b).

2

Is Applied Ethics Worth Doing?

Throughout most of this century philosophers have sharply distinguished moral theory from moral practice, and many have held that moral theory has little or nothing to do with acting morally. It was commonly said that the proper domain of moral philosophy is moral theory: moral practice is the province of Everyman. The following passage from C. D. Broad (1959: 285) is a characteristic expression of this view.

We can no more learn to act rightly by appealing to the ethical theory of right action than we can play golf well by appealing to the mathematical theory of the flight of the golf-ball. The interest of ethics is thus almost wholly theoretical, as is the interest of the mathematical theory of golf or billiards.[1]

Anticipating the disappointment some might feel about the irrelevance of moral philosophy to practical concerns, Broad quotes the following Latin phrase, *Non in dialectica complacuit Deo salvum facere poplum suum*, commenting that "salvation isn't everything".

Although salvation may not be everything, it is certainly something, and something quite important. It seems inevitable that sooner or later philosophers would again try to bring their methods to bear on matters of salvation. What was needed was a spark, and it was provided by the civil rights and

This essay was largely written in 1983. For this reason some of the examples may seem dated, though I believe that the substantive points they are meant to illustrate still hold. Since this essay is a kind of personal apology, it seemed natural at the time I was writing it to use male pronouns to refer to the applied philosopher. I hope that this will not give offence to any of my readers. I am heavily indebted, especially in Section I, to Richard Sharvy's unpublished classic, "Who's to Say What's Right or Wrong? People Who Have Ph.Ds in Philosophy, That's Who." Section 7 largely follows Peter Singer (1972*b*). In addition, I have benefited from the suggestions of Nancy Davis, John A. Fisher, James W. Nickel, Elizabeth Robertson, David M. Rosenthal, Anita Silvers, and especially Tom Regan.

[1] The most striking exception to the dominant view is John Dewey and the pragmatist tradition.

anti-war movements of the 1960s. By the 1970s philosophers were, for better or worse, "back on the job".[2]

I first became acquainted with this new work in applied ethics when I heard Roger Wertheimer read "Understanding the Abortion Argument".[3] Wertheimer's paper had not yet appeared in *Philosophy and Public Affairs*, and indeed that journal had not as yet published a single issue. I was both intrigued and irritated by Wertheimer's paper. On the one hand he was using his philosophical skills to address a real issue in people's lives. On the other he seemed to conclude in a fit of Wittgensteinian despair: we could and should appreciate both sides of the abortion argument, but there was little or nothing that philosophers could do to help bring it to a rational conclusion. It seemed to me that, if philosophers could only kibitz while real people had it out, then we might as well stick to the Problem of Universals.

Wertheimer's article was just an opening shot in what soon became a deafening barrage. Undoubtedly different pieces moved different people in different ways. For me the crucial year was 1975. The first publications that made me think that there might be a place for philosophers in the real world were Peter Singer's *Animal Liberation* and Tom Regan's "The Moral Basis of Vegetarianism".[4] It is no doubt true that, in part, the power of these works comes from their vivid portrayal of animal suffering. Before 1975 most of us thought of happy chickens and contented cows rather than of battery hens and totally confined, anaemic veal calves. Probably we also thought that all or most experimentation on animals was necessary and carried out in the most humane way possible. But, in addition to confronting us with the facts of animal exploitation, itself an important departure from mainstream ethics, these works were also solid pieces of "analytic" philosophy. What was striking was that they arrived at utterly unintuitive conclusions about how we ought to live. When I first read them I didn't think there was a chance in a hundred that they could be right. A year later I concluded, with lots of minor quibbles and qualifications, that they were right.

I mention the work of Singer and Regan and its effect on me for one reason. If it is the case that philosophers can construct sound arguments about how people ought to live which lead to conclusions that would seem ludicrous to most people who have not studied moral philosophy, then it must be the case that, in some sense and to some degree, there is some connection between being a moral philosopher and being a moral expert. And, just as there is

---

[2] "Philosophers Are Back on the Job" is the title of an influential article by Peter Singer (1974).
[3] 1971: 67–95.   [4] Singer (1975/2001). Regan (1975).

reason for architectural experts to do architecture, so there is reason for moral experts to do applied ethics.

In a remarkably short period of time the view that moral philosophers are moral experts has become very prominent, and applied ethics is one of the few growth areas in a depressed academic job market. A glance at *Jobs for Philosophers* shows that virtually every philosophy department in the country wants someone in applied ethics. Several universities, like my own, have established new centres for research in applied ethics or in the philosophical foundations of social policy. Philosophers have also successfully insinuated themselves into schools of public policy, medicine, law, engineering, business, journalism, environmental science, and so forth. They have also done well with funding agencies. During the Carter administration the National Endowment for the Humanities looked upon programmes in philosophy and public policy with great favour, and many private foundations continue to do so.

Undoubtedly many of our patrons in government and business have affection for us for all the wrong reasons. They think of us as secular priests or as technocrats whose field is ethics rather than, say, public finance. Many of us have probably felt all along that, when and if our patrons find out what we really do, the jig will be up. But our severest critics have been not professionals in business or government, but rather ideologues of the political right and left. The right dislikes us because we are left-leaning irreligious college professors who are usurping the role of the church and family in moral education. The left dislikes us because we treat individual morality as if it were important, instead of focusing on the economic structures and class divisions which are the real forces of history.[5] Some of our colleagues are also dubious about what we do. Worldly success is viewed with suspicion in a discipline whose founding father was rewarded for his work with execution.

Most of the criticisms of applied ethics that I have heard have been expressed in conversation. It is only recently that articles critical of this field have begun to be published in professional journals. Still, it seems clear that times have changed and reaction has begun. There are signs all around us: the shift in direction at the National Endowment for the Humanities away from public policy towards more traditional concerns; articles critical of applied ethics in such journals of opinion as *Commentary* and the *Public Interest*; the revival of virtue theories in the philosophical literature. It would not be too surprising if applied ethics, which had a meteoric rise in the 1970s, suffered an equally meteoric decline in the 1980s.

[5] For criticism from the right, see Lilla (1981); from the left, see Noble (1982).

This might make us wonder whether the decline and fall of applied ethics would be lamentable. I think it would indeed be lamentable, even though applied ethics as it is usually practised is open to well-founded criticisms. But, before I discuss some criticisms of applied ethics, well-founded and otherwise, some misunderstandings about it should be put to rest.

First, much of what is said about applied ethics, and probably much of what I have said so far, suggests a picture in which the distinction between the theoretical and the applied is very sharp and clear. Unfortunately life is more complicated than that. Still, the difference between the theoretical and the applied can be illuminated to some degree in the following way. Theoretical and applied ethics have the same subject-matter: the moral lives of agents and patients. What is different about them is their perspective on this subject-matter. Theoretical ethics takes the broad view; it is the telescope through which we observe the phenomena. Applied ethics views a narrow band of the same terrain in greater detail. It is the microscope through which we examine our moral lives.

A second misunderstanding concerns the relationship between applied ethics and the history of moral philosophy. Some people write as if applied ethics were something very new and different which appeared from out of nowhere about 1970 and as if, before this time, ethics just was theoretical ethics. Such a view cannot survive even a casual reading of the history of moral philosophy.

The *Groundwork of the Metaphysics of Morals* is certainly a paradigm work in theoretical ethics; yet Kant applies his theory to such practical matters as capital punishment, suicide, and the duty to tell the truth. Both Bentham and Mill move quickly from discussions of fundamental principles to disquisitions on particular cases, and back again. There is nothing new about applied ethics as a subject of philosophical concern. The banishment of applied ethics in this century, a position for which I invoked Broad as a spokesman, was a relatively brief and novel interlude in the history of moral philosophy. What is new about the recent revival of applied ethics is the way in which it has become entrenched in our educational and cultural institutions, but that is part of the larger social and cultural history of philosophy rather than the history of moral philosophy proper. Kant, Bentham, and Mill discussed practical matters in the same breath as theoretical issues because they understood that doing ethics in the full sense involves both. Applied ethics requires theoretical ethics as a foundation for its claims and arguments. Theoretical ethics is vacuous if it does not bear on human conduct. To paraphrase something Kant might have said but didn't: applied ethics without theoretical ethics is blind: theoretical ethics without applied ethics is empty.

Finally, we should be aware that many different things go on under the rubric of applied ethics. My work in this area centres on teaching courses in environmental ethics and contemporary moral problems and on doing research on the morality of killing. I am also involved in trying to bring the results of philosophical investigation to bear on issues of social policy. Other practitioners of applied ethics do not teach in philosophy departments, but work in a variety of other settings, some of them non-academic. Some practitioners even wear white coats and beepers and help make life-and-death decisions in clinical situations. Quite obviously, my problems are different from theirs and theirs from mine. In what follows, my remarks will be from the perspective of one who does "academic" applied ethics rather than the "clinical" version.

I shall discuss six criticisms of applied ethics. Some of these criticisms are good ones, and I shall try to say what we should learn from them. Others are not so good, and I shall try to say why. In the concluding section I shall say why I think applied ethics is worth doing.

1. RELATIVISM AND SUBJECTIVISM

Much of the hostility towards applied ethics is rooted in metaethical views concerning the possibility of moral knowledge. A class of freshmen, asked whether it is wrong to let people starve in the Third World while we destroy most of our vegetable protein in the process of converting it into meat, all too often will not say "yes" or "no" or even plead agnosticism. Instead their response is: "Who's to say what's right or wrong?" Although this response has the grammatical form of a question, it is meant as an assertion: the only conceivable answer is that no one can say what's right or wrong. This is a depressing experience for an ethics teacher, but there is a bright side. Freshmen are in college in order to learn, among other reasons, and usually by the end of the semester this particular response has been purged from their behavioural repertoires. What is more depressing is that the views of untutored freshmen on the subject of morality are often no more or less sophisticated than the views of social scientists and non-academics. Even many people who favour the teaching of ethics in professional schools do not believe in the possibility of moral knowledge. They have the peculiar view that it is a good thing to spend one's time trying to answer questions that are in principle unanswerable. Although there is no right answer about, say, whether or not it is permissible to take a bribe from Lockheed, reflection upon the question functions as ersatz justification. From this it is a short step to the view that it doesn't matter what you do so long as you know what you are doing. By this process the callous and calculating are transformed into the virtuous.

The position that drives the question, "Who's to say what's right or wrong?", is what I shall call the *denial of moral expertise*. On this view ethics is importantly different from accounting, surgery, carpentry, and so forth. In these areas there are experts. In matters of morality there are not. We are all equal. I take it that research and teaching in applied ethics is directed towards the development of moral expertise, at least in so far as that is taken to mean greater understanding of moral truths concerning practical issues. If moral expertise is not possible, then applied ethics is not worth doing.

There are at least two bases for the denial of moral expertise. One is subjectivism, and the other is relativism.

Subjectivism can take at least two forms. One holds that ethical "statements" are the expressions of non-propositional inner states. They do not have truth conditions, so the concepts of verification and proof do not apply to them. A second version holds that ethical statements really are statements, but they are about the beliefs, desires, feelings, and attitudes of the speaker. On both views an apparent dispute about the morality of suicide, for example, is not really a dispute about suicide, but at best a dispute about the sincerity of those who are arguing.

Relativism holds that ethical statements are true or false only relative to particular cultures. Just as ' Snow is white.' is true in English, so 'Murder is wrong.' is true in England. Unsophisticated relativists think of cultures as very small, perhaps constituted by the speaker and his friends. When a "culture" has only one member, relativism collapses into subjectivism, or at least is pragmatically indistinguishable from it.

We should see first that, if subjectivism or unsophisticated relativism can be sustained, then not only applied ethics is threatened but also theoretical ethics in the grand tradition of Aristotle, Kant, and Mill. If either of these views is correct, the task of the moral philosopher is just to pick up the pieces that are strewn about by the moralist and the casuist, who, unencumbered by philosophical knowledge, can continue to claim the authority to tell people what to do. Neither of these positions, then, provides the ground from which critics of applied ethics can mount an attack, if they also wish to defend theoretical ethics as it has traditionally been conceived.

For familiar reasons which I shall not rehearse here, both subjectivism and unsophisticated relativism are false.[6] Still it is striking that, despite our best efforts to keep them down, these views keep bouncing back. I believe that part of the reason it is so difficult to exterminate them completely is that, though false, they are based on real insights. Morality is subjective in that moral rules, principles, and judgements are ultimately validated by reference to the welfare of individual beings. Morality is relative in that there is a class of possible moralities for societies of intelligent social animals such that all members of the class are adequate and all can be defended on rational grounds. What is important to see is that we can give both subjectivism and relativism their due without being driven to the denial of moral expertise.

Thus far I have claimed that the denial of moral expertise is often based on subjectivism or relativism and that both of these views, at least in the forms that directly support the denial of moral expertise, are false. Moreover, I have argued that these views can be espoused only by those who are also prepared to reject theoretical ethics as it has traditionally been conceived.

2. VIRTUE CANNOT BE TAUGHT

Another reason often cited for believing that applied ethics is not worth doing is that virtue cannot be taught. Put this way, however, the claim is overstated. What people who say this usually mean is that virtue cannot be taught by the classroom methods of the moral philosopher with their emphasis on reason and argument. This view is not new. We can find its origins in the work of Aristotle and the eighteenth-century Scottish philosophers. The following passage from C. S. Lewis (1947: 33–4) expresses it eloquently.

It still remains true that no justification of virtue will enable a man to be virtuous. Without the aid of trained emotions the intellect is powerless against the animal organism. I had sooner play cards against a man who was quite skeptical about ethics, but bred to believe that "a gentleman does not cheat," than against an irreproachable moral philosopher who had been brought up among sharpers.

Much of what Lewis says in this passage is true, but it does not show that applied ethics isn't worth doing. To suppose otherwise is to misunderstand the role of applied ethics in moral thinking. R. M. Hare's distinction between two levels of moral thinking, the "intuitive" and the "critical", can help us see that this is true.[7]

---

[6] Refutations of subjectivism and unsophisticated relativism occur in almost every introductory ethics book. See e.g. Williams (1972).

[7] Hare (1982, part I).

The intuitive level is characterized by deeply entrenched dispositions and the feelings that go along with them. We are trained not to cheat at cards, and we may have feelings of guilt at the mere thought of cheating. Most of our moral life is conducted at the intuitive level. We do not ordinarily reason about what to do. We follow our heart's command. But there is also a role for critical thinking, and that is the level at which we do applied ethics.

The first reason why critical thinking is important is that sometimes the head should overrule the heart. Lewis seems to suggest that this is impossible, but that is surely wrong. It may well be my duty to cheat at cards, if it would not seriously harm my victim and my family would otherwise starve. That this is my duty could be shown only by reasoning about this particular case in conjunction with some knowledge of moral theory. Our emotions are not likely to be convinced, however. We might feel as sickened by cheating in a good cause as by cheating in a bad one.

A second reason why critical thinking is important is that we need to know which moral dispositions to encourage in ourselves and in our children. Perhaps Southern plantation owners did not feel remorse for the pain they caused their slaves. Perhaps they raised their children to feel remorse when they harmed whites but not when they harmed blacks. Critical thinking could show them they were wrong.

A third reason why critical thinking is important is that many of the moral problems we face today are novel; we have no deeply entrenched dispositions to guide us. It may well be wrong to keep alive for years someone with no hope of recovery who is barely conscious and in pain, but the opportunity to do this is so recent in our history that it is not surprising that our dispositions concerning cases like this tend to be contradictory, vague, and ill focused.

Finally, critical thinking is important because some practitioners of applied ethics are interested in evaluating alternative social policies as well as in providing moral advice about personal problems. Our moral psychology, however, is remarkably unresponsive to complicated large-scale issues, especially those which involve people and events that are not close at hand. We do not respond strongly to the suffering of distant strangers in Assam or to issues like the New Federalism. Yet there are important moral dimensions to these issues which can be appreciated only by reason, since they outrun our capacity for heartfelt response.

There is another point that should be made, though too much should not rest on it. A professor of philosophy is not just a machine for producing and evaluating arguments. He is also a person whose behaviour while teaching and lecturing reveals his conscientiousness, his intellectual honesty, his willingness to treat others with respect, and his commitment to his ideals. For these reasons he, like all people, is continually involved in moral education by example as well as by argument. Because of the nature of the subject and the fact that he is guaranteed an audience, a moral philosopher is often an especially important role model for his friends and students.

Although not everything important to behaving morally can be taught in a classroom by a moral philosopher, some of it can be. Applied ethics is worth studying and teaching even if it is only part of a complete moral education.

3. DIVERSITY OF OPINION

A third argument against applied ethics is really a moral argument. Virtually everyone has moral beliefs. These are obtained from our interactions with parents, schools, religious institutions, and so forth. These beliefs do not always, or perhaps even usually, form a consistent set. Nor can most of us articulate the reasons we have for holding the beliefs we hold. Despite this, we succeed in muddling through with a fair degree of success. There is of course plenty of room for improvement in our moral thinking. But the problem is that applied ethics is not conducive to such improvement. Indeed, it is often harmful.[8]

When a student takes a course in applied ethics he immediately finds that his moral beliefs are under attack. They are shown to be inconsistent, and he discovers that he cannot do a very good job of defending most of them. Simultaneously he is confronted with a whole cafeteria of competing moral theories and beliefs. Some august thinkers say that acts are justified by their consequences: others vigorously disagree. Some speak of natural rights; others condemn such talk as "nonsense upon stilts". Some claim that the foetus's potential is sufficient for ascribing to it full moral rights; others hold that killing foetuses is morally equivalent to killing fish. This maelstrom of radically different conflicting views emanates from the very people who are supposed to be moral experts. If they cannot get their act together, is it any wonder that an intelligent student who has been argued or perhaps browbeaten out of his naïve morality retreats to scepticism? His old views have been

---

[8] Bennett (1980) makes this argument.

discredited, and the new ones have committed "fratricide". He is left with nothing, and it is the fault of the practitioner of applied ethics, who turns out to be responsible for contributing mightily to the thing he abhors: the denial of moral expertise. In order to save theoretical ethics from scepticism and in order to preserve a society in which people have moral beliefs and ideals, we should jettison applied ethics.

There are really two arguments here. One is that widespread disagreement among practitioners of applied ethics is sufficient for thinking that applied ethics isn't worth doing. The other is that widespread disagreement among practitioners of applied ethics has pernicious consequences, and that is sufficient for thinking that applied ethics isn't worth doing. We shall examine the first argument first.

The problem with this argument is that it underestimates the amount of agreement among people working in applied ethics, overestimates the disagreement, and makes too much of both. There are probably few important propositions to which every moral philosopher assents, just as there are probably few important propositions to which every physicist or chemist assents. Still, there are propositions about which there is considerable agreement. Perhaps more importantly, the views of moral philosophers on many issues diverge sharply from those of most ordinary people. Consider some examples. Most moral philosophers reject the view that moral problems can be resolved by appeal to divine commands. They know that justifying ultimate ends is very different from justifying instrumental ends. They know that pleasure is not a sensation and that no simple version of hedonism is true. Concerning more practical issues, most moral philosophers agree that abortion is not murder. Most would deny that life itself, independent of its quality, has value. Most would hold that the distinction between acting and omitting is without moral significance in a broad range of cases. They would say that we should do more to help desperate people even if they are not citizens of our country. And most would agree that the interests of non-human animals should be taken more seriously than they are usually taken. Let me say again that I do not mean to suggest that every person working in applied ethics holds these views. Philosophers are cranky by profession, and any statement of the form "Most philosophers believe that *P*" is certain to provoke a flurry of activity on behalf of not-*P*. My claim is just that there is some consensus among people working in applied ethics and that this consensus is unlikely to be mirrored in the thinking of non-philosophers.

But even if I am wrong in supposing that there is consensus about some issues in applied ethics, the fact of widespread disagreement would not be sufficient for thinking that applied ethics is not worth doing. Such an argument, if it proves anything at all, proves too much. There is no unanimity among interpreters of Plato. Metaphysicians and epistemologists do not speak with a single voice, nor do physicists or biologists. Perhaps it is true that moral philosophers disagree more among themselves than physicists do, but, if that is so, one reason is that in certain respects moral philosophy is harder than physics. Whether an action or a policy is right depends on many things: the welfare of those affected by it; how it is institutionally embedded; the pre-vailing beliefs, desires, and expectations of those in the affected community; the intentional states of the actor; and undoubtedly much more besides. Regularities concerning these matters are very difficult to discover because they involve the behaviour of intelligent social animals. Secular moral philosophy is in its infancy. It is a wonder that we know as much as we do.

The second argument is more interesting. It claims that widespread dis-agreement among those who do applied ethics has pernicious consequences and that, for that reason, applied ethics is not worth doing. We might for-mulate this as the charge that the practitioners of applied ethics are guilty of corrupting the youth.

Note first that the question of whether or not applied ethics is worth doing is itself a question in applied ethics, for it concerns the value of one of our everyday activities. Perhaps applied ethics can be avoided only by remaining silent.

More importantly, I doubt that applied ethics has the pernicious conse-quences that this argument attributes to it. I have seen many cases in which study and research in this area improve the moral sensibility of those who undertake them. I have even seen people's behaviour change radically for the better when they became convinced of the soundness of an argument. When the study of applied ethics does have pernicious consequences I think it is almost always because of the way in which the subject is taught and studied. But, ultimately, I and the critic are at a standoff on this point. The question of whether or not studying applied ethics is conducive to moral improvement is an empirical question which is not easily settled. For its answer depends in part on what our conception of moral improvement is, which is itself a moral question. But there is another point that I think is telling against the argument. Other things are valuable besides maintaining a culture in which people believe in the possibility of moral knowledge. One of them is the attainment of moral knowledge. If the price of such knowledge is the creation of some moral sceptics, that is a price we should be willing to pay.

4. SINGLENESS OF OPINION

A fourth argument against applied ethics denies a crucial premise of the previous argument. This fourth argument holds that applied ethics is worthless because only a narrow range of views is usually countenanced. It is not worth our while to study a field that, after a lot of hot air and bother, merely reinforces our prior beliefs. Cheryl Noble has claimed: "Starting from a position of political and historical naiveté, they [applied ethicists] inevitably arrive at conventional and tame conclusions, drawn from a preexisting range of alternatives" (1982: 8). It is hard to see how someone could believe this. In the last ten years philosophers have defended a host of views that most people would consider shocking. Here are some examples. Peter Singer has argued that we should give until it hurts to relieve world hunger; Tom Regan that it is wrong to harm any animals at all in the course of scientific research; Holmes Rolston that even a smallpox virus has intrinsic value; Michael Tooley that infanticide is often permissible; Hugh LaFollette that parents should be licensed.[9] Noble (1982: 15) has responded to such obvious counter-examples by claiming that most of them "could be joined together to form a good profile of one garden variety liberal". This claim is just false. Peter Singer's prescriptions concerning our duties to the Third World go far beyond those of anyone who could reasonably be called a liberal. The reordering of our relationships to the natural world that Regan and Rolston advocate would be as shocking to Stewart Udall as to James Watt. And only the most extreme feminists have gone as far as Michael Tooley in defending infanticide as well as abortion. Still, much work in applied ethics is open to serious criticism, and there is something important that is on Noble's mind, as we shall see in the next section.

5. PROBLEMS OF METHOD

Work in applied ethics has often been criticized for placing too much weight on moral intuitions. The critics echo Mill's attack on those who make "ethics not so much a guide as a consecration of man's actual sentiments".[10] Noble takes Thomas Nagel as an exemplar. He defends the "conventional, modern Western view of how wars should be fought" on the basis of intuited absolutist principles. "Whether he is discussing war or equality, Nagel ends up saying that the way things are is pretty much the way they ought to be." He

---

[9] Singer (1972a); Regan (1983); Rolston III (1982); Tooley (1973); LaFollette (1980).

[10] Mill (1863/1993: 3).

lays out "general principles of fairness and represent[s] them as independently derived and justified" when they are not (Noble 1982: 8). Phillip Abbot similarly criticizes philosophical treatments of abortion: "[D]espite their [philosophers'] flaunted independence from moral convention, they may only be intuiting conclusions already determined by an increasing atomistic society".[11]

These criticisms raise difficult questions about method in moral philosophy. These questions are some of the most vexing in all of philosophy. They are especially problematical for applied ethics because it is the nature of the enterprise that they are not often confronted or even acknowledged, yet everything that is said or written about practical moral problems rests on some presuppositions about method.

R. M. Hare is one of the few philosophers working in applied ethics who has explicitly discussed these problems. He has argued that appeal to moral intuitions is always illicit and that only linguistic intuitions can provide the bedrock for moral theory (1982, ch. 1). I have serious doubts about Hare's positive view. I don't believe that his sharp distinction between moral and linguistic intuitions can be sustained. Nor do I see how linguistic intuitions can be pure so long as moral ones are tainted. Nevertheless, he and Noble are right in thinking that too much work in applied ethics is just a restatement of the writer's prior beliefs in the guise of something else. Arguments must rest on some unargued assumptions, but we have been too permissive in granting controversial assumptions that are quite fundamental.

The appeal to intuition takes many forms. Sometimes moral intuitions provide the limits beyond which the conclusions cannot stray. If a theory implies that animals have rights, then some would say that the theory must be rejected. Intuitions also enter arguments in response to imagined cases that bear only the slightest resemblance to anything we have ever experienced. We are then instructed as to what our intuitions are, and the conclusion is drawn. Sometimes we are given cases that are close to our actual experience, but we are told to purge our minds of all the contingent associations we are likely to have with such cases. If we drag any of these real-world assumptions into the conversation we are told that we are not thinking philosophically.

Despite the dangers, it is doubtful that moral philosophy can be done without relying on a stock of prior moral beliefs or "intuitions". We must always begin from where we are, and we are always somewhere. This is true of epistemology in general, not just of moral epistemology. There is no

---

[11] Abbot (1978: 331).

harm in relying on prior beliefs and intuitions, however, so long as each individually is open to revision. When we think about moral questions, it is also important that the route from the stock of prior beliefs to the conclusion of an argument not be too direct. Although this point cannot be pursued further here, I hope that enough has been said to make plausible the view that problems about the role of intuition in moral philosophy are not different in kind from problems that arise in general epistemology; and just as these problems do not lead us to the conclusion that epistemology is not worth doing, neither should they lead us to the conclusion that applied ethics is not worth doing.

Another methodological trap for the practitioner of applied ethics is baited by the very name of the field. The expression 'applied ethics' suggests a field in which ethical theories are applied to particular cases in much the same way that a mechanic applies automotive theories to the transmission of a Volvo. Inspired by this picture, classes in applied ethics often centre on laying out the deontological, consequentialist, and contractarian views of various contemporary problems. Although it is undeniable that some moral theories are more at home with some conclusions than with others, this simple-minded way of "applying" theories to cases is indefensible. It ignores the fact that these are all families of theories. 'Consequentialism' refers to a class of theories of which utilitarianism is a member. But utilitarianism too admits of many varieties. There is no unique utilitarian view of affirmative action, euthanasia, or abortion. All the great moral theories are too complicated for that, and so are the practical issues to which they are "applied".

Although there are dangers and temptations that the practitioner of applied ethics must seek to avoid, this is true in all areas of philosophy. Applied ethics can be done badly, but so can epistemology or metaphysics. These considerations concerning method do not show that applied ethics isn't worth doing.

6. APPLIED ETHICS AND THE REAL WORLD

Most of the work that has been done in applied ethics has focused on individual rather than societal responses to ethical problems. The main concern has usually been to say what individuals should do about various problems like world hunger and abortion. Questions about what social policies we should adopt or what individuals should do as members of a democratic society hardly ever get addressed. This is especially striking in the literature on professional ethics. Philosophers have written voluminously on various aspects of the physician/patient relationship while virtually ignoring questions about the role of medical institutions in the life of society. Although philosophers have written quite a lot about the difficulties faced by individual doctors and hospitals in the distribution of resources, they have said little about the larger problems concerning the proportion of our total resources that go to the medical sector or about the problems of justly distributing those resources across the entire population. Similarly, the literature on engineering ethics exemplifies a single-minded devotion to the problems of the whistle-blower while saying very little about the role of engineering in society.

One reason why philosophers tend to avoid the social dimensions of ethical issues is their reluctance to appear politically and socially committed. Applied ethics is welcomed into the halls of government and business because it seems to be another specialization. An employer might say: we have someone who does economic analysis, someone who does policy analysis, and someone who does systems analysis; why not hire someone who does ethical analysis? It is very easy for philosophers to adopt the role of the technocrat, since much of our recent history has conceived of the philosopher as the disinterested analyst, sorting out conceptual muddles. Some people are soil engineers, others are electrical engineers. We are conceptual engineers. After all, what is letting the fly out of the fly-bottle but a low-level engineering job? I am not sure to what extent this model was ever a viable description of what anyone did in any area of philosophy. I do know, however, that it is not a viable model for someone in applied ethics. The positions we take in our work have political and social consequences, and it would be dishonest to pretend otherwise.

A better reason why philosophers have focused on the individual dimensions of moral problems while neglecting the social is that philosophers are primarily college professors. They speak to students rather than to presidents or legislators. They write mainly for other professors. Even those who wear white coats and beepers typically address medical students and individual physicians. Given the institutional location of most philosophers, writing about individual responses to ethical problems makes good sense. We might succeed in changing the behaviour of a few students and colleagues, but, if our goal is to change the world, our prospects are bleak. As philosophers fan out into policy-making contexts they will begin to write for different audiences, and the character of their work will change. Already this is occurring.

But this response will take us only so far. Even if we take into account the institutional background in which philosophy is embedded, it still seems to many people that philosophical writing on most contemporary issues usually misses the heart of the matter and, for that reason, is less effective than it might otherwise be.

Thomas Nagel (1979, p. xiii) seems largely to agree with this, but he doubts that it could be otherwise. He writes:

I am pessimistic about ethical theory as a form of public service. The conditions under which moral argument can have an influence on what is done are very special, and not very well understood by me.

It certainly is not enough that the injustice of a practice or the wrongness of a policy should be made glaringly evident. People have to be ready to listen, and that is not determined by argument. I say this only to emphasize that philosophical writing on even the most current public issues remains theoretical, and cannot be measured by its practical effects. It is likely to be ineffective; and if it is theoretically less deep than work that is irrelevant to the problems of society, it cannot claim superior importance merely by virtue of the publicity of its concerns. I do not know if it is more important to change the world or to understand it, but philosophy is best judged by its contribution to understanding.

It is certainly true that most of us would not know how to make our words change the world even if that were what we wanted. The gap between individual morality and public policy is awesome, as Nagel suggests. It is not even easy to grasp what makes a society lurch in one direction rather than another. Nagel is also right in saying that philosophical work should not be judged by its influence on public life. To suppose otherwise threatens to collapse the distinction between philosophy and advocacy journalism. Still, I am disquieted by Nagel's words. He does not seem disappointed that "philosophical writing on even the most current public issues remains theoretical", but this, perhaps more than anything else, is what has disturbed the critics of applied ethics, and it deserves a sympathetic response.

Consider first the words of Mark Lilla:

We have always been a moralistic nation, but seldom before have we conducted our political arguments in full academic regalia . . . [t]his sort of moral discourse is now so pervasive that even the moral obligations of government officials . . . are now discussed in the obscure and formal analytic language of the contemporary theoretical philosopher . . . While angels dance on pins, these thinkers ponder such questions as: if a group of people are hopelessly trapped in a tunnel by a fat man stuck in the opening . . . is it right to blow the man to bits to save the group? (1981: 10–11)

Cheryl Noble has written that recent work in applied ethics is "devoid of interest in other traditions of social and cultural criticism—historical, social, scientific, literary, or psychological". Because of this, she believes that its "conception of the kind of knowledge and insight needed to shed light on moral issues is unavoidably inadequate" (1982: 8). To a very great extent the remarks of Noble and Lilla are unfair, and based on serious misunderstandings. As I suggested at the outset, theoretical and applied ethics are complementary; good work in one requires the other. And it is not surprising that the methods and approaches of theoretical ethics strike many non-philosophers as "formal" and "obscure". Still, there is something important that Lilla and Noble are on to.

Much recent work in applied ethics is not really about the problems it seems to address. Some philosophers write about animal rights because they are concerned with the nature and scope of rights in general. Other philosophers address the physician/patient relationship because of their interest in arguments for and against paternalism and coercion. Problems of world hunger provide a convenient backdrop to discussions of action theory and its relation to moral responsibility. The list could go on. I do not mean to suggest that everyone working in applied ethics has a hidden agenda, only that much of the work that seems to be about "real issues" is not. All too often we have tried to have it both ways. We have wanted the public support and attention that comes from addressing issues of real public concern; at the same time we have been more interested in impressing our peers than in making a difference in the world. To put the point in another way: some of the critics of applied ethics have noticed, perhaps obliquely, that most work in *Philosophy and Public Affairs*, for example, is really about philosophy rather than public affairs.

To some degree this can be explained by the defensive position of applied ethics within professional philosophy. Although most philosophy departments have created courses in applied ethics within the last ten years and many have hired specialists in this area, often this has been a grudging concession to student demand or administration pressure to increase enrolments. Running hundreds of students through courses in contemporary moral problems has become a popular strategy for trying to save "real" philosophy courses—logic, philosophy of science, philosophy of language—in an era of shrinking budgets. Although applied ethics has become institutionalized in philosophy departments, to a great extent the relationship is very much like the result of a shotgun wedding. Given the widespread scepticism about applied ethics within the profession, it is not surprising that practitioners of applied ethics have been anxious to demonstrate their philosophical *bona fides*; and this can be done only by writing articles directed towards philosophers and relying on philosophical sources published in philosophical journals. Two results of this have become apparent.

First, while practitioners of applied ethics have been concerned to show that they are real philosophers rather than half-breeds, their colleagues in philosophy of science have been busily studying physics, biology, psychology, and cognitive science. It is ironical that, although most philosophers are willing to admit that a logician has more in common with some mathematicians than he has with many of his fellow philosophers, they resist the view that in order to do applied ethics well it might be necessary to spend more time talking to economists, sociologists, activists, and street people, than to other philosophers.

Secondly, it is becoming increasingly clear that much work in applied ethics exemplifies the worst of both worlds. Writing traditional philosophical articles under the guise of doing applied ethics will never satisfy traditionally minded philosophers. For they understand that, for the most part, the deepest and most interesting philosophical work will be done by people who honestly and directly take on the fundamental problems. Nor, as we have seen, does this hybrid work satisfy those who are concerned with the real issues. For they rightly see that much of this work consists in a dance between philosophers rather than a conscientious attempt to address the issues.

Philosophers are moving in the direction of the real world, but they have not yet landed. For reasons I will discuss in the next section, I believe that philosophers can do important work on issues of great public moment. Ultimately, however, this belief will stand or fall on the basis of our attempts. So far we have barely tried. We have isolated ourselves by ignoring the social dimensions of ethical problems. As to our ultimate effectiveness, the jury is still out.

7. WHY PHILOSOPHERS SHOULD DO APPLIED ETHICS

Thus far my project has been mainly negative. I have resisted the view that applied ethics is by its very nature so deeply flawed that it is not worth doing. I would like to conclude by briefly saying why philosophers should do applied ethics. My claim is really very simple: philosophers have advantages that most people do not have which make philosophers natural candidates for the role of moral expert.

First, philosophers are trained in logic. They can detect fallacies and separate good arguments from bad. They can identify premises and point to those which require additional support. Anyone who reads the newspaper knows how ubiquitous logical mistakes are in the discussion of public issues. Often it is an important contribution just to identify the logic of the arguments that people employ.

Secondly, philosophers are trained in thinking about moral concepts. We know, for example, the difficulties involved in negotiating the supposed chasm between "facts" and "values". It can be a great service to point out those premises that people employ which spring from deep value commitments, since their adherence to those premises is unlikely to be sensitive to new factual information. Consider an example. Many people are in favour of capital punishment because they believe that murderers deserve to die. Any rational discussion of their views must engage this value commitment. No number of studies about the inefficacy of capital punishment as a deterrent will move them. Although analytically this point is very simple, it is often obscured by the rhetorical flak that surrounds real arguments. Philosophers also know that the relationship between the good and the right is really very complicated. Ordinary people often think it is quite simple: if something is good then it is right to bring it about. Sensitivity to the full range of possible relationships makes philosophers specially qualified trail guides on the road from the good to the right.

Thirdly, philosophers have knowledge of moral theories. Although, as I have suggested, these theories cannot be trotted out and "applied" to real problems, they do provide a storehouse of sophisticated thinking about how particular judgements may be unified into a larger framework. This is important because people often make moral decisions on a piecemeal basis. (For example, it is sometimes said that, for a policy-maker, the time horizon is the next five minutes.) The result is that people often hold obviously inconsistent views about what ought to be done. The knowledge of moral theories which philosophers have can influence people to recognize the necessity of thinking about the fundamental principles that underlie their particular judgements.

Fourthly, philosophers have the leisure to think about real moral problems, whereas many other people do not. The thinking of ordinary people usually remains at the intuitive level because the press of circumstance does not allow the time for the hard work that critical thinking requires. Most people rightly believe that it is better to rely on one's intuitions than to do a poor job of working out all the complications involved in a difficult issue. Philosophers are moral experts, in part, for the same reason that physicians are experts in medicine: both moral philosophers and physicians devote themselves full-time to their areas of expertise.

Finally, philosophers are sufficiently insulated from the pressures of ordinary life that they can think about moral issues in a relatively impartial way. Very few people in any society can follow their thinking about practical issues wherever it might lead, without fear of reprisals. Many people avoid moral crisis by avoiding moral thinking. Since moral philosophers are paid to think through moral questions, they are less likely to be threatened if they come up with the "wrong" answers. We should not be too sanguine about this, however. There is a history of political interference in American universities. Moreover, as philosophers increasingly work outside universities and as support for universities becomes more politicized, this advantage will erode.

These, then, are the advantages that philosophers have in thinking about real issues. It adds up to a kind of moral expertise. Applied ethics is worth doing for philosophers because philosophers are moral experts. This does not imply, however, that philosophers should be the only ones to do applied ethics, that people should always defer to philosophers, or that philosophers always do applied ethics well. Nor does it imply an excessively optimistic view about the place of reason in ethics. When all is said and done, people will continue to make difficult decisions about real moral issues. They will consult policy analysts, theologians, astrologers, physicians, politicians, and bartenders. Philosophers may not be ideally suited for the role of moral adviser, but they are better suited than their rivals. For this reason applied ethics is more than worth doing. Philosophers have a duty to bring their expertise to bear on the problems of real life.

3

Great Apes and the Human Resistance to Equality

Questions about the nature and limits of the community of equals are controversial in both theory and practice. As I write these words, a bloody war between Serbs and Croats is continuing in the former Yugoslavia. Many fear that this is a preview of what may happen in what was once the Soviet Union. Tensions between Czechs and Slovaks are running high, and "the troubles" continue in the northern part of Ireland. Here in New York, where I am writing this essay, relations between Hasidic Jews and African-Americans in the Crown Heights section of Brooklyn have deteriorated to the point where a cycle of reprisal killings may have begun. Relations between blacks and Koreans are generally very bad, and all over America there are incidents of white racism against blacks and Asians.

Most people would express regret about all of these cases, and say that in the highly interconnected world in which we live different groups are going to have to learn to get along with each other. They don't have to like each other, but they must respect each other as equals. Whether Croat or Serb, black or Hispanic, all humans are members of the community of equals and have the right to live in peace and tranquillity, without threats to their lives and liberty.

The cases of inter-ethnic struggle that I have mentioned pose practical problems of community: how can we bring it about that people will act on the basis of what they believe to be true and recognize the equality of others? At the level of theory the battle mostly has been won. Not many people would

I am grateful to Paula Cavalieri, Peter Singer, and Richard Sorabji for their comments on earlier drafts of this essay.

seriously argue that it is permissible to treat Serbs or Australian Aborigines badly on grounds of their race or ethnicity. But human beings are often better at theory than practice.

We have a long way to go even in theory towards recognizing our equality with the other great apes. The idea that chimpanzees, gorillas, and orang-utans should be recognized as members of our community of equals strikes many people as bizarre or outrageous. Yet, like the other contributors to the Great Ape Project, I believe that we have very good reasons for including them.[1]

In this essay I will not try to say specifically what the community of equals is or to what its members are entitled. Instead I simply endorse the general sentiments of the Declaration on Great Apes: the community of equals is the moral community within which certain basic moral principles govern our relations with each other; and these moral principles include the right to life and the protection of individual liberty.[2]

My main interest in this essay is in exploring why the moral equality of the great apes is so difficult for many humans to accept. What follows can be viewed as a speculative diagnosis of the sources of human resistance to recognizing our moral equality with the other great apes. My hope is that once the sources of this resistance have been exposed, they will to some extent have been disabled, and we can then move towards the difficult task of putting our moral ideas into practice. I will discuss what I take to be five sources of resistance to recognizing our moral equality with the other great apes.

One source of our resistance may be this: we are unsure what recognizing our equality with the other great apes would mean for our individual behaviour and our social institutions. Would they be allowed to run for political office? Would we be required to establish affirmative action programmes to compensate for millennia of injustices? To some extent this unclarity comes from the narrowness of our vision, and to some extent because there are significant questions involved that cannot be answered in advance. Humans often seem to have failures of imagination when considering radical social change. A world without slavery was unfathomable to many white southerners prior to the American Civil War. Life without apartheid is still unimaginable to many South Africans. One reason we may resist radical social

---

[1] The Great Ape Project, founded in 1993 by Paula Cavalieri and Peter Singer, is directed towards winning the recognition of basic rights for all the great apes, not only humans. In 1993 a book was published which included a "Declaration on Great Apes" signed by prominent scientists, philosophers, and other scholars (Cavalieri and Singer 1993). For further information visit http://www.greatapeproject.org

[2] Cavalieri and Singer (1993: 4–7).

change is because we cannot imagine the future, and we fear what we cannot imagine.

But having said this, it is true that it is very unclear exactly what recognizing the moral equality of great apes would mean. Clearly it would end our use of chimpanzees in medical research, and our destruction of areas in which mountain gorillas live, but what other changes would it bring? We can benefit here from reflecting on the American experience of social change. Once slaves were emancipated and recognized as citizens, it remained unclear what exactly their rights and protections were. For more than a century various court decisions and legislative acts have continued to spell them out. This is an ongoing process, one that cannot entirely be envisaged in advance. If we are to change social practices that cannot be defended, then we must accept the unavoidable uncertainty that follows.

A second source of resistance may generally be connected to the sources of racism and sexism. Humans often tolerate diversity more in theory than in practice. The prevalence of inter-ethnic violence and the abuse of women by men is surely related to brute differences between the groups in question. Yet the differences among humans seem slight compared with differences between humans and chimpanzees, gorillas, or orang-utans. The idea of admitting our moral equality with such creatures seems outlandish in the face of such differences.

However, it is interesting to note that perception of difference often shifts once moral equality is recognized. Before emancipation (and still among some confirmed racists) American blacks were often perceived as more like apes or monkeys than like Caucasian humans. Once moral equality was admitted, perceptions of identity and difference began to change. Increasingly blacks came to be viewed as part of the "human family", all of whose members are regarded as qualitatively different from "mere animals". Perhaps some day we will reach a stage in which the similarities among the great apes will be salient for us, and the differences among them will be dismissed as trivial and unimportant, or perhaps even enriching.

A third source of human resistance to equality for great apes is the lack of voices calling for such equality. The recognition of equality is deeply affected by empathy and sympathetic identification. It is difficult to identify or empathize with creatures who are remote, and whose plight is not directly articulated. Indeed the psychological importance of nearness is part of the reason why the plight of African humans is so often overlooked. Many Africans currently face famine, yet the industrialized would seems much more concerned with the less serious plights of its own victims of recession.

Even when the oppressed or disadvantaged have powerful and articulate champions, the victims themselves are often much more effective than their advocates. This aspect of human psychology has been repeatedly exploited by promoters of animal research whose public relations campaigns often feature children who claim to be alive and happy because of experimentation on animals. These individuals who have been victims of disease or disability are often more effective advocates for research than scientists. The problem with the other great apes, however, is that they are not in a position to communicate effectively with humans. As a result their case must be made by humans, and such appeals have limited efficacy.

A fourth source of the human resistance to equality is the recognition of the setback to human interests that would result. The broader the membership of the community of equals, the fewer the benefits that accrue to the members. This is part of the reason that there has been historical resistance to expanding the circle of moral concern. Societal elites have resisted claims of equality from the inferior classes; men have resisted such claims from women; and whites have resisted the claims put forward by blacks. The loss of unjust advantage is part of the cost of life in a morally well-ordered society, but those who stand to bear the cost typically try to evade it.

Perhaps the deepest source of human resistance is that claims of equality among the great apes involve a fundamental conflict with the inherited Middle Eastern cultural and religious world-view of most Western societies. Judaism, Christianity, and Islam all grant humans a special place in nature. In orthodox Christian views humans are so special that God even took the form of a human; it would be unthinkable that he would have taken the form of a chimpanzee, gorilla, or orang-utan. Even unbelievers live with the legacy of these traditions. The specialness of humans in nature is part of the background of our belief and action. Yet, as James Rachels (1990) has powerfully argued, this picture in which human uniqueness plays such an important role is being undermined by the emerging world-view of science and philosophy. A secular picture which takes evolutionary theory seriously provides no support for human privilege. On this view, humans are seen as one species among many, rather than one species over many; in the long run humans are destined to go the way of other extinct species, and there is nothing in the scientific picture that directly supports the idea that this would be a loss. Of course there is no direct logical contradiction between the scientific world-view and claims about human uniqueness: one can continue to hold both, as many people do. What the scientific world-view does, however, is to remove much of the background which once gave plausibility to claims about human uniqueness.

Without this background, such claims increasingly seem ad hoc and unsupported.

In this essay I have tried to identify some of the sources of human resistance to acknowledging the moral equality of the great apes. Seen from a certain perspective, what is surprising is not that a distinguished group of scientists and philosophers are willing to assert such equality, but rather that such claims seem absurd to so many people. What I have suggested is that this initial impression of absurdity may be an expression of deep-seated fears and anxieties about our place in nature and our relations with those who are different. Even if this diagnosis is correct, such fears and anxieties will not instantly disappear. We have a long way to go before our emerging naturalistic worldview will fully inform our relations with the rest of nature. But before our demons can be tamed they must be identified and understood. I have tried to take a first step towards such identification and understanding.

4

Science, Knowledge, and Animal Minds

1. INTRODUCTION

David Hume is remembered by many philosophers as the great sceptic who called into question causality, necessity, and even the existence of the self. It is striking, then, that Hume writes that "no truth appears to me more evident, than that beasts are endow'd with thought and reason as well as men".[1] He goes on to ascribe to animals such idea-mediated indirect passions as pride and love as well as such direct passions as desire, contentment, and fear. Hume also attributes anger, grief, and courage to animals and writes that " 'Tis evident, that *sympathy*, or the communication of passions, takes place among animals, no less than among men".[2] Since Hume writes that the object of love must be a person and that animals can love their conspecifics, he goes so far as to imply that animals are persons.[3]

Hume's view of animals is dramatically different from that of some other philosophers. Descartes famously believed that animals do not have thought or "real feeling".[4] In our own day R. G. Frey holds that animals do not have

This essay began life as a contribution to the Cornell Workshop on Comparative Cognition. Subsequent versions were presented at the Pacific Division of the American Philosophical Association, Duke University, the University of Colorado, Monash University, La Trobe University, and the University of Melbourne. I was helped by those who took part in these discussions; especially Colin Allen, Marc Bekoff, Carl Ginet, Kristina MacRae, Paul Moriarity, and Sydney Shoemaker. Comments by Elizabeth Fricker, Douglas C. Long, Margaret Dauler Wilson, and Steven Yalowitz on various versions of the manuscript also occasioned revisions. My greatest debt is to John A. Fisher with whom I have discussed these issues for many years.

[1] Hume (1738/1888: 176).   [2] ibid. 398.
[3] ibid. 329, 397. For discussion of these passages and Hume's view of animals generally, see Baier (1983). See also Arnold (1995).
[4] On Descartes's view of animals see Radner and Radner (1989); and Wilson (1995/1999).

desires and Donald Davidson teaches that animals do not think.[5] While Peter Carruthers grants that animals have experiences, he strangely claims that all of these experiences are non-conscious.[6]

Scepticism about animal minds is even more prominent in science than in philosophy. The ascription of mental states to animals by Darwin, Romanes, and other early evolutionary biologists is commonly viewed these days as embarrassing anthropomorphism that has no place in serious science. Donald Griffin's attempts to resurrect some of their ideas and to formulate a cognitive ethology are frequently viewed as naïve, and perhaps even a little crazy.[7] J. S. Kennedy, a leading animal behaviourist, speaks for many when he writes that "although we cannot be certain that no animals are conscious, we can say that it is most unlikely than any of them are".[8] Kennedy attacks contemporary advocates of cognitive ethology for promoting what he calls the "new anthropomorphism", which he regards as damaging science by turning back the clock to the prebehaviourist era.[9] Even many scientists who are sympathetic to the idea of cognitive ethology are wary of ascribing mental states to animals. They are happier talking about animal "minds" than animal minds.

It is striking that what the (supposed) sceptic Hume considers evident is thought by many philosophers and scientists to be false or at least controversial. He himself provides a key to understanding this dispute in the sentence succeeding the one quoted at the beginning of this paper. "The arguments are in this case so obvious, that they never escape the most stupid and ignorant."[10] It is clear that when Hume says that "beasts are endow'd with thought and reason" he means to be reporting common-sense beliefs about animals. He has a philosophical point to make—that humans and animals are both part of the natural order—but here he is buttressing his view by calling on beliefs that he thinks are held by even "the most stupid and ignorant". He sees no need for rolling out heavy philosophical or scientific artillery to prove that animals have thought and reason.

Hume is right in thinking that it is quite evident to most people (in our culture anyway) that animals have thought and reason.[11] As in his own day it

[5] Frey (1980); Davidson (1984).

[6] Carruthers (1989); for a reply see Jamieson and Bekoff (1992).

[7] See Humphrey's (1977) review of Griffin (1976/1981). See also Essay 5.

[8] Kennedy (1992: 31).

[9] For an alternative perspective on anthropomorphism see Fisher (1990/1996).

[10] 1738/1888: 176. There is some irony here since Hume was quite aware of the Cartesian denial of animal minds.

[11] For evidence that these views have been widely shared in Britain over the last half millennium, see Thomas (1983). For discussion of how animals were viewed in antiquity see Sorabji (1993).

is typically philosophers and scientists who call this view into question. I will try to show that the reluctance of some philosophers and scientists to embrace the view that animals have minds is primarily a fact about these philosophers and scientists rather than a fact about animals. Our ordinary practices of ascribing mental states to animals are quite defensible. It is the failure to see this that damages science.

2. ANIMAL MINDS IN EVERYDAY LIFE

In this section I will remind us of some of these practices. But before going on, those of us who are philosophers or scientists should take a deep breath and relax some of our concerns about the use of mental language—it's OK, sometimes anyway, to speak with the vulgar. In particular we should lighten up about the use of some highly charged nouns. It is obvious that most of us believe in animal minds. This does not mean that we believe that animals have Cartesian souls or that their bodies are in some way "occupied" by some unbreakable substance called "consciousness". Some people believe this, but strange views about the mind are not the price of admission for supposing that dogs miss their people, cats like to be fed, and tigers hope to be freed from their cages. We often confidently say that animals have thoughts, beliefs, intentions, desires, attitudes, emotions, feelings, or sensations. Often we claim to know what mental state obtains with respect to a particular creature on a particular occasion. Sometimes we don't even worry about "content". Call these practices "ascribing or attributing mental states to animals".

We ascribe mental states to animals explicitly and implicitly. Grete (a dog) scratches the door after having just been out. What does she want? We might have a spirited discussion about this, with different views being put forward. Perhaps we reach agreement, perhaps not. But we are co-conspirators in attributing mental states to Grete. Later, without comment or explicit thought, I get Grete's ball out from under the bed because I know that she wants it. I implicitly attribute a mental state to her. In addition to such explicit and implicit attributions, much of our behaviour towards animals simply presupposes that they have minds. We take the intentional stance towards them; more than that, we take the "affective stance": we relate to them not only as intentional creatures, but also as beings who experience pain and pleasure. Much of our behaviour presupposes that what happens to animals matters to them.

We have these practices not only with companion animals, but also with farm animals and wild animals. Farmers and ranchers often pride themselves on understanding their animals and being able to identify their wants and needs. When we go to zoos or watch nature films, we sometimes try to think ourselves into the place of the creatures. Such thought experiments are often rewarded by predictive success or the feeling that some behaviour has been made intelligible.

Even philosophers and scientists who are professionally sceptical about animal minds engage in these everyday practices when interacting with their animals and orally presenting their research. It is when publishing their official views that they purge mentalistic language from their vocabularies. It is reported that Descartes had a dog, Monsieur Grat, whom he treated with great kindness.[12] Apparently Descartes's philosophy did not prevent him from appreciating the wants of his animal companion.

The fact that we have these everyday practices of ascribing mental states to animals does not mean that every ascription is correct. If someone were to say that Grete is contemplating the concept of an imaginary number he would be wrong. There is no reason to think that Grete has the conceptual equipment for such cogitation, nor that she would be interested in imaginary numbers even if she were able to think about them.

Beyond what seems obviously true or false about animal minds is a large domain of uncertainty, indecision, and indeterminacy. Deep questions about the mind and the application of mental predicates appear in our everyday discourse and reappear in philosophical discussion. Some of these involve large questions about whether there are any such things as minds; and if there are, how they should be understood and conceptualized. Others involve small questions about attributing particular mental states on particular occasions to particular creatures. Is it a tennis ball that Grete wants, any old ball, or just a round object that rolls? Does she have the second-order mental state of believing that I miss Toby (a human) or is she capable of only first-order mental states? Such questions arise with languageless humans and in some cases even with linguistically competent creatures. Debates about the minds of infants can be eerily reminiscent of discussions of animal thought. Moreover, the mental states of some humans remain quite opaque despite our best efforts. I do not always know even what I think about various issues, much less what Newt Gingrich thinks about them. I'm not even always sure that the questions that I raise about the minds of myself and others are sensible ones.

To a great extent these difficulties in attributing mental states are

---

[12] Radner and Radner (1989: 60). I am not aware of any such stories about Malebranche, however.

conceptual. They cannot be solved simply by attending closely to behaviour.[13] Since there is a diversity of views about the mind and how it should be conceptualized, it is not surprising that our practices give out at some stage and fail to determine clear answers to difficult questions. This indeterminacy explains why, within limits, questions about the attribution of mental states are irreducibly open.

Thus far we have been discussing questions about the minds of mammals and other animals who are biologically close to us. Conundrums also arise about where various lines should be drawn and about what we should say concerning animals whom we think of as biologically remote. Most people would not hesitate in denying mentality to an amoeba and attributing it to a gorilla.[14] But what about insects? Our initial response might be that a minded bug is out of the question. However, there is a literature that suggests that insects and spiders may sensibly be thought of as feeling pain.[15] We may dismiss this possibility as outlandish, change our behaviour, or simply come to think that the world is a stranger place than we had thought. All of these possibilities are open to us.

The fact that we can be wrong in attributing mental states to animals and that we can face unanswerable questions about them should not obscure the fact that we are quite sure that many animals have minds and that on particular occasions we know what is in them. This raises the question of how we come to know what an animal is thinking. This is connected to how we justify particular claims about particular animals on particular occasions, but it should not be confused with the question of how we can justify the entire practice of attributing mental states to animals. (This broad question about the justification of our practices will be addressed in Section 3.)

Some people think that the way we come to know what an animal is thinking is quite different from the way in which we come to know what a human is thinking. Call this the Asymmetry View (AV). Although the AV can take different forms, its adherents typically say that while humans tell us what is on their minds we must infer what is on the minds of animals, and that the

---

[13] Dupré (1990/1996) argues a similar point. Later I shall argue that we often see mental states expressed in behaviour, but that it does not follow from this that attending closely to behaviour will rationally compel a confirmed sceptic to believe that an animal is minded.

[14] But would we be so confident if amoebae were the size of dogs or humans? H. S. Jennings writes "that if Amoeba were a large animal, so as to come within the everyday experience of human beings, its behavior would at once call forth the attribution to it of states of pleasure and pain, of hunger, desire, and the like, on precisely the same basis as we attribute these things to the dog" (1906: 336).

[15] See e.g. Eisemann et al. (1984); Wigglesworth (1980); Fiorito (1986); and Eisner and Camazine (1983).

former route to knowledge of other minds is much more reliable than the latter.

First consider this view of how we know what is on the minds of animals: call it the Inferential View (IV).[16] The IV holds that all knowledge claims about animal minds are based on probabilistic inferences to hidden mental states from observations of behaviour. For example, on this view my claim that Grete wants to play is an inference about Grete's mental state drawn on the basis of her behaviour. Behaviour is what is presented to us; inner mental states may be associated with behaviour, but whether or not they are (in general or on a particular occasion) is a matter of inference.

It is easy to see how the IV can lead naturally to scepticism about animal minds. If mental states float free of behaviour in this way, then we can never be sure that they exist. Grete could be empty-headed now or always. She and all of her friends could be mindless Cartesian automata. We can speculate or infer that they are not, but the heavy-duty machinery of reliable knowledge production cannot be brought to bear on the issue. No wonder people who hold the IV use scare quotes when they talk about animal minds.[17]

The IV is based on the assumption that rather than seeing Grete, a cheetah, or an elephant what I see when I look at an animal is a behaving body. This body may or may not be animated in some way or another by a mind. Whether it is or not is what is in question. But it may reasonably be argued that this is not a fair account of what goes on when I look at animals. Grete, the real object of my perception, has been displaced by a philosophical monster—the idea of a behaving body.[18] This is what needlessly "problematizes" the question of animal minds. If mental states are hidden entities whose existence can only be inferred from behaviour, then we should be quite mystified much of the time about what and whether an animal is thinking. But it is mainly scientists and philosophers who are mystified, not "the most stupid and ignorant". Unless there is a more compelling account available, the most

[16] Many scientists hold the IV, including some who are friendly to the idea of animal minds. For example, both Griffin (1992) and Kennedy appear to hold this view, as does Bertrand Russell (1921: 27).

[17] David Sanford has pointed out in conversation that various aspects of the IV are logically distinct. For example, the view that mental states are inferred from behaviour does not imply that they are inner or hidden; the view that mental states are inner does not imply that they are hidden or inferred; and so on. Despite the logical independence of these views, they tend to hang together as part of a broadly Cartesian picture of mind. At any rate the view I am considering involves the conjunction of at least these three propositions.

[18] This point is an extension of claims made by Long and Cook that scepticism about other human minds often gets going by substituting the philosophical concept of a human body for the everyday notion of a human being. See Long (1964); and Cook (1969).

plausible explanation is that philosophers and scientists have been seduced by their own ideology and concepts. It is the "stupid and ignorant" who have it right.

In addition to this epistemological point a further reason for rejecting the IV, already hinted at, is that it fails to be true to the phenomenology of our experience of animal minds. Sometimes we are uncertain about what is on an animal's mind and on those occasions we may try out an inference. But in many cases our knowledge of what an animal is thinking seems immediate and non-inferential. We experience an animal's behaviour not as a set of premises that support an inference, but as expressing the animal's mental state. When my dog Ludwig was running in the woods and stepped into a leghold trap, I heard in his howl that he was in pain. The irritated meow of my (late) cat Sassafras expressed her hunger and displeasure at me for not feeding her sooner. When a caged gorilla in a zoo throws faeces at the gawkers there is little question about what is on his mind—not because the behaviour implies a particular mental state ascription, but because our seeing the behaviour in context as an expression of boredom and anger is virtually irresistible.

It may be objected that our failure to have the phenomenology of inference means little. In recent years we have become increasingly sceptical of phenomenology and have got used to the idea that mental processes may involve lots of non-conscious inferring, computing, rule-following, and so on.[19] Whatever is true of these claims, it is useful to distinguish two senses of 'inference'. In the broad sense an inference may involve a wide range of transitions between states. In the narrow sense an inference is a transition that is made on the basis of reasons. When I deny the IV I am denying that our knowledge claims about animal minds are typically matters of inference in the narrow sense.

One reason for hanging on to the IV is that the alternative may be viewed as even less plausible. It might be thought that if our knowledge of animal minds is not an inference from behaviour then it must be a matter of perception—and it is certainly not that. I am not sure that perception and inference exhaust the alternatives but, understood in a certain way, I don't think that it is out of the question to suppose that some of our knowledge of human and animal minds is perceptual.[20]

---

[19] For example, Marr writes that "the true heart of visual perception is the inference from the structure of an image about the structure of the real world outside" (1982: 68). For an argument that transitions between representations in the visual system do not constitute inferences see Crane (1992).

[20] The following philosophers have endorsed some version of the view that some of our knowledge of other human minds is perceptual: Dretske (1969: 183–9); Luntley (1988: 222); McDowell (1983); Merleau-Ponty (1962: 346–65); Scheler (1954: 10), and Wittgenstein (1980: 100). According to

It is very difficult to set firm limits on what counts as perceptual know-ledge. We can see stars now even though they may have gone out of existence millions of years before. We can see Susan even though she is a religious Muslim and her body is completely covered. We see Jake on his way to work, even though only the dust kicked up by his truck is visible. On the other hand seeing the Auckland airport is not seeing New Zealand. Seeing someone's heart exposed for surgery is not seeing his body. Seeing a flea-ridden dog doesn't count as seeing fleas. Contemplation of these examples and others should show how difficult it is to give an account of what is and what is not seen.[21] Ditto for the other senses.

In everyday life we often use perceptual language in talking about our knowledge of other minds. I have already given some examples of this in the case of animals. In the case of humans we say that we see when people are happy, sad, or disappointed. As Wittgenstein reminds us, " 'We *see* emotion.'— As opposed to what?—We do not see facial contortions and make inferences from them."[22] It seems that there is a prima-facie case for supposing that we can sometimes see that people and animals are in particular mental states. However, it might be objected that we should not take such language at face value. Our knowledge of other minds cannot be perceptual, it might be said, because mistakes in the ascription of mental states are not perceptual mis-takes. I thought that Toby was upset but she was only pretending. Grete looked hungry but she was just being greedy. In both cases I am mistaken but in neither case have my senses failed me. What I see is the same whether Toby is upset or pretending, whether Grete is hungry or greedy. Since Toby's and Grete's mental states are underdetermined by what I see, any knowledge I have of their mental states is not perceptual knowledge.

One response is to deny that such problematical cases can ever arise.[23] The story might go like this. What I see when Grete is hungry is not the same as

Follesdal, Husserl also belongs in this camp (see Follesdal (1994: 300–1)). A similar view has also been defended by the following psychologists: Baron-Cohen (1995), and Hobson (1990: 205). The *gestalt* psychologist Werner claimed that we perceive the "inner life" of both humans and "higher animals" (1948: 69, 76); and the classical ethologist Kortlandt (1954) claimed that we see the viciousness or friendliness of a dog just as we see colour (unpublished English translation available from the author).

[21] Many of these examples are drawn from Ziff (1970, ch. 7). See also Hanson (1958, ch. 1); and Churchland (1992).

[22] 1970, sect. 225.

[23] This response is discussed sympathetically in McDowell (1983) as part of an attempt to under-stand some remarks of Wittgenstein's, but it is not clear whether McDowell himself endorses this view. Austin was also inclined toward such a response, but granted that "there may be cases in which 'delu-sive and veridical experiences' really are 'qualitatively indistinguishable'" (1962: 52). These issues are usefully discussed by Millar (1996).

what I see when she is greedy. To believe otherwise is to assume that a visual experience that is a "mere appearance" can be qualitatively identical with a visual experience that reveals a fact. But a visual experience that is fact-revealing is thereby qualitatively different from one that is a "mere appearance". So we should reject the initial description of the problem cases as ones in which we are presented with qualitatively identical appearances.[24]

This line may be correct as a matter of metaphysics but it doesn't help with our epistemological problem. Once I know that Toby is pretending I may come to think of her behaviour as having been quite different from what it is when she is upset. But this ability to "retrofit" my judgements doesn't help me to sort out the cases upfront. When I'm looking at Grete and Toby, it may appear to me that they behave in exactly the same way in cases in which I am right and cases in which I am wrong. It may seem that my senses have done their job but I've still made a mistake. Therefore, it may be thought, my mistakes in these cases are not perceptual ones.

However, totting up the blame for mistakes is not as easy as it may seem. Different explanations can be given for the same mistake at different times, to different audiences, depending on our purposes. I may say to my mother that I see the North Star, but when grilled by an astronomer I may be more discreet in reporting what I saw. Generally, if the possibility of error becomes magnified in our minds, we begin to think of perceptual claims as inferential ones. Courtroom lawyers are often very good at forcing witnesses to recast claims in this way (e.g. "Did you actually see my client kick Rodney King or did you draw an inference from the fact that you saw his foot move in the direction of King's head?"). The problem with supposing that the retreat from claiming perceptual to inferential grounding for our assertions is a move towards greater truth and literalness is that there is no natural stopping point for this retreat short of sense-data (if that is a natural stopping point), and most of us no longer believe that we really perceive only shapes and colours and everything else is built up by inference. A better way to look at our epistemic mistakes involves seeing our claims to knowledge as part of a network of beliefs and commitments that are informed by theories, attitudes, and insights gained from particular experiences. When something goes wrong the blame can be located at various points in the network. For certain purposes we may hold everything else fixed and say that it was perception that misfired. For other purposes we may fix other elements in our cognitive

---

[24] For discussion of some similar points regarding authentic artworks and forgeries, see Nelson Goodman (1968, ch. 3).

economy and blame inference, or other beliefs or commitments. Of course, not anything goes. Any bad arguments that I may give in this essay are probably not due to perceptual failings. Still, what I am suggesting is that for many mistakes about the minds of animals it seems as natural or unnatural, depending on context or circumstance, to blame perception as inference. For example, I might say "How stupid of me not to see that the elephant is feeling nasty today; you saw it immediately". Or I may say "I guess the elephant is feeling nasty today".

Another reason for objecting to the idea that we sometimes have perceptual knowledge of animal minds is that this view may seem to fail to account for the importance of behaviour in making mental attributions. As Sydney Shoemaker claims about the human case, "while we can be said to observe or perceive facts about another's mental states, we do this *by* observing his behavior (and the circumstances in which it occurs). It is *from* a man's behavior (including his facial expressions) that I see that he is angry."[25] What Shoemaker says in this passage is true: behaviour is important to mental attributions. Indeed, to say that it is important understates the close linkages between behaviour and mental attributions. What is at issue, however, is not whether behaviour is important to mental attributions but rather the way in which it is important. My claim is that the close connection between observations of behaviour and the attribution of mental states is often perceptual rather than inferential. Behaviour does not typically provide premises for mental attributions; often we see mental states as expressed in behaviour and we see behaviour as confirming our reading of a creature's mind. The fact that behaviour is important to attributions of mental states is indifferent between the inferential and perceptual views.

It is also important to be clear about what constitutes behaviour. One important strand of our conception of humans and many other animals is that we relate to them as animated creatures rather than disembodied Cartesian souls.[26] If we see a creature as minded we see it as behaving, even if it is sitting around not doing much of anything. Gross movements are not always needed for attributing mental states. A listless body will do in many cases.[27]

---

[25] Shoemaker (1975: 216).

[26] Here I echo Strawson: "We simply react to others as to other *people*. They may puzzle us at times; but that is part of so reacting" (1985: 21). But, perhaps contrary to Strawson, I think that a similar point is also true of our reactions to many non-human animals on many occasions, but that there are various strands in our practices with respect to both humans and other animals, not all of which are obviously consistent.

[27] Hornsby (1986) makes a similar point.

It may be that our practices of seeing mental states as expressed in behaviour have properties of both perceptual and inferential knowledge and perhaps some unique characteristics of their own.[28] What I insist is that the perceptual model is not so inferior to the inferential model that we should embrace the IV out of embarrassment at the alternative. If I am right about this, no case will yet have been made for the plausibility of the IV as an account of our knowledge of animal minds.

The second part of the AV holds that language is key to our understanding the minds of human beings: they tell us what is on their minds. Call this the Linguistic Thesis (LT). On one interpretation the LT is unobjectionable, perhaps even trivial: in "the normal case" Toby's uttered sentence expresses what is on her mind. But if the LT is taken as asserting that linguistic expression is essential to knowing the minds of others then it is clearly false.

The "normal case" may involve saying what is on one's mind but abnormal cases abound. Speakers lie and use tropes. I may not know what is on a speaker's mind by attending to her use of language. I may even form false beliefs as a result. In other cases we possess knowledge of the mental states of others through language-independent modalities. When someone winces at something I say I know that they are displeased. Linguistic behaviour is neither necessary nor sufficient for knowing what is on someone's mind.

For these reasons I reject both parts of the AV as it is typically developed. In my view there is no good reason to believe that there is a difference in kind as to how we come to know the mental states of humans and animals. With respect to both humans and animals, sometimes such knowledge is based on some form of inference, but often it comes from recognizing what is expressed in the behaviour of the organism in question. As I have already suggested, many animals express various mental states through a wide range of behaviour. When dogs want to play they characteristically bow with their heads down and their tails up. When primates want something they often put their hands out and cock their heads to the side. Many animals express surprise with wide open eyes and dropped tails. Understanding both humans and animals involves placing their behaviour in broad interpretive frameworks. We aim to fit their behaviour into a pattern, linguistic or otherwise, to find

---

[28] Shoemaker has recently argued that although there is a "stereotype" of sense perception, not everything we count as sense perception conforms to it. Even so, some of our knowledge of the mental states of others seems to conform to what Shoemaker calls "the broad perceptual model". For further discussion see Shoemaker (1994: 249–314).

the "project" to which it belongs.[29] Different creatures behave in different ways, but the basic task of interpretation remains the same.[30]

Success in interpretation rests on many factors including background knowledge, appreciation of context, specific information about the creature in question, familiarity with his or her way of life, and general knowledge about the relationship between mental states and behaviour.[31] The rather bland fact is that knowing the mental states of others (whether human or animal) requires knowing what things are like around here.

Consider some examples of how interpretation works. Even though in most respects she appears to be behaving normally, I can see that Nina is still depressed after losing her job in the box factory. I know that Ivan, the gorilla who has lived in a shopping mall in Tacoma, Washington for nearly thirty years, is desperately unhappy although at the moment he appears to be coping. If I knew nothing about how depressed humans and unhappy gorillas behave I would not be in a position to make such attributions. Nor would I be able to make them if I had no knowledge of the effects of unemployment on humans and being caged in shopping malls on gorillas.

We are better at reading the minds of creatures whom we know well than those who are foreign to us. I can identify Toby's mental states more reliably than those of the President of my College. I know Grete's mind better than that of a random spaniel. I have more confidence about the mental states of a dog than of a koala. Most of us are more confident of our judgements about the mental states of another human than we are about those of most non-humans. But if we know the animal well and the human not at all, this may not be the case. Many people are better at identifying the mental states of their animal companions than those of an animal control officer.

Cultural differences among humans can make the identification of mental states difficult. Often the inability to read the mental states of other humans is associated with racism. Caucasians sometimes claim to find Asians inscrutable or give highly improbable accounts of what they think (e.g. "They

---

[29] In the wake of Sue Savage-Rumbaugh's work with bonabos and Lou Herman's work with dolphins, the linguistic/non-linguistic distinction looks increasingly dubious. At the very least the range and depth of non-linguistic expressions looks richer all the time. See their essays in Bekoff and Jamieson (1996*b*).

[30] Gareth Evans discusses the broad, interpretive project involved in attributing psychological states to humans (1982: 130).

[31] See Austin's comments about the role of familiarity and experience in knowledge claims (1970). Dretske (1969: 179–90) makes similar points about specialization and its role in perception. Searle (1983) discusses the importance of what he calls "the network" and "the background" for understanding intentional states.

don't value human life like we do in the West"). When the Spanish arrived in the Americas they were very bad at reading the behaviour of the indigenous people. There were scholarly arguments about whether the native peoples were degenerate humans, therefore rational animals who could and should be converted; or savage beasts, who could and should be enslaved.[32]

Mental attributions are based on behaviour but they occur against a large and complex set of empirical and conceptual structures. Some of these structures involve knowledge about the natural expressions of mental states and others involve knowledge about relevant conventions. Linguistic behaviour is important in mental attributions to humans because language use and interpretation is so conventionalized that it wrings out indeterminacy and reduces the ground available for supporting sceptical challenges. In so far as there are asymmetries in our knowledge of human and animal minds they are based on our lack of familiarity with animals and the paucity of shared conventions. There is nothing about human language use in itself that underwrites essential differences in our knowledge of human and animal minds.

In this section I have been claiming that we have practices that involve seeing both human and non-human members of our community as expressing mental states in their behaviour. This is not to say that our attributions of mental states are always correct or unproblematical, or that it is entirely clear what it is to be a member of our community. What is clear is that most of us live in society with normal adult humans, languageless humans, and non-human animals. In a great many cases we have no trouble identifying what is going on in the minds of others, whether they are human or non-human.

It might be wondered whether everyone in our community is party to these practices. In order to try to answer this question we need to imagine what it would be like to find these practices alien. It is not enough to imagine oneself as an animal torturer. Someone who tortures animals has no trouble reading their minds. What gives him pleasure is knowing that he is causing animals pain. A better example would be someone who is in a certain way autistic. Although it comes in varieties and degrees, it is said that the heart of autism is the inability to read the minds of others.[33] Interestingly, sometimes it is

---

[32] For discussion see Hanke (1959).

[33] There is a huge literature on autism. For a variety of views and perspectives see Baron-Cohen *et al.* (1993). Baron-Cohen has suggested that autistic humans "may have a purely behavioural notion of the function of the brain, and may even be completely unaware of the distinction between mental and physical entities" (1991: 233–4). See also Baron-Cohen (1989, 1995). For further discussions of autism, see e.g. Leslie (1990), and Hobson (1990). For a popular account, see Sacks (1995). For what it is like to be autistic, see Williams (1992); and Grandin (1995).

claimed that autistic people find the minds of animals more transparent than those of humans. But imagine a variety of autism that makes opaque the inner lives of animals while leaving those of humans open to view. Dogs, cats, cows, spiders, mice, and monkeys would all present an overwhelming challenge to such a person. She might even have trouble with cartoons, nature shows, and *Beethoven's Second*. It is not easy to imagine what it would be like to be such a person. It is especially difficult to imagine that her inability to read animal behaviour would not spill over to the behaviour of humans as well. What would she make of infants, the infirm, those whose lives are profoundly different from hers? If there were such a person our differences with her would not primarily be philosophical. Rather, they would be psychological: we would say that she is disordered in an important way. Normal people in our culture sometimes see mentality expressed in the behaviour of some animals who are close to them. This is a feature of our practices. A person with whom we do not share these practices is, in an important way, not one of us.

3. THE DEMAND FOR JUSTIFICATION

Someone might agree with what I have said thus far but still want to know how our practices can be justified. Perhaps as a matter of fact we do see at least some animal behaviour as expressing mentality. Perhaps someone who did not could be described as disordered. But that is mere name calling. No argument has been given for why we ought to see animal behaviour as expressing mentality rather than as mere bodily movements. Perhaps the correct view is one that in these ignorant times we would describe as disordered.

We should first appreciate just how strong a demand is being made. Particular claims about the minds of animals can be justified or not within the context of our present practices. Many questions are left open and there is a great deal of room for reformers of various persuasions to build upon, revise, or try to revolutionize the practices that we have. But what is now being asked is why we should have these practices at all. We are being asked to defend our whole form of life in so far as it involves ascribing mental states to animals.

There is a question about who has the burden of proof here. The sceptic about animal minds may view himself as saying: "We have minds. Do other animals? Prove it to me!" But a truer account of what he is saying might be this: "Granted, we believe that other animals have minds. But we could be wrong. Prove to me that we're not." When the sceptic's challenge is framed in this way it is not clear what would count as meeting it or that we are even obliged to try.[34]

One response to the demand for justification would be to say that none can be given but none is required: our practices with regard to animals are an ineluctable fact about our form of life. J. S. Kennedy, oddly enough a sceptic about animal minds, appears to think that we cannot help but believe in them. He writes that

... anthropomorphic thinking about animal behaviour is built into us. We could not abandon it even if we wished to. Besides, we do not wish to. It is dinned into us culturally from earliest childhood. It has presumably also been "pre-programmed" into our hereditary make-up by natural selection ... (Kennedy 1992: 4–5)

"Anthropomorphic thinking"—Kennedy's term for attributing mental states to animals—is demanded both by our genes and our culture. Yet Kennedy wants us to change our ways. "If the study of animal behaviour is to mature as a science, the process of liberation from the delusions of anthropomorphism must go on." Kennedy is bound to be disappointed. If our practices with regard to attributing mental states to animals are determined by our genes and culture, then they are not going to change. And if this is true, no justification for these practices is needed. Demands for justification are moot in the face of the inevitable.

Let us suppose, however, that in some way or another, at some cost however heavy, our practices with regard to animals could be overthrown. What we would have to imagine is that the right-minded succeed in mounting a cultural revolution, in consequence of which we come to see animals as (something like) Cartesian automata. While we would continue to view the behaviour of infants as expressing mindedness we would come to see the behaviour of birds and monkeys as akin to the movements of aeroplanes and wind-up toys. What would motivate the abolition of our practices of ascribing mental states to animals is some philosophical argument that showed that these practices were unjustified. What such an argument would be like is far from clear, but let us suppose that one were available.[35] We would then face a clash between the demands of everyday life and the deliverances of philosophy. Which should win?

It is far from obvious that philosophy should win. To suppose that it should reflects the view that the practices of everyday life require philosophical jus-

---

[34] This way of framing the sceptic's challenge is suggested by Ziff's account of the "other minds" sceptic (1966).

[35] The philosophical arguments that I have seen for such a conclusion fail. For discussion of some of them see Jamieson and Bekoff (1992), and Bekoff and Jamieson (1991).

tifications. But this is a controversial assumption. In fact it is a metaphysical assumption that itself requires justification. It is just as plausible to suppose that everyday practices that have their own internal resources for justifying claims and reforming behaviour require no further justification—that these practices are ultimately legitimated by "showing their worthiness to survive on the testing ground of everyday life".[36]

Fortunately, however, our everyday practices that involve attributing mental states to animals can be defended. Whether what can be said constitutes a full-scale philosophical justification for them I will not try to say. Nevertheless it is clear to me that quite a lot more can be said on behalf of these practices than against them. Here I will briefly review four kinds of reasons for our having practices that involve ascribing mental states to animals.

The first reason is that these practices are useful.[37] Part of why even behaviourists find it natural to attribute mental states to animals is that mentalistic language plays a role in anticipating, explaining, and modifying behaviour that could not easily be replaced by the language of learning theory, neuroscience, or anything else that is currently available. That these practices have a payoff is clearly a reason to have them, although people may disagree about the character and strength of this reason.

The second reason for supposing that our practices are justified appeals to similarities between humans and many other animals.[38] Given that we behave in ways that are similar to many other animals and that there is remarkable continuity in the structure of various nervous systems, it is plausible to suppose that if we have mental states so do they. Given these facts about biological continuity and similarity, it would be quite surprising if human psychology in all of its depth and richness were completely unique. Indeed, it would be the biological equivalent of the immaculate conception.

The third reason for supposing that our practices are justified involves

[36] Johnston (1993: 85). It would be a different matter if someone claimed to produce an argument that showed that our everyday practices are not only unjustified but plain wrong. Although I am in great sympathy with a view that Johnston calls "minimalism", his conflation of this distinction vitiates his reply to Parfit in Johnston (1992). Here he defends our everyday practices that involve views of personal identity against Parfit's strictures. Johnston conflates the claim that our everyday practices stand in need of philosophical justification with the claim that philosophical argument shows that these practices are incorrect. Since I take Parfit as arguing the latter, at least in part, Johnston's invocation of minimalism fails to defeat Parfit's arguments. Something more needs to be said to defend our everyday practices against the second sort of assault.

[37] This is a point that Dennett (1987) and Fodor (1981) have made in different ways over the years. Shoemaker's Informed Agency condition (in his 1975) may provide an explanation of why attributing mental states to animals is useful.

[38] This view goes back to Charles Darwin (1871, 1896). For discussion of Darwin's views regarding animals see Rachels (1990). On the similarity argument generally see Crisp (1990/1996), and Matthews (1978).

scientific theory.[39] That humans have mental lives is a fact that must ultimately yield to evolutionary explanation. Various accounts of the evolution of mind appeal to the sorts of environmental and social problems that our ancestors would have faced. These involve such matters as the pressures of group-living and the need to engage in cooperative hunting and foraging. But the ancestors of many other animals faced similar problems as well. Thus the same evolutionary forces that might have selected minded human ancestors could be expected to have selected minded ancestors of various other animals as well.

Finally, attributing mental states to creatures is part of an outlook that recognizes them as morally significant. The relations between having a mind and being an object of moral concern are logically quite complex, but they are psychologically very strong. While favourable moral attitudes towards animals may not in themselves justify the ascription of mental states to animals, the existence of such feelings may lead us to see various facts about an animal as constituting or supporting such attributions. In addition there are all sorts of good reasons from the perspective of diverse moral theories for embracing a moral outlook that takes animals seriously.[40] Some philosophers may balk at the idea that our morality should play any role at all in shaping our view of the mind, but that view requires justification and it seems to me to rest on dubious foundationalist views about the relations between various areas of philosophical inquiry, as well as on the possibility of clearly distinguishing the descriptive from the normative.[41]

These reasons for attributing mental states to animals might constitute a justification if one is needed. If we wanted to give a name to this justification we might call it "inference to the best explanation". However it is important not to confuse this inferential defence of our practices taken as a whole with an inferential defence of particular claims about the mental states of particular animals on particular occasions. When I say that Grete is lonely I am not ordinarily making an inference on her bodily movements. What I am suggesting here is that our practices of ascribing mental states to animals, taken as a whole, serve to unify our moral sensibilities, our scientific understand-

---

[39] Alison Jolly and Nicholas Humphrey have separately given evolutionary accounts of how consciousness might have evolved that appeal particularly to the social demands of life in primate communities. Their early papers are reprinted in Byrne and Whiten (1988).

[40] The literature on this subject is now overwhelming. Jamieson (1993) is a concise introduction. Also for an overview see DeGrazia (1996).

[41] Ancestors of this paragraph have produced quizzical looks and sceptical questions on every occasion on which I have presented this paper (Peter Singer and Michael Smith have been the most quizzical or sceptical). I hope this version puts these concerns to rest but "the induction is depressing". See also Papineau (1993: 126–7).

ings, and our practical concerns. If a justification for our practices is required, this ought to do it.

However the voice of the sceptic is not so easily stilled. Couldn't we be wrong about animals having minds? Yes, we could be wrong, but so what? We could be wrong about all sorts of things. The sceptic wants to seduce us into taking the epistemological stance towards animal minds.[42] But from here all sorts of things are in question—other human minds, causality, substance, personal identity, to name just a few. There may be philosophical reasons for taking this stance on particular occasions, but it should not be allowed to cast doubt on our commitment to animal minds. Nor should this kind of scepticism be permitted to infect science. For the purposes of everyday life and science we should rebuff the sceptic. He can take his stance and go dance with the philosophers.

4. CONCLUDING REMARKS

For reasons of space my concluding remarks will be relatively brief.[43] I have already suggested that what I have called the AV inhibits the scientific study of animal minds. We are now in a better position to see why. When scientists assume that what we observe is bodily movements and then worry about whether any inference to internal mental states is justified, they wrap themselves in the garb of hard-headed empiricism. But really they are recommending a disorder as a methodological stance. The inferential view of animal minds is part of a normative objectifying programme that demands that we see animals in a way that is difficult for us to fulfil and one that we ought to reject.

It is striking to compare the successes of cognitive psychology with the sloganeering of cognitive ethology. Many ethologists still work with behaviourist and reductionist assumptions. They feel that cognitive language is a temptation to resist rather than a theoretical vocabulary to deploy. Their preference is for evolutionary or neurophysiological explanations, which they typically view as replacing cognitive ones. But a cognitive approach to animals divides up the world in different ways than these other approaches. It makes different generalizations possible and provides different kinds of explanations. I would even say that cognitive approaches help us to appreciate animals from their own points of view.

Cognitive psychologists, on the other hand, do not worry about the

---

[42] Searle (1994) discusses the epistemological stance.

[43] Some of the themes in this section are further elaborated in Essay 5.

problem of other minds. They take for granted that they are studying cognitive creatures and design experiments that try to shed light on the cognitive capacities they presume to exist. This is the path that should be followed by cognitive ethologists: rather than getting in a twist about whether animals have minds, instead design experiments that study the cognitive capacities of animals.[44] Ultimately the tenability of various scientific views about animal minds will be demonstrated by the fruitfulness of the research. It may be that the best cognitive vocabulary for humans or other animals will depart from folk psychological concepts. Perhaps at the "end of neuroscience" mentality will have been explained away. Our everyday practices of attributing mental states to animals is where cognitive ethology should begin, not where it should end. But whatever the future may hold, a science of animal minds cannot get going without presupposing that it has an object of study.

Having said this, it is important to recognize that the tenability of our everyday practices of ascribing mental states to animals does not rest on the possibility of a science of animal minds. In the present intellectual climate it is tempting to suppose that we should believe only in what can be vindicated by scientific methods. This may even be thought to follow from the role that science plays in our culture as the provider of reliable knowledge. But although science may be a high-class producer of quality cognitive products, there is little reason to believe that it has a monopoly on them. In order to suppose that, we would need to be convinced that the only form of knowledge is scientific knowledge. Not only is this unproven, but it seems to me to be false. Furthermore, as I have suggested, ascribing mental states to animals is an important part of our moral outlook. The persistence of this moral outlook does not depend on the possibility of a science of animal minds.

In this essay I have claimed that many of us know that many animals are in various mental states on various occasions and that there can be a science that studies these states. Even if I am wrong about the latter claim, the former claim is not thereby undermined. The conception of animals as minded creatures, encoded and expressed in our everyday practices, is currently too well entrenched for scepticism to overcome. The recognition of this fact is the beginning of any serious investigation of animal minds.

[44] Some of the best cognitive ethologists are beginning to do this. See the work collected in Cummins and Allen (1998).

5

On Aims and Methods of Cognitive Ethology
(with Marc Bekoff)

1. INTRODUCTION

In 1963 Niko Tinbergen published a paper, "On Aims and Methods of Ethology", dedicated to his friend Konrad Lorenz. This essay is a landmark in the development of ethology. Here Tinbergen defines ethology as "the biological study of behavior" and seeks to demonstrate the "close affinity between Ethology and the rest of Biology" (p. 411). Building on Huxley (1942), Tinbergen identifies four major problems of ethology: causation, survival value, evolution, and ontogeny. Concern with these problems, under different names (mechanism, adaptation, phylogeny, and development), has dominated the study of animal behaviour during the last half century.[1]

With his emphasis on the importance of innate structures internal to animals, Tinbergen was resolutely anti-behaviourist. Yet he remained hostile to the idea that ethology should employ any form of teleological reasoning or make reference to "subjective phenomena" such as "hunger" or the emotions. He wrote that teleological reasoning was "seriously hampering the progress of ethology" and that "[b]ecause subjective phenomena cannot be observed objectively in animals, it is idle to either claim or to deny their existence" (1951: 4).[2]

We are grateful to all those who participated in discussions of this material at the University of Wyoming and the 1992 Philosophy of Science Association meetings. We especially thank Colin Allen, Marc Hauser, David Resnik, and Carolyn Ristau.

[1] Dawkins *et al.* (1991); Dewsbury (1992).

[2] However, Tinbergen seems to suggest only a page later that "the study of subjective phenomena" is "consistent in the application of its own methods" but that this study should be kept distinct from the study of causation (1951: 5).

Since the 1976 publication of Donald Griffin's landmark book, *The Question of Animal Awareness*, a growing band of researchers has been attempting to study the cognitive states of non-human animals.[3] Although vigorous debate surrounds this research, cognitive ethology as a field has not yet been clearly delineated, adequately characterized, or sufficiently explained.

Our goal in this essay is to attempt for cognitive ethology what Tinbergen succeeded in doing for ethology: to clarify its aims and methods, to distinguish some of its varieties, and to defend the fruitfulness of the research strategies that it has spawned.

The remainder of this essay is divided into five main sections. In Section 2 we briefly sketch the history of ethology and explain the motivation behind the cognitive turn. Next we discuss the groundbreaking work of Donald Griffin and the rise of cognitive ethology. In Section 4 we distinguish two varieties of cognitive ethology ("weak" and "strong") and provide some reasons for preferring the latter to the former. Section 5 of the essay is a discussion of one area of research in cognitive ethology: social play. Finally we make some concluding remarks.

2. THE STORY OF ANIMAL BEHAVIOUR

During the third quarter of the nineteenth century, Charles Darwin was the most important contributor to the foundations of animal behaviour.[4] Darwin argued for mental continuity between humans and other animals, and claimed that "the lower animals, like man, manifestly feel pleasure and pain, happiness, and misery" (Darwin 1871: 448).[5] According to Darwin monkeys are capable of elaborate deceit (1896), insects can solve problems, and many animals can deliberate about what to do (1871, 1896).

Darwin's approach can be characterized as "anecdotal cognitivism". He attributed cognitive states to many animals on the basis of observation of particular cases rather than controlled experiments or manipulations. Darwin's follower, George Romanes, followed in this tradition although he was more critical than Darwin of various cognitive attributions to non-human animals. Even Lloyd Morgan, mainly remembered for his canon—"in no case may we interpret an action as the outcome of the exercise of a higher psychical faculty,

---

[3] For samples of this work see Bekoff and Jamieson (1990), and Ristau (1991).

[4] Boakes (1984); Richards (1987).

[5] However there is a passage in Darwin (1871, ch. 2) where he seems to suggest discontinuity between humans and other animals. Humans are dominant, according to Darwin, because of language, and language in part depends on human intellectual faculties. This suggests that discontinuities in power between humans and other animals may reflect discontinuities in intellect.

if it can be interpreted as the outcome of the exercise of one which stands lower in the psychological scale" (Morgan 1894: 53)—accepted the Darwin–Romanes view of the continuity of mental states. Indeed, as Rollin (1989) points out, Morgan's canon is not only consistent with the view that animals have mental states, it actually presupposes it.

Behaviourism arose in part as an attempt to overcome the anecdotal approach and to bring rigour to the study of behaviour. Controlled experiments rather than field observations provided the primary data, and basic concepts were supposed to be grounded in direct observation. Against this background, animal consciousness came to be seen as "mystical, unscientific, unnecessary, obscure, and not amenable to study" (Rollin 1989: 68).

Jacques Loeb, who was active from about 1890–1915, was an influential forerunner of behaviourism in biology. Although he believed that consciousness was an emergent property of higher organisms, he argued that all animal behaviour could be explained non-teleologically in terms of tropisms.[6] Throughout the 1920s, with the work of Watson and others, behaviourism became increasingly influential. By 1930 the behaviourist revolution was complete and anecdotal cognitivism had virtually vanished from mainstream science.

Classical ethology developed in Europe with the work of Lorenz and Tinbergen, and arrived in America in the post-World War II period (although as Dewsbury 1992 points out, there were contacts before the war). The roots of classical ethology were in the investigations of Darwin, Charles Otis Whitman, and Oskar Heinroth. Classical ethology signified a return to some of the ideas of Darwin and the early anecdotal cognitivists, especially in its appeals to evolutionary theory, the close association with natural history, and the reliance on anecdote and anthropomorphism in motivating more rigorous study.

Lorenz, who was trained as a physician, comparative anatomist, psychologist, and philosopher, did little fieldwork but his knowledge of animal behaviour was enormous. His method was to watch various animals, both domestic and wild, who lived near his homes in Austria and Germany. He freely used anecdotes and did very little experimentation. Lorenz thought that empathy, intuition, and emotion were important in understanding animals and that science should not be pursued "in the belief that it is possible to be objective by ignoring one's feelings" (Lorenz 1988/1991: 7). He attributed to animals such states as love, jealousy, envy, and anger.

---

[6] Pauly (1987).

Tinbergen complemented Lorenz's naturalistic and anecdotal approaches by doing elegant, simple, and usually relatively non-invasive field experiments. Tinbergen also worked with Lorenz on several classical problems, including egg-rolling in geese.

Theoretically what was most important about Lorenz and Tinbergen was the emphasis they placed on internal states such as "instincts", "drives", "motivational impulses", and "outward flowing nervous energy". On their view behaviour is typically caused by internal states; external stimuli mainly release or block behaviour. This emphasis on internal states was in sharp contrast with the behaviourist tradition.

However by 1973 when Lorenz and Tinbergen were awarded the Nobel Prize (shared with Karl von Frisch), many thought that their grand theory was already in tatters.[7] As early as 1968 Patrick Bateson wrote that "[w]orship of the old gods and the intellectual baggage that went with it still survives quaintly in odd corners. But for the most part proponents of a Grand Theory have either been forced to close their eyes to awkward evidence or modify their ideas to the point of unfalsifiability" (p. 89). Marian Dawkins has written that "[m]ost contemporary textbooks on animal behavior tend to dismiss 'instinct' altogether and attempt to consign it to honorable retirement" (Dawkins 1986: 67).

In recent years no grand theory has arisen to replace the Lorenz–Tinbergen theory of instinct. However, the question of adaptation (survival value) has become increasingly central in animal behaviour studies. Indeed, many researchers write as if a behaviour is completely explained if it can be shown that it might contribute to inclusive fitness. This is surprising since adaptationist explanations are often radically underdetermined by empirical evidence; and when they are not, the availability of a good adaptationist story does not drive out other forms of explanation.

The Lorenz–Tinbergen theory of instinct was meant to be an account of the mechanisms of behaviour. With the decline of the "grand theory" some researchers have turned to neuroethology as the replacement for the study of instinct. However, despite great advances in neuroethology, much of what we want to know about animals cannot be explained in these terms alone. If we want to know why Grete (the dog) barked at the postman, an explanation in terms of neural pathways may not be very helpful.[8]

Like many of the animals it studies, animal behaviour needs all four legs (mechanism, adaptation, phylogeny, and development). And perhaps as never

---

[7] Kennedy (1992).   [8] Dennett (1987).

before animal behaviour needs to countenance a variety of forms of explanation. Cognitive ethology has the potential to make important contributions to our understanding in a number of areas, for the cognitive vocabulary can help to deliver important insights about animals that may otherwise not be available.

3. GRIFFIN AND THE RISE OF COGNITIVE ETHOLOGY

Many of the same forces that led to the development of cognitive psychology in the 1960s began to gather in animal behaviour in the 1970s. Lorenz and Tinbergen had already made appeals to "unobservable" internal states respectable, and philosophers such as Hilary Putnam (1960/1975) and Jerry Fodor (1968) had shown that materialism and mentalism could be made compatible. In addition, Jane Goodall and Dian Fossey were popularizing the idea that the other African apes, including chimpanzees and mountain gorillas,[9] have rich cognitive and emotional lives.[10]

The rise of cognitive ethology can conveniently be dated from the publication of Donald Griffin's *The Question of Animal Awareness* (1976). In view of its historical significance it is surprising that the expression 'cognitive ethology' occurs only twice in the first edition of this landmark book, and then only in the last four pages. By 1978, however, this term figured in the title of Griffin's *Behavioral and Brain Sciences* target article. In each succeeding book (Griffin 1984, 1992) this expression has become more frequent.[11]

One explanation for Griffin's apparent reluctance to use the term 'cognitive ethology' is his hostility to cognitive psychology. This hostility may be surprising since, as we have suggested, the cognitive turn in ethology can be related to similar developments in psychology. However Griffin appears to think of cognitive psychology as a variety of behaviourism. Indeed, he claims that "conspicuously absent from most of contemporary cognitive psychology is any serious attention to conscious thoughts or subjective feelings" (Griffin 1984: 11). Yet it is "conscious thoughts" and "subjective feelings" that Griffin is most interested in exploring. Griffin writes that the challenge of cognitive ethology "is to venture across the species boundary and try to gather satisfactory information about what other species may think or feel" (ibid. 12).

Griffin's picture is of a world of creatures with different subjectivities leading their own individual lives. Trying to learn about the minds of other

---

[9] See Cavalieri and Singer (1993).   [10] Montgomery (1991).
[11] On Griffin's development see Bekoff (1993a); Hailman (1978).

animals involves trying to get "a window" on their minds (ibid. ch. 8). Griffin seems to think that communication offers such a window, and in his writings he focuses on the communication systems of various animals.

Griffin's cognitive ethology has been attacked from several directions. Scientists, especially those of a behaviourist persuasion, often argue that cognitive or mental concepts cannot be operationally defined, thus there are no researchable questions in cognitive ethology. On this view cognitive ethology should be banished from the citadel of science and consigned to the scrapheap of idle speculation.[12]

Griffin seems to be of two minds about this objection. In much of his work he has been concerned to satisfy his critics by framing definitions. Yet he seems impatient with the demand for definition and sometimes dismissive of it. In his early work (1976/1981) Griffin is concerned to define such terms as 'conscious awareness' and 'mental experience'. In Griffin (1982, 1984) he tries to define 'mind', 'aware', 'intend', 'conscious', 'feeling', and 'think'; but he is most concerned to define 'consciousness'. Although Griffin seems to think that it is important to define these key terms, he never seems completely happy with the definitions that he gives. In 1981 he writes that "almost any concept can be quibbled to death by excessive insistence on exact operational definitions" (p. 12). By 1991 he is claiming that "it is therefore neither necessary nor advisable to become so bogged down in quibbles about definitions that the investigation of animal cognition and consciousness is neglected altogether" (pp. 4–5). But despite his interest in getting on with it, even if the central terms cannot precisely be defined, Griffin returns again and again to the problem of definition.

In our view classical definitions cannot be given for key terms in cognitive ethology but it is not necessary to give them in order to have a viable field of research. Classical definitions preserve meaning and provide necessary and sufficient conditions for the application of a term. An area in which there is controversy is likely to be one in which the definitions of key expressions are contested. It is not only the application of cognitive terms that is contested, there are also competing definitions of such terms as 'fitness', 'recognition', 'communication', 'play', 'choice', 'dominance', 'altruism', and 'optimality'. With respect to mental concepts, a huge literature has developed over the years about whether or not it is part of the meaning of mental terms that what they refer to is private, introspectable, incorrigible, and so on. One result of scientific inquiry is to help fix and refine definitions. As science advances,

---

[12] For discussion see Bekoff and Allen (1996).

definitions change and become more precise and entrenched. In order to get an area of inquiry going, what is needed is some common understanding of the domain to be investigated, not agreement about the meaning of key terms. Key terms in cognitive ethology are well enough understood to begin inquiry, even if classical definitions are difficult to come by.

Griffin's cognitive ethology is not sunk by the failure of definition. Yet it should be clear from this discussion that Griffin is tempted by some key assumptions of his critics. It is another assumption, one that Griffin shares with some of his critics, that is especially problematical for his version of cognitive ethology.

Griffin appears to accept a fundamentally Cartesian notion of the mind, at least with respect to its epistemological status. Although he formulates his central question in different ways, what Griffin really wants to know is whether animals are conscious. He assimilates the question of consciousness to the question of whether animals have subjective states. When the question is posed in this way, the link between mind and behaviour seems highly contingent: two creatures many be in the same subjective (i.e. mental) state, but in only one does this have any objective (i.e. behavioural) consequence; two creatures may be in the same objective (i.e. behavioural) state, but in only one is the behaviour caused by a subjective (i.e. mental) state. Knowledge of the minds of others is, on this view, inferential and probabilistic (Griffin 1992: 260). From our observations of objective states we make inferences to unobservable, subjective states. But since the connections between observable, objective states and unobservable, subjective states are weak and contingent, these inferences can be incorrect. On this view the passage from behavioural observations to the attribution of mentality is always uncertain and possibly treacherous. Nevertheless Griffin believes that many animals are conscious and he appeals to three sorts of evidence in support of his view.

The first sort of evidence can be viewed as a generalization of an argument given by Mill (1865/1884) for the existence of other human minds. It involves noting that in my own case various forms of consciousness are associated with various behaviours, physical states, and structures; and inferring that these behaviours, states, and structures are probably associated with various forms of consciousness in other creatures as well. It has often been pointed out that this argument fails in its goal of establishing the existence of other human minds; for generalizing to countless cases from my own involves a very large generalization from a very small sample.[13] When the analogies are weaker, as

---

[13] See the papers in Rosenthal (1991, part II.A).

they are when drawn between humans and non-humans, the induction is even more suspect.

Other arguments that Griffin gives involve appeals to novel or flexible behaviours. These appeals often have the rhetorical power of "gee whiz" stories. When people hear about the neat things that animals do they are often inclined to infer consciousness. But such inferences are open to the following objection. If flexible and novel behaviours can be fully explained by reference to non-cognitive states or processes whose existence is relatively uncontroversial, then it is reasonable to explain them in these non-cognitive terms. In many cases such behaviour can be explained in such non-cognitive terms.[14] In other cases it cannot, but Griffin's critics say that cognitive explanations are just temporary placeholders for the "real" explanations of which we are currently ignorant. Put in these terms, the dispute appears to be a standoff.

In the light of these difficulties with other forms of argument, it is not surprising that the evidence that Griffin most relies on involves communication. Just as Descartes placed a great deal of weight on the importance of language, so Griffin views communication as providing a window on other minds.

Communication can provide important evidence for various views about the nature of animal minds.[15] But this concept as it is used in the ethological literature has its problems.[16] Communication is not a transparent window that permits us to see into another "subjectivity". Thus facts about animal communication do not always provide support for views about the kinds of minds that Griffin believes that animals have.

So the objectors are right (in a way) but for the wrong reasons. They point out that the existence of Griffin-style minds in non-human animals is highly speculative and cannot convincingly be demonstrated by inferences from behavioural data. From this they conclude that animals do not have minds, or that if they do, they cannot systematically be studied. Instead the correct conclusion is that animals do not have Griffin-style minds, but for that matter neither do we. Our minds are closely tied to behaviour and so are the minds of other animals. However, our knowledge of other minds is not generally a matter of inference from behaviour.

We agree with Griffin that many animals have mental states and that this belief is supported by close observations of their behaviour. As we shall suggest in Section 4, minds that are closely tied to behaviour can systematically be

---

[14] See e.g. Galef (1990/1996).   [15] See Cheney and Seyfarth (1990); Smith (1990/1996, 1991).
[16] Philips and Austad (1990/1996).

studied. In our view cognitive ethology is not only possible, but it is an active field of ongoing research.

In summary, Griffin's great contributions are to insist that questions about animal minds be addressed, to argue that what we say about animal minds must be continuous with our views about human minds, to bring a fully comparative perspective to bear on these questions, and to have motivated empirical research in a neglected area. However, despite his contributions and his immensely important historical role, cognitive ethology must develop more sophisticated conceptions of the mind and its relation to behaviour, and develop research programmes that are capable of answering some very specific questions. In the next two sections we will take some initial steps towards discharging these obligations.[17]

4. TWO CONCEPTS OF COGNITIVE ETHOLOGY[18]

Cognitive ethology is an area that is undergoing growth and expansion. Among the different sorts of practices, two kinds of cognitive ethology can be distinguished. We will refer to them as "weak cognitive ethology" and "strong cognitive ethology", and discuss them in turn.

4.1 Weak Cognitive Ethology (WCE)

WCE is the most common form of cognitive ethology. WCE countenances the use of a cognitive vocabulary for the explanation of behaviour, but not its description. The following passage is a characteristic expression of WCE (although in this passage it is offered as a "definition" of cognitive psychology).

[I]t is the study of the mental processes that result in behavior. These internal processes act on sensory input: transforming, reducing, elaborating, storing, retrieving, and combining. Because these processes are usually not directly observable, their

---

[17] There is an important strand in Griffin's work that we have not addressed: he wants to understand creatures from "the inside out", he wants to know what it is like to be a bat (for example), and he assumes (following Nagel 1974) that such knowledge does not consist in knowing some set of "objective" facts about bats (for a contrary view see Akins 1990). If Griffin is right in supposing that such radical subjectivity exists, cognitive ethology as we understand it will not deliver a deep appreciation of it. Griffin's concerns about radical subjectivity may be of profound importance, but they go beyond the boundaries of science as it is currently understood.

[18] In what follows we make several simplifying assumptions including these: first, that cognitive ethology is directed towards explaining behaviour rather than cognitive competencies; secondly, that for many organisms in many cases intentional interpretations and explanations count as cognitive ones; and thirdly, that information processing in many organisms counts as cognitive activity. All of these assumptions warrant further discussion.

characteristics and the information upon which they act are inferred from behavior. Hypotheses about internal events (i.e. cognitive theories) generate predictions of how environmental inputs will be transformed in the production of behavior.[19]

WCE is an advance over behaviourism because it takes information processing seriously. Behaviourists typically treated organisms as "black boxes" whose internal states were irrelevent to the real job of science which involves mapping environmental inputs on to behavioural outputs. WCE prises the lid off the black box and treats its contents as important.

However the description of the contents of the black box often relies on fashionable computer metaphors. Indeed, one might say that WCE simply replaces the mechanical metaphors of the behaviourist tradition with the computer metaphors of cognitive science. It may be, as many think, that the computer metaphor marks a real advance over mechanical ones. Digital computers have impressive formal powers that old-fashioned machines that rely on gears and pulleys do not. But Griffin and others[20] remain unimpressed. They say that something is left out even in these very sophisticated models (e.g. "consciousness", "intrinsic intentionality").

Whether or not something has been left out, there appears to be a double standard between humans and non-humans that is implicit in much work that is done in WCE. Non-humans are often assimilated to computers in a way in which humans are not. But the significant border, if there is one, is not between animals and computers on the one hand and humans on the other, but between biological creatures and non-biological entities. Both may process information but they seem importantly different. The capacity for having affective states is a feature of many biological creatures, but one that computers do not seem to share. Many biological creatures suffer pain, distress, fear, and can be happy or contented. WCE leaves out the affective states of biological organisms. Cognition may play a role in emotion, but emotional and affective states cannot simply be reduced to cognitive states.

Another weakness of WCE is that it attempts to protect the description of behaviour from the cognitive vocabulary. Researchers in the tradition of WCE seem to share the behaviourist presumption that the behaviour that is to be explained can and should be described in a cognitive-free language that makes reference only to bodily movements. Appeals to cognitive states enter only with attempts at explanation. We believe that a great deal of animal behaviour cannot meaningfully be described without using cognitive and affective vocabularies. What distinguishes strong cognitive ethology from WCE (in

---

[19] Yoerg (1991: 288).   [20] e.g. Searle (1992).

part) is the willingness to deploy these vocabularies in the interpretation of behaviour as well as in its explanation.

4.2 Strong Cognitive Ethology (SCE)

SCE underwrites a range of research programmes in which both cognitive and affective vocabularies are willingly employed for purposes of interpretation and explanation. We will explain these concepts of interpretation and explanation in turn.

One important function of ethological investigation is to describe the behaviour of animals. This role is not as highly prized as it was in the early days of ethology and is often dismissed as a hangover from natural history and sometimes likened to stamp-collecting. Yet any science must provide a description of its domain and it is important to know what animals do if we are to explain why they do it.

In recent animal behaviour studies there has been a search for canonical descriptions that reflect the basic categories of behaviour.[21] The idea is that for any behaviour it is possible to produce a description in a common vocabulary that is solely based on what is observable. Other descriptions of behaviour, though they may be useful, involve "reading into the behaviour" and are ultimately eliminable. This view is untenable for a number of reasons.

First, although we cannot argue the point in detail here, we believe that the search for basic non-human behaviours is doomed for the same reasons that the search for basic human actions is doomed. At time t_1 Kelly presses the button, rings the doorbell, and displaces some molecules. Did Kelly do one thing or many things? If one thing, which thing? If many things, which thing is basic? Grete (the dog) may simultaneously engage in a play behaviour, bow, bend her front legs, kick up some dust, and displace some molecules. The same questions arise about how many things Grete did and which they are. We believe that no plausible answers to these questions can be given that are independent of pragmatic factors. What an animal does and how this is conceptualized is a contextual matter.

A second reason why this approach is untenable is related to this point. In our view descriptions of behaviour are intrinsically plural and multi-dimensional. What counts as "the best" description is relative to the questions being asked and the interests of the interrogator. It would be unfruitful and perhaps impossible to constrain all descriptions of animal behaviour by a set of basic categories.[22] This point is perhaps most obvious with respect to

---

[21] Golani (1992); see also Purton (1978).   [22] Mason (1986).

primates. Primatologists virtually always describe the behaviour of their subjects in highly abstract and functional terms. Later, often for purposes of publication, they may try to translate these descriptions into the vocabulary of bodily movements. But if primatologists were forbidden to use abstract, functional vocabularies, one wonders if they could describe the behaviour of their subjects at all.[23] Indeed, what would be the title, or the subject for that matter, of a classic book like de Waal's *Peacemaking among the Primates*.

A third problem with this approach is that in many cases descriptions of an animal's behaviour in the canonical language would deprive us of insights into the meaning of the behaviour. Predator-avoidance may take many forms, and since non-human animals are no more infallible than human animals, such behaviour may fail, or occur when no predator is within striking distance. In many cases we might be disposed to say that the animal is trying to avoid a predator, yet a description of the animal's behaviour just in terms of her observable bodily movements would not allow this insight.

Finally, an animal's behavioural repertoire is organized functionally as well as in other ways. The same bodily movements may have different meanings; and the same behaviour, defined in functional terms, may involve different bodily movements. For example, the same bodily movements involved in canid play are also involved in aggression and reproduction.[24] And the same behaviour from a functional point of view, for example, predator avoidance, may involve tree climbing in one case and running in another.

For these reasons we believe that the search for canonical descriptions of animal behaviour fails. This approach is rooted in the positivist dream of a value-free observation language that can be used to characterize the phenomena that covering laws are supposed to explain. Whatever the plausibility of this model for the physical sciences, it is highly implausible for ethology.

Because the attempt to describe behaviour in a canonical vocabulary that reflects basic categories is unsuccessful, we favour the use of the term 'interpretation' where others use the term 'description'. This acknowledges the fact that describing what animals do involves interpreting their behaviour.

A central role of explanation is to specify why something happened. Although we cannot tell the story here, we would defend a view of explanation that is similar to our account of interpretation: explanations can be plural, non-competitive, and occur at different levels of abstraction. In our view appeal to generalizations that involve cognitive and affective states can genuinely be explanatory.

However, a word of caution is in order. We have tried to defeat a picture of

---

[23] Bekoff (1995a).   [24] See Section 5.

ethology that leaves no room for cognitive and affective interpretations and explanations. But even if what we have said is correct, no one is compelled to employ such vocabularies. It is still open to someone to object that such vocabularies are illegitimate—neither suitable for interpretation nor explanation. The rejection of the "canonical description view" does not imply the legitimacy—much less the fruitfulness—of the SCE alternative. A second objection is weaker. It may be admitted that although cognitive and affective vocabularies can be employed legitimately in interpretation and explanation, we are not compelled to use them and indeed would do better if we did not.

With respect to the second objection, we concede that no one is driven to apply cognitive and affective vocabularies to animals on pain of logical contradiction. Quine and Skinner could write their autobiographies as narratives of their bodily movements without falling into logical inconsistency. No doubt the same would be true of Digit and Koko. But Quine's autobiography is boring: it lacks insight and inspiration. One has the feeling that much of what is important has been left out. In our view the same is true with respect to interpreting and explaining the behaviour of many non-human animals: one can avoid cognitive and affective vocabularies, but as we will try to show in the next section, in many cases one does this on pain of giving up interesting and insightful perspectives.

With respect to the first objection, this charge most plausibly comes either from those who espouse a double standard with respect to humans and non-humans (or languageless creatures and those with language),[25] or eliminativists with respect to cognitive and affective vocabularies. We have argued elsewhere, as have many others, that a principled double standard cannot be maintained, so we will not repeat those arguments here.[26] With respect to eliminativism, if it is true that cognitive and affective vocabularies will one day bite the dust, then SCE would cease to exist. But SCE is not singularly vulnerable. The elimination of cognitive and affective vocabularies would fell other scientific enterprises as well and be part of a radical revision of the way that we think about the world. It is enough here to defend SCE against those who are more modest in their claims.[27]

---

[25] e.g. Carruthers (1989).

[26] Bekoff and Jamieson (1991); Jamieson and Bekoff (1992).

[27] As suggested in the text, the existence of a cognitive vocabulary is a necessary condition for the persistence of cognitive ethology. However cognitive ethology is not committed to "folk psychology". Cognitive ethology is committed to the view that the behaviour of non-human animals can usefully be interpreted or explained in ways consistent with our best understanding of cognitive states, whether these involve folk-psychological concepts or not. If our best understanding of cognitive states involves some alternative to folk psychology, then cognitive ethology should embrace the alternative.

In this section we have distinguished two concepts of cognitive ethology, spoken in favour of one, and defended it against two objections. The heart of the case for SCE, however, rests with its fruitfulness as a conceptual guide to empirical research. In the next section we will discuss one area of research in cognitive ethology.

5. SOCIAL PLAY

Space does not allow us to cover the many areas of research (e.g. mate choice, habitat selection, individual recognition and discrimination, injury-feigning, assessments of dominance, foraging for food, caching food, various types of social communication, observational learning, tool use, imitation, teaching) in which cognitive ethological approaches have been useful in gaining an understanding of the behaviour of animals.[28] Here we will discuss only one area: social play.

Social play is a behaviour that lends itself to cognitive studies, and poses a great challenge to researchers.[29] In particular, the question of how mammals communicate their intention to engage in social play presupposes cognitive states, without which it would be difficult or impossible to describe the social encounter.[30]

The canid "play bow" is a highly stereotyped movement that seems to function to stimulate recipients to engage (or continue to engage) in social play.[31] When an animal performs a play bow she crouches on her forelimbs, leaves her hind legs fairly straight, and may wag her tail and bark. Such play-soliciting signals appear to transmit the message that "what follows is play". Play-soliciting signals are used to communicate to others that actions such as biting, shaking the head from side to side, and mounting are to be taken as play and not as aggressive, predatory, or reproductive behaviour.

Play-soliciting signals appear to foster cooperation between players so that each responds to the other in a way consistent with play and different from the responses that the same actions would elicit in other contexts.[32] This cooperation may occur because each of the participants has a belief about the intentions of the other animals who are involved in the social encounter. For example, in coyotes the response to a threat gesture is very different if it is

---

[28] For examples see Griffin (1984, 1992); Mitchell and Thompson (1986); Byrne and Whiten (1988); Cheney and Seyfarth (1990); Bekoff and Jamieson (1990, 1991); Ristau (1991); Bekoff (1995a).
[29] Mitchell (1990); Bekoff and Allen (1992).
[30] Bekoff (1995a).   [31] Bekoff (1977).   [32] Bekoff (1975).

immediately preceeded by a play signal or if a play signal is performed at the beginning of the interaction.[33] The play signal can be viewed as altering the meaning of a threat signal by establishing (or maintaining) a "play mood". When a play signaller bites or mounts the recipient of a play signal, the recipient is not disposed to injure or to mate with the signaller.

It is difficult to describe canid play behaviour without using a cognitive vocabulary. One and the same bodily movement can be aggression or play. The difference between a movement that is aggressive and one that is playful is naturally described in terms of one animal's intention and another animal's appreciation of the intention.

Similarly the cognitive vocabulary appears to provide the resources for explaining some play behaviour. For example, suppose that we want to know why Grete permitted Jethro to nip at her ears. One explanation may be that Grete believes that Jethro is playing. This gives rise to further questions, such as whether Jethro believes that Grete believes that Jethro is playing. One of the challenges of research in cognitive ethology is to investigate the extent to which such questions are well-formed and what the possible answers to them might be.

In this section we have been able to provide only a brief summary of some questions about social play. Because of the brevity of this account, we have not been able to discuss behaviours in which the affective vocabulary gains a foothold. Nor did we discuss what might be reasonable empirical constraints on cognitive interpretations and explanations.

It is important to remember that we are pluralists with respect to both explanation and interpretation. Cognitive explanations do not exclude other causal ones, nor do they rule out explanations that are adaptationist, phylogenetic, or developmental. In our view we need to employ a large range of conceptual resources in order to understand behaviour.

6. CONCLUDING REMARKS

We have argued that cognitive ethology can be defended against its critics. In addition, we have discussed some of its varieties and forms and briefly sketched one area of research in cognitive ethology. Before closing, it is worth mentioning what cognitive ethology can contribute to cognitive studies generally.

Cognitive ethology can help to broaden the perspective of cognitive studies in two ways. First, cognitive ethology can help to situate the study of

---

[33] ibid.

cognition in an evolutionary framework. It should be a necessary condition for postulating a cognitive state in a human that the existence of this state is at least consistent with evolutionary history. Although lip service is sometimes given to this constraint, talk of evolution in cognitive science is too often metaphorical. Cognitive ethology has the potential to make cognitive science take evolution seriously. Second, the fact that cognitive ethology is fully comparative can help to make cognitive science less parochial. Although there has been a great deal of concern about parochialism with respect to non-biological systems, this concern has often coexisted with a surprising degree of "chimpocentrism".[34] Many people are more willing to countenance cognition in computers or space aliens than in rodents, amphibians, or insects. Even in cognitive studies there is a tendency to view cognition as "essential" to humans and instantiated in various (lesser) degrees only in those who are phylogenetically close to humans. With its view of cognition as a strategic evolutionary response to problems that might have been faced by a variety of diverse organisms, cognitive ethology can help to overcome this form of parochialism.

There is no question but that the issue of animal minds is difficult and complex. Like questions about the human mind, it is tangled in issues of definition, conception, relation to behaviour, and so on. Yet in our view cognitive ethology is here to stay. For the adoption of cognitive and affective vocabularies by ethologists opens up a range of explanations, predictions, and generalizations that would not otherwise be available. As long as there are animals to behave and humans to wonder why, cognitive interpretations and explanations will be offered. In our view this is not only permissible, it is often enlightening. Sometimes it is even science.

[34] Beck (1982).

6

Cognitive Ethology at the End of Neuroscience

Eliminative Materialism is the thesis that our common-sense conception of psychological phenomena constitutes a radically false theory, a theory so fundamentally defective that both the principles and the ontology of that theory will eventually be displaced, rather than smoothly reduced, by completed neuroscience.

(Churchland 1981: 67)

1. A SHORT, SIMPLE HISTORY

In the beginning, humans were animals. Accounts of the belief systems of aboriginal peoples often emphasize the fact that these peoples viewed themselves as continuous with the rest of nature.[1] Animals were worshipped, hunted, and respected. They were also agents with whom one made agreements,[2] and in some cases even entered into conjugal relationships.[3] Of course aboriginal peoples distinguished between those who were members of their own group and those who were outsiders. But, in many cases, some animals were considered insiders and other humans were treated as outsiders. Thus, for many aboriginal peoples, life was fully lived in inter-species communities.

Then along came humanism. There are many ways of characterizing humanism and dating its arrival. Viewed historically, it was a cultural movement that arose during the Italian Renaissance, though it looked back to the classical world. Protagoras' oft-quoted remark, "man is the measure of all

I thank Colin Allen, Marc Bekoff, Gordon Burghardt, and especially Brian Keeley for their stimulating comments on an earlier draft.

[1] See Whitt *et al.* (2001).   [2] See Martin (1978).   [3] See Passmore (1974).

things", however it was originally intended, conveys the spirit of humanism. Humanism can broadly be characterized as "[a]ny philosophy concerned to emphasize human welfare and dignity, and optimistic about the powers of unaided human understanding".[4] On this view, humans are seen as morally distinctive, and the moral difference between humans and other animals is typically thought to rest on a non-moral categorical distinction—for example, that humans are different from other animals in being rational; or that only humans are capable of language, tool use, or some other favoured activity.

The rise of humanism and modern science was temporally coincident, and humanism's optimism about human understanding helps to explain this association. Humanism advocated science on the ground that scientific knowledge contributes to human welfare. Humanism thus provided a justification for modern science's inauguration of the large-scale, systematic infliction of pain and death on non-human animals in the pursuit of knowledge. Indeed, since there are no elephant Galileos, the very practice of science itself also helped to distinguish humans from other animals. Some might say that humanism was the theory and science was the practice.

The great exemplar of humanism's attitude towards animals was the seventeenth-century thinker, René Descartes. Descartes, who is often regarded as the founder of modern philosophy, also did important work in optics and analytical geometry. He emphasized the importance of reason, and exalted humans over other animals.

Descartes was a dualist in at least the two following respects. First, he taught that humans are composed of two interacting substances: a material substance that is the body, and an immaterial substance that is the mind. Secondly, he was a dualist with respect to the relation between humans and the rest of nature. Humans and other animals are distinct because, while non-human animals are material substances, humans are essentially immaterial substances associated with material substances. Stated simply, his view was that while humans are minded creatures, non-human animals are organic automata who are not harmed when they are subjected to invasive procedures. An unknown contemporary wrote of the scientist followers of Descartes that

[t]hey administered beatings to dogs with perfect indifference; and made fun of those who pitied the creatures as if they felt pain . . . They nailed poor animals up on boards by their four paws to vivisect them and see the circulation of the blood which was a great subject of controversy.[5]

---

[4] Blackburn (1994: 178).   [5] As quoted in Rosenfield (1968: 54).

Humanism died in 1859 with the publication of Darwin's *On the Origin of Species*, but it has not yet become extinct: it remains a "dead man walking". Various philosophers, for example, James Rachels (1990), have shown how evolutionary theory undermines the human claim to categorical uniqueness, thus rendering views about the moral distinctiveness of humans implausible. Whether we look at humans behaviourally, taxonomically, or genetically, the categorical distinction that is supposed to underwrite the moral difference between humans and other animals does not seem to obtain. Behaviourally, the overwhelming similarities between humans and many other animals are obvious to anyone who bothers to pay close attention.[6] Taxonomically, humans are one of several species of great ape, more closely related to chimpanzees than chimpanzees are to gorillas or orang-utans. Genetically, the similarities are overwhelming. Commenting on the publication of the human genome, Svante Pääbo (2001: 219) wrote:

The first comparisons will be between the human genome and distantly related genomes such as those of yeast, flies, worms, and mice . . . [w]e share much of our genetic scaffold even with very distant relatives. The similarity between humans and other animals will become even more evident when genome sequences from organisms such as the mouse, with whom we share a more recent common ancestor, become available. For these species, both the number of genes and the general structure of the genome are likely to be very similar to ours . . . [T]he close similarity of our genome to those of other organisms will make the unity of life more obvious to everyone. No doubt the genomic view of our place in nature will be both a source of humility and a blow to the idea of human uniqueness.

However, the most obvious challenge to the notion of human uniqueness is likely to come from comparisons of genomes of closely related species. We already know that the overall DNA sequence similarity between humans and chimpanzees is about 99%. When the chimpanzee genome sequence becomes available, we are sure to find that its gene content and organization are very similar (if not identical) to our own. The result is sure to be an even more powerful challenge to the notion of human uniqueness than the comparison of the human genome to those of other mammals.

For much of the twentieth century behaviourism held sway. It became the "normal science" of university psychology departments, and for the most part happily co-existed with prevailing humanist values. Although many behaviourists considered themselves materialists, in some respects their doctrine was oddly unbiological. While they emphasized the importance of learning, they minimized the role of underlying biological structures, and seldom attempted evolutionary explanations. The word 'evolution' rarely appears in

---

[6] See e.g. Bekoff (2000).

the foundational treatises of the movement, with six occurrences in the index of Skinner (1953), and no occurrences at all in the index of Watson (1930). However Watson and Skinner did not flinch from the radical anti-humanist implications of their theory. Watson (1930, p. v), reflecting on his Columbia University lectures of 1912 and the storm of criticism they provoked, wrote that

> We believed then, as we do now, that man is an animal different from other animals only in the types of behavior he displays . . . Human beings do not want to class themselves with other animals . . . The raw fact that you, as a psychologist, if you are to remain scientific, must describe the behavior of man in no other terms than those you would use in describing the behavior of the ox you slaughter, drove and still drives many timid souls away from behaviorism.

The very title of Skinner's book, *Beyond Freedom and Dignity*, indicates the lengths he was willing to go to in articulating the anti-humanist case.

At least two sources contributed to the decline of Behaviourism. One was the development of more biological understandings of behaviour in the work of such classical ethologists as Konrad Lorenz and Niko Tinbergen.[7] The other was the cognitive revolution that originated with the work of Noam Chomsky in linguistics, and then migrated into philosophy and psychology. Chomsky's cognitivism was developed in direct response to Skinner's Behaviourism. In his devastating review of Skinner's *Verbal Behavior*, Chomsky (1959) showed that Behaviourist learning theory, which neglected the innate endowment of organisms, was not powerful enough to explain human linguistic behaviour.

2. THREE QUESTIONS ABOUT COGNITIVE ETHOLOGY

The cognitive turn came late to ethology, dating perhaps from Griffin (1976/ 1981). Although most of the central concepts and claims in this field are contested, we can start with the simple thought that cognitive ethology proposes that some behaviour of some animals can be explained by appeal to their cognitive and affective states. Cognitive states are typically understood as representational states produced by natural selection. Representational states are in turn characterized by their semantic content. So, cognitive ethology proposes to explain some animal behaviour by appeal to semantic content. A simple example of such an explanation is this: Grete (the dog) walks to the door

---

[7] For further discussion see Essay 5.

because she wants to go out. Wanting to go out is a representational state that figures in the explanation of the behaviour.

There are many different ways of filling in the details of this programme. The proffered explanations could be causal or non-causal. They may or may not involve psycho-behavioural laws. Content could be wide or narrow. A story must also be told about the relationship between cognitive explanations and those that might be given for the phototropic behaviour of plants or the heat-seeking behaviour of missiles. However, these are questions that I shall put aside. Instead, in the space that remains, there are three questions that I wish to explore. The first two questions are relatively straightforward: first, what is the relation between cognitive ethology and folk-psychological explanation? Secondly, how can we discover the content of an animal's thought? Finally, I wish to return to my epigraph and comment on the very large question of whether the rise of neuroscience is a threat to cognitive ethology.

On the first question, it may appear that the future of cognitive ethology is essentially linked to the fate of folk psychology. Certainly part of the intuitive case for cognitive ethology flows from the naturalness of applying folk psychological categories and generalizations to non-human animals. Grete, like my mother, sometimes gets jealous, and both Grete and my mother get testy when they are frustrated. Some cognitive ethologists do not shrink from explicitly endorsing such folk-psychological explanations of animal behaviour. This is apparent in *The Smile of a Dolphin*,[8] a remarkable book in which eminent ethologists, behavioural ecologists, psychologists, sociologists, and anthropologists let their hair down and describe their most memorable encounters with non-human animals. The chapter headings say it all: "love"; "fear, aggression, and anger"; "joy and grief"; and "fellow feelings". I myself am not at all chary about applying folk psychological vocabularies and generalizations to both my mother and to Grete. However, the question here is whether cognitive ethology necessarily stands or falls with the tenability of folk psychology. I claim that it does not.

Folk psychology provides one way of providing cognitive explanations, but it is not the only way. Perhaps concepts such as jealousy and frustration will be replaced by ones that more adequately individuate states and explain behaviour. Someday more useful generalizations may be found for making behaviour intelligible. Cognitive ethology can avail itself of improved cognitive and psychological theories without subverting itself. It is essential to

---

[8] Bekoff (2000).

cognitive ethology that its explanations appeal to representational states of organisms, but these states need not be the familiar ones of folk psychology. Thus, the demise of folk psychology does not in itself portend the end of cognitive ethology.

This takes us to the second question of how we can identify the content of animals' cognitive states. Work on this issue has proceeded both from the top down and from the bottom up. Some, including me (e.g. in Essay 4), have insisted that animals think, but generally avoided serious discussion of what they think. Others, such as Colin Allen (1999), have sketched specific approaches for empirically characterizing concepts that might figure in an animal's cognitive economy. The first sort of work sometimes seems unconvincing since the best evidence for the claim that an animal is thinking involves some account of the content of its thought. On the other hand the second kind of work doesn't always seem very cognitive. Content that is inferred from fairly crude discrimination experiments and concepts that are straightforwardly reducible to neural states all seem rather remote from human cognition. However, in my view, the difficulty in systematically characterizing the content of animals' cognitive states is not so much because there are problems with the various research strategies that have been employed, as with the notion of content itself.

The concept of content plays a role in a particular way of conceiving the mind. On this view a mental state involves a three-place relation between a creature, an attitude, and a content. For example, when Grete believes that her treats are in the cupboard, Grete is the creature, she has the attitude of believing, towards the content, "my treats are in the cupboard". When the matter is stated this way, it is easy to see why many are sceptical about whether languageless creatures can have cognitive states. If cognitive states are attitudes, and if contents are sentences, as they appear to be in the example given, then some fancy footwork is required to resist this scepticism. This is not the concern I wish to address here, however.[9] My point at present is simply that the notion of content occurs as part of a particular way of looking at the mind.

What I want to suggest is that content ascription is part of a practice deployed in order to make ourselves and others intelligible. Within this practice, content ascription is a heuristic that is fundamentally interpretative and interest-relative. These features are reflected in "the holism of the mental" (Davidson 1999: 10), a feature noted by Quine (1960/1975) and vigorously

---

[9] For discussion of this point see Allen and Bekoff (1997: 63 ff.).

advocated by Davidson throughout his career. Grete's behaviour of walking to the door can variously be explained by mutually adjusting beliefs and desires. If we fix a desire, for example, that Grete wants to urinate, then we can specify a belief (for example, that on the other side of the door is a place in which it is appropriate for her to urinate) that will make the behaviour intelligible. But if we fix a different desire (for example, that Grete wants to play with Jethro), then we will have to adjust Grete's beliefs accordingly in order to explain the behaviour. This story about the interactions between contents and attitudes ramifies. While not anything goes, content ascriptions answer to various pragmatic concerns, including those involving other content ascriptions, and not only to what is known about the organism's body and the world in which it is embedded. For this reason we should not expect content ascriptions to be uniquely determined by empirical observation.

If I am right about this, then assigning content is as much a matter of marshalling conceptual considerations as empirical ones. There will not be a decisive observation or critical experiment that will uniquely determine what an animal "really" thinks. However, it does not follow from this that what an animal thinks is unknowable, or a matter of inference or guesswork. For such a sceptical view presupposes that there is some determinate fact of the matter to know, infer, or guess. What I am suggesting is that it is the very nature of content specification, thus cognitive explanation, to be plural and indeterminate, and therefore conceptually, not just empirically grounded. To be blunt: there is no unique fact of the matter about what a non-human animal "really" thinks.

This is not a weakness of cognitive ethology. For there is no unique fact of the matter about what you or I "really" think. The same slackness that is at work in content attributions to non-human animals is at work in content attributions to humans as well. However, this is obscured by familiarity, deference, and especially language. But linguistic behaviour is behaviour none the less, and the task of the interpreter is not in principle different when faced with me verbalizing or Grete tail-wagging.[10]

The view that I am urging is not entirely original. Its origins are in Quine and Wittgenstein, and it owes a lot to philosophers who have already been cited. In substance, my view may be closest to Dennett's. The key idea is that we should not expect to find the propositional attitudes or their ilk written in the brain or anywhere else. Instead propositional attitudes are attributed by interpreters who take the "intentional stance".[11] These

---

[10] For further discussion see Essays 4 and 5.
[11] For discussion of the intentional stance see Dennett (1987).

attributions are ways of keeping track of what the organism is doing, has done, and might do. The propositional attitudes are like a grid projected on to a field. What gives the grid-points their significance is their relations to other grid-points, not their absolute locations in the field. Grid-points and propositional attitudes are means of sorting, classifying, and assessing rather than invariant, sober, descriptions of aspects of the world. On this view we attribute propositional attitudes to humans and non-humans for the same reason: in order to keep track of behaviour.

Since his earliest writings on cognitive ethology, Dennett has attempted to balance "romantic" intepretations of animal behaviour with "killjoy" understandings (1987: 245). In his recent work the killjoy seems to have gained the upper hand. He has become more scientistic in his views, and seems now to believe that there are real biological differences that count against attributing propositional attitudes to many non-human animals.[12] He has also come to think, as many did before him, that the hyperintensionality afforded by language marks an important difference in the cognitive possibilities of humans and other animals (1996: 159). Finally, perhaps motivated in part by the scientism, he seems uncomfortable with the moral uses to which cognitive attributions to non-humans have been put (ibid.: 161 ff.).

This is not the place to attempt to thwart Dennett's slide into the conventional orthodoxies about non-human animals. I will confine myself to two remarks. First, a thoroughgoing interpretivist should not be scientistic (here I side with Davidson against Quine). Scientific statements must also be interpreted, and they are as indeterminate and inscrutable as non-scientific statements. Secondly (as I have already noted), in principle for an interpreter, the task is the same whether confronted with me verbalizing or Grete tail-wagging. Davidson (1986: 446) provides a surprising reason for this (especially in light of his own views with respect to animal minds): "we have erased the boundary between knowing a language and knowing our way around the world generally . . . I conclude that there is no such thing as a language, not if a language is anything like what many philosophers and linguists have supposed."

This brings us to our final and deepest question. What would be the fate of cognitive ethology in a world in which every behaviour yielded to neuroscientific explanation? My own view is that while this would bring an end to cognitive science generally, including cognitive ethology specifically, it would not necessarily put a stop to the productive deployment of cognitive

---

[12] See Dennett (1996: 132).

vocabularies. For these vocabularies have a place in everyday discourse, whatever their status as theoretical terms. In particular, they often carry our evaluational attitudes. Cognitive language is closely tied to practices of moral appraisal—of blaming, praising, and so on. Thus, if such language were to outlive its scientific usefulness, it would not necessarily vanish. It may still have other roles to play in everyday life.

Consider the analogue from physics. We have been instructed by our epistemological betters that space and time do not exist as independent dimensions with linear structures. Yet, this has not led to the abolition of the alarm clock. Even in the face of relativity theory we speak usefully and responsibly of the sun rising and setting, though no reasonable person thinks that these notions should figure in a scientific conception of the world.

These considerations seem to suggest an important moral for cognitive ethology. If the logic of neuroscientific explanation is quite different from that of cognitive explanation, as I seem to be suggesting, then it will be a dangerous mistake to mix them in an unreflective way. Yet much of the literature of cognitive ethology does just this. Many scientists seem to go back and forth between neural and cognitive explanations, as if they were working with the same vocabularies, at the same levels of description, employing the same logic of explanation.[13] They seem to assume that micro-level explanations simply reveal what subserves macro-level phenomena, while leaving macro-level phenomena untouched. But that is far from obvious. As Paul Churchland points out in the epigraph, macro-level phenomena are sometimes displaced, rather than smoothly reduced, by micro-level explanations. This is exactly the concern that many people have about the Human Genome Project, fearing that genetic-level explanations will drive out the language of responsibility.

The suggestion of confusion can be resisted by showing that in fact cognitive and neuroscientific explanations work in the same way. One strategy would be to construe cognitive explanation in a way that is as determinate and mechanical as neuroscientific explanation. The second strategy would be to show that neuroscientific explanation is itself as pluralistic and indeterminate as cognitive explanation. There might be two reasons for thinking this. One reason would be because explanation itself is pragmatic and pluralistic (perhaps this view is implicit in Quine 1960/1975). A second reason would involve claiming that neuroscientific explanation itself appeals to content, and thus has the same features as any other content explanation. Patricia Churchland (1986: 361) seems to suggest this when she writes:

---

[13] For some examples, see Griffin (1992).

It is important . . . to emphasize that when neuroscientists do address such questions as how neurons manage to store information, or how cell assemblies do pattern recognition, or how they manage to effect sensorimotor control, they are addressing questions concerning neurodynamics—concerning information and how the brain processes it. In doing so, they are up to their ears in theorizing, and even more shocking, in theorizing about representations and computations.

What I have been suggesting could be summarized by saying that cognitive explanations are appropriate when we are too ignorant to give real (i.e. neural) explanations. I resist this way of putting the point for the reasons suggested in the preceeding paragraph, but there is something right about this view. Once we achieved a physical understanding of the occurrence of lightning we no longer had to appeal to the moods of the gods.[14] However, even if things inexorably move towards micro and mechanical explanations of behaviour, and away from macro and functional ones, cognitive ethology will still have performed a great service. Some of its contributions are methodological: it returns scientists to the field, requires that they watch animals, reflect on behavioural similarities and singularities, and so on. But from a larger cultural perspective, the real contribution of cognitive ethology is that it completes the circle and restores unity to our picture of nature.

3. CONCLUSION

I opened this chapter with a short, simple history of human attitudes towards animals. Some may quarrel with the history, disagree with my account of the science, or rightly claim that it is all much more complicated than I suggest. What cannot be denied or evaded is that this science has a moral dimension. How we study animals and what we assert about their minds and behaviour greatly affects how they are treated, as well as our own view of ourselves. Humanism is dead and its foundation is in tatters, yet the full force of this fact has not yet been felt. Cognitive ethology helps us to accept this by showing that the same explanations that apply in one case often apply in the other as well. This is an important scientific lesson, but it also carries deep and profound moral lessons. Indeed, it is because of these moral lessons that some people find this science to be subversive.

[14] Dennett (1969: 89).

7

Pain and the Evolution of Behaviour

1. INTRODUCTION

I begin with what I will call "the truism":

Pain is bad and therefore should be avoided or minimized.

While almost everyone would initially claim to subscribe to this truism, it appears to have sweeping implications that are quite at odds with most people's behaviour or beliefs. We live in a world that is characterized by vast amounts of preventable human suffering caused by war, poverty, and persecution. The resources devoted to one night's up-market dining in any major European or American city could reduce the suffering of vast numbers of people in Africa, Asia, or Latin America. Moreover, the production of food for one night's up-market dining directly entails vast amounts of animal suffering. *Foie gras* is expensive for the geese as well as for the humans. If we really subscribed to the truism, it appears that we would refrain from such excesses.

One response would be to confess to practical irrationality. We sometimes fail to do what we have most reason to do, and this is an example. While practical irrationality is no doubt a fact about our lives, there is something strange about such a confession in this case. Practical irrationality is something to be avoided and deplored, not affirmed with a shrug of the shoulders. Imagine a man who both abuses his wife, and believes that abuse is bad and should be avoided. Reflecting on his behaviour he confesses to practical irrationality. At the very least we would expect him to struggle to change his behaviour. He should be in therapy, a support group, or perhaps even plead guilty to violating the law and go to jail. Regret and often remorse are proper responses to the confession of practical irrationality. Yet regret and remorse do not seem much in evidence at Europe's and America's up-market restaurants. While most of us may claim to embrace the truism, we don't seem willing to confess to practical irrationality. We seem to think that we can have the truism, and the *foie gras* too.

In what follows I will mainly be interested in cases in which the truism seems to conflict with our attitudes towards, and treatment of, non-human animals. I will explore four alternative strategies for maintaining that there is no plausible truism about pain and its avoidance that is inconsistent with our everyday treatment of animals.

2. FUZZ UP THE TRUISM

The first strategy is to "fuzz up" the truism. It is obvious that there is something right about this approach. Pain isn't the only thing that is bad, and in concrete cases the good of pain reduction would have to be balanced against other goods. For example, suppose (not implausibly) that when painting the Sistine Chapel, Michelangelo came home from work each night suffering from various aches and pains. Not many of us would say that he should have given up painting the chapel in order to avoid the pain. The value of Michelangelo's creation outweighs whatever aches and pains he might have suffered in creating it. Of course, it also matters to us that Michelangelo willingly painted the frescos. If he were a suffering slave some people's opinions about this case might shift (but not mine).

The point is this. No doubt there are various ways in which the truism should be fuzzed up. However, on most plausible revisions, it is still going to be a truism and it is still going to have implications that are at odds with many of our ordinary beliefs and much of our everyday behaviour. Getting the truism into philosophically respectable shape may help to dull the contradiction between the truism and our ordinary lives, but it will not remove it entirely. It is difficult to see how I could maintain any plausible version of the truism while cheerfully chomping away on the *foie gras*.

3. LIMIT THE SCOPE OF THE TRUISM TO PAIN SUFFERED BY HUMANS

A second strategy is to limit the scope of the truism to pain suffered by humans. The basic intuition behind this may be the common view that we should apply a transpersonal discount rate to pain. On this view, the suffering of a stranger should be less important to me than the suffering of a friend, and the suffering of a friend ought to be less important to me than my own suffering. I believe that such a view has less going for it than one might think,[1] but even if it is God's own truth it does not directly support excluding altogether concerns about the suffering of non-human animals. What would be needed is a further argument to the conclusion that the pain of non-humans should be discounted away entirely.

Such an argument seems to me to be not forthcoming. If pain is bad and has implications for action, this cannot plausibly be said to depend on who experiences the pain. Imagine a surgeon who would want an anaesthetic if he were to undergo an otherwise painful procedure, but denies it to someone else on the grounds that the pain that would be suffered is not his pain. Of course it is open for someone to admit that the individual solipsism of the surgeon is irrational while trying to maintain that some version of species-solipsism is plausible.

Consider two versions of species-solipsism: *Homo sapiens* species-solipsism, and indexical species-solipsism. *Homo sapiens* species-solipsism holds that the truism applies only to pain suffered by humans; indexical species-solipsism holds that the truism applies only to pain suffered by the conspecifics of those who embrace the truism. *Homo sapiens* species-solipsism is implausible for many reasons, not least because it implies that highly sentient, advanced life forms in remote galaxies should only be concerned about human suffering, even if there is enormous suffering on their planet and they have no idea that earth and its humans exist. Indexical species-solipsism is implausible for the same reasons that individual solipsism is implausible. If one believes the truism and grants that humans and some non-humans are alike in having pain, then it seems indefensible to say that the truism only applies to human pain. That pain should be avoided or minimized follows from its being pain, not from any taxonomical facts about who has the pain. To suppose otherwise is like saying that sugar is sweet only when it is my sugar.

4. REJECT THE TRUISM

A third strategy is to reject the truism. This is the most radical strategy that I will consider, and it relies on a certain understanding of evolution for support. Here is one version of the argument.

---

[1] See Parfit (1984) for discussion.

Pain and pleasure seem to have nothing to do with good and evil if our appraisal is taken from the vantage point of ecological biology. Pain in particular is primarily information. In animals, it informs the central nervous system of stress, irritation, or trauma in outlying regions of the organism . . . The doctrine that life is the happier the freer it is from pain and that the happiest life conceivable is one in which there is continuous pleasure uninterrupted by pain is biologically preposterous. A living mammal which experienced no pain would be one which had a lethal dysfunction of the nervous system. The idea that pain is evil and ought to be minimized or eliminated is as primitive a notion as that of a tyrant who puts to death messengers bearing bad news on the supposition that his well-being and security is improved.[2]

One point that should be made at the outset is that the correlation between sensations of pain and useful information is much weaker than one might think.[3] Those who suffer from phantom limb pain, chronic pain, and referred pain often suffer without tissue damage. On the other hand wounded soldiers, accident victims, and those who suffer from SIB (self-injurious behaviour) often fail to have pain sensations despite serious physical damage. This suggests that evolutionary considerations, brought to bear in this way, are consistent with a version of the truism that focuses on unnecessary pain. Unnecessary pain is pain which does not provide useful information to an organism, either because it is not correlated with physical damage, or because the organism is unable to flee or resist the cause of the damage of which it is being made aware. It is obvious that much of the pain suffered by non-human animals as a result of human action is of exactly this type. The pain of the goose from which the *foie gras* is extracted is clearly unnecessary, on this understanding. Thus it remains difficult to see how I can have the truism and the *foie gras* too.

However, there is a more serious difficulty with this argument. What is presupposed here is that showing that something has a biological function defeats any claim about its value. But this presupposition conflates the descriptive question of why something came to be with the normative question of whether or not we should value it. Consider some examples. Several different accounts have been given of the function of social play.[4] Surely it does not follow that if social play has a biological function, then it is not good. A lot of play is harmless fun, and that surely counts as something good. Similarly, there may be evolutionary explanations for rape and other aggressive behaviour, but the fact that there are such explanations in no way implies that these behaviours are not bad and should be avoided or minimized. This way of

[2] Callicott (1989: 32–3).   [3] See Hardcastle (1999) for discussion.
[4] See the essays collected in Bekoff and Byers (1998).

rejecting the truism founders because it conflates (supposed) facts with values. Pain may have evolved as a conveyor of useful information, but it still may be bad. It would be irrational for the tyrant to put to death the messenger for the reason that the messenger bears bad news, but the tyrant may have other, better, reasons for putting him to death. The messenger may bear bad news that is otiose, and he may be a royal pain.

5. DENY THAT NON-HUMANS SUFFER PAIN

A fourth strategy is to deny that non-humans suffer pain. On this view the truism applies to all creatures who suffer pain, but it happens that humans are the only such creatures. On the face of it this strategy, reminiscent of Descartes's denial of animal minds, may seem singularly unpromising. But it is not as absurd as it may seem.

It is becoming increasingly clear that our everyday concept of pain is at least troubled and perhaps incoherent. We think of pain as essentially a sensation, yet we also think that I may enjoy a respite from my headache without supposing that I have suffered from two distinct headaches. My headache was there all along but for a while I didn't feel the pain. Indeed, our language suggests that pains are there to be felt and so, presumably, not to be felt. Just as I may perceive or not perceive a tree, so I may feel or not feel a pain. This way of speaking suggests that the pain is an object of perception rather than a sensation whose essence is in being experienced. But can there really be unfelt pains? We often think of pain as essentially bad, yet people sometimes report various drug experiences as not extinguishing a pain but of making the sufferer care about it less or not at all. Some drugs extinguish pains; others allow us to better tolerate them. Can we feel pain without the sensation being bad?

In the face of such conflicting intuitions philosophers have moved in different directions. Some have insisted that pain is essentially "subjective", and tried to explain away the "objectivist" intuitions. Others have insisted that pains are essentially objective and tried to dismiss subjectivist intuitions. Others have argued for complex relational views, and still others have opted for eliminativism, insisting that there is really nothing that corresponds to our everyday notion of pain.[5]

In light of these considerations some might say that pain can only be predicated of humans, since there is no coherent substratum which can support

---

[5] See Hardcastle (1999: 95 ff.) for discussion.

the projection of the predicate to other animals. On this view a large enough chunk of the peculiar collection of sentences about pain that we hold to be true about humans cannot meaningfully be applied to non-humans. What would be the grounds for saying that Bessie (the three-legged dog) suffers from phantom limb, or that she still feels her toothache but no longer cares about it so much? I am not entirely sceptical about the possibility of answering such questions, but the supposed inability does provide some ground for denying that the truism has any relevance to non-human animals.

At this stage it is hard to be confident about what will turn out to be the best account of our pain intuitions, especially in light of the growing evidence that they are also quite culturally relative. But in my opinion this dispute should not shake our confidence in the truism nor lead us to question its widespread application. The feature of pain that undergirds the truism is the fact that it hurts. Perhaps there are pains that do not hurt, in which case the truism may not apply to them. But many pains do hurt and these are bad for that reason, and should be avoided or minimized. And as Broom (2000) has shown, there is every reason to believe that pains that hurt are widely distributed among various species of animals.

6. CONCLUSIONS

In this essay I have defended a widely accepted truism that appears to be inconsistent with many of our everyday attitudes and practices regarding animals. There is quite a lot more to say on this subject. However, I hope that enough has been said to make plausible the view that a simple, widely accepted truism about pain may have sweeping implications regarding our treatment of non-human animals.

8

On the Ethics of the Use of Animals in Science
(with Tom Regan)

As you read this, animals are being killed, burned, radiated, blinded, immobilized, and shocked. They are being locked and strapped into the Noble-
Collip drum, tossed about at the rate of 40 revolutions per minute and thrust
against the iron projections that line the drum. This procedure crushes bones,
destroys tissues, smashes teeth, and ruptures internal organs. Right now,
somewhere, animals are in isolation, deprived of all social contact, while
others are in alien environments, manipulated into cannibalizing members of
their own species. It is not just a few animals at issue. In the year 1978 alone,
about 200 million animals were used for scientific purposes, about 64 million
of these in the United States. This number includes 400,000 dogs, 200,000
cats, and 30,000 apes and monkeys.[1] From anyone's point of view, these are
disagreeable facts, but some will say they are the concern of scientists only. We
who are not scientists cannot get off the hook so easily, however. The use made
of animals in science frequently is carried out in the name of improving the
quality of human life: to find cures for cancer, heart disease, and a thousand
other ailments; to develop safe new products for our consumption; and to
instruct others in, and to advance our knowledge of, the world in which we

We wish to thank Barbara Orlans and Andrew Rowan for helpful comments on an earlier draft of this
essay. Professor Jamieson's work on this project was assisted by a grant from the University Awards
Committee of the State University of New York, while Professor Regan's was assisted by a grant from
the National Endowment for the Humanities. It is a pleasure to express our gratitude in a public way
to these respective agencies.

[1] For documentation and additional information see Diner (1979); and Ryder (1975).

live. Because these things are done in our name, ostensibly to help us live better lives, and because these activities frequently are financed by public monies (approximately $5 billion dollars in federal support in the United States for 1980) we cannot in good faith or with good sense avoid confronting the facts about the use of animals in science, and assessing its morality.

In the past this debate has usually been put in terms of being for or against vivisection. But this term, 'vivisection', is ill-suited for our purposes. To vivisect an animal is to dissect it, to cut it, while it is alive. Not all practices that demand our attention involve vivisection. Animals placed in the Noble-Collip drum or those that are radiated or shocked, for example, are not dissected while they are alive. For this reason it would be misleading at best to pose our central question in terms of whether one is for or against vivisection. Our interest lies in assessing the use made of animals in science in general, not just in those cases where they are vivisected.

There are three major areas of science in which animals are routinely used. These are (1) biological and medical education; (2) toxicology testing, where the potential harmful affects for human beings of various chemicals and commercial products are first tested on animals; and (3) original and applied research, including not only research into the causes and treatment of various diseases but also into the basic biochemical nature and behaviour of living organisms.[2] All of us are familiar with the use of animals in education from our time spent in laboratory sections in biology, for example, and most of us have an outsider's inkling of what goes on in original and applied research from what we read in the newspapers and are exposed to by the other media. As for the use of animals in toxicity testing, that will become clearer as we proceed, when we discuss various toxicity tests, including the so-called Draize Test and the LD_{50} test.

It is possible that some people might object to our including all three uses of animals under the general heading of the use of animals in science. In particular, some scientists might have a narrower view of science, according to which only original and applied research counts as "genuine science"; the use of animals in educational contexts or in toxicological testing isn't science, on this view, or not "real" science at any rate. This narrower conception of science is understandable, if science is viewed exclusively in terms of the devising and testing of original hypotheses. The fact remains, however, that it is not by witchcraft or astrology, say, that the acute or chronic toxicity of pesticides, food additives, hair sprays, and oven cleaners are determined; it is a matter of

---

[2] These three areas are identified and discussed more fully by Rowan (1980).

applied science. And it is not to turn out persons educated in, say, philology or accounting that lab sections are held in connection with standard courses in biology; it is to educate persons in biological science. So, while there may be a sense in which neither toxicity tests nor instructional labs are "science", there is certainly another sense in which they are a recognized part of those activities carried out by scientists, in their capacity as scientists or as teachers of science, and it is this more general but still proper sense of 'science' that we shall have in mind throughout the pages that follow. Thus, when we inquire into the morality of how animals are used in science or for scientific purposes, we intend to include their use in all three areas—in biological and medical education, in toxicology testing, and in original and applied research—though we shall feel free occasionally to emphasize their use in one area over their use in the others.

Before setting forth our own view regarding the ethics of the use of animals in science, two extreme positions will be characterized and debated. By subjecting their supporting arguments to criticism, we hope to show the need for a more reasonable, less extreme position. We shall call the two positions "The Unlimited Use Position" and "The No Use Position". The former holds that it is permissible to use any animal for any scientific purpose, so long as no human being is wronged. The latter holds that no use of any animal for any scientific purpose is morally permissible. We shall first examine the leading arguments for the Unlimited Use Position.

1. THE UNLIMITED USE POSITION

The first argument that we shall consider is the Cartesian Argument. It is named after the seventeenth-century philosopher, René Descartes, who held that animals are mindless machines. Here is the argument.

1. If a practice does not cause pain, then it is morally permissible.
2. Unlimited use of animals for scientific purposes would not cause them any pain.
3. Therefore, the use of any animal for any scientific purpose is morally permissible.

So simple an argument is not without far-reaching consequences. The tacit assumption of the Cartesian Argument by the scientists of Descartes's day helped pave the way for the rapid growth of animal experimentation in the seventeenth and eighteenth centuries. The following passage, written by an unknown contemporary of Descartes's, gives a vivid and unsettling picture of science at that time.

They [i.e., scientists] administered beatings to dogs with perfect indifference; and made fun of those who pitied the creatures as if they felt pain. They said the animals were clocks; that the cries they emitted when struck, were only the noise of a little spring that had been touched, but that the whole body was without feeling. They nailed poor animals up on boards by their four paws to vivisect them and see the circulation of the blood which was a great subject of controversy.[3]

It is well to remember this passage whenever we doubt that ideas can make a difference. Clearly Descartes's idea that animals are mindless machines profoundly influenced the course of science. The influence of an idea, however, is not a reliable measure of its truth, and we need to ask how reasonable the Cartesian Argument is.

A moment's reflection is enough to show that some crucial qualifications must be added if the Cartesian Argument is to have any plausibility at all. Inflicting pain is not the only way to harm an individual. Suppose, for example, that we were to kill humans painlessly while they are asleep. No one would infer that because such killing would be painless it would therefore be quite all right. But even if the necessary qualifications were introduced, the Cartesian Argument would still remain implausible. The evidence for believing that at least some animals feel pain (and it is only those animals with which we shall be concerned) is virtually the same as the evidence for believing that humans feel pain. Both humans and animals behave in ways that are simply, coherently, and consistently explained by supposing that they feel pain. From a physiological point of view, there is no reason to suppose that there are features that are unique to humans that are involved in pain sensations. Veterinary medicine, the law, and common sense all presuppose that some animals feel pain. Though some seem to accept the Cartesian Argument implicitly, it is doubtful that many would try to defend it when it is clearly stated.

The failure of the Cartesian Argument has important implications regarding the moral status of animals. Once we acknowledge the reality of animal consciousness and pain, we will be hard pressed indeed to exclude animals from membership in the moral community. Membership in the moral community might be thought of as in some ways analogous to membership in a club, with both qualifications and possible benefits. The key potential benefit of membership is that limits are placed on how others may treat you. For example, as a member, your life and property are protected by moral sanctions. Who belongs to the moral community? Evidently all those individuals

---

[3] As quoted in Rosenfield (1968: 54).

who can themselves be treated wrongly qualify as members. But which individuals are these? A variety of answers have been proposed, including the following:

- all and only rational beings;
- all and only autonomous beings (individuals having free will).

It will not be possible to discuss these views in detail.[4] It is sufficient to note their common failing: infants and severely enfeebled human beings, for example, are neither rational nor autonomous, and yet we treat them wrongly if we cause them significant pain for no good reason. Thus, since we can treat these individuals wrongly, they qualify as members of the moral community; and since they qualify as members of this community despite the fact that they are neither rational nor autonomous, neither rationality nor autonomy are requirements for membership in the moral community.

Still, infants and the enfeebled are human beings, and it might be suggested that membership in the moral community is determined by species membership. In other words, it might be suggested that all and only human beings are members of the moral community. This requirement for membership is also unsatisfactory. To restrict membership in the moral community to those who belong to the "right" species is analogous to the racist's attempt to restrict membership to those who belong to the "right" race, and to the sexist's effort to exclude those of the "wrong" gender.[5] Racism and sexism are today recognized as unacceptable prejudices. Rationally, we recognize that we cannot mark moral boundaries on the basis of such biological differences. Yet this is precisely what those who attempt to restrict membership in the moral community to all and only *Homo sapiens* are guilty of. They assume that membership in a particular species is the only basis for deciding who does and who does not belong to the moral community. To avoid this prejudice of "speciesism", we must reject this way of setting the boundaries of the moral community, and recognize that when needless pain and suffering are inflicted on infants and enfeebled humans, it is wrong, not because they are members of our species, but because they experience needless pain and suffering. Once this is acknowledged we may then come to see that it must be wrong to cause any individual, human or otherwise, needless pain or suffering. Thus, since many animals are conscious beings who can experience pain, as was argued in response to the Cartesian Argument, we must recognize that we can wrong them by causing them needless pain or suffering. Since they

---

[4] These views are discussed more fully in Regan (1975).
[5] Richard Ryder was the first to argue in this way in his (1975).

themselves can be wronged, they themselves must be members of the moral community.

The failure of the Cartesian Argument, therefore, does indeed have important implications regarding the moral status of animals. We shall have occasion to remind ourselves later of these implications.

But now let us consider a second argument that might be urged on behalf of the Unlimited Use Position. We shall call this the "Might Makes Right Argument".

1. If a practice is in the interests of the stronger, then it is morally permissible.
2. Humans are stronger than animals.
3. Unlimited use of animals in science would be in the interests of humans.
4. Therefore the use of any animal for any scientific purpose is morally permissible.

Even if we accept the view that only human interests determine how animals ought to be treated, what premise 3 asserts is false. Sometimes it is not in our interests to allow the use of just any animal for just any scientific purpose. Some animals are members of species that many people care about. Our reasons for caring are sometimes romantic or sentimental. Sometimes they are educational or aesthetic. Increasingly they are prudential. The more we learn about the interrelatedness of life on this planet, the more we recognize that the quality of our lives is inextricably linked to the welfare of other species. Because we care about some animals, we have an interest in how they are treated, and therefore their unlimited use cannot be said to be in the interests of humans. Consider, too, that the first premise, that what is permissible is determined by what is in the interest of the stronger, implies that strong humans do nothing wrong when they pursue their ends by using weaker humans, however badly they might treat them. Thus the Might Makes Right Argument would permit, not just unlimited use of animals, but unlimited use of weak and defenceless humans as well. If we are unwilling to swallow this repugnant conclusion, we must reject this argument. If, on the other hand, we are willing to accept unlimited use of weak and defenceless humans, then most and possibly all animal experimentation and toxicity testing performed in the name of human welfare is unnecessary. However useful animal experimentation or toxicity tests might be in improving the quality of the lives of stronger humans, surely the use of weaker humans would be even more useful. When animals are used, the problem of "extrapolating the data", that is, applying the results to humans, inevitably arises. (We shall have occasion to return to this problem in the pages that follow.) The problem of extrapolation could be overcome, however, if weaker humans instead of animals were used. After all, what could be a better experimental model of a human than another human? But no one, presumably, will seriously argue that weak humans should be exploited in this way. Thus no one will seriously espouse the Might Makes Right Argument.

A third argument, the Soul Argument, overcomes some of these difficulties.

1. Moral constraints only apply to beings who have souls.
2. All humans have souls.
3. No animals have souls.
4. Therefore moral constraints apply to what may be done to humans but not to what may be done to animals.
5. Therefore, unlimited use of animals for scientific purposes is morally permissible.

One who accepts this argument can use it to avoid the unsavoury implications for weaker humans of the Might Makes Right Argument. Since premise 2 states that all humans have souls, it follows that even weak humans have souls; thus the Soul Argument would not permit unlimited use of weak humans by stronger humans. Animals, however, are not protected by morality since they allegedly lack souls. Thus, according to the Soul Argument, morality permits us to use any animal for any scientific reason.

This argument is open to numerous objections. To begin with, the claim that all humans have souls is both vague and difficult to support. What is a soul? How do we know that humans have them but animals don't? On any account, these are not easy questions to answer. Moreover, although the dominant religions of the Western world typically deny that animals have souls, other religions, for example, Hinduism and some Native American religions, do attribute souls to animals. Just as there is great controversy concerning the nature of the soul and the very coherence of the concept, so there is controversy about which individuals have souls.

Suppose, however, that we were to accept the view that all and only humans have souls. Now, having a soul clearly would make an important difference to an individual's chances for a life beyond the grave. Those lacking a soul will have no chance for a future life. Thus the bodily death of an animal, assuming all animals lack souls, would mark its complete annihilation as a conscious individual. The influential Christian writer, C. S. Lewis (1971), argues that this fact would have the opposite implication from the one drawn in the Soul

Argument. If animals have no souls and no possible life beyond the grave, then the pain and suffering that they are made to endure in this life cannot possibly be balanced or overcome by the pleasures and enjoyments of an afterlife. In other words, if animals have no souls there is no possibility that the travails of their earthly existence can be recompensed in a world beyond. Thus the obligation to minimize the pain and suffering of animals during this their only life would seem to be, if anything, increased rather than diminished by their lack of a soul. If this is true, then we shall certainly fail to discharge that obligation if we permit the use of any animal for any scientific purpose. The Soul Argument, rather than providing grounds for the Unlimited Use Position, actually contains the seeds of an argument that can be used to criticize that position.

A fourth argument for unlimited use is the Knowledge Argument.

1. If a practice produces knowledge, then it is morally permissible.
2. Unlimited use of animals for scientific purposes would produce knowledge.
3. Therefore unlimited use of animals for scientific purposes is morally permissible.

Here we should balk at the first premise. Torturing suspects, spying on citizens, vivisecting cousins, all could produce knowledge, but surely that alone would not make these activities morally all right. Some knowledge is simply not worth the price in pain required to get it, whether those who suffer the pain are humans, as in the activities just listed, or animals, as in the case about to be described.

The Draize Test is a procedure employed by many manufacturers to determine whether proposed new products, most notably new cosmetics, would irritate the eyes of humans.[6] The most recent Federal guidelines for the admin-

---

[6] In January 1981 Revlon, Inc., the world's largest cosmetics manufacturer, announced that it had awarded Rockefeller University $750,000 to research and develop an alternative to the Draize Test. The company also granted $25,000 to establish a trust, the purpose of which is to fund further research into alternatives. Thus other cosmetic companies can join Revlon's pioneering move (this is the first time a commercial firm has funded the search for alternatives to the use of live animals for testing) by the simple expedient of contributing to the trust. The political realities being what they are, chances are good that Revlon's efforts will soon be imitated by other firms in the cosmetics industry. Revlon's actions were prompted by an uncommonly well-organized campaign, involving more than 400 separate animal welfare-related organizations, conducted over a two-year period. Through meetings with representatives of Revlon, through the media, through petitions to the Congress, through letter-writing campaigns, and through protest marches and rallies, the Coalition to Stop the Draize Rabbit Blinding Tests, Inc. helped to persuade Revlon to take its revolutionary step. The Coalition's success gives a clear demonstration of what can be done on behalf of animals and what must be done to succeed. When the money required to seek alternatives is on hand, there will be no lack of persons willing to do it.

istration of the Draize Test recommend that a single large volume dose of the test substance be placed in the conjunctival sac in one eye of each of six albino rabbits. The test substance is to remain in the eyes of the rabbits for a week, and observations are to be periodically recorded. The guidelines recommend that in most cases anaesthetics should not be used. The rabbits are often immobilized in restraining devices in order to prevent them from clawing at their eyes. At the completion of a week, the irritancy of the test substance is graded on the basis of the degree and severity of the damage in the cornea and iris.

The Draize Test is not a very good test by anyone's standards. It is unreliable and crude. In fact, a 1971 survey of twenty-five laboratories employing the Draize Test concluded that the Draize Test is so unreliable that it "should not be recommended as standard procedures in any new regulations".[7] But even if the Draize Test were a reliable test, the most that we would gain is some knowledge about the properties of some inessential new products. Can anyone really believe that there is a scarcity of cosmetics already on the market? The value of whatever knowledge is provided by the Draize Test is insignificant compared to the cost in animal pain required to obtain it. Indeed, no less a figure than Harold Feinberg, the chairperson of the American Accreditation For the Care of Laboratory Animals Committee, has stated that "the testing of cosmetics is frivolous and should be abolished".[8]

A fifth argument seeks to remedy this deficiency of the Knowledge Argument. Here is the Important Knowledge Argument.

1. If a practice produces important knowledge, then it is morally permissible.
2. Unlimited use of animals for scientific purposes would produce important knowledge.
3. Therefore unlimited use of animals for scientific purposes is morally permissible.

The Important Knowledge Argument fares no better than the Knowledge Argument. Consider an example. Surely it cannot be denied that it is important to know what substances are carcinogenic in humans. But animal tests for carcinogenicity in humans are often inconclusive. For example, in recent years there has been great controversy over whether one can infer that saccharin or oral conceptives are carcinogenic in humans on the basis of data

---

[7] Weil and Scala (1971: 352).

[8] Dr Feinberg made this claim while serving on a panel discussion on animal experimentation, sponsored by the Anti-Cruelty Society of Chicago, in October 1980.

collected in animal tests. Some have argued that because of the methods used in such research, such an inference cannot be made.[9] Massive doses are administered to rats and mice in these studies over short periods of time; there is no reason to believe that human cancers develop in response to similar conditions. Moreover, unlike humans, rats and mice tend spontaneously to develop a high incidence of tumours. One prominent medical journal remarked with respect to the oral contraceptive controversy: "It is difficult to see how experiments on strains of animals so exceedingly liable to develop tumors of these various kinds can throw useful light on the carcinogenicity of a compound for man."[10] If, however, we were to adopt the policy of unlimited use of humans, we could conclusively determine which substances are carcinogenic in humans. Moreover, such a policy would be sanctioned by the Important Knowledge Argument, since unlimited toxicology testing and experimentation on humans would unquestionably produce important knowledge. If the production of important knowledge makes a practice permissible, then unlimited testing and experimenting on humans is permissible. But again, this is a repugnant conclusion. If we are unwilling to accept it, we must give up the Important Knowledge Argument. If, on the other hand, we are willing to accept it, then most and possibly all toxicology tests and experiments carried out on animals in the name of human interests are unnecessary, since better models, namely humans, are available.

Finally there is the Freedom Argument. The Freedom Argument does not seek to show directly that unlimited use of animals is permissible. Rather it seeks to show that limitations on a researcher's freedom to use animals are wrong. Here is the argument.

1. Outside limits placed on the scientist's right to freedom of inquiry or academic freedom are not permissible.
2. Any outside restriction placed on the use of animals for scientific purposes would place limits on the scientist's right to freedom of inquiry or academic freedom.
3. Therefore, no outside restrictions on how animals may be used for scientific purposes are morally permissible.

This argument focuses attention away from the value of the goal of science (knowledge or important knowledge) to the value of the freedom to inquire. But though this change is noteworthy, and though this freedom is important

---

[9] Some of these issues are explored in a rather extreme way in Epstein (1979).

[10] *British Medical Journal*, 28 Oct. 1972: 190. We have taken this example as well as several others from Deborah Mayo (1983).

and ought to be one among a number of factors considered in the course of examining the ethics of the use of animals in science, it is clear that freedom of inquiry is not the only morally relevant consideration. The right to freedom of inquiry is no more absolute than, say, the right to freedom of speech. There are limits on what can be done by individuals in exercising their rights. To say precisely just what these limits are is difficult; but limits there are. Almost no one would say that the right to freedom of inquiry would sanction some of the things that have been done to humans in the name of science. For example, in the eighteenth century "charity children" were infected with smallpox in experiments conducted by Princess Caroline. Early in the twentieth century condemned criminals in the Philippines were injected with plague bacillus. And as recently as the 1960s, black prisoners in Alabama were left untreated to suffer from syphilis while researchers documented the course of the disease. That there are limitations on what can be done in the name of science is a principle that is enshrined in international agreements, including the Nuremberg Code of 1947 and the World Medical Association's Declaration of Helsinki adopted in 1964. Since some limits on the right to freedom of inquiry clearly are justified, the unlimited use of animals cannot be defended by appealing to some supposed absolute right to freedom of inquiry. For this reason the Freedom Argument, like the others before it, fails to provide a rational defence of the Unlimited Use Position.[11]

Although we haven't canvassed all possible arguments that might be given in support of the Unlimited Use Position, we have examined those that seem most common. None of these arguments provides any rational support for this position. It is now time to examine an alternative view.

2. THE NO USE POSITION

The No Use Position holds that no use of any animal for any scientific purpose is ever permissible. Is this position rationally defensible? We think not. We propose to argue for this conclusion in ways analogous to the case made against the Unlimited Use Position. We shall characterize some representative arguments for this position, indicating where and why these arguments go wrong.

Before addressing these arguments, it is worth noting that the reasonableness of the No Use Position does not follow from the inadequacy of the

---

[11] Recently even many scientists have become concerned about the possibilities inherent in certain kinds of research. The interested reader should see the essays collected in the following volumes: Holton and Morison (1978); Wulff (1979); Richards (1978); and Jackson and Stich (1979).

Unlimited Use Position, any more than it follows, say, that no men are bald because it is false that all men are. Those who accept the No Use Position may take some comfort in our critique of the Unlimited Use Position, but they cannot infer from that critique that their own position is on the side of the truth.

We shall discuss four arguments for the No Use Position. Here is the Pain Argument.

1. If an action causes pain to another being, then it is not morally permissible.
2. The use of animals for scientific purposes causes animals pain.
3. Therefore no use of any animal for any scientific purpose is morally permissible.

We should note first that not all scientific uses made of animals cause them pain. For example, some experimental uses of animals involve operant conditioning techniques, and most of these do not cause pain at all. Other experiments call for minor modifications in animals' diets or environments. Still others require killing anaesthetized animals. The Pain Argument does not provide a basis for objecting to any of these uses of animals. Because the Pain Argument cites no morally relevant consideration in addition to pain, it cannot provide a thoroughgoing defence of the No Use Position.

More importantly, the Pain Argument is defective from the outset. Contrary to what the first premise states, it is sometimes permissible to cause pain to others. Dentists cause pain. Surgeons cause pain. Wrestlers, football players, boxers cause pain. But it does not follow that these individuals do something that is not permissible. Granted, the presumption is always against someone's causing pain; nevertheless, causing pain is not itself sufficient for judging an act impermissible.

Suppose, however, that, unlike the case of dentists, pain is caused against one's will or without one's informed consent. Does it follow that what we've done is wrong? This is what the Informed Consent Argument alleges. Here is the argument.

1. If an action causes pain to another being without that being's informed consent, then it is not morally permissible.
2. The use of animals for scientific purposes causes animals pain without their informed consent.
3. Therefore no use of any animal for any scientific purpose is morally permissible.

The second premise is open to the same objections raised against the corresponding premise in the Pain Argument: not all scientific uses made of animals cause them pain. Thus, one cannot object to every use made of animals on this ground. Besides, animals are not the sort of beings who can give or withhold their informed consent. Explanations of what will be done to them in an experiment or test cannot be understood by them, so there is no possibility of "informing" them. Thus, there is no coherent possibility of causing them pain "without their informed consent".

The first premise also falls short of the truth. Suppose that a small child has appendicitis. If not operated on, the condition will worsen and she will die. Scary details omitted, the situation is explained to the child. She will have none of it: "No operation for me," we are told. The operation is performed without the child's consent and causes some amount of pain. Was it wrong to perform the operation? It is preposterous to answer affirmatively. Thus, we have a counter-example to the basic assumption of the Informed Consent Argument, the assumption that it is not permissible to cause others pain without their informed consent.

Still, one might say that there is a difference between hurting others (causing them pain) and harming them (doing something that is detrimental to their welfare). Moreover, it might be suggested that in the example of the child and appendicitis, what we've stumbled upon is the fact that something that hurts might not harm. Accordingly, it might be held that what is always wrong is not causing pain, or causing others pain without their informed consent; rather, what is always wrong is harming others. This suggestion gains additional credence when we observe that even a painless death can be a great harm to a given individual. These considerations suggest another argument. Here is the Harm Argument.

1. If an action harms another being, then it is not morally permissible.
2. The use of animals for scientific purposes harms animals.
3. Therefore, no use of any animal for any scientific purpose is morally permissible.

This argument, like the ones before it, has gaping holes in it. First, it is clear that it will not even serve as a basis for opposing all animal experimentation, since not all animal experimentation harms animals. More fundamentally, it is simply not true that it is always wrong to harm another. Suppose that while walking alone at night, you are attacked and that through luck or skill you repel your assailant who falls beneath your defensive blows, breaks his neck, and is confined to bed from that day forth, completely paralysed from the neck down. We mince words if we deny that what you did harmed your assailant.

Yet we do not say that what you did is therefore wrong. After all, you were innocent; you were just minding your own business. Your assailant, on the other hand, hardly qualifies as innocent. He attacked you. It would surely be an unsatisfactory morality that failed to discriminate between what you as an innocent victim may do in self-defence, and what your attacker can do in offence against your person or your property. Thus despite the initial plausibility of the first premise of the Harm Argument, not all cases of harming another are impermissible.

The difficulties with the Harm Argument suggest a fourth argument, the Innocence Argument.

1. If an action causes harm to an innocent individual, then it is not permissible, no matter what the circumstances.
2. Animals are innocent.
3. The use of animals for scientific purposes harms them.
4 Therefore no use of any animal for any scientific purpose is morally permissible.

This argument, unlike the Harm Argument, can account for the case of the assailant, since by attacking you the assailant ceases to be innocent, and therefore in harming him you have not wronged him. In this respect if in no other, the Innocence Argument marks a genuine improvement over the Harm Argument. Nevertheless, problems remain. Again, since animals are not always harmed when used for scientific purposes, the Innocence Argument does not provide a foundation for the No Use Position. It could also be argued that animals cannot be viewed as innocent. We shall return to this issue in the following section. The more fundamental question, however, is whether the basic assumption of this argument is correct: is it always wrong to harm an innocent individual, no matter what the circumstances?

Here we reach a point where philosophical opinion is sharply divided. Some philosophers evidently are prepared to answer this question affirmatively.[12] Others, ourselves included, are not. One way to argue against an affirmative answer to this question is to highlight, by means of more or less far-fetched hypothetical examples, what the implications of an affirmative answer would be. The use of such "thought experiments" is intended to shed light on the grey areas of our thought by asking how alternative positions would view far-fetched hypothetical cases. The hope is that we may then return to the more complex situations of everyday life with a better understanding of how

---

[12] Baruch Brody is apparently one such philosopher. See his (1975).

to reach the best judgement in these cases. So let us construct a thought experiment, and indicate how it can be used to contest the view that it is always wrong to harm an innocent individual, no matter what the circumstances. (A second thought experiment will be undertaken near the beginning of Section 3.)

Imagine this case.[13] Together with four other friends, you have gone caving along the Pacific coast. The incoming tide catches your group by surprise and you are faced with the necessity of making a quick escape through the last remaining accessible opening to the cave or else all will drown. Unfortunately, the first person to attempt the escape gets wedged in the opening. All efforts to dislodge him, including his own frantic attempts, are unsuccessful. It so happens that one member of your party has brought dynamite along, so that the means exist to widen the opening. However, to use the explosive to enlarge the escape route is certain to kill your trapped friend. The situation, then, is this: if the explosive is used, then it is certain that one will die and likely that four will escape unharmed. If the explosive is not used, it is certain that all five will die. All the persons involved are innocent. What ought to be done? Morally speaking, is it permissible to use the dynamite despite the fact that doing so is certain to harm an innocent person?

Those who think it is always wrong to harm an innocent individual, no matter what the circumstances, must say that using the dynamite would be wrong. But how can this be? If the death of one innocent individual is a bad thing, then the death of considerably more than one innocent individual must be that much worse. Accordingly, if it is claimed that you would be doing wrong if you performed an act that brought about the death of one innocent individual because it is wrong to act in ways that harm an innocent individual, then it must be a more grievous wrong for you to act in ways that will bring equivalent harm to a greater number of innocent individuals. But if this is so, then we have reason to deny that it is always wrong to harm an innocent individual, no matter what the circumstances. What our thought experiment suggests is that it is possible that some circumstances might be so potentially bad that morality will permit us to harm an innocent individual. In the thought experiment it would be permissible to use the dynamite.

Those who incline towards viewing the prohibition against harming the innocent as absolute, admitting of no exceptions whatever, are not likely to be persuaded to give up this view just by the weight of the argument of the

[13] The example is given by Richard Brandt (1975). The philosophical propriety of using more or less unusual hypothetical examples in assessing moral principles is critically discussed by G. E. M. Anscombe (1958/1968), and by Jamieson (1991a).

previous paragraphs. The debate will—and should—continue. One point worth making, however, is that those who like ourselves do not view this prohibition as absolute can nevertheless regard it as very serious, just as, for example, one can view the obligation to keep one's promises as a very serious moral requirement without viewing it as absolute. Imagine that you have borrowed a chain-saw from a friend, promising to return it whenever he asks for it. Imagine he turns up at your door in a visibly drunken state, accompanied by a bound and gagged companion who has already been severely beaten and is in a state of terror. "I'll have my chain-saw now," he intones. Ought you to return it, under those circumstances? The obligation to keep one's promises can be regarded as quite serious without our having to say, yes, by all means, you ought to fetch the chain-saw! There are other considerations that bear on the morality of what you ought to do in addition to the fact that you have made a promise. Similarly, the fact that some action will harm an innocent individual is not the only consideration that is relevant to assessing the morality of that action. In saying this we do not mean to suggest that this consideration is not an important one. It is, and we shall attempt to develop its importance more fully in the following section. All that we mean to say is that it is not the only morally relevant consideration.

There would appear to be cases, then, whether they be far-fetched hypothetical ones or ones that might arise in the real world, in which morality permits us to harm an innocent individual. Thus, even in those cases in which animals used for scientific purposes are harmed, and even assuming that they are innocent, it does not follow that how they are used is morally wrong. Like the other arguments reviewed in this section, the Innocence Argument fails to provide an acceptable basis for the No Use Position. Assuming, as we do, that these arguments provide a fair representation of those available to advocates of this position, we conclude that the No Use Position lacks a rationally compelling foundation, either in fact, or in logic, or in morality.

3. THE MODIFIED INNOCENCE PRINCIPLE

The previous two sections criticized two extreme positions, one favouring, the other opposing, all uses of animals for scientific purposes. In the present section, and in the one that follows, two different arguments will be developed for less extreme positions, positions which though they place severe limitations on when animals may be used in science, do allow for the possibility that some animals may sometimes be used for some purposes, even some that harm them. The argument of the present section takes up where

the argument of the last one ended: with the wrongness of harming the innocent. The argument of the next section is based on the different idea of max-
imizing the balance of good over evil. The differences between the two
arguments will be sketched in Section 5.

The prohibition against harming innocent individuals is a very serious, but
not an absolute, prohibition. Because it is not absolute, it has justified exceptions. The problem is to say under what circumstances an exception is
permitted. Perhaps the best way to begin formulating an answer is to again
consider the caving example. Notice first that in that case we assumed that
other alternatives had been exhausted; for example, every effort had been
made to find an alternative route of escape and to dislodge your trapped
friend. Secondly, we assumed that you had very good reason to believe that
all would be drowned if the only remaining exit was not widened. Very dread-
ful consequences—death—would obtain, therefore, for five as compared with
one person, if the dynamite was not used. These considerations suggest a
modified principle concerning the harming of those who are innocent. We
shall call this principle the Modified Innocence Principle (MIP), and formulate it in the following way.

(MIP) It is wrong to harm an innocent individual unless it is reasonable to
believe that doing so is the only realistic way of avoiding equal harm for
many other innocents.[14]

The role of this principle can be illustrated by means of another regrettably
not too far-fetched thought experiment.

Imagine that a terrorist has possession of a well-armed tank and is systematically slaughtering forty-five innocent hostages whom he has fastened to
a wall.[15] Attempts to negotiate a compromise fail. The man will kill all the
hostages if we do nothing. Under the circumstances, there is only one reasonable alternative: blow up the tank. But there is this complication: the terrorist has strapped a young girl to the tank, and any weapon sufficient to blow
up the tank will kill the child. The girl is innocent. Thus to blow up the tank
is to harm an innocent, one who herself stands no chance of benefiting from
the attack. Ought we to blow up the tank?

MIP would sanction doing so. If, as we argued in the previous section, it is
worse that harm befalls many innocent individuals than that an equal harm

---

[14] MIP would probably have to be reformulated to account for a range of cases (e.g. 'innocent
threats') with which we are not primarily concerned in this essay. Insane persons can kill just as surely
as sane ones and, though they are innocent, morality surely allows us to defend ourselves against their
threatening attacks.

[15] Here we develop an example introduced by Nozick (1974, ch. 3).

befall one, then surely it would be worse if all the hostages were killed rather than just the one innocent child. Moreover, we have assumed that other alternatives to the attack have been tried, that they have failed, and that the only realistic way to prevent the slaughter of the remaining hostages is to blow up the tank. Thus MIP should not be understood as sanctioning a policy of "shooting first and asking questions later". It is only after other non-violent or less violent alternatives have been exhausted that we are permitted to do what will harm an innocent individual.

Problems remain, however. Consider the notion of "equal harm". MIP will not permit harming an innocent just so that others might avoid some minor inconvenience. We cannot, for example, confine innocent vagrants to concentration camps just because we find their appearance aesthetically displeasing. Still, not all harms are equal. It is a matter of degree how much a given harm will detract from an individual's well-being, and problems will arise concerning just how serious a given harm is, or whether two or more different harms are "equal". Moreover, there is also certain to be a problem concerning the number of innocents involved. The thought experiment involving the terrorist and the tank was a clear case of harming one innocent in order to prevent equal harm to many other innocents. But how many is many? If the only way to avoid the death of two innocents is to kill one, ought we to do this? This question, and others like it, would have to be explored in a comprehensive examination of MIP. We bypass them now, not because they are unimportant, but because they are less important than another question which cannot be passed over. This concerns the very intelligibility of viewing animals as innocent. The fundamental nature of this issue is clear. If no sense can be made of the idea of the "innocence of animals", then whatever else may be said of MIP, at least this much could be: it simply would be inapplicable to our relations with animals. So let us ask whether sense can be made of the view that animals are innocent.

One argument against the intelligibility of animal innocence is the Moral Agent Argument.

1. Only moral agents can be innocent.
2. Animals are not moral agents.
3. Therefore animals cannot be innocent.

By 'moral agents' is meant individuals who can act from a sense of right and wrong, who can deliberate about what they ought to do, who can act and not merely react, and who thus can be held accountable or responsible for what they do or fail to do. Normal adult human beings are the clearest examples of individuals having the status of moral agents.

The first premise states that only moral agents can be innocent. Why might this be claimed? The most likely explanation is the following. Because moral agents are responsible for their actions, they can be accused of acting wrongly. Individuals who are not moral agents, however, can do no wrong. If a tree falls on someone causing death or injury, it makes no sense to condemn the tree. Since the tree "had no choice", it cannot be faulted. Moral agents can be faulted, however. If a moral agent commits murder, then he has done what is wrong; he is guilty of an offence. Suppose, however, that a moral agent is falsely accused of committing murder; he is not guilty; he is (and here is the crucial word) innocent. Thus, it makes perfectly good sense to say that a moral agent is innocent because moral agents can be guilty. It makes no sense to say that a tree is innocent because trees cannot be guilty.

The second premise denies that animals are moral agents. This seems true. Granted, we reward and punish animals for their behaviour, hoping to incline them towards behaving in ways we prefer and away from those we do not; but it is doubtful that many, if any, animals meet the requirements of moral agency.[16] Thus, if the first premise of the Moral Agent Argument is accepted, and assuming as we shall that the second premise is true, then there would seem to be no way to avoid the conclusion that animals cannot be innocent. If, like trees, they cannot be guilty, then they cannot be innocent either. And if this conclusion cannot be avoided, a conclusive case would have been made against viewing MIP as bearing on the morality of how animals may be treated. Since MIP is concerned with how innocent individuals may be treated, it has no bearing on how animals may be treated, if animals cannot be innocent.

But is it true that animals cannot be innocent? The preceding argument at most establishes only that they cannot be innocent in the sense that moral agents can be said to be innocent. Is this the only intelligible sense of 'innocence' that plays a role in our moral thought? The answer is definitely no, if we take our actual practice as our guide. Much of the debate over the morality of abortion, for example, centres on the alleged "innocence of the foetus". If only moral agents can be innocent, then referring to the fetus as "innocent" cannot make sense. The same is true when very young children who are killed or maimed are referred to as "innocent victims". Since they are not moral agents, it ought to be senseless to refer to them in this way. But in actual practice we do speak this way, which suggests that the concept of innocence is not restricted in its application to moral agents only, but can be meaningfully applied to those individuals who are "moral patients".[17] These are those indi-

[16] The possibility that certain species of animals have a morality of their own, based on mutual sympathy, is explored and defended by Rachels (1976/1989).

[17] For further comments on this term, see Warnock (1971).

viduals who, though they are not moral agents and thus can do no wrong, can be the undeserving recipients of wrongs done to them by others. That is, they can be wronged, even though they can do no wrong. Children are the innocent victims of war, in this sense, not because they can be falsely accused of some wrongdoing, but because they can be made to suffer undeserved harm, in this case, undeserved harm done to them by those who make war.

A question arises regarding what individuals qualify as moral patients. Our answer hearkens back to our earlier discussion of the moral community. An individual qualifies as a member of that community, we claimed, if it is possible for others to wrong her directly. Thus, moral agents qualify, but so do moral patients. Young children, the aged and helpless, the mentally enfeebled and the emotionally deranged of all ages, qualify as members of the moral community if it is possible to wrong them. In order to avoid the prejudice of speciesism we must also recognize that all those animals who can be harmed must likewise be recognized as members of the moral community, not because they can do what is wrong, but because, as moral patients, they can suffer wrongs.

An argument has been offered for the intelligibility of the idea of animal innocence. This is a controversial subject, and we shall return to it again at the beginning of the following section. If we assume for the moment that animals can be innocent in a morally relevant way, then we may also assume that MIP does apply to how we may treat them, and thus develop the implications of its applicability to the use of animals in science by means of the following argument, the Modified Innocence Argument.

1. It is wrong to harm the innocent unless we have very good reason to believe that this is the only realistic way to prevent equal harm for many other innocents.
2. Animals are innocent.
3. Therefore, it is not permissible to harm them unless the conditions set forth in premise (1) are satisfied.
4 At least a great deal of the use of animals in science harmful to them fails to meet the conditions set forth in premise (1).
5. Therefore at least a great deal of this use is wrong.

The first and second premises have already been addressed. The conclusion drawn in step three follows from steps one and two. The step that remains to be examined is the fourth one, and it is to the task of defending it that we shall now turn.

As a minimal condition, MIP requires that it be reasonable to believe that the harming of an innocent will prevent equal harm to many other innocents. Apart from the issue of experimentation, it is clear that not all uses of animals in science harmful to them satisfy this requirement. For example, very many animals are harmed for instructional purposes in school and laboratory settings and in science fairs. The fulfilment of these purposes cannot reasonably be viewed as an essential step leading to the prevention of equal harms for many other innocents.[18] As for experimentation, it is clear that there are many cases in which animals are harmed to obtain trivial bits of knowledge. For example, recently the Canadian Department of Indian Affairs and Northern Development spent $80,000 to determine the effect of oil spills on polar bears.[19] The procedure involved immersing three polar bears in a container of crude oil and water. One polar bear died after licking oil from her fur for twelve hours. A second polar bear was killed for "humane reasons" after suffering intense pain from kidney failure. The third survived after suffering from severe infection that was caused by injections that the bear was given through her oil-stained skin by veterinary surgeons who were attempting to treat her for the kidney and liver damage that was caused by her immersion in oil. The Canadian government, with the cooperation of the American government, is now planning to conduct similar experiments on dolphins.

The polar bear experiment is not an isolated incident. There is a growing body of literature that documents the triviality of much that routinely passes for "original scientific research".[20] The situation in toxicology testing is regrettably similar, as the following test illustrates.

The standard measure of the toxicity of a substance (i.e. the accepted measure of the degree to which a given substance is poisonous to humans) is its median lethal dose. The median lethal dose, or the LD_{50} as it is called, is defined as the amount of a substance needed to kill 50 per cent of the test animals to which it is administered. The United States government requires that the LD_{50} be determined for each new substance bound for the market. The substances in question are not just exotic life-saving drugs, but include such ordinary products as the latest household detergent, shoe polish, oven cleaner, deodorants, and soda pop. There are at least two reasons for believing that these tests, which cause great harm to the test animals, will not prevent

---

[18] For a fuller discussion of these issues, see McGiffin and Brownley (1980).

[19] The results have not been published in a professional journal. But see the reports published in the Vancouver, BC newspapers (*The Province* and *The Vancouver Sun*) on 28 March 1980 and 8 April 1980, respectively. This case and the relevant documentation were brought to our attention by David Rinehart of the *Greenpeace Examiner*.

[20] See again Diner (1979) and Ryder (1975), as well as Singer (1975/2001).

equal harm to many other innocents. First, many of the substances for which the LD_{50} is obtained are already known to be relatively non-toxic. As a result, enormous quantities of these substances must be forcibly fed or otherwise administered to the test animals in order to cause 50 per cent fatalities. In such cases it is often very clear long before 50 per cent of the test animals have died, that the substance poses no serious threat to human beings. To put the point baldly: determining the toxicity of substances which are never likely to harm anyone except the test animals to whom they are initially administered, is blatantly impermissible, given MIP. There is no good reason to believe that these tests will prevent equal harm to many other innocents.

But secondly, the data obtained in LD_{50} tests are often just not reliable. There are a number of reasons why. (1) It is not always possible to extrapolate toxicity data from animals to humans. As an expert in the field has noted, "(t)here are countless known examples of . . . species differences".[21] Penicillin is highly toxic to guinea pigs but not to humans, while strychnine is highly poisonous to humans but not to guinea pigs. Dinitrophonol will not cause cataracts in most laboratory animals but will in humans, and morphine, which is an effective sedative for humans, has the exact opposite effect on cats. (More will be said about the problem of extrapolation in the next section.) (2) LD_{50} tests are not performed in a uniform way. Differences in the test animals' strain, sex, age, ambient and nutritional condition, and so forth, often result in the reporting of different LD_{50}s for the same substance. Studies of four household chemicals conducted in six different laboratories produced toxicity data that were inconsistent, not just with respect to the absolute toxicity of the four substances but with respect to their relative toxicity as well.[22] Though this is perhaps an extreme case, the phenomenon is not uncommon, and serves to illustrate why a test like the LD_{50} fails to comply with MIP: we simply do not have good reason to believe that the harm done to the test animals will prevent equal harm to many other innocents.

MIP also requires that other realistic alternatives be exhausted before it is permissible to harm an innocent individual. This requirement does make a difference. If, prior to attempted negotiations with the terrorist, for example, we blew up the tank, we would be morally culpable. We would have resorted to violence, knowing this would harm the innocent child, without having first determined whether we could have acted to prevent harm being done to all the innocents. So let us ask whether all scientific uses of animals harmful to them are undertaken only after other realistic alternatives have been tried.

Unfortunately, the answer is no: a great deal of the use made of animals in

---

[21] Levine (1978: 258).   [22] These studies are reported in Loosli (1967).

science clearly fails to satisfy this requirement, though of course we cannot say exactly how much, anymore than we can say exactly how much water there is in the Pacific. What we can say is that the amount in each case is a lot. "But there are no alternatives", it is often said. This is an answer that we shall examine more fully shortly. Sometimes, however, there are well-established alternatives to the use of animals. These alternatives include tissue and cell cultures, mathematical modelling, chemical analysis, mechanical models, clinical examination, and epidemiological surveys.[23] In cases where there are established, scientifically viable alternatives to using animals and other innocent individuals who can be hurt or harmed (e.g. humans), MIP requires that these alternatives be employed and not the innocents.

However, it remains true that sometimes, in some cases, there are no known alternatives that have been proven to be scientifically reliable. What does MIP imply about these cases? Here we must take note of an important disanalogy between the scientific enterprise and our thought experiments. Those experiments presented us with crisis situations in which the alternatives are clearly defined, in which neither time nor circumstances allow for the investigation of new options, and in which we could not reasonably be expected to have done anything before the crisis developed so that we might have another realistic option at our disposal. (There is nothing we could reasonably be expected to do today, for example, to increase the options that would be available to us in the extremely unlikely event that we should find ourselves in the predicament we imagined in the caving example.) There is, however, a great deal that science can begin to do today and could have done in the past in an effort to explore alternatives to the use of animals for scientific purposes. Time and circumstances do allow for the scientific investigation of such alternatives; indeed, it is part of the very essence of the scientific enterprise to search for new ways to approach old (and emerging) problems. The longer the life sciences, including psychology,[24] are delayed in making a conscientious effort to search for alternatives, the greater the wrong, given MIP, since an insufficient commitment in this regard itself offends against the spirit of MIP. To harm the innocent is so serious a moral matter that we must do all that we can reasonably be expected to do so that we can avoid causing this harm. If the life sciences, through lack of will, funding, or both, fail to do all that can reasonably be expected of them in this regard, then we have no reason to assume that the use made of animals in science is justified "because there are no available alternatives". On the contrary, we have reason to deny the moral propriety of such use. To put this same point differently: since we are justified in

---

[23] These methods are reviewed in e.g. Rowan (1980) and Ryder (1975).
[24] For a critical assessment of the use made of animals in psychological research, see Bowd (1980).

believing that it is wrong to harm the innocent unless we can be shown that it isn't, we are justified in regarding the harm caused to animals in science as unjustified unless we can be shown that all that reasonably could be done has been done to avoid causing it. If we cannot be shown that these efforts have been made, then we are right to regard their use as wrong, given MIP.

Viewed from this perspective, at least most harmful use of animals in science ought to be regarded as morally unjustified. The "search for alternatives" has been a largely token effort, one that has not been given a priority anywhere approaching that required by MIP. But this is not the fault only of those involved in the life sciences. As a society we have not seriously thought about the moral status of animals. We have failed to recognize that animals are members of the moral community, or we have minimized the importance of their membership. As a result, we have not funded the search for alternatives sufficiently. Since (as it is well said) "research goes where the money is", the investigation of alternatives has not prospered.

Those involved in the life sciences are not entirely free of responsibility, however. Though they do not control the flow of money from public and private sources, their voice is not without its influence. Moreover, the voices of scientists carry more weight in determining what research finds funding than do the voices of ordinary citizens, or even the voices of those active in the humane movement. A demand on the part of scientists that the search for alternatives be given the priority MIP requires is essential, if this search is to have any chance of receiving the funding that acceptance of MIP would require.

We may conclude the present section, then, as follows. About much use of animals in science that harms them, it is false to suppose that it will prevent equal harm befalling many other innocents. About some harmful use that might prevent such harm, it is false to suppose that these uses are known to be the only realistic way to achieve such results. And about most use of animals that causes them harm, it is false to suppose that as a society we have made the conscientious effort to search for alternatives that the MIP requires. Thus, if MIP should guide our behaviour with respect to animals, we cannot avoid concluding that at least most of the uses made of animals in science that harms them are not morally permissible—indeed, they are morally wrong.

4. THE PRINCIPLE OF UTILITY

The argument of the previous section relied heavily on the idea that animals are innocent. The attempt to undermine this idea by means of the Moral

Agent Argument was considered and found wanting. There are other ways to contest this idea, however. The Rights Argument is one.

1. Only those individuals who have rights can be innocent.
2. Animals cannot have rights.
3. Therefore animals cannot be innocent.

A defence of the first premise might proceed along the following lines. To speak of individuals as innocent assumes that they can suffer *undeserved* harm. But undeserved harm must be harm that is unjust or unfair, and what is unjust or unfair is what violates an individual's rights. Thus, only those individuals who have rights can be the recipients of undeserved harm. As for the second premise, not very long ago it was assumed to be so obvious as not to require any supporting argument at all. Recently, however, the idea of animal rights has been debated, and there is a steadily growing body of literature, in an expanding number of prestigious professional journals from scientific and humanistic disciplines, devoted to the reflective assessment of this idea.[25] It will not be possible to review this debate on the present occasion. We mention it only in order to indicate how the idea of the innocence of animals is relevant to the more widely discussed idea of animal rights. A thorough examination of the former idea would have to include a thorough examination of the latter one as well.

It is possible to approach the question of the ethics of animal use in science from a perspective that does not place fundamental importance on innocence and the allied idea of rights. Utilitarianism is one such perspective. It is a view that has attracted many able thinkers, and represents today, in the English speaking world at least, the primary alternative to views of morality that place central importance on individual rights. Moreover, utilitarianism's most influential advocates, from Jeremy Bentham and John Stuart Mill to the contemporary Australian philosopher Peter Singer, have explicitly recognized the membership of animals in the moral community. It will be instructive, therefore, to sketch the utilitarian position in general and to mark its implications for the use of animals for scientific purposes in particular.

Utilitarianism is the view that we ought to act so as to bring about the greatest possible balance of good over evil for everyone affected. Utilitarianism is thus not a selfish doctrine; it does not prescribe that each individual is to act so as to maximize his or her own self-interest. For the utilitarian, your neighbour's good counts the same as yours; in Bentham's words, "Each to count for one, no one for more than one". In trying to decide what ought to be done,

---

[25] See "A Select Bibliography on Animal Rights and Human Obligations", *Inquiry*, 1–2 (1978).

therefore, we must consider the interests of everyone involved, being certain to count equal interests equally. The point of view required by utilitarianism is uncompromisingly impartial; we are not allowed to favour our own interests, or those of our friends, or say, White-Anglo-Saxon-Protestants, over the like interests of others. It is, in the words of the nineteenth-century utilitarian Henry Sidgwick, "the point of view of the universe". For the utilitarian, the ideas of the innocence and the rights of individuals are not independent considerations to be used in determining what ought to be done. They have a role only if they bear on the determination of what the best consequences would be. Utilitarianism recommends a "forward-looking" morality. Results are the only things that matter in the determination of right and wrong.

Utilitarians have disagreed over many points, including the nature of the good consequences they seek and the evil ones they seek to avoid. Classical utilitarians, including Bentham and Mill, viewed goodness as pleasure and evil as pain. Some recent utilitarians understand goodness as the satisfaction of an individual's preferences.[26] On either view, many animals must find a place in the utilitarian calculation of the best consequences, if, following these thinkers, we agree that many animals can experience what is pleasant or painful, or have preferences. For the sake of simplicity, in what follows we shall think of good consequences (utility) as pleasure, and bad consequences (disutility) as pain.

Bentham, in an oft-quoted and justly famous passage, declares the relevance of the pain of animals in the following way.

The French have already discovered that the blackness of the skin is no reason why a human being should be abandoned without redress to the caprice of a tormentor. It may come one day to be recognized, that the number of the legs, the villosity of the skin, or the termination of the *os sacrum*, are reasons equally insufficient for abandoning a sensitive being to the same fate . . . [T]he question is not, Can they *reason*? nor, Can they *talk*? but, Can they *suffer*? (Bentham 1789/1989: 26)

If we assume, as we have throughout, that the animals of which we speak can suffer, how might a utilitarian such as Bentham argue against their use for scientific purposes? Clearly no utilitarian would accept the principal assumption of the Pain Argument; the assumption that it is always wrong to cause another pain. The permissibility of causing pain, like the permissibility of performing any other act, must depend for the utilitarian on the utility of doing it, and since it could be true in any given case that we will bring about the best consequences for everyone involved by an act that causes pain to

---

[26]   e.g. Hare (1976); and Singer (1979/1993).

some individuals(s), the utilitarian will not accept the prohibition against causing pain as absolute (as impermissible at all times, no matter what the consequences).

It remains true, nevertheless, that utilitarians will regard causing pain as a negative feature of an act. Any action which causes pain and fails to bring about a greater amount of pleasure will be ruled out by the utilitarian as morally wrong, except when every other alternative action would bring about an even greater balance of pain over pleasure. Thus, one way of formulating the Utilitarian Argument against the use of animals in science is the following.

1. Acts are not morally permissible if they cause pain to some individuals and yet fail to bring about the best possible consequences for everyone involved.
2. A great deal of the scientific use of animals causes them pain and fails to bring about the best possible consequences.
3. Therefore a great deal of this use is not morally permissible.

There are many reasons for accepting the second premise of this argument. Even in the case of animal-based experimentation or research, much is redundant, and is carried on well beyond the threshold needed for replication. Experimental studies of shock are a good example. As early as 1946 a survey of the literature indicated that over 800 papers had been published on experimental studies of shock. These studies induced shock by various means, including: tourniquets, hammer blows, rotations in the Noble-Collip drum, gunshot wounds, strangulation, intestinal loops, burning, and freezing. By 1954 a survey article reported that although "animal investigations in the field of traumatic shock have yielded diversified and often contradictory results," the investigators looked forward to "future experimentation in this field".[27] In 1974 researchers still described their work as "preliminary". Presumably such work will continue as long as someone is willing to fund it.

There is no question but that much animal experimentation, like the research on shock described in the previous paragraph, continues from habit, convenience, desire for professional advancement, and so forth. Dr Roger Ulrich, one of the leading researchers in aggression studies, has performed experiments on rats that involve blinding, mutilation, and castration, as well as the administration of electric shock and bursts of intense noise. Recently, in a letter to the American Psychological Association's *Monitor*, he wrote:

---

[27] Rosenthal and Milliean (1954: 489). See also Singer (1975/2001).

Initially my research was prompted by the desire to understand and help solve the problem of human aggression but I later discovered that the results of my work did not seem to justify its continuance. Instead I began to wonder if perhaps financial rewards, professional prestige, the opportunity to travel, etc., were the maintaining factors.[28]

Other experiments are performed in order to confirm hypotheses that almost everyone already knows are true. The experiments on polar bears discussed in the previous section are an obvious example. As one Vancouver newspaper editorialized: "The experts wanted to determine the effects of oil spills on the polar bears. Apparently no children of, say, 12 years of age were on hand to give them a pretty good idea."[29] Moreover, similar experiments had been conducted in Canada on seals only five years before. To the surprise of no one except possibly the researchers, most of the seals died after being immersed in oil.

Other experiments are performed in order to falsify hypotheses that almost everyone knows are false. Here is the voice of David Hubel of Harvard Medical School reporting one such case.

A few years ago the notion was advanced that memories might be recorded in the form of large molecules, with the information encoded in a sequence of smaller molecules, as genetic information is encoded in DNA. Few people familiar with the highly patterned specificity of connections in the brain took the idea seriously, and yet much time was consumed in many laboratories teaching animals tasks, grinding up their brains and either finding differences in the brain chemistry of the trained animals or finding "statistically significant" improvement in the ability of other animals, into which extracts of the trained animals' brains were injected, to learn the same tasks. The fad has died out . . . (1979: 53)

Many animal experiments are rendered useless by the unreliability of the data obtained. Experimental results have been found to vary depending on the time of day that the experiment was performed, the appearance of the researcher, the temperature of the room, and other equally subtle factors. It is almost impossible to control such complex background variables.[30] Moreover, even when the data are reliable with respect to the test animals, the problem of extrapolating the results to humans remains severe. As two prominent researchers from the Institute of Experimental Pathology and Toxicology of

---

[28] *Monitor*, Mar. 1978: 16. The view that science develops mainly through habit, convenience, desire for prestige, and so forth is one that has gained currency in contemporary science studies. See Kuhn (1970); Feyerabend (1975); and Laudan (1977).

[29] *The Vancouver Sun*, 28 Mar. 1978.

[30] The literature concerning such difficulties has been proliferating. See e.g. Magalhaes (1974).

the Albany Medical College have written: "At the present time . . . the legitimate question can still be asked, for we do not have the answer: 'How can we be sure that the extrapolation of animal data to man is accurate?'"[31] After noting substantive difficulties in extrapolating data, the authors conclude:

To be sure, these data may have little or no relevance to man, but they are the best basis for prediction of hazard to man that we have at the present time . . . Unfortunately. Alexander Pope's remark of many years ago, "The proper study of mankind is man" is still true. Various committees of the World Health Organization and of the National Academy of Sciences are in general agreement with this statement.[32]

In another paper, one of the co-authors goes so far as to advance the proposal that routinely using animals as test or experimental models is premature at best.

Species differences in metabolism is one of the primary reasons why projection of animal data to man is not always possible. Differences in the metabolic pathways and the rate of detoxification are observed among the animal species and between animals and man. That is why early trial in man, to learn something of the metabolic rate and pathway in man, as compared to animals, is recommended before long-term animal studies are initiated.[33]

The extrapolation problem is so severe, then, that at least one prominent toxicologist has advocated human studies before long-term animal studies! This suggestion, of course, raises ethical issues of its own. But one must certainly wonder why and how animal tests would be necessary at all in a situation in which a substance had already been administered to humans.

The utilitarian argument could go even further. John Cairns, Director of the Imperial Cancer Research Fund's Mill Hill Laboratory in London, has pointed out that during the last 150 years in the Western world, there has been an enormous increase in life expectancy.[34] He notes that this increase in life expectancy began before the advent of "what we would call medical science" and argues that it is primarily due to better nutrition and hygiene rather than to the development of exotic new drugs and surgical procedures. He goes on to say that the chance of dying of cancer in the United States has not altered appreciably in the last thirty-five years, in spite of intense research activity. Claims to the contrary are based on statistical gimmicks: Since 'cure' is defined as survival five years after diagnosis, the earlier a cancer is diagnosed the greater the likelihood of cure, even if the course of the disease and the time

---

[31] Coulston and Serrone (1969: 682).   [32] ibid. 682–3.   [33] Coulston (1980).
[34] Cairns (1978).

of death are unaffected in any way. In commenting on the eradication of infectious diseases, Cairns claims: "It is significant, however, that what is often thought of as one of the accomplishments of sophisticated medical science was, in large part, the product of some fairly simple improvements in public health. In the end, history may well repeat itself and the same prove to be true for cancer."[35]

Cairns is not the only prominent figure in the scientific establishment to have made such an argument. Perhaps it goes too far, but it does suggest how thoroughgoing a utilitarian critique of animal experimentation, or the use of animals in toxicology experiments or in education, can be. If most of our use of animals in these activities is largely irrelevant to producing longer and pleasanter lives, then there is no justification for using animals in ways that cause them pain.

But it is not just the unreliability and redundancy of the data that utilitarians will contest. They can also object to the kind of animal used for scientific purposes. Rocks cannot feel pleasure or pain. Only conscious beings can. Nevertheless, there are great differences among conscious beings regarding the degree or level of their consciousness. Some conscious beings have a conception of their own identity, a self-concept: they can make plans for the future, regret the past, and envision their own bodily death. Beings that lack a concept of self might experience something like pleasure, but they cannot anticipate future pleasure, nor regret those pleasures they have missed in the past. It is for this reason that we think of some beings as having more complex, richer, and "higher" states of consciousness than other conscious beings. Beings with a sense of self are utility "hot spots", so to speak. Because they have the kind of consciousness they do, they can experience richer, fuller pleasures and pains, and because of this we should take special care to maximize their pleasures and minimize their pains. That would seem to be a winning strategy for bringing about the best consequences.

Where, precisely, we draw the line between animals who do, and those who do not, have a concept of self is unclear. Probably there is no precise line to be drawn. That problem is not what demands our attention just now. The point to notice is that utilitarianism will not allow the use of animals having higher levels of consciousness, even if their use would bring about a net balance of good over evil, if these same (or better) results could be obtained by using animals of less highly developed consciousness. Wherever possible, that is, utilitarianism requires that science deal with the most rudimentary

[35] Cairns (1978: 7).

forms of conscious life and as few of these as possible, or, most preferable by far, with non-conscious beings, living or otherwise. Since there is ample evidence that most chimpanzees, for example, have a sense of self,[36] and growing evidence that some species of Cetaceans do,[37] the case for regarding these animals as having higher consciousness is increasingly reinforced and the utilitarian grounds for cautioning against the use of these animals for scientific purposes is correspondingly strengthened. It is exceedingly doubtful that the 30,000 primates used for scientific purposes in America in 1978 were used justifiably, given the Utilitarian Argument.

There is welcome evidence that contemporary scientists, unlike Descartes's contemporaries, are becoming increasingly sensitive to the issues discussed in the previous paragraph. Talk of "the three Rs" is in the air. The goal of research, it is said, is replacement, reduction and refinement. Commenting on these ideas, D. H. Smyth (1978: 14) writes that "Replacement [means] the substitution of insentient material for conscious living higher animals. Reduction [means] reduction in the number of animals used to obtain information of given amount and precision. Refinement [means] any decrease in the incidence or severity of inhumane procedure [i.e., pain or suffering] applied to those animals which still have to be used." These are goals that both utilitarians and supporters of the Modified Innocence Principle can endorse. But both positions can be used to press the case for justification of the use of animals in science at a deeper level. The question is, how can any use of any animal for any scientific purpose be justified? To be told that, whenever possible, we ought to replace, reduce, or refine, does not address this question. Built into the three Rs is the assumption that the use of animals in science sometimes is justified, and it is precisely this question that must be addressed rather than begged. Utilitarianism provides us with one way of answering it, the Modified Innocence Principle provides us with another; but the three Rs provides us with no answer at all.

Perhaps it will be replied that the goal of refinement gets at the heart of the matter. "Only that suffering that is absolutely necessary for the scientific integrity of an experiment or test is allowed", it may be said. Suppose this is true. Does it follow that, judged on utilitarian grounds, the animal's use is permissible? It does not. The larger question is whether the experiment, test, or other use of the animal is itself justified. Only if it is can the pain involved be justified. Until the issue of the moral justifiability of the animal's use is

---

[36] On chimpanzees, see Gallup (1977).
[37] On Cetaceans, see the essays collected in Norris (1966) and McIntyre (1974).

addressed, therefore, the justification of the animal's pain, even if the pain is "kept to a minimum", remains in doubt.[38]

In summary, the principle of utility demands that stringent requirements be met before we can be justified in using any animal for any scientific purpose that causes it pain. It must be shown that a proposed use will promote the utilitarian objective of bringing about the greatest possible balance of good over evil for everyone involved. If it does not, then, as premise 2 of the Utilitarian Argument asserts, the procedure is morally wrong. There is ample reason to believe that at least a great deal of the use of animals in science does not satisfy this requirement. Thus, if utility be our guide, there is strong reason to condemn much of the current use made of animals in science.

5. INNOCENCE AND UTILITY CONTRASTED

In the two preceding sections we sketched two moral perspectives that converge on the same general conclusion: at least much of the scientific use made of animals is morally wrong and ought to be stopped. Despite their agreement in a broad range of cases, however, the Principle of Utility and the Modified Innocence Principle (MIP) support conflicting judgements in some cases.

Recall that MIP will allow harming an innocent only if we have very good reason to believe that this is the only realistic way to prevent equivalent harm to many other innocents. MIP does not sanction harming innocents so that others may reap positive goods (e.g. pleasures); it is limited to the prevention or elimination of harms or evils (e.g. pain). Thus, in principle, MIP will not allow, say, contests between a few innocent Christians and hungry lions so that great amounts of otherwise unobtainable pleasure might be enjoyed by large numbers of Roman spectators. MIP does not permit evil (the harming of innocents) so that good may come. In principle, utilitarianism could allow this. Classical utilitarianism is aggregative in nature: it is the total of goods and evils, for all the individuals involved, that matters. Theoretically, then, it is possible that achieving the optimal balance of good over evil in any given case will necessitate harming the innocent. The point can be illustrated abstractly by imagining that we face a choice between two alternatives, A_1 which will harm an innocent individual and A_2 which will not. A utilitarian, we may assume, will assign some disutility, some minus score, to the harm caused in A_1. Suppose this is -20. Suppose further, however, that A_1 would bring about much better consequences for others than A_2; suppose that the difference is a mag-

---

[38] For further comments on the ambiguity of 'unnecessary suffering', see Regan (1980).

nitude of 100 to 1, A_1 yielding benefits that total +1,000, A_2 yielding only +10. A greater balance of good over evil would result if we did A_1 than if we did A_2. Utilitarians, therefore, must choose the former alternative, but not those who accept MIP: they must favour the latter alternative (A_2).

The Principles of Utility and that of Modified Innocence do differ in theory, therefore, despite their agreement in many practical cases. Which principle ought we to accept? That is far too large an issue to be decided here. It is enough to realize that utilitarianism theoretically could allow more use of animals in science that harms the animals than MIP allows. Whether or not this difference is a sign of the moral superiority or inferiority of utilitarianism in comparison to MIP, at least this much is clear: there is a difference.

6. CONCLUDING REMARKS

Some general points should be kept in mind as we conclude. First, given either the Principle of Utility or MIP, to harm an animal is in need of moral defence: both principles view the harming of an individual as presumptively wrong, as something that is wrong unless it can be shown that it isn't. Given either principle, therefore, the burden of proof must always be on those who cause harm to animals in scientific settings. Unless these persons can show that what they do is morally permissible, we are entitled to believe that it is not. This burden, obvious as it may seem, has not always been recognized. Too often it has been "those who speak for the animals" who have been called upon to shoulder the burden of proof. But it is not the critics, it is the advocates of animal use in science who should bear it. This fundamental point must never be lost sight of in the debate over the ethics of the use of animals in science.

Secondly, the kind of knowledge (one might better say "wisdom") sometimes required to determine the permissibility of using an animal, especially in experiments in basic research, clearly is not the exclusive property of any particular profession, let alone any particular branch of science. For that reason we should draw upon the expertise of many people, from many fields, to review experimental proposals before they are funded. It is very important that these decisions not be left just to those who have a professional interest in their outcome. Not very long ago in the United States experiments were performed on humans with impunity. Today we have recognized the merits of the idea that decisions about the permissibility of research that might harm human subjects must be made on a case-by-case basis, involving the best judgement of persons from diverse areas of expertise; we wouldn't dream of leaving these decisions entirely in the hands of those doing the research. Because animals cannot, except by prejudice, be excluded from the moral community, it is reason, not "mere sentiment", that calls for similar procedural safeguards for their use in science generally and in scientific experimentation in particular. It is not enough, even if it is a salutary development, that principles for the care and maintenance of laboratory animals are in place,[39] though even here one should raise questions about how conscientiously these principles are enforced. How often, for example, has a scientific establishment been found in violation of these principles? And how impartial are those in whose hands the business of enforcement rests? One need not prejudge the answers to these questions by insisting upon the propriety of asking them.

At this point someone will accuse us of being "anti-scientific" or, more soberly, perhaps it will be argued that instituting procedural safeguards of the kind we recommend, in which research proposals are considered case by case by a panel of experts from diverse fields, would "rein in science", thus having a chilling effect on important research. The "anti-science" accusation will be answered in this essay's final paragraph. As for the "chilling effect" argument, it is true that adopting the kind of procedural safeguards we recommend would place limits on what scientists would be permitted to do. These safeguards would thus restrict the scientists's "freedom to inquire". The right to inquire, however, as was argued earlier, is not absolute; one may not do anything one pleases in the name of this right; it can and should be limited by other, weightier moral concerns. It is no longer possible in this country, for example, to lie to poor black males in Alabama, telling them that they were being treated for their syphillis, when in reality effective treatment was being withheld so that the course of the disease could be documented. This is a restriction on science, but one which ought to be viewed as welcome and appropriate. An unfortunate consequence of instituting and effectively enforcing procedural safeguards for the use of animals in science, it is true, is that research proposals would have to be screened by another, interdisciplinary committee, requiring that yet another set of forms be filled out and so forth. Both the bureaucracy and the red tape are almost certain to increase if our call for safeguards is heeded. Researchers may see "Big Brother" at work, and descry, in the words of a leader in brain transplant research, Robert J. White, "the ever-present

---

[39] These federal regulations are part of the Animal Welfare Act. The physical facilities in which animals used in science are housed and the attention given to some of their basic needs (food, water) have improved as a result of these regulations. Not all animals are covered by the Act, however, rats and mice being notable exceptions; and the regulations apply to, and thus are enforceable only in the case of, federally supported programmes.

danger of government control of biological research through the limitation of animal availability and experimental design".[40] But the inconvenience "red tape" causes would seem to be a comparatively small price to pay to ensure that scientific practice meets the demands of morality. The life sciences are not physics, and the costs that must be borne in the conduct of biological and psychological research cannot be measured merely in dollars and cents.

In reply it may be objected that the kind of safeguards we propose would be impracticable, and, in any event, would cost too much to implement. Neither objection is well-founded. In July of 1977 some initial procedural safeguards for experimental animals were put into place in Sweden. It has been noted that simply by establishing ethics committees to review research proposals, research designs have been improved; and these designs often require the use of fewer animals than was formerly the rule.[41] In addition, greater use is being made of animals with less highly developed conscious lives, animals which, not surprisingly, are cheaper to procure and maintain; and the employment of less harmful procedures is growing. It has been reported that the Swedish approach has proved satisfactory to many, both in the scientific and in the animal welfare communities. The "Swedish experiment" suggests that it is possible to develop a framework that is practical and financially sound, a framework which, though not a panacea, does go some way towards protecting the interests of animals while at the same time nurturing our interest in the growth and maintenance of science.

Two final points. First, nothing that we have said should be taken as condemning the motives, intentions, or character of those engaged in scientific research. We are not saying that these people are nasty, vicious, cruel, dehumanized, heartless, depraved, pitiless, evil people. No one who uses animals in science has been accused of being, in White's terminology, a "monster-scientist, perpetrator of abominable crimes" (1971: 166). Neither are we saying that "all scientists" are on an ego-trip, motivated to do their work only to pump out another publication, to be used to secure yet another grant, to be parlayed into yet a bigger name, yet another promotion, yet another rise, and so forth and so forth. These accusations may have powerful rhetorical force in some quarters, but they have no place, and have found none, here, in a reflective assessment of the ethics of the use of animals in science. Our concern throughout has been to assess the ethics of what scientists do, not why they do it. The point that must be recognized is that people can do what is wrong

---

[40] White (1971: 164).
[41] For a discussion of the Swedish experiment, see Ross (1978).

even though they have the best motives, the best intentions, even though they are "the nicest people". The question of the moral status of animal use in science thus is not to be decided by discovering the motives or intentions of those who do it or of those who criticize it. The sooner all the parties to the debate realize this, the better.[42]

Lastly, there is the idea of alternatives again. The search for alternatives to using animals in science is only in its infancy. Many scientists tend to scorn the idea and to believe that the number and utility of alternatives are very limited. One would have thought that recent developments would have put this attitude to rest. To cite just one encouraging example, a promising new bacterial test for carcinogens has been developed by Professor Bruce Ames at the University of California. Whereas animal tests for carcinogenicity typically take two to three years and cost in excess of $150,000, the Ames test takes two to three days, uses no animals, and costs just a few hundred dollars.[43] Ames himself stops short of claiming that his test is 100 per cent accurate, and he does not rule out the present need to use animals as an ancillary part of research into carcinogens. Yet his test does much to suggest the potential benefits to be realized from the search for alternatives, both in terms of the savings in animal pain and in dollars and cents. Those sceptical of "alternatives" ("impossible" it may be said) may hold their ground, but we should not be discouraged. Yesterday's "impossibilities" are today's commonplaces. We must press on despite the sceptics, acting to ensure that adequate funds become available to those qualified to search for alternatives. The call to intensify the search is not "anti-scientific". In fact, it is just the opposite. It is a call to scientists to use their skill, knowledge, and ingenuity to progress towards our common aspirations: a more humane approach to the practice of science. It is a call to do science, not to abandon it. The commitment to search for alternatives should be viewed as an index both of our moral and our scientific progress.

Postscript

Since 1982, when this essay was originally published, both the practice of animal experimentation and reflection upon it have evolved. Any paper written on this topic now would have to take these changes and the subsequent literature into account. Notable changes include the apparent reduction in the total number of animals used in science (though reliable data for the

---

[42] Some of these matters are discussed in Regan (1980).
[43] See Devoret (1979).

United States are difficult to obtain), and the virtual abandonment of some of the worst practices (though new invasive procedures, e.g. xenotransplantation, are becoming increasingly common). Salem and Rowan (2001) provide a good starting-point for the contemporary investigation of these issues. Despite these changes, the fundamental philosophical questions posed by the use of animals in science remain unchanged.

Since co-authoring this article Regan has revised his views on animal experimentation; see his book, *The Case for Animal Rights* (1983). For my more recent reflections on this topic, see Essays 9 and 10.

9

Experimenting on Animals:
A Reconsideration

We live in a world that is morally horrific by almost anyone's standards. In the Third World millions of people suffer from malnutrition, and due to inefficiency, stupidity, or venality many of them will literally starve to death. Even those of us fortunate enough to live in affluent countries are threatened daily with annihilation. Through madness or miscalculation, Reagan or Gorbachev could turn the entire planet into a fiery oven. The survivors would have nothing to look forward to but slow death in a nuclear winter.

In such a world, is it any wonder that many people do not think that animal welfare is a high priority? With so many other causes competing for our limited attention, some say that devoting time and energy to animal welfare is just a way of avoiding the more pressing problems of people.

This is a common attitude that is not easily overcome. Most of us conveniently forget how pervasive our use of animals really is. We prefer our childhood images of "Old Macdonald" to the realities of factory farms. Even when the facts are brought to our attention—seventy million lab animals used in the United States each year and four billion animals slaughtered for food—the lesson seldom sinks in.[1] Many people continue to believe that serious concern for animals is either beyond the call of duty or a way of avoiding the call of duty altogether.

Animal liberationists, on the other hand, do not understand how sensitive, caring people can be indifferent to animal suffering. Many of us who pamper

For ease of reference, I refer to members of the scientific establishment with male pronouns and members of the animal liberation movement with female pronouns.

[1] This estimate of the number of animals used in laboratories is taken from Rowan (1984, ch. 5). The estimate of the number of animals slaughtered for food is taken from various Fact Sheets published by Food Animal Concern Trust, PO Box 14599, Chicago, IL 60614.

dogs and cats eat cows and pigs. We would have the next-door neighbour arrested for doing the sorts of things we do not object to when they are part of a scientific protocol. How can people who show concern for some animals show such contempt for others?

In such an environment, neither abstract moral theorizing nor raw emotional appeal has much force. For neither side is open to the arguments or exhortations of the other. Nowhere is this clearer than in the debate over the use of laboratory animals.

Several years ago Tom Regan and I wrote an essay in which we discussed various views concerning the ethics of using animals in science. We argued against both the "unrestricted use" view characteristic of the scientific establishment, and the "abolitionist" view often held by animal liberationists. Our claim was that two very different but independently plausible moral principles lead to a moderate position: that it is sometimes permissible to use some animals in scientific experiments. We argued further that our present practices with respect to animals are so abhorrent and extreme that even this moderate position implies that "at least much of the scientific use of animals is morally wrong and ought to be stopped".[2]

It is not easy to come up with final answers to moral questions, and further reflection often leads philosophers to revise their views. Regan (1983, ch. 9) has changed his mind about animal experimentation, and he now thinks that the abolitionist position is the only defensible one. While I agree that there are mistakes in our original essay, I think they are merely mistakes of detail rather than substance. I continue to believe that a moderate view is the correct one, and continue to think that it has sweeping implications.

Still, there is an important oversight in the original essay. We assumed without argument that most people would agree that the use of animals in science raises moral problems that should at least be discussed, and that anyone who agreed with this would be committed to the patterns of reasoning and discourse that are characteristic of rational discussion. It is now clear to me that many people do not share these assumptions. The most important and neglected aspect of the dispute between animal liberationists and the scientific establishment concerns whether the question of animal experimentation is really a moral question at all, and if it is, what implications this has for the kinds of positions that can be rationally defended. Only after these issues are resolved, can we go on to construct a logical framework that has the potential to affect people's behaviour.

[2] Essay 8.

My main purpose in this essay is to address these questions. I hope that the result will be a clearer understanding of which positions are defensible and which are not, and how argument and discussion should proceed if we are to make progress.

In Section 1 I discuss the dispute as I think it is typically seen by the scientific establishment. In Section 2 I discuss what I take to be the views of the mainstream of the animal liberation movement. Finally, in Section 3 I draw some conclusions.

1. THE VIEW FROM THE TOP

Some in the scientific establishment have recently become concerned about the activities of the animal liberationists. In 1982 Harvard University's Office of Government and Community Affairs produced a report entitled *The Animal Rights Movement in the United States: Composition, Funding Sources, Goals, Strategies, and Potential Impact on Research*. This report, which was intended for internal distribution only, warned that although these groups are disorganized and competitive, they present a "formidable threat" to university research.[3] Donald Kennedy, a former head of the Food and Drug Administration and now President of Stanford University, issued a more serious warning in a speech to the Comstock Club entitled, "The Great American Science Venture: Will It Survive?" Of all the problems facing American science, according to Kennedy, "None is more troubling than some actions promoted in the name of 'animal rights'".[4]

Animal liberationists are threatening, it is often thought, because they are the vanguard of a large anti-science movement. This movement has been said to include, at various times, astrologers, food faddists, and natural healers, as well as opponents of recombinant DNA research. A recent example of such a view can be found in Dr Maurice Visscher's critical notice of Bernard Rollin's *Animal Rights and Human Morality*. Writing in the *New England Journal of Medicine*, Visscher claims that "Few physicians will care to read this book . . . but its appearance at this time is evidence that the anti-science group in America is becoming more vociferous".[5] Visscher calls on the "rational

---

[3] The Harvard Report is available from the International Society for Animal Rights, 421 South State Street, Clarks Summit, PA 18411.

[4] Parenthetical page references are to a typescript of Kennedy's speech released by his office at Stanford.

[5] Visscher (1982: 1303–4). For further discussion of Visscher's review, see my review of Rollin (1981) in Jamieson (1983a).

segment of society" to "diligently counter [the animal liberationists'] pernicious influences on biologic science".[6]

Since the time of Visscher's review, the preparation of the Harvard Report,
and Kennedy's address to the Comstock Club, animal liberationists have
become increasingly militant in their tactics. In the last year, the Animal
Liberation Front has freed animals from laboratories on both coasts. Recently
the ALF obtained some videotapes, made by researchers, of head injury
experiments performed on baboons at the University of Pennsylvania.[7] The
purpose of these experiments, according to Dr Thomas Langfitt, Chair of the
Department of Neurosurgery, was to discover what happens to the brain at
the moment of injury. The experiments involved deliberately inflicting head
injuries on baboons by strapping them to a table, encasing their heads in a
steel cylinder, and then violently accelerating the cylinder with a piston-driven
pneumatic device. This causes the brain to slam against the skull with such
force that the baboon suffers massive concussive injuries which result in
paralysis and usually death. The experiments documented by these tapes were
appalling, but even more shocking was the behaviour of the researchers. They
treated their animal subjects with what can only be described as great ruth-
lessness and insensitivity. The tapes even show one researcher teasing another:
"better hope the anti-vivisectionists don't get a hold of this".

The scientific establishment has responded to this escalation of animal
liberationist activity in several ways.

Some have tried to take the moral high ground. They agree with the animal
liberationists that there are serious moral issues involved in animal experimentation. What they claim, however, is that morality is on the side of the
researchers. I shall call these people Moral Humanists (or Humanists for
short).

Those in the second group also believe that animal experimentation raises
moral issues, but they have a different conception of what moral principles
are: they see them simply as preferences, rather than as overriding commitments. Disputes about the morality of animal experimentation are, in their
view, conflicts between people with different preferences about how animals
should be treated in scientific contexts. Since conflicts of preferences can often
be resolved by simple compromise, those in this second group are more

---

[6] Visscher (1982: 1304).

[7] A thirty-minute compilation of these tapes is available from People for the Ethical Treatment of
Animals, PO Box 56272, Washington, DC 20011. My discussion of this case is based on these tapes and
accounts published in various newspapers from 28 July 1984 until the beginning of August of that year.
Articles published in the PETA *Newsletter* and in *Agenda* have also been helpful.

willing to try to find common ground with the animal liberationists than the Humanists are. I shall call these people Moral Democrats (or Democrats for short).

A third group does not see animal experimentation as a moral issue at all. They think that the domain of morality is very narrow; it concerns only private stances on fundamentally private issues. These people regard animal liberationists as irrational fanatics who do not understand science or recognize its authority. They see themselves as victims of these "animal crazies" who are out to harrass them and disrupt their work. I shall call this group, which I believe to be the largest of the three, Moral Privatists (or Privatists for short). I shall discuss each of these groups in turn.

Humanists typically claim that the behaviour of animal liberationists is immoral. It violates a fundamental principle that must be respected. One oft-cited candidate for such a fundamental principle is freedom of inquiry.

At the height of the controversy over recombinant DNA research, Carl Cohen, a philosopher at the University of Michigan, published two influential articles defending a strong right to freedom of inquiry (1977, 1978). He claimed that unless an overwhelmingly strong case can be made against a line of research, it may go forward. Cohen believes that the abolitionists have failed to make an overwhelming case against animal experimentation just as the opponents of recombinant DNA research failed to make their case. Indeed, in conversation, Cohen has expressed the opinion that there should be more animal experimentation rather than less.

Sometimes the argument on behalf of unrestricted research appeals to values that are less lofty than freedom of inquiry. In his Comstock Club speech, Kennedy's defence of scientific research seems to rest on its contribution to GNP. He begins by saying: "It is a real pleasure to appear before you. I shall use the opportunity to tell you a tale of extraordinary American success. It has to do with the relationship between productivity and innovation, and in particular with the function on which both depend: basic research" (p. 1). He goes on to quote Herbert Hoover approvingly: "A nation with output of fifty million [sic] annually of commodities which could not be produced but for the discoveries of pure science could well afford, it would seem, to put back a hundredth of one percent as an assurance of further progress" (p. 2). Later in the speech, when animal liberationists are identified as "perhaps the major threat to scientific research", Kennedy seems to imply that they are to be faulted for impeding commerce.

Were Kennedy not an important and influential man, the view he seems to be advancing in this address would hardly be worth taking seriously. Our economy is perhaps threatened by cheap imports, high interest rates, and large budget deficits, but it is ludicrous to suppose that animal liberationists present the same sort of threat. Moreover, what is at issue in this dispute is whether or not our treatment of animals in scientific contexts can be justified. To point out that we benefit from our treatment of animals does not in itself constitute a justification.

Cohen's position seems more plausible on the face of it. Most of us would agree that freedom of inquiry is an important value which we should seek to preserve and extend. But three considerations cast doubt on the plausibility and force of this argument.

First, it is not clear that restricting the use of animals in science would result in less freedom of inquiry. In fact, by redirecting resources away from entrenched institutions and calcified research programmes, such restrictions could well contribute to greater effective freedom of inquiry for really creative scientists with new and exciting ideas. It is important to remember that social forces—whether economic, political, sociological, or moral—always play an important role in guiding scientific research. They profoundly affect the goals set, the methods employed, and the questions asked. Which research programmes are pursued and which are not is often determined by funding decisions, which in turn are heavily dependent on policy decisions in both the public and private sectors, as well as on the decisions and judgements of those researchers who are well-established in their fields (the "old boy" network). The introduction of a new consideration into the funding game—restrictions on animal experimentation—would undoubtedly be devastating to those who have been trained in animal research and are unwilling or unable to effect a transition. But it might also provide more opportunity for many other researchers to pursue exciting new projects.

These are only speculations, of course, but they cannot be dismissed out of hand. It would require considerable argument and evidence to show that restricting animal research really would result in diminished freedom of inquiry. In the absence of such argument and evidence, we should resist the temptation to make the all-too-ready inference that restrictions on the use of animals would constitute restrictions on freedom of inquiry. Still less should we conclude that such restrictions would impede the growth of knowledge.

Even if restrictions on animal experimentation constituted restrictions on freedom of inquiry, it does not follow that it would be wrong to initiate such restrictions. Freedom of inquiry is not an absolute value. We accept and even demand some restrictions on freedom of inquiry, even when this stands in the way of obtaining valuable knowledge. We do not allow research on unconsenting prisoners, unwanted children, or unloved old people. We find the research conducted by Nazi doctors in concentration camps utterly repugnant, however valuable the information they obtained might be. Freedom of inquiry is an important value, but not the only value.

The final point is this. Respecting freedom of inquiry is one thing; being compelled to support particular research programmes which employ particular methodologies is another. Animal liberationists are accused of trying to curtail scientific research because they oppose the use of their tax dollars to support research that harms animals. But this charge is no more just than the charge that those people who opposed the use of their tax dollars to bail out Chrysler were attempting to destroy the American automobile industry.

It might be thought that I have overlooked an important premise in the arguments of the Moral Humanists. The argument from GNP would not be successful, it might be admitted, if there were substantial values on the other side of the scale. But since there are only animals on the other side of the scale, and since animals count for nothing or for next to nothing, economic considerations and the value of free inquiry are important enough to sustain this position.

But, if this is how these arguments are to be understood, then the Moral Humanist begs the question. For these arguments were introduced in order to show why animals do not matter. If, in order to succeed, they must assume that animals do not matter, then the demonstration will have failed. The suggestion that it is legitimate simply to assume that animals count for nothing is especially troubling since an impressive body of work over the last decade argues otherwise.[8] For this work to be dismissed out of hand with no argument is a poor way to defend a position, and an even poorer way of trying to arrive at the truth.

Moral Democrats have recently become more prominent within the scientific establishment. They recognize that there is a deep and serious division in our society about how animals may be treated in scientific contexts, and they seek to compromise this division. Democrats view the issue as one of the "few crucial interfaces between the operations of science and the concerns of the public as a whole". Consequently, they believe that "the scientific community must ensure that the issue is handled sensitively and credibly".[9] The quoted words are from a recent article by Thomas Moss, Director of Research Administration at Case Western Reserve. According to Moss, some scientists

---

[8] See e.g. Singer (1985) and the sources cited therein.
[9] Moss (1984: 51). Parenthetical page references are to this article.

are beginning to perceive "the reality and legitimacy of public feelings about laboratory animals, even if those feelings seem irrational in some scientific or logical frameworks", and he points out that "public attitudes toward respect for animal life are no more irrational than many broader attitudes towards the sacredness of life" (p. 52). This movement within the scientific community leads him to an optimistic conclusion: "both sides appear to be moving toward a beneficial mutual understanding" (p. 56).

I find Moss's optimism encouraging. I, myself, have argued that reasonable people should be able to agree immediately to a three-quarter reduction of the number of animals used in science, and only then get down to the hard cases. Still, I fear that Moss's optimism is based on a misconstrual of the animal liberationists, and a misunderstanding of what it is to take a moral position. This is suggested by what is missing in Moss's article. He seems to understand that people's feelings about animals matter, but he doesn't seem to accept the fact that animals matter. And for the animal liberationists, the heart of the struggle is to get that second point across. Animals matter in their own right because of what they are, regardless of any ties they may have to humans.

The Democrats' view seems to be this: moral principles are preferences that can be balanced against other preferences with a view to satisfying those which are most intense and widely held. But moral principles are not mere preferences. Rather, they embody commitments to work for the development of certain kinds of character, the establishment of certain ways of life, or the bringing about of a certain kind of world.

Moral commitments need not be absolutist in principle nor lend themselves to uncompromising tactics. I may think that it is wrong to lie, kill innocent people, or experiment on animals without thinking that it is always wrong to do these things; thus, my principles may support a moderate view. But if I hold a moderate view, it does not mean that I must be willing to split the difference with those who disagree with me: kill a few innocent people here, spare a few there. Rather, to have a moral commitment to a moderate position is to subscribe to a set of principles which implies that it is permissible to kill an innocent person or experiment on an animal under some conditions; but when those conditions are not satisfied, such conduct is wrong. I may be willing to compromise in order to minimize the number of unjustified lies or killings of innocents; but in so far as my commitments are moral commitments, whether absolutist or not, I cannot rest with such compromise. My end is the elimination of evil, not accommodation with those whose views I regard to be incorrect.

What this means for the present case is that animal liberationists will not finally be satisfied with the sort of compromise that the Democrats seek—not because liberationists are fanatics—but because their commitment to ending what they regard as our immoral treatment of animals is a moral commitment. This does not mean, however, that reasonable compromise is impossible. Each side could find itself in a situation in which it could only lose if it does not come to terms with the other, just as two nations each convinced of the moral turpitude of the other may reach accommodation if both are vulnerable. But to expect people who view this issue as one of great moral gravity to reach accommodation easily or to compromise simply for the sake of reducing conflict is to fail to respect their views as moral views.

The Moral Privatists do not see the issue of animal experimentation as a moral issue at all. In their view, it is my business how I treat my dog and your business how you treat your cat. What goes on in the lab is nobody's business but the researchers'.

The Privatist position seems strange to a moral philosopher.[10] The Humanist can be seen as someone who has moral principles which he cannot defend, and the Democrat as someone who misunderstands the force and authority of moral principles, but the Privatist seems to be off the map altogether. His misunderstanding of the nature of morality and the force of moral reasons is so thoroughgoing that he seems to stand in need of diagnosis and therapy rather than argument.

Moral philosophers typically believe in the sovereignty of morality. Moral reasons, whether or not they are different in kind from non-moral reasons, always win: they take precedence over all other considerations. If morality demands my presence or yours at a "hands-off Nicaragua" rally, then it would be wrong for me or you to go to the opera instead.

This is a conception of morality that is foreign to the Privatist. If he thinks about morality at all, he thinks of it as something which is very personal and private—how he lives his life, how he treats his wife and kids, and so on. From this perspective, the very idea of public morality looks strange and dangerous.

Whatever our politics, most of us share something of the Privatist's conception. We tend to resent those who want to intrude in our lives whether they are advocates of restrictive abortion laws, prayer in public schools, or legislation intended to protect laboratory animals. Although the Privatist might

---

[10]   Recently, however, some philosophers have begun to challenge the sovereignty of morality. For further discussion, see Davis and Jamieson (1987), and the references cited therein.

try to parry the animal liberationist with the charge that she should care more about people and less about animals, the Privatist is really just as opposed to those who would compel him to do good for people. He might say that our time and energy is better spent on people than animals, but he would resent us just as much if we were to argue that he should be forced to do what he can to relieve starvation in Ethiopia.

In my view, none of these groups really engages constructively with the animal liberationist. The Humanist fails because he assumes at the outset that animals do not matter; the Democrat fails because he treats moral principles and commitments as if they were mere preferences; the Privatist fails because he has such an impoverished conception of morality and moral discussion.

2. THE VIEW FROM THE BARRICADES

There are three key ideas that are characteristic of animal liberationist thought.

First, animals are like us in ways that count. They are conscious beings who can suffer and enjoy their lives. And just as it is a bad thing for us to suffer, so it is a bad thing for them to suffer. Secondly, animals are innocent. They have done nothing to deserve their fate at the hands of experimenters, and they do not benefit from whatever results are obtained. Finally, animal liberationists suggest that our treatment of animals both expresses what kind of people we are and contributes to making us worse.

Animal liberationists give other arguments as well. They point out that animals are often used in research that is stupid, pointless, or redundant (the Draize Test and the LD_{50} are good examples). They claim that alternatives to animals are available if only researchers would use them; and that where alternatives are not available, it is because we have had no real interest in developing them. And sometimes animal liberationists impugn the motives of researchers. This will probably become more common as the University of Pennsylvania videotapes are more widely viewed.

I think it is clear that the arguments in this second group rest on more fundamental premises. The worries about the failure to use alternatives and the pointlessness of much research would not matter were it not the case that animals are important creatures who are like us in ways that are morally relevant. The belief that researchers have malign motives is related to the view that what we do to animals expresses what is bad about us and also makes us worse.

There is quite a lot to be said about these three fundamental arguments, but what I say here will have to be brief.

The first argument concerns our continuity with other animals. From the point of view of animal liberationists, the scientific establishment has not learned the moral lesson implicit in the Darwinian Revolution. We are merely one species among many; from "the point of view of the universe", we are not fundamentally different in kind from many other animals. Indeed, this is what makes animals plausible "models" for humans in experimental situations. Now that we are free of the behaviourist blinkers that distorted our view for the first half of this century, we can see that our similarities to other animals are not just physical but extend to our conscious lives, as well. Many animals experience pleasure and pain, act on the basis of their beliefs and desires, and communicate by means of highly complex representational systems. To deny animals moral standing is to make an arbitrary distinction between our species and all other species. It is this line of argument which views our treatment of animals as the same kind of moral failing as racism and sexism.

The second argument concerns innocence. Laboratory animals have done nothing to deserve their fates. They are victims of science in consequence of having been victims of irresponsible owners, or because they were brought into existence for commercial purposes or kidnapped and transported from their natural habitats. It is wrong to do what we do to innocent animals for the same reason that it is wrong to imprison and execute innocent humans— whether conscious or self-conscious, rational or irrational. When the lives of innocents are at stake, appeals to "levels of consciousness" are not decisive and perhaps not even relevant.

The final argument concerns the effect of our practices on the development of character. Most of us value certain traits and dispositions. We admire people who are gentle, loving, benevolent, appreciative of nature and beauty, loyal, and so on. Yet we think that deliberately destroying and causing pain to animals is an important part of the education of many people, especially of those who are to become healers (for example, veterinary surgeons and physicians). It is not that all researchers are bad people, or that those who deliberately break the necks of baboons will do the same to humans; but rather, a society concerned to develop good people does better to educate them in the practice of those virtues. In the long run, a society which does not will be morally bankrupt. Indeed, some may think that the ills which I mentioned at the beginning of this essay are to be expected in a world which mistreats animals. From this perspective, there is no conflict between liberating animals, and liberating what is best in human beings.

These arguments, which are at the heart of the animal liberation position, are essentially moral arguments. They are not primarily appeals to self-interest, our desires, or our emotions. Rather, they ask us to think in an impartial way about all of those creatures who are the proper objects of moral concern. It is this point of view, the moral point of view, which provides the ultimate reasons for action.

3. CONCLUSION

What I have suggested is that there is a real failure of understanding between the scientific establishment and the animal liberationists. The scientific establishment for the most part appeals to our collective self-interest, or their authority, in trying to defeat the animal liberationists. When they try to engage in moral discussion, the arguments they advance are typically less than cogent. When they make overtures towards compromise, they often presuppose false views about the nature of the dispute.

The animal liberation movement is a movement with a moral foundation. It is directed towards radically altering our principles and practices in the light of moral theory. In this respect (as in many others), it is truly the heir of the progressive social movements of the last century.

The animal liberation movement is not necessarily committed to an abolitionist position, however. One can accept some or all of the arguments sketched in the previous section without supposing that they lead to the conclusion that it is never permissible to experiment on an animal, whatever the consequences. Nor is this movement necessarily uncompromising. But if meaningful compromise and accommodation are to be possible, it is important to understand what is at stake on both sides of the issue. And so far, the scientific establishment has failed to understand the force and power of the moral position on which the animal liberation movement is founded. Until that happens, meaningful dialogue will be difficult to achieve.

10

Ethics and the Study of Animal Cognition
(with Marc Bekoff)

In the heyday of logical empiricism (*c*.1930–60), science was seen as the purest of human activities. There was a single thing that was "the scientific method"; observations were distinct from and unaffected by theoretical commitments; theories were "sets of sentences" that made no essential reference to knowers; explanation and prediction were regarded as formal relations between sentences that in principle could be made mechanical; and all of this theorizing, explaining, and predicting was thought to be uncontaminated by values.

While many scientists continue to give obeisance to some such picture, it has long since met its demise in the broader intellectual community. Beginning with Quine (1951/1961), influential philosophers argued forcefully against almost every tenet of logical empiricism. Next came historians, abetted by the testimony of important scientific figures. Books such as J. D. Watson's (1968) *The Double Helix* painted a very different picture of scientific discovery than was suggested by the logical-empiricist model. Scientists were seen to be sometimes selfish, irrational, motivated by power and prestige rather than The Pursuit of Truth—in other words, all too human. In the wake of these critiques have come moral philosophers, sociologists, and most recently feminists.[1] Although many scientists may not be aware of it, there is a swirl of activity addressing almost every feature of the scientific life.[2]

Science, like all human practices and institutions, is a proper subject for moral scrutiny, and there is growing concern about issues that centre on

---

[1] See e.g. Gruen (1990/1996).   [2] Alberts and Shine (1994).

human relationships with non-human animals.[3] Scientists such as Richard Dawkins (1993) have called for legal rights for chimpanzees, gorillas, and orang-utans. Top-level administrators in the United States such as President Clinton's science adviser, John Gibbons, have indicated the need for greater ethical reflection on the use of animals in research.

In this chapter we briefly consider two difficult, overlapping issues about the relationship between ethics and the study of animal cognition. These are (i) the vexing connection between cognition and moral status and (ii) the ethics of various experimental practices in studies of animal cognition and behaviour.

1. COGNITION AND MORAL STATUS

The philosophical roots of the contemporary animal protection movement can be traced to Peter Singer's (1975/2001) book, *Animal Liberation*. One important factor influencing the reception of Singer's book is that it appeared against a background of changing attitudes in philosophy, psychology, and linguistics about the appropriateness of appeal to cognitive states in the explanation of human behaviour. Chomsky's (1959) review of Skinner's *Verbal Behavior* was widely regarded as devastating to behaviourist attempts to explain human linguistic competence. By the time *Animal Liberation* was published, behaviourism was dead in much of the intellectual world. It was no longer out of the question for scientists to explain human behaviour in mentalistic terms. If the social lives of many animals were as complex as some researchers suggested and if there were no good theoretical reasons for eschewing talk of mental states, then it seemed natural to explain animal behaviour in mentalistic terms as well.

Viewed in this light, the development of cognitive ethology was inevitable, and perhaps even tardy. The years 1974–6 saw the publication of Nagel's (1974) provocative paper "What is it Like to be a Bat?," Wilson's (1975) *Sociobiology: The New Synthesis*, and Griffin's (1976/1981) *The Question of Animal Awareness: Evolutionary Continuity of Mental Experience*. In only two years students of animal behaviour were presented with major new ideas in overlapping fields concerned with the comparative and evolutionary study of animal behaviour. In *Animal Liberation* Singer discussed research on animals at great length, and although much of the discussion is negative and disapproving, he relied on the ethological work of Jane Goodall, Konrad Lorenz, and Niko

---

[3] References can be found in Bekoff (1994*a*, 1995*b*) and Bekoff and Jamieson (1996*a*).

Tinbergen to show that many animals have much more complex cognitive and social systems than were previously attributed to them, especially by the behaviourist mainstream, and that they were capable of pleasure and pain. Singer himself noted the irony that scientific research on animals has discovered features of animals such that, in virtue of them, a great deal of behavioural research cannot be justified. Indeed, the very research that resulted in these discoveries may appear immoral in light of their own results.

Questions about the relation between what animals are like and how they should be treated are often in the background of discussions about the complexity of behaviour and the "inner" lives of animals.[4] These questions should move from the background to the foreground and be openly discussed. While there is no purely logical connection between views about mental continuity and views about moral continuity, there are important psychological connections. A culture that recognizes its behavioural and emotional kinship with non-human animals is one that is likely to recognize its moral kinship as well.[5]

Some have gone as far as to claim that if gaining knowledge of the cognitive skills of wild animals does nothing more than inform the debate about animal welfare, then these efforts are worthwhile.[6] Those who study behaviour and behavioural ecology in the field are in a good position to make important contributions to animal welfare, although unfortunately they often play only a minor role in informing legislation and regulation. Field workers can help to provide guidelines concerning dietary requirements, space needs, and the type of captive habitat that would be the most conducive to maintaining the natural activity budgets of the animals being held captive, as well as information on social needs in terms of group size, age and sex composition, and about the nature of the bonds that are formed between animals and human researchers. One important result of research in cognitive ethology is that even if animals are physically well-maintained, the individual's state of mind—his or her psychological well-being—must be given serious consideration.[7]

2. RESEARCH ETHICS FOR ETHOLOGISTS

Studies on cognition are performed both under controlled laboratory conditions and in the field. Often research not motivated by an interest in animal

---

[4] Bekoff and Jamieson (1991); Jamieson and Bekoff (1992); Bekoff (1994a, 1995a).
[5] Rollin (1989); Bekoff et al. (1992); Cavalieri and Singer (1993).   [6] Byrne (1991).
[7] Bekoff (1994a, 1995b).

cognition but by an interest in behaviour suggests that animals are "smarter" than had been previously realized; that they are conscious, have expectations, desires, and beliefs, make assessments and choices based on fine discriminations among various alternatives, and have subjective feelings.[8] Even though apparently clever behaviour does not imply cognition, often the attribution of mental predicates is irresistible in these cases. Even those who are officially sceptics about animal cognition often fall into using cognitive language when discussing their work. In some cases they would not know what to say otherwise.

Both laboratory and field research can involve intrusions into the privacy of animals' lives. Because animals living under field conditions are generally more difficult to observe than individuals living under more confined conditions, various manipulations are often used to make them more accessible to study. These include activities such as handling, trapping (often using various sorts of mechanical devices that might include using live animals as bait), and marking individuals, none of which is unique to field studies, but all of which can have important and diverse effects on wild animals who may not be accustomed to being handled by humans or even to their presence. Simply observing and visiting individuals, groups, nests, dens, and ranging areas can also have a significant influence on behaviour. Filming animals can have a negative influence on the animals being filmed; reflections from camera bodies, the noise of motor-driven cameras and other sorts of video devices, and the heat and brightness of spotlights[9] can all be disruptive. In a long-term study of coyotes,[10] it was found that shiny cameras and spotting scopes made the animals uneasy, so this equipment was painted dull black so that it would not reflect much light. In this study, the same clothes were worn when visiting dens so that similar odours and visual images were presented to the coyotes on each visit.

Here are some examples of how what seem to be minor or insignificant intrusions from our point of view can actually disrupt the lives of animals.[11]

1. Kenney and Knight (1992) found that magpies who are not habituated to human presence spend so much time avoiding humans that this takes time away from essential activites such as feeding.

2. Major (1990) reported that in white-fronted chats, nests that were visited daily by humans suffered higher nest predation than nests that were visited only once at the end of a typical period of incubation.

[8] Bekoff and Jamieson (1991); Ristau (1991); Griffin (1992); M. Dawkins (1993).
[9] A. Pusey, personal communication.   [10] Bekoff and Wells (1986).
[11] See also Kirkwood et al. (1994).

3. Wilson *et al.* (1991) found that Adélie penguins who were away from their nests when exposed to aircraft and directly to humans showed profound changes in behaviour including deviation from a direct course back to a nest as well as increased nest abandonment. Overall effects due to exposure to aircraft included a decrease of 15 per cent in the number of birds in a colony and an increase of 8 per cent in active nest mortality when compared to undisturbed conditions, as well as substantial increases in heart rates.

4. Henson and Grant (1991) found that trumpeter swans do not show such adverse effects to aircraft. However, the noise and visible presence of vehicles did produce changes in incubation behaviour by trumpeter females that could result in decreased productivity due to increases in the mortality of eggs and hatchlings.

5. Gales *et al.* (1990) found that the foraging efficiency of little penguins (average mass of 1,100 grams) was decreased by their carrying a small device (about 60 grams) that measured the speed and depth of their dives. They referred to the changes in behaviour as the "instrument effect". Davis (1991) also found that Adélie penguins fitted with small transmitters showed reduced swimming speed and probably foraging efficiency as well.

6. Pietz *et al.* (1993) found that free-ranging radio-equipped female mallard ducks, when compared to females who were not radio-equipped, "tended to feed less, rest and preen more, initiate nests later, and lay smaller clutches and eggs" (p. 696).

7. Kinkel (1989) reported that fewer wing-tagged ring-billed gulls returned to their colony site when compared to leg-banded individuals, pair bonds of tagged birds were also broken more frequently than pair bonds of banded birds, and most tagged females who returned to their colony were unable to acquire mates.

8. Burley *et al.* (1982) showed that mate choice in zebra finches is influenced by the colour of the leg band used to mark individuals. Females with black rings and males with red rings had higher reproductive success than birds with other colours. Blue and green rings were especially unattractive on both females and males.

9. Gutzwiller *et al.* (1994) found that in some species of birds, human intrusion influenced normal singing behaviour, the result of which could lower the reproductive fitness of males who are sensitive to this type of disturbance.

10. Bertreaux, Duhamel, and Bergeron (1994) observed that the weight of

radio collars influenced dominance relationships in adult female meadow voles. There was a significant loss of dominance when voles wore a collar that was greater than 10 per cent of their live body mass.

11. Laurenson and Caro (1994), in perhaps the most careful and extensive analysis available for a large mammal, analysed the long-term effects of wearing a radio collar, aerial radio-tracking, and lair examination in wild cheetahs on the central plains of the Serengeti National Park, Tanzania. They concluded that "the behaviour and reproduction of even sensitive mammals need not be affected by field techniques" (p. 547). However, they caution that some of their measures might have been too crude and they note that there might be individual differences in response to stress (for example) that demand close attention. Furthermore, they state (p. 556) that "Recording and reporting such measures should be a routine part of any study using intrusive techniques, as the onus is on fieldworkers to show that their methods have no impact, or at least an acceptable impact, on their study animals".[12] Needless to say, much more work and discussion is needed to flesh out just what "an acceptable impact" consists in.

While there are many problems that are encountered both in laboratory and field research, the consequences for wild animals may be different from and greater than those experienced by captive animals, whose lives are already changed by the conditions under which they live. This is so for different types of experiments that may or may not entail handling, trapping, and marking individuals. Consider experimental procedures that include (i) visiting the home ranges, territories, or dens of animals, (ii) manipulating food supply and other resources, (iii) changing the size and composition of groups (age, sex ratio, kin relationships) by removing or adding individuals, (iv) playing back vocalizations, (v) depositing scents, (vi) distorting phenotypes, (vii) using dummies, and (viii) manipulating the gene pool. These manipulations can change the behaviour of individuals and groups with respect to movement patterns, how space is used, the amount of time that is devoted to various activities including hunting, foraging, anti-predatory behaviour, and social encounters including care-giving, play, and dominance interactions. These changes can also influence the behaviour of non-target individuals. Consider, for example, the consequences of reintroducing red wolves into areas in which coyotes already live.

Many specific questions can be asked about the ethics of animal research

----

[12] See also Travaini et al. (1993).

and we briefly discuss several of these questions in what follows. Although there may be little consensus about the answers to these questions at this time, we believe that better and worse answers can be given.

1. Do wild animals have a different moral status than domestic animals? This is an important question because field studies are performed on both domestic and wild animals, often in the same habitat. Callicott (1980/1989: 30) writes that "Domestic animals are creations of man. They are living artifacts, but artifacts nonetheless, and they constitute yet another mode of the extension of the works of man into the ecosystem." Callicott thinks that domestic animals are "stupid" and are not owed the kind of respect due to wild animals. Others, however, argue that there is no distinction in moral status between wild and domestic animals, or that we owe more to domestic animals than we do to wild animals. We may owe more to certain domesticated animals because of the trust these animals invest in humans and the strong reciprocal bonds that develop.[13] Colwell (1989: 33) maintains that "Our moral responsibility for the appropriate care of *individual* organisms in agriculture, zoos, or gardens does not depend on whether they are wild or domesticated in origin". He also writes: "I contend, however, that the role of domesticated *species* as coevolved members of our ancestral component community . . . places them in a biologically and ethically distinct class from 'wild' species".

2. Is it ever justified, and if so under what conditions, to bring wild animals into captivity? The most frequently cited reason for bringing animals into captivity is to preserve endangered species by allowing individuals to live in a protected environment that facilitates breeding and maintains the species' gene pool. It is sometimes said that the goal of these programmes is the eventual return of these animals to the wild. While there are serious philosophical questions involved here (e.g. Do animals have a right to liberty? Do species have interests? Can the welfare of individuals be sacrificed in the interests of species?[14]), it should be noted that some of the most severe critics of captive breeding programmes are the scientists themselves who have dedicated their lives to these efforts and who sincerely want them to succeed.[15] No one should deny the extreme importance of the goals of captive breeding programmes. However, half-hearted, haphazard, or incorrect approaches both waste resources and harm the animals involved.

3. How can the number of animals used in research be minimized? In cases in which animals are followed or located repeatedly, it is worth asking whether

---

[13] Bekoff (1995a).   [14] See Essays 11–13.
[15] e.g. Peterson (1989); Rabinowitz (1986); Schaller (1993).

only one individual has to be marked or fitted with a radio collar if all other animals are individually identifiable using reliable behavioural or other markers. Not only would this entail less handling of individuals, but minimal labelling of the animals might also lead to less disruption of ongoing behaviour. If studies produce results whose validity can be legitimately questioned, because, for example, the data come from stressed animals, then attempts to repeat the studies, in one form or another, will result in yet more animals being used.

4. Should individuals be subjected to harmful or painful staged encounters so that we can learn how animals deal with these situations and how their behaviour is influenced?[16] There are many studies of this kind, including those in which researchers intentionally stimulate predatory, agonistic, infanticidal, or other types of encounters. While these sorts of studies can result in useful knowledge, there are many difficult issues involved, and reflecting on them can make people change their minds. As an example, one of us (MB) performed staged encounter studies on the development of predatory behaviour in captive coyotes, but on reflection found it impossible to justify them and decided that he would no longer do this sort of research. His decision centred on the psychological pain and suffering to which the prey (mice and young chickens) were subjected by being placed in a small arena in which there were no possibilities for escape, as well as the physical consequences of being stalked, chased, caught, maimed, and killed. One result of his decision is that additional detailed information about the development of predatory behaviour could not be obtained because similar data cannot be collected under non-staged field conditions. Staged-encounter studies are also performed in the field. For example, in a recent study, Small and Keith (1992) released radio-collared Arctic and snowshoe hares to learn how Arctic foxes preyed on them. Infanticide is also often studied using staged encounters. In one study of experimentally induced infanticide in birds, mothers were "collected"—that is, shot dead—to determine how replacement females would treat the young of the females who had been killed.[17] Many motherless chicks were maimed or killed, and the ethics of such a study have been called into question.[18]

Live trapping is also an activity that can be incredibly inhumane, and the experience of being caught in a live trap can be quite painful for an animal. In order to learn about the physiological (endocrinological, haematological) and behavioural responses of captive and free-ranging red foxes to padded and unpadded foothold traps, Kreeger et al. (1990) conducted a three-year

---

[16] Huntingford (1984).   [17] Emlen et al. (1989).   [18] Bekoff (1993b).

study in which trapped foxes were "euthanized" (killed) by shooting them and non-trapped free-ranging foxes who were used as controls were also shot dead. Kreeger and his colleagues found (p. 147) that "foxes caught in unpadded traps had higher physical injury scores to the trapped limbs than foxes caught in padded traps" and that "heart rate and body temperature increased rapidly after foxes were caught, but returned to mean pretrapped levels after 80 minutes". There were also some important biochemical differences between trapped and control foxes (generally, trapped foxes had "higher levels of adrenocorticotropin, β-endorphin, and cortisol and lower levels of thyroxine and insulin" as well as higher leukocyte counts with a significant neutrophilia and leukopenia, and higher incidences of adrenal and kidney congestion and haemorrhaging in their adrenal glands, lungs, and hearts) and between foxes caught in padded versus non-padded traps (foxes caught in padded traps generally had higher cortisol levels, but lower β-endorphin levels). There was no significant difference in the mean time spent resisting traps during an eight-hour period between foxes caught in padded (mean of 85.4 minutes) and unpadded traps (mean of 63.8 minutes). Note that animals were allowed to resist traps for cumulative periods of over one hour!

As a result of their efforts, Kreeger et al. concluded that "Red foxes caught in foothold traps developed 'classical' stress responses characterized by increased HR, increased HPA hormones, elevations of serum chemicals, and neutrophilia" (p. 159). Most of the changes in trapped animals were due to resisting traps. The results of their study led the researchers to recommend the use of padded traps in future work. There is no mention at all about the ethics of either the research that they did or that trapping of all kinds is an activity that should be carefully scrutinized and is often ill-advised. That padded traps do, indeed, produce fewer serious injuries had previously been shown by Olsen et al. (1986, 1988) and McKenzie (1989), and one wonders why Kreeger et al.'s research was even necessary. McKenzie modified steel foothold traps and tested them on seven free-ranging black-backed jackals in Botswana. While there were fewer injuries when padded traps were used, six (85.7 per cent) of the jackals trapped still showed lameness of the leg which had been trapped.

Unfortunately, the guidelines of most professional societies are not very explicit about what humaneness consists in nor about schedules of checking traps, nor for that matter, about schedules for checking on animals who are fitted with bands, tags, radio collars, or implanted telemetric devices. For example, the American Society of Mammalogists' guidelines for acceptable field methods (1987: 7) state that humane scientific methods, those "that keep the captured mammals alive, uninjured, and in a comfortable microenvironment while contained for subsequent handling", must be used when trapping live animals and that "Live traps must be checked frequently". The (undefined) schedule of checking depends on the type of trap that is used. In the booklet on ethics published by the Association for the Study of Animal Behaviour and the Animal Behavior Society (Dawkins and Gosling 1992) there is no discussion of recommended trapping procedures. Perhaps developing stringent guidelines for checking trap lines and also for checking marked or instrument-equipped animals should be on the immediate agenda of these and other associations. It seems highly unlikely that anyone who has ever worked with trapped animals could claim that being trapped is not both physically and psychologically harmful or painful for the individuals involved. Alternatives to leghold traps and other devices that restrict an animal's movements should be developed.

   5. What responsibility does the research community have to prevent ethical misconduct, and how should this responsibility be exercised? In recent years various communities of researchers have taken steps to deal with problems of misconduct by adopting codes of professional ethics and refusing to publish papers that violate ethical guidelines. At the same time researchers have too often behaved like physicians in being reluctant to take steps against their own. In cases of conflict there has been a tendency for many scientists to side with more powerful members of the community against the less powerful. Unfortunately, there still is not much agreement about what the collective ethic should be with regard to many of the questions that we ask, nor much sense that the research community has the obligation to encourage high ethical standards within its own community. In many circles there is even a sense of complacency about research misconduct. Yet, in the most exhaustive empirical study to date on the reported incidence of misconduct, Swazey et al. (1993) found that reports of fraud, falsification, and plagiarism occur at a surprisingly high rate. They conclude that this is a serious problem that needs immediate attention.[19]

   6. What is the proper relationship between researchers and the animals they study? Because some form of bonding between the animals who are being studied and the researchers is probably inevitable, these bonds should be exploited in such a way as to benefit the animals.[20] As L. E. Johnson (1991: 122) notes: "Certainly it seems like a dirty double-cross to enter into a relationship of trust and affection with any creature that can enter into such

[19] See also Bulger et al. (1993); Silverman (1994).
[20] Davis and Balfour (1992); Bekoff (1994b).

a relationship, and then to be a party to its premeditated and premature destruction". Indeed, double-crossing is routinely done as part of many research projects including exploiting the trust of domesticated animals in human beings so that they can be harmed for experimental purpose. Trapping can also compromise the trust that wild animals develop in humans.

7. What principles should we use as ethical guides? Rolston III (1988) has suggested that if human-caused pain in animals is less than or equal to what the animal would experience in the wild, then it is permissible to inflict the pain. For many animals it is difficult to know whether this condition is satisfied, for we do not know how most individual animals in nature experience pain.[21] For this reason we must be careful that this principle is not just a rationalization for researchers doing what they really want to do on other grounds.[22] Many other principles have been proposed that perhaps should guide us in our treatment of animals: utilitarian ones, rights-based ones, and so forth.[23] Scientists often operate on the basis of implicit principles and guidelines that are not discussed that should be brought out into the open.

8. Are scientists responsible for how their results are used? This is not purely an "academic" question, since a great deal of research on animals is funded by agencies that want to reduce populations and control behaviour. Information about the behaviour of tigers or wolves may be useful to those who simply want to make a rug out of them. Those who study marine mammals have been struggling with the question of researchers' responsibilities to the animals they study for more than a decade. Purely scientific information about populations, migration routes, and behaviour can be used by those who are involved in the commercial exploitation of animals. Even when there are hunting bans and restrictions, these may only be temporary.

One idea worth considering is that a scientist who studies particular animals may be morally required to be an advocate for them in the way that physicians are supposed to be advocates for their patients. On this view, the welfare of the animals whom a scientist studies should come first, perhaps even before the goal of obtaining peer-reviewed scientific results. Some scientists such as Jane Goodall and Dian Fossey have examplified this ethic, but they have had many critics from within the scientific community.

9. Perhaps the most fundamental question is why do research on animals at all. Even the least invasive research can be disruptive and costs time and money. In recent years anthropology has been going through a disciplinary soul-searching, and it is time for behavioural biology to go through one as

---

[21] Hettinger (1994).   [22] Hettinger (1989).
[23] For further discussion see Jamieson (1993).

well. Many people study animals for deeply personal reasons—they like being outdoors, they like animals, they don't know what else they would do with their lives—but this hardly amounts to a justification. Several other reasons for doing this research are also frequently given: that animal research benefits humans, that it benefits animals, and that it benefits the environment.

Animal research that benefits humans falls into two categories. One category includes research that contributes to human health; the other category includes research that provides economic benefits. Little field research can be defended on the grounds that it contributes to human health. Animal models for human diseases and disorders are better constructed under laboratory conditions, and even then many of them are quite controversial both on scientific and moral grounds. Animal research that contributes economic benefits often concerns predator control. Much of this research employs morally questionable methods, and also raises questions about where science ends and industry begins. Predator management may be informed by science but in itself it is not science; and if producing direct economic benefits were the only justification for studying animals then very little behavioural research would be justified.

The idea that behavioural research benefits animals and the environment is an appealing one. The thought is that only by studying animals in nature will we know how to preserve them, and only by preserving animals can we protect the natural environment. As noble as these sentiments are, they are rife with dangers. For this attitude can lead very quickly to transforming science into wildlife management; and wildlife management poses important moral challenges.[24]

Humans face an environmental crisis in part because of their attempts to control, dominate, and manage nature. These attempts have led to the destruction of important aspects of nature, and even to serious threats to human well-being. In attitude and intention, much wildlife management is more of the same. A new generation seems to think that in the past we were incompetent managers but now we know what we are doing. However, as Ziff (1960, p. vii) wrote in a different context, "the induction is depressing". Ludwig et al. (1993) call into question the idea that we can manage animal populations in a sustainable way. They argue that science is probably incapable of predicting sustainable levels of exploitation of an animal population, and even if it were possible to make such predictions human shortsightedness and greed would prevent us from acting on them.

---

[24] Jamieson (1995a).

The purest motivation for studying animals may be simply the desire to understand them. But even if this is our motivation, we should proceed cautiously and reflectively. For in quenching our thirst for knowledge we impose costs on the animals. In many cases they would be better off if we were willing to accept our ignorance, secure in the knowledge that they are leading their own lives in their own ways.[25] However, if we do make the decision to study animals we should recognize that we are doing it primarily for ourselves and not for them, and we should proceed respectfully and harm them as little as possible.

3. CONCLUDING REMARKS

There is a continuing need to develop and improve general guidelines for research on free-living and captive animals. These guidelines should be aspirational as well as regulatory. We should not be satisfied that things are better than they were in the bad old days, and we should work for a future in which even these enlightened times will be viewed as the bad old days. Progress has already been made in the development of guidelines, and the challenge is to make them more binding, effective, and specific. If possible, we should also work for consistency among countries that share common attitudes towards animals; research in some countries (e.g. the United States) is less regulated than research in other countries (e.g. the United Kingdom).[26] In this evolving process, interdisciplinary dialogue between field workers and philosophers is necessary; no single discipline can do the necessary work alone. Researchers who are exposed to the pertinent issues, and who think about them and engage in open and serious debate, can then carry these lessons into their research projects and import this knowledge to colleagues and students. Not knowing all of the subtleties of philosophical arguments—details over which even professional ethicists disagree—should not be a stumbling block nor an insurmountable barrier to learning.

Perhaps what is most important is to teach well by precept and example. Those who are now students will live and work in a world in which increasingly science will not be seen as a self-justifying activity, but as another human institution whose claims on the public treasury must be defended.[27] It is more important than ever for students to understand that questioning science is not to be anti-science or anti-intellectual, and that asking how humans should interact with animals is not in itself to demand that humans never use

---

[25] Jamieson and Regan (1985).   [26] Gavaghan (1992).   [27] Jamieson (1995b).

animals. Questioning science will make for better, more responsible science, and questioning the ways in which humans use animals will make for more informed decisions about animal use. By making such decisions in an informed and responsible way, we can help to ensure that in the future we will not repeat the mistakes of the past, and that we will move towards a world in which humans and other animals may be able to share peaceably the resources of a finite planet.

11

Against Zoos

1. ZOOS AND THEIR HISTORY

We can start with a rough-and-ready definition of zoos: they are public parks which display animals, primarily for the purposes of recreation or education. Although large collections of animals were maintained in antiquity, they were not zoos in this sense. Typically these ancient collections were not exhibited in public parks, or they were maintained for purposes other than recreation or education.

The Romans, for example, kept animals in order to have living fodder for the games. Their enthusiasm for the games was so great that even the first tigers brought to Rome, gifts to Caesar Augustus from an Indian ruler, ended up in the arena. The emperor Trajan staged 123 consecutive days of games in order to celebrate his conquest of Dacia. Eleven thousand animals were slaughtered, including lions, tigers, elephants, rhinoceroses, hippopotami, giraffes, bulls, stags, crocodiles, and serpents. The games were popular in all parts of the empire. Nearly every city had an arena and a collection of animals to stock it. In fifth-century France there were twenty-six such arenas, and they continued to thrive until at least the eighth century.

In antiquity rulers also kept large collections of animals as a sign of their power, which they would demonstrate on occasion by destroying their entire collections. This happened as late as 1719 when Elector Augustus II of Dresden personally slaughtered his entire menagerie, which included tigers, lions, bulls, bears, and boars.

The first modern zoos were founded in Vienna, Madrid, and Paris in the eighteenth century and in London and Berlin in the nineteenth. The first American zoos were established in Philadelphia and Cincinnati in the

1870s. Today in the United States alone there are hundreds of zoos, and they are visited by millions of people every year. They range from roadside menageries run by hucksters, to elaborate zoological parks staffed by trained scientists.

The Roman games no longer exist, though bullfights and rodeos follow in their tradition. Nowadays the power of our leaders is amply demonstrated by their command of nuclear weapons. Yet we still have zoos. Why?

2. ANIMALS AND LIBERTY

Before we consider the reasons that are usually given for the survival of zoos, we should see that there is a moral presumption against keeping wild animals in captivity. What this involves, after all, is taking animals out of their native habitats, transporting them great distances, and keeping them in alien environments in which their liberty is severely restricted. It is surely true that in being taken from the wild and confined in zoos, animals are deprived of a great many goods. For the most part they are prevented from gathering their own food, developing their own social orders, and generally behaving in ways that are natural to them. These activities all require significantly more liberty than most animals are permitted in zoos. If we are justified in keeping animals in zoos, it must be because there are some important benefits that can be obtained only by doing so.

This conclusion is not the property of some particular moral theory; it follows from most reasonable moral theories. Either we have duties to animals or we do not. If we do have duties to animals, surely they include respecting those interests which are most important to them, so long as this does not conflict with other, more stringent duties that we may have. Since an interest in not being taken from the wild and kept confined is very important for most animals, it follows that if everything else is equal, we should respect this interest.

Suppose, on the other hand, that we do not have duties to animals. There are two further possibilities: either we have duties to people that sometimes concern animals, or what we do to animals is utterly without moral import. The latter view is quite implausible, and I shall not consider it further. People who have held the former view, that we have duties to people that concern animals, have sometimes thought that such duties arise because we can "judge the heart of a man by his treatment of animals", as Kant (1930/1980: 240) remarked in "Duties to Animals". It is for this reason that he condemns the man who shoots a faithful dog who has become too old to serve. If we accept

Kant's premise, it is surely plausible to say that someone who, for no good reason, removes wild animals from their natural habitats and denies them liberty is someone whose heart deserves to be judged harshly. If this is so, then even if we believe that we do not have duties to animals but only duties concerning them, we may still hold that there is a presumption against keeping wild animals in captivity. If this presumption is to be overcome, it must be shown that there are important benefits that can be obtained only by keeping animals in zoos.

3. ARGUMENTS FOR ZOOS

What might some of these important benefits be? Four are commonly cited: amusement, education, opportunities for scientific research, and help in preserving species.

Amusement was certainly an important reason for the establishment of the early zoos, and it remains an important function of contemporary zoos as well. Most people visit zoos in order to be entertained, and any zoo that wishes to remain financially sound must cater to this desire. Even highly regarded zoos, like the San Diego Zoo, have their share of dancing bears and trained birds of prey. But although providing amusement for people is viewed by the general public as a very important function of zoos, it is hard to see how providing such amusement could possibly justify keeping wild animals in captivity.

Most curators and administrators reject the idea that the primary purpose of zoos is to provide entertainment. Indeed, many agree that the pleasure we take in viewing wild animals is not in itself a good enough reason to keep them in captivity. Some curators see baby elephant walks, for example, as a necessary evil, or defend such amusements because of their role in educating people, especially children, about animals. It is sometimes said that people must be interested in what they are seeing if they are to be educated about it, and entertainments keep people interested, thus making education possible.

This brings us to a second reason for having zoos: their role in education. This reason has been cited as long as zoos have existed. For example, in 1898 the New York Zoological Society resolved to take "measures to inform the public of the great decrease in animal life, to stimulate sentiment in favor of better protection, and to cooperate with other scientific bodies . . . [in] efforts calculated to secure the perpetual preservation of our higher vertebrates".

Despite the pious platitudes that are often uttered about the educational efforts of zoos, however, there is little evidence that zoos are very successful in educating people about animals. Stephen Kellert's paper "Zoological Parks in American Society", delivered at the annual meeting of the American Association of Zoological Parks and Aquariums in 1979, indicates that zoo-goers are much less knowledgeable about animals than backpackers, hunters, fishermen, and others who claim an interest in animals, and only slightly more knowledgeable than those who claim no interest in animals at all. Even more disturbing, zoo-goers express the usual prejudices about animals; 73 per cent say they dislike rattlesnakes, 52 per cent vultures, and only 4 per cent elephants. One reason why some zoos have not done a better job in educating people is that many of them make no real effort at education. In the case of others the problem is an apathetic and unappreciative public.

Edward G. Ludwig's (1981) study of the zoo in Buffalo, New York revealed a surprising amount of dissatisfaction on the part of young, scientifically inclined zoo employees. Much of this dissatisfaction stemmed from the almost complete indifference of the public to the zoo's educational efforts. Ludwig's study indicated that most animals are viewed only briefly as people move quickly past cages. The typical zoo-goer stops only to watch baby animals or those who are begging, feeding, or making sounds. Ludwig reported that the most common expressions used to described animals are "cute", "funny-looking", "lazy", "dirty", "weird", and "strange".

Of course, it is undeniable that some education occurs in some zoos. But this very fact raises other issues. What is it that we want people to learn from visiting zoos? Facts about the physiology and behaviour of various animals? Attitudes towards the survival of endangered species? Compassion for the fate of all animals? To what degree does education require keeping wild animals in captivity? Couldn't most of the educational benefits of zoos be obtained by presenting films, slides, lectures, and so forth? Indeed, couldn't most of the important educational objectives better be achieved by exhibiting empty cages with explanations of why they are empty?

A third reason for having zoos is that they support scientific research. This too, is a benefit that was pointed out long ago. Sir Humphrey Davy, one of the founders of the Zoological Society of London, wrote in 1825: "It would become Britain to offer another, and a very different series of exhibitions to the population of her metropolis; namely, animals brought from every part of the globe to be applied either to some useful purpose, or as objects of scientific research—not of vulgar admiration!" Zoos support scientific research in at least three ways: they fund field research by scientists not affiliated with zoos; they employ other scientists as members of zoo staffs; and they make otherwise inaccessible animals available for study.

The first point we should note is that very few zoos support any real scientific research. Fewer still have staff scientists with full-time research appointments. Among those that do, it is common for their scientists to study animals in the wild rather than those in zoo collections. Much of this research, as well as other field research that is supported by zoos, could just as well be funded in a different way—say, by a government agency. The question of whether there should be zoos does not turn on the funding for field research which zoos currently provide. The significance of the research that is actually conducted in zoos is a more important consideration.

Research that is conducted in zoos can be divided into two categories: studies in behaviour and studies in anatomy and pathology.

Behavioural research conducted on zoo animals is very controversial. Some have argued that nothing can be learned by studying animals that are kept in the unnatural conditions that obtain in most zoos. Others have argued that captive animals are more interesting research subjects than are wild animals: since captive animals are free from predation, they exhibit a wider range of physical and behavioural traits than animals in the wild, thus permitting researchers to view the full range of their genetic possibilities. Both of these positions are surely extreme. Conditions in some zoos are natural enough to permit some interesting research possibilities. But the claim that captive animals are more interesting research subjects than those in the wild is not very plausible. Environments trigger behaviours. No doubt a predation-free environment triggers behaviours different from those of an animal's natural habitat, but there is no reason to believe that better, fuller, or more accurate data can be obtained in predation-free environments than in natural habitats.

Studies in anatomy and pathology are the most common forms of zoo research. Such research has three main purposes: to improve zoo conditions so that captive animals will live longer, be happier, and breed more frequently; to contribute to human health by providing animal models for human ailments; and to increase our knowledge of wild animals for its own sake.

The first of these aims is surely laudable, if we concede that there should be zoos in the first place. But the fact that zoo research contributes to improving conditions in zoos is not a reason for having them. If there were no zoos, there would be no need to improve them.

The second aim, to contribute to human health by providing animal models for human ailments, appears to justify zoos to some extent, but in practice this consideration is not as important as one might think. There are very severe constraints on the experiments that may be conducted on zoo animals. In a 1982 article, Montali and Bush drew the following conclusion:

Despite the great potential of a zoo as a resource for models, there are many limitations and, of necessity, some restrictions for use. There is little opportunity to conduct overly manipulative or invasive research procedures—probably less than would be allowed in clinical research trials involving human beings. Many of the species are difficult to work with or are difficult to breed, so that the numbers of animals available for study are limited. In fact, it is safe to say that over the past years, humans have served more as 'animal models' for zoo species than is true of the reverse.

Whether for this reason or others, much of what has been done in using zoo animals as models for humans seems redundant or trivial. For example, the article cited above reports that zoo animals provide good models for studying lead toxicity in humans, since it is common for zoo animals to develop lead poisoning from chewing paint and inhaling polluted city air. There are available for study plenty of humans who suffer from lead poisoning for the same reasons. That zoos make available some additional non-human subjects for this kind of research seems at best unimportant and at worst deplorable.

Finally, there is the goal of obtaining knowledge about animals for its own sake. Knowledge is certainly something which is good and, everything being equal, we should encourage people to seek it for its own sake. But everything is not equal in this case. There is a moral presumption against keeping animals in captivity. This presumption can be overcome only by demonstrating that there are important benefits that must be obtained in this way if they are to be obtained at all. It is clear that this is not the case with knowledge for its own sake. There are other channels for our intellectual curiosity, ones that do not exact such a high moral price. Although our quest for knowledge for its own sake is important, it is not important enough to overcome the moral presumption against keeping animals in captivity.

In assessing the significance of research as a reason for having zoos, it is important to remember that very few zoos do any research at all. Whatever benefits result from zoo research could just as well be obtained by having a few zoos instead of the hundreds which now exist. The most this argument could establish is that we are justified in having a few very good zoos. It does not provide a defence of the vast majority of zoos which now exist.

A fourth reason for having zoos is that they preserve species that would otherwise become extinct. As the destruction of habitat accelerates and as breeding programmes become increasingly successful, this rationale for zoos gains in popularity. There is some reason for questioning the commitment of zoos to preservation: it can be argued that they continue to remove more animals from the wild than they return. Still, zoo breeding programmes have had some notable successes: without them the Père David Deer, the Mongolian Wild Horse, and the European Bison would all now be extinct. Recently, however, some problems have begun to be noticed.

A study by Katherine Ralls, Kristin Brugger, and Jonathan Ballou (1979) convincingly argues that lack of genetic diversity among captive animals is a serious problem for zoo breeding programmes. In some species the infant mortality rate among inbred animals is six or seven times that among non-inbred animals. In other species the infant mortality rate among inbred animals is 100 per cent. What is most disturbing is that zoo curators have been largely unaware of the problems caused by inbreeding because adequate breeding and health records have not been kept. It is hard to believe that zoos are serious about their role in preserving endangered species when all too often they do not even take this minimal step.

In addition to these problems, the lack of genetic diversity among captive animals also means that surviving members of endangered species have traits very different from their conspecifics in the wild. This should make us wonder what is really being preserved in zoos. Are captive Mongolian Wild Horses really Mongolian Wild Horses in any but the thinnest biological sense?

There is another problem with zoo breeding programmes: they create many unwanted animals. In some species (lions, tigers, and zebras, for example) a few males can service an entire herd. Extra males are unnecessary to the programme and are a financial burden. Some of these animals are sold and end up in the hands of individuals and institutions which lack proper facilities. Others are shot and killed by Great White Hunters in private hunting camps. In order to avoid these problems, some zoos have been considering proposals to "recycle" excess animals: a euphemism for killing them and feeding their bodies to other zoo animals. Many people are surprised when they hear of zoos killing animals. They should not be. Zoos have limited capacities. They want to maintain diverse collections. This can be done only by careful management of their "stock".

Even if breeding programmes were run in the best possible way, there are limits to what can be done to save endangered species. For many large mammals a breeding herd of at least a hundred animals, half of them born in captivity, is required if they are to survive in zoos. As of 1971 only eight mammal species satisfied these conditions. Paul and Anne Ehrlich (1981) estimate that under the best possible conditions American zoos could preserve only about a hundred species of mammals—and only at a very high price: maintaining a breeding herd of herbivores costs between $75,000 and $250,000 per year.

There are further questions one might ask about preserving endangered species in zoos. Is it really better to confine a few hapless Mountain Gorillas in a zoo than to permit the species to become extinct? To most environmentalists the answer is obvious: the species must be preserved at all costs. But this smacks of sacrificing the lower-case gorilla for the upper-case Gorilla. In doing this, aren't we using animals as mere vehicles for their genes? Aren't we preserving genetic material at the expense of the animals themselves? If it is true that we are inevitably moving towards a world in which Mountain Gorillas can survive only in zoos, then we must ask whether it is really better for them to live in artificial environments of our design than not to be born at all.

Even if all of these difficulties are overlooked, the importance of preserving endangered species does not provide much support for the existing system of zoos. Most zoos do very little breeding or breed only species which are not endangered. Many of the major breeding programmes are run in special facilities which have been established for that purpose. They are often located in remote places, far from the attention of zoo-goers. (For example, the Bronx Zoo operates its Rare Animal Survival Center on St Catherine's Island off the coast of Georgia, and the National Zoo runs its Conservation and Research Center in the Shenandoah Valley of Virginia.) If our main concern is to do what we can to preserve endangered species, we should support such large-scale breeding centres rather than conventional zoos, most of which have neither the staff nor the facilities to run successful breeding programmes.

The four reasons for having zoos which I have surveyed carry some weight. But different reasons provide support for different kinds of zoo. Preservation and perhaps research are better carried out in large-scale animal preserves, but these provide few opportunities for amusement and education. Amusement and perhaps education are better provided in urban zoos, but they offer few opportunities for research and preservation. Moreover, whatever benefits are obtained from any kind of zoo must confront the moral presumption against keeping wild animals in captivity. Which way do the scales tip? There are two further considerations which, in my view, tip the scales against zoos.

First, captivity does not just deny animals liberty but is often detrimental to them in other respects as well. The history of chimpanzees in the zoos of Europe and America is a good example.

Chimpanzees first entered the zoo world in about 1640 when a Dutch prince, Frederick Henry of Nassau, obtained one for his castle menagerie. The chimpanzee didn't last very long. In 1835 the London Zoo obtained its first chimpanzee; he died immediately. Another was obtained in 1845; she lived six months. All through the nineteenth and early twentieth centuries zoos obtained chimpanzees who promptly died within nine months. It wasn't until the 1930s that it was discovered that chimpanzees are extremely vulnerable to human respiratory diseases, and that special steps must be taken to protect them. But for nearly a century zoos removed them from the wild and subjected them to almost certain death. Problems remain today. When chimpanzees are taken from the wild the usual procedure is to shoot the mother and kidnap the child. The rule of thumb among trappers is that ten chimpanzees die for every one that is delivered alive to the United States or Europe. On arrival many of these animals are confined under abysmal conditions.

Chimpanzees are not the only animals to suffer in zoos. In 1974 Peter Batten, former director of the San Jose Zoological Gardens, undertook an exhaustive study of two hundred American zoos. In his book *Living Trophies* he documented large numbers of neurotic, overweight animals kept in cramped, cold cells and fed unpalatable synthetic food. Many had deformed feet and appendages caused by unsuitable floor surfaces. Almost every zoo studied had excessive mortality rates, resulting from preventable factors ranging from vandalism to inadequate husbandry practices. Batten's (1976, p. lx) conclusion was: "The majority of American zoos are badly run, their direction incompetent, and animal husbandry inept and in some cases non-existent".

Many of these same conditions and others are documented in Lynn Griner's (1983) review of necropsies conducted at the San Diego Zoo over a fourteen-year period. This zoo may well be the best in the country, and its staff is clearly well-trained and well-intentioned. Yet this study documents widespread malnutrition among zoo animals; high mortality rates from the use of anaesthetics and tranquillizers; serious injuries and deaths sustained in transport; and frequent occurrences of cannibalism, infanticide, and fighting almost certainly caused by overcrowded conditions. Although the zoo has learned from its mistakes, it is still unable to keep many wild animals in captivity without killing or injuring them, directly or indirectly. If this is true of the San Diego Zoo, it is certainly true, to an even greater extent, at most other zoos.

The second consideration is more difficult to articulate but is, to my mind, even more important. Zoos teach us a false sense of our place in the natural order. The means of confinement mark a difference between humans and animals. They are there at our pleasure, to be used for our purposes. Morality and perhaps our very survival require that we learn to live as one species among many rather than as one species over many. To do this, we must forget what we learn at zoos. Because what zoos teach us is false and dangerous, both humans and animals will be better off when they are abolished.

12

Zoos Revisited

The possibility of perpetual reinvention is deeply embedded in the American psyche. Waiters can become movie stars, gangsters can be transformed into respectable businessmen, and corrupt White House officials can return as fundamentalist preachers. One California governor, who signed the most liberal abortion law in the nation, became a fiercely born-again anti-abortionist; another former California governor, one of the leading political fund-raisers of his generation, ran for president on a platform that denounced political fund-raising as the root of all evil. Despite its attractions, reinvention is not always successful. In F. Scott Fitzgerald's the *Great Gatsby*, the title character emerges from a shady past to assume the life of a Long Island gentleman. Yet despite the trappings of wealth and power, his new identity is fragile. In the end he succumbs to his past.

In their drive to reinvent themselves, American zoos are very American. Early zoos were explicitly meant to demonstrate and celebrate the domination of nature by man. They included all sorts of exotics, both human and non-human.[1] As the control of zoos moved from rich and powerful individuals to communities and governments, they were increasingly seen as sources of urban amusement. But in these enlightened times many zoo professionals no longer see amusement and entertainment as roles that are worthy of zoos. Indeed, in this spirit, the New York Zoological Society has abolished its zoos;

Discussions with many people have affected my views about zoos. I thank the participants in the conference Animal Welfare and Conservation: Ethical Paradoxes in Modern Zoos and Aquariums, at which a version of this essay was presented, especially Bryan Norton, Michael Hutchins, and Terry Maple for inviting me to participate, and Don Lindburg, who was an intellectual and moral inspiration. Over the years I have learned a great deal about various topics touched on in this essay from Marc Bekoff, Anna Goebbel, Sue Townsend, and John Wortman. Despite my debts to all of these people, I alone am responsible for the views that I have expressed.

[1] For a moving account of an African Pygmy who was confined to the New York City Zoo, see Bradford and Bloom (1992).

however, wildlife conservation parks have risen, phoenix-like, to replace them. In their current reinvention zoos are being pitched as the last best hope for endangered wildlife. For advocates of zoos, as for Jay Gatsby, the past is evil but fortunately always behind us. The present is good, and the future promises to be even better—assuming the money holds out.

Critics of zoos rightly see this attitude as self-serving and disingenuous. Most zoos are still in the business of entertainment rather than species preservation. Despite protestations to the contrary, most zoos are still more or less random collections of animals kept under largely bad conditions. Although the best zoos have been concerned to position themselves as environmental heroes, they have done little to promote this ethic in the zoo industry as a whole. There are many bad exhibits and many bad zoos, but not much is being done to shut them down. Even the best zoos have problems with preventable mortality and morbidity due to accidents or abuse and are too often in league, wittingly or unwittingly, with people whose idea of a good animal is one that turns a quick profit. The rhetoric of science, favoured by the best people in the best zoos, has not yet penetrated the reality of most zoos and indeed carries with it new possibilities for abuse. Even now, with the bad old days presumably behind us, there is not much ground for complacency.

Still, it is clear that zoos are changing. They are becoming more naturalistic in environment, focusing more on species preservation and scientific research and less on entertainment. Zoos in the future, at least the better ones, will increasingly become more like parks.

Parks and preserves are changing as well. They are becoming more like zoos. In 1987 Kenya's Lake Nakuru National Park was completely fenced.[2] It is only a matter of time until large East African mammals are managed in much the same way as domestic animals, as has already been suggested by the World Conservation Union.[3] This tendency towards management is also at work in the national parks in this country.

What will become of wild nature in this proliferation of miniparks or megazoos?[4] Wild nature may be done for. Human population growth remains out of control. The effects of human consumption and production are modifying fundamental planetary systems in what may be irreversible ways. We are probably already committed to a climate change that will have profound effects on both nature and human society. Extremely remote areas in the arctic and antarctic regions are suffering the effects of human-induced ozone depletion. Today no part of the planet is unaffected by human action. Nature may not

---

[2] Conway (1990).   [3] See Conway (1995); Hutchins *et al.* (1995).   [4] Conway (1990).

yet be tamed, but she is no longer wild.[5] The evolution of every animal species, to some degree, is now affected by human action.[6]

One of the most dramatic effects of human action is the epidemic of extinctions currently sweeping the earth. Increasingly zoos have attempted to position themselves as the guardians of wild nature, as the boy with his thumb in the dike trying to hold back the flood-waters. I do not believe that zoos can successfully play this role. Establishing genetic warehouses is not the same as preserving wild animals. Highly managed theme parks are not wild nature.

Although in the bad old days zoos may have made their contributions to extinction, they are not responsible for the current wave. Nor are they directly to blame for our pathetic response to it. What is to blame is the peculiar moral schizophrenia of a culture that drives a species to the edge of extinction and then romanticizes the remnants. Until a species is on the brink of extinction it seems to have little claim on our moral sensibility.

Consider the northern spotted owl. Most people probably agree with the Denver newspaper, the *Rocky Mountain News*, which editorialized (16 March 1992) that loggers need jobs as much as the spotted owls need trees. This is what passes for a moderate position, carefully balancing the unsustainable lifestyle of a few thousand humans against the very existence of another form of life. Once the owl is extinct or a few stragglers have been moved indoors, people will sing a different song. No steps will be too extreme to save this endangered species.

In the bad old days I published a paper with the subtle, highly nuanced title "Against Zoos" (Essay 11). For my effort I was virtually accused of child abuse by a local television station. Its correspondents interviewed children visiting the Denver Zoo, eliciting their reactions to some pointy-headed philosopher who wanted to take their fun away. The responses were predictable. A column in the *Chicago Tribune* (28 April 1991) said that my ideas were so absurd that "only an intellectual could believe them". No less a journal than *Time Magazine* (24 June 1991) called me a "zoophobe" and suggested that I am indifferent to the fate of endangered species.

What I tried to do in that much-maligned essay was to set forth as rationally as possible the case against zoos. I examined the arguments that have been given on their behalf: that they provide amusement, education, opportunities for scientific research, and help in preserving species. I saw some merit in each argument, but in the end I concluded that these benefits

---

[5] McKibben (1989).   [6] Borza and Jamieson (1990); Jamieson (1990); Essay 18.

were outweighed by the moral presumption against keeping animals in captivity. I also claimed that despite the best intentions of zoo personnel, the profound message of zoos is that it is permissible for humans to dominate animals, for the entire experience of a zoo is framed by the fact of captivity.

Serious people have taken issue with my claims and arguments.[7] Because some of my critics place more weight on the role of zoos in preserving endangered species than I do, I want to discuss that issue in some detail. However, I first want to reconsider whether there is a presumption against keeping animals in captivity, since this claim is foundational to my argument against zoos.[8]

1. IS THERE A PRESUMPTION AGAINST KEEPING ANIMALS IN CAPTIVITY?

In Essay 11 I argued that there is a presumption against keeping animals in captivity. My argument was rather intuitive. Keeping animals in captivity usually involves restricting their liberty in ways that deny them many goods including gathering their own food, developing their own social orders, and generally behaving in ways that are natural to them. In the case of many animals captivity also involves removing them from their native habitats and conditions. If animals have any moral standing at all, then it is plausible to suppose that depriving them of liberty is presumptively wrong, since an interest in liberty is central to most morally significant creatures.

My claim that there is such a presumption has recently been challenged.[9] If Leahy is correct in thinking that there is no such presumption, then there is no general reason for being opposed to zoos. The acceptability of keeping animals in captivity would turn entirely on a case-by-case examination of the conditions under which various animals are kept. Before considering Leahy's arguments against this presumption, let us first consider the view to which he is committed.

The idea that there is a presumption against keeping animals in captivity implies that it is not a matter of moral indifference whether animals are kept captive. But it carries no implication about how strong the presumption is.

---

[7] See e.g. Chiszar et al. (1990); Hutchins et al. (1995).

[8] Although I prefer to avoid the language of rights, my work on zoos has been greatly influenced by Rachels (1976/1989). For a good discussion of the concept of freedom, see Taylor (1986: 105–11). It should also be noted that for the purposes of this essay I use the terms 'liberty' and 'freedom' interchangeably.

[9] Leahy (1991).

People who agree that there is a presumption against keeping animals in captivity can disagree about the strength of the presumption or about whether it is permissible to keep an animal in captivity in a particular case. What Leahy is committed to is the view that everything else being equal, it is a matter of moral indifference as to whether animals are kept in captivity; we might as well flip a coin. I believe that this view is implausible.

Although it is difficult to perform this thought experiment, imagine that we could guarantee the same or better quality of life for an animal in a zoo than the animal would enjoy in the wild. Suppose further that there are no additional benefits to humans or animals that would be gained by keeping the animal in captivity. The only difference between these two cases that might be relevant is that in one case the animal is confined to a zoo and in the other case the animal is free to pursue his or her own life. Would we say that the fact of confinement is a morally relevant consideration? I believe that most people would say that it is, and that it would be morally preferable for the animal to be free rather than captive. In my opinion this shows that most of us believe that there is a moral presumption against keeping animals in captivity. That we believe that there is such a presumption is indicated in various ways. For example, sometimes it is said that keeping an animal in captivity is a privilege that involves assuming special obligations for the animal's welfare. This expresses the sense, I believe, that in confining an animal we are in some way wronging him or her, and thus owe him or her some compensation.

With this result in mind, let us consider Leahy's arguments. He appears to offer two. The first (following Hediger 1964) involves the claim that animals are not truly free in the wild. They are constrained by ecological and social pressures and are "struck down by natural predators and diseases which, quite reasonably, can be said to limit their freedom" (Leahy 1991: 242). Since animals are not truly free in the wild, keeping them in captivity does not deprive them of liberty. The second argument is a conceptual one. According to Leahy, animals do not have language and are not self-conscious; therefore they cannot make choices or raise objections. Since they cannot make choices or raise objections, they cannot be said to live their own lives. Since they cannot live their own lives, they can never really be free. Since animals can never really be free, confining them in zoos does not deprive them of their freedom.

The first argument is intended to show that as a matter of fact animals are not free in their natural habitats while the second argument is intended to show that animals can never be free under any circumstances. There is no presumption against keeping them in captivity because in neither case does captivity deprive them of something that they have in the wild.

We should see first that these arguments do not really question the view that there is a presumption against depriving animals of liberty. What these arguments are supposed to show is that animals do not or cannot have liberty, thus they are not deprived of it by captivity. If it could be shown that animals do have liberty in the wild but not in captivity, then Leahy might agree that there is a presumption against keeping animals in captivity on grounds that it deprives them of liberty. At least he has said nothing that counts against this view.

The core of the issue, then, is the plausibility of the common-sense view that animals lose their liberty when they are removed from the wild and kept in zoos. I affirm the common-sense view; Leahy denies it. Who is right?

Consider Leahy's second argument first. Two steps in the argument that invite objection are these: the claim that animals are not self-conscious, and the claim that self-consciousness or language is required for making choices.

The topic of self-consciousness is a difficult one. Philosophers and psychologists often use this concept in different ways. One approach, characteristic of Descartes and much of the philosophical tradition, associates self-consciousness with the ability to use language or other complex symbol systems. But even if it were agreed that the use of complex symbol systems is required for self-consciousness, it would appear that various primates and cetaceans satisfy this criterion and thus would be excluded from the scope of Leahy's conclusion.[10] For those animals who use complex symbol systems, Leahy would have no argument for supposing that they are not free in the wild. Thus with respect to those animals at least, my claim that there is a presumption in favour of liberty would appear to survive unscathed. A second approach, characteristic of work in cognitive ethology, regards attributions of self-consciousness as underwritten by such factors as behaviour, evolutionary continuity, and structural similarity. Researchers have argued that a wide range of behaviour in a variety of animals involves self-consciousness, including social play, deception, and vigilance.[11] Whichever approach is adopted, the claim that only humans are self-conscious appears doubtful.

The second dubious step in this argument involves the claim that self-consciousness is required for making choices. The philosopher's paradigm of choice may involve listing alternatives on a yellow pad with the pros and cons of each fully described in the margins, but this is only one way of making choices. Many of our choices are made without explicitly representing

---

[10] Herman and Morrel-Samuels (1990/1996); Savage-Rumbaugh and Brakke (1990/1996).
[11] Mitchell and Thompson (1986); Byrne and Whiten (1988); Griffin (1992); Essay 5.

alternatives and totting up pluses and minuses—for example, when we choose coffee rather than tea, hit the brake rather than the accelerator, or immediately agree to give a lecture in Iowa in response to a telephone call. In these kinds of cases it is hard to see exactly how self-consciousness is supposed to be involved. Moreover, important work on animal behaviour has purported to address such topics as mate choice,[12] habitat choice,[13] and the choice of nest sites.[14] For the most part this work has been done without presupposing that animals are self-conscious. It may be that these researchers misuse the term 'choice' or are simply wrong in supposing that animals make choices in these situations. However, I believe that it is more plausible to suppose that it is Leahy's claim that is false and that self-consciousness is not required for choice. Since at least two steps in Leahy's second argument appear dubious, it is plausible to suppose that the argument fails.

Leahy's first argument attempts to show not that animals cannot be free under any conditions but that as a matter of fact they are not free in the wild. The idea is that if they are not free in the wild, then they lose nothing when they are confined in zoos. The evidence for the claim that animals are not free in the wild is that they are constrained by ecological and social pressures and are struck down by natural predators and disease.

If pointing to ecological and social pressures were sufficient for showing that an animal is not free, it would prove too much, for all organisms, including humans, are constrained by ecological and social pressures. The most that this claim could establish is that social and ecological pressures restrict animals to such an extent that they are more free in captivity than they are in the wild.

Are animals more free in zoos than in the wild? On the face of it, this claim is wildly implausible. It is like saying that humans are more free in prison than on the street because they are not subject to the same pressures as people on the street. The argument seems to overlook the fact that social pressures exist in zoos as well as in the wild, and in many cases such pressures are more intense in zoos because individuals are inhibited from responding to them in the ways in which they would in the wild. But more important, even if it could be shown that caged animals, whether human or non-human, live longer than those who are uncaged, this would not provide evidence for the claim about freedom. Nor could the claim be established by showing that caged animals are happier than uncaged animals. Liberty is not the same as longevity or happiness, nor does it always manifest itself in these ways. Moreover, there is very

[12] Bateson (1983).   [13] Rosenzweig (1990/1996).   [14] Bekoff et al. (1989).

little evidence for supposing that captive animals live longer or are happier in zoos than they are in the wild. It seems plain that most animals have less freedom in zoos than in the wild. Indeed, the very point of systems of confinement is to deprive them of freedom.

For reasons that I have given it seems to me that Leahy's arguments fail. The common-sense position, that everything else being equal it is better for animals to be free, is vindicated. However, there is another line of argument that might be thought to be more challenging than those pursued thus far. It might be granted that there is a presumption of liberty with respect to animals who are born in the wild, but denied that there is any such presumption with respect to those who are born in captivity. It might be argued that captive-bred animals have never known freedom, so they are denied nothing by captivity.

In my view there is a presumption in favour of liberty with respect to all animals, whether bred in captivity or in the wild. Imagine humans who have never known liberty. Would it be plausible to deny that there is a presumption of liberty for them on the grounds that they do not miss what they have never known? An affirmative answer would be absurd. Indeed, we might think that the tragedy of their captivity is all the greater because they have never known liberty. Transferring these intuitions to non-human animals, we can see that there is a presumption in favour of liberty even with respect to animals born in captivity. Indeed, the presumption may even be stronger in their case. Still, some people would argue against this presumption, pointing out that many animals bred in captivity would not survive liberation, despite attempts at preparation. Their lives in nature would be nasty, brutish, and short. Even if this is true it fails to show that there is no presumption in favour of liberty for these animals. At most it shows that in these cases the presumption in favour of liberty is outweighed by concerns about the welfare of these animals. The presumption for liberty exists, but it may be wrong to release these animals into the wild.

What I have argued in this section is that a basic claim of Essay 11, that there is a presumption in favour of liberty for animals, still stands. The burden of proof rests on those who would confine animals in zoos. The most compelling reason for confining animals in zoos, in some people's eyes, is the need to preserve endangered species. It is to this justification that I now turn.[15]

---

[15] In a recent book Bostock agrees that there is a presumption against keeping animals in captivity, but claims that "we can go a long way towards providing good conditions in zoos" (1993: 50). For the presumption to be overcome however, it must be shown that the benefits of confining animals in zoos are greater than the burdens. This is not established by speculative claims about the possibility of creating good conditions for animals in zoos.

2. CAN ZOOS PRESERVE ENDANGERED SPECIES?

There are a number of arguments against zoos as meaningful sites for pre-serving endangered species. First, such preservation is needed, it is rightly pointed out, because we are losing species at an enormous rate. But although estimates differ and not all the facts are known, it is obvious that not more than a tiny fraction of these species can be preserved in zoos. Ehrlich and Ehrlich estimate that American zoos could preserve about one hundred mammals under the best conditions (1981: 211). Secondly, only a small number of the species preserved in zoos could ever be reintroduced into their natural habitats. Indeed most attempts at reintroduction have failed.[16] For many species, zoos are likely to be the last stop on the way to extinction. Finally, over many generations the genetic structure and behaviour of captive popu-lations change. Captivity substitutes selection pressures imposed by humans, either intentionally or inadvertently, for those of an animal's natural habitat. Indeed, under some definitions of domestication, confining animals in zoos and breeding them in captivity transforms them into domesticated animals.[17] Whether we count zoo animals as domesticated or not, it is clear that in fifty, one hundred, or a thousand years we may not have the same animal that was placed in captivity, much less the animal that would have existed had it evolved in nature. Taken together these arguments show that the role that captive breeding and reintroduction can play in the preservation of endangered species is at best marginal. Thus the benefit of preservation is not significant enough to overcome the presumption against depriving an animal of its liberty.

Against arguments such as these,[18] it is sometimes objected that they are entirely hypothetical. Where are the data? it is sometimes asked, and then we hear anecdotes abut species that have been saved by captive breeding pro-grammes. Such arguments are made against Varner and Monroe by Hutchins and Wemmer, who go on to assert that "there are many problems facing captive breeding and reintroduction programs, but they are not insurmount-able" (1991: 6). But how do they know? Where are the data that show that such problems are not insurmountable? Is this a scientific statement or the expres-sion of a quasi-religious faith in the idea that humans have the ability to tech-nofix everything, even the threatened extinction of other species?[19]

---

[16] Beck (1995).

[17] See e.g. Rodd (1990: 113); Clutton-Brock (1992); but see also Norton (1995b).

[18] Essay 11; Varner and Monroe (1990).

[19] Proponents of zoos seem especially given to making unsubstantiated, sweeping claims. Wolfe attacks my Essay 11 for failing to consider "that one function of zoos may be to help children make

The point is that demands for data can be made by either party to the dispute. The fact is that there are anecdotes on both sides, qualitative material that different people evaluate in different ways, but very little that looks like hard data. The sceptic about captive breeding programmes will say that the defender of zoos has the burden to show that such programmes can really be successful. If there is a presumption against keeping animals in captivity, then it is wrong to do so unless a case can be made that the benefits outweigh this presumption. From the perspective of a sceptic, an inconclusive argument on this point is one that the sceptic wins.

Defenders of zoos say that the burden is on the other side, for captive breeding keeps options open. True enough. We ought to keep options open, not only for ourselves but for future people as well. But at what cost? Unless the presumption that animals should not be kept in captivity can be overcome by the moral case for keeping options open, this observation does not carry much weight. It certainly does not establish a burden of proof.

There is another dimension to this dispute. The critics of zoos point out that breeding and reintroduction programmes can be extremely invasive, involving not just denials of liberty but sometimes pain and suffering for individuals. Defenders of zoos sometimes say that this suffering is for the good of the species. This is the manoeuvre that in Essay 11 I called sacrificing the interests of the lower-case gorilla for those of the upper-case Gorilla.

There is a lot of confusion about the concept of species and its proper role in our biological and moral thinking.[20] Yet law, policy, and common morality take the concept very seriously. An animal that is part of an endangered species may have millions spent to protect her, but if she is a member of an endangered subspecies or a hybrid she may be exterminated as a pest. Some of these issues are explored by May (1990), O'Brien and Mayr (1991), Vane-Wright *et al.* (1991), Geist (1992), and Rojas (1992).

One confusion in our biological thinking concerns the relation between variability and species diversity. Species diversity is one kind of variability but not the only kind. Within most species there is an enormous amount of

---

symbolic sense of the world around them". He then goes on to conclude. "Children learn to use their powers of fantasy and imagination—to love animals—by going to the zoo. Strip them of this rich source of their interpretive life and, as adults, they will likely be more unfeeling, not less" (Wolfe 1991: 116–17). This is all very nice, high-minded rhetoric, and may even be true. But what I claimed in Essay 11 is that there are very few data to support the educational claims that are made on behalf of zoos. Whether zoos indeed have the uplifting effects on children claimed by Wolfe is an empirical question. I ask again: where are the data?

[20] Ereshefsky (1992); Hargrove (1992).

variability—think of dogs or coyotes, for example.[21] The evolutionary story requires variability, but it is not clear that it requires a very strong conception of species. Richard Dawkins writes that "'the species' [is] an arbitrary stretch of continuously flowing river, with no particular reason to draw lines delimiting its beginning and end" (1986: 264). Darwin himself was quite conventionalist about the concept of species, writing that "I look at the term species, as one arbitrarily given for the sake of convenience to a set of individuals closely resembling one another" (Darwin 1859/1958: 67). The demotion of the concept of species from the exalted role that it played in Aristotelian biology was one consequence of the Darwinian revolution. Like other consequences of the Darwinian revolution, we are still struggling to grasp its full significance.[22]

Variability is important to us as well as to the evolutionary process. We value variability, but just as we often focus on the charismatic megafauna and overlook other creatures that are as important to nature, so we often fix on species variability as the only kind of diversity that matters. We compound the problem when we think that it is species to which we have obligations rather than the creatures themselves. This is an instance of the general fallacy of attributing to species the properties of individual creatures. Individual creatures have hearts and lungs; species do not. Individual creatures often have welfares, but species never do. The notion of a species is an abstraction; the idea of its welfare is a human construction. While there is something that it is like to be an animal there is nothing that it is like to be a species.

I am a Darwinian about the concept of species, but I am not callous about the survival of nature. I am as concerned about saving wild nature as any defender of zoo breeding programmes. But I believe that the only hope for doing this is to put large tracts of the earth's surface off-limits to human beings and to alter radically our present lifestyles.[23] I agree with Ehrenfeld that "the true prospects for conservation ultimately depend not on the conservation manipulations of scientists but on the overarching consideration of how many people there will be in the world in the next century, the way they live, and the ways in which they come to regard and use nature" (1991: 39).

I believe further that attempts at preserving wild nature through zoo breeding programmes are a cruel hoax. If zoo breeding programmes are successful

---

[21] Bekoff and Wells (1986).

[22] Dewey (1910); Rachels (1990).

[23] For this reason I endorse the general concepts put forward by the Wildlands Project, PO Box 455, Richmond VA 05477.

they will not preserve species but rather transform animals into exhibits in a living museum. "This is what used to exist in the wild", we can say to our children while pointing at some rare creature alienated from her environment, "before the K Mart and the biotechnology factory went in". Zoo professionals like to say that they are the Noahs of the modern world and that zoos are their arks. But Noah found a place to land his animals where they could thrive and multiply. If zoos are like arks, then rare animals are like passengers on a voyage of the damned, never to find a port that will let them dock or a land in which they can live their lives in peace and freedom. If we are serious about preserving wild nature we must preserve the land, and not pretend that we can bring nature indoors.

In my darker moments I believe, not just that zoos are in the business of perpetuating fraud with their rhetoric about preserving animals, but that, knowingly or not, they are deeply implicated in causing the problem that they purport to be addressing. Zoo professionals are often eager to remove animals from the wild to more controlled environments where they can be studied. But as more and more animals are taken out of the wild, the case for preserving wild nature erodes. Why save a habitat if there is nothing to inhabit it? Advocates of zoos like to point out that they are not just in the business of removing animals from the wild, but increasingly they are also involved in trying to preserve animals in nature as well. Although zoos boast of their programmes in the developing world, very few can withstand scrutiny.[24] The truth is that very few zoos make meaningful attempts to preserve animals in nature, and most zoos spend more on publicity and public relations than they do on programmes involving animals. This is especially appalling because in many cases programmes to preserve animals *in situ* are relatively cheap. For example, the Bonobo Protection Fund estimates that the bonobo population in Zaire could be effectively protected for an initial investment of $185,000 and $60,000 per year thereafter. This is a small amount to spend for the protection of the rarest of ape species.

In my opinion we should have the honesty to recognize that zoos are for us rather than for the animals. Perhaps they do something to alleviate our sense of guilt for what we are doing to the planet, but they do little to help the animals we are driving to extinction. Our feeble attempts at preservation are a matter of our own interests, values, and preoccupations rather than

---

[24] *Newsweek* (12 April 1993) documents the ineffectiveness and corruption of various programmes to save endangered species, several of them involving major zoos. For a case study, see Schaller (1993).

acts of generosity towards those animals whom we destroy and then try to save. In so far as zoos distract us from the truth about ourselves and what we are doing to nature, they are part of the problem rather than part of the solution.

3. SUMMARY AND CONCLUSIONS

Much of what I have said may sound like an aggravating stew of idealism and curmudgeonliness. Hutchins and Wemmer speak for many people when they say that philosophers seem "more concerned with logical arguments than with practical solutions to real problems" (1991: 5). Although I wish non-philosophers were more concerned with logical arguments, I sympathize with their sentiments. It is a fact that despite the arguments that I and others have given, zoos are not going to go away. It is easier to try to change large institutions that are adept at fund-raising than it is to abolish them. At any rate we are responsible for the lives of a great many animals, and more are being bred all the time. Given that zoos exist, there is a great difference between good ones and bad ones. I would like to close by expressing some of my hopes and fears about how zoos may develop in the future.

As I have already said, the best zoos in the future will be increasingly indistinguishable from small parks. The conditions under which animals will be kept for breeding purposes and scientific study will be naturalistic. While the idea of a *naturalistic* environment should not be confused with a *natural* environment, it is clear that human-designed naturalistic environments rule out some of the worst of the abuses to which captive animals traditionally have been subject. For example, naturalistic environments would not permit animals to be constantly observed by hundreds of small boys who feed them Cracker Jacks and hurl various objects at them. This obviously would be an improvement over many exhibits that exist today.

In my opinion there will be increasing tension between what zoos do to gain public support (entertain) and what they must do in order to justify themselves (preserve species). This tension will emerge within zoos as those who are interested in animals and science will increasingly come into conflict with those whose charge is budgets and public relations. This conflict already prevents zoos from being as good as they can be, and it will become more pronounced in the future. This is a fear.

One hope that I have for the future is that we will recognize that if we keep animals in captivity, then what we owe them is everything. Whatever else we may believe about the morality of zoos, I hope we can come to a consensus that these animals are in our custody through no wish or fault of their own. They are refugees from a holocaust that humans have unleashed against nature. There should be no question of culling these animals or trading off their interests against those of humans. If we are to keep animals in captivity, then we must conform to the highest standards of treatment and respect. My hope is that zoo professionals will accept this principle and that an enlightened and aggressive public will keep them to it, for the animals themselves have no voice in human affairs, and as nature recedes their voices become ever more silent.

13

Wild/Captive and Other Suspect Dualisms

1. INTRODUCTION

Dualisms have had a hard time in recent years. Philosophers used to think that facts and values were distinct, and that philosophy and science were radically different enterprises. While scientists employed empirical methods to discover the way the world happens to be, the job of philosophers was to use conceptual analysis to reveal how the world necessarily is. In the wake of the revolution unleashed by Quine in the early 1950s, philosophers either had to learn some science, find another job, or fight an irredentist action on behalf of conceptual analysis that is mainly of interest only to a few other philosophers.[1]

The loss of these comfortable dualisms has upset the complacency of scientists as well as philosophers. Ethics cannot be ignored when the National Institutes of Health require ethics modules as part of all new training grants, when human and animal research must be approved by university committees, and when both the general public and "opinion leaders" feel free to comment on a wide range of issues that a generation ago might have been regarded as purely scientific.

2. DUALISMS AND ENVIRONMENTAL PHILOSOPHY

The attack on these dualisms has also had an effect on various political and social movements, including the environmental movement. Classical

I thank Claudia Mills, Steve Kramer, and Mark Woods for helpful discussions of these topics.

[1] See Quine (1951/1961); for discussion see Burge (1992).

Environmentalism (CE), the dominant view in the American environmental movement of the 1960s and 1970s, seemed to suppose that there was an all or nothing distinction between clean and polluted air, that wilderness is wild nature untrammelled by humans, and that wild animals are those who live lives that are completely independent of humans. For the CEs the distinction between the natural and the human was fundamental. Beaver dams are natural but Glen Canyon Dam is not. Nature is stable and self-regulating; change, lack of balance, and disequilibrium are the effects of human intrusion. The ultimate goal of the environmental movement is to protect nature from human beings, and human beings from themselves.

In recent years the New Environmentalists (NEs), many of whom are scientists or economists, have denigrated CE as a naïve or outmoded view. With that special wrath that siblings and sectarian Marxists reserve for their next of kin, some NEs seem to see CEs as the enemy of the environment. By holding out for confused and unrealistic goals, CEs spurn the opportunities to make a difference that are available. They demand what they cannot have and, despite their good intentions, nature is crushed between the CEs on one side and the "wise use" movement on the other.

At least three influences have contributed to the rise of the NE.

One influence is the generalized cultural effects of Postmodernism (PM). For better or worse PM has become the reigning intellectual perspective of our time and its influence is felt in a variety of ways. Our current tendency to see change as constant, difference as dramatic, and categories as slipping, sliding, colliding, and melting into each other is an expression of PM; so is our suspicion of ideals and our tendency to see logic and rhetoric as continuous or even as the same thing. In some circles arguments and armies are evaluated on the same basis: how effective they are in changing people's behaviour. PM hovers in the background of all contemporary cultural work and conditions the responses even of those who claim to have no idea of what it is.[2]

A second influence that has contributed to NE is the rise of environmental history and the new ecology. It has become common to say that the kind of wilderness envisioned by the CEs hardly ever existed anywhere at any time in which there have been human inhabitants. Stories are told about how the ecologies that we now associate with wilderness were created by aboriginal populations acting on the land in Australia, North America, and Great Britain. Not only do CEs have a false conception of wilderness, but on this view they also have an ethnocentric one.[3] Their conception of wilderness could only

---

[2] For further discussion see Jamieson (1991b).
[3] See Callicot and Guha, both reprinted in Gruen and Jamieson (1994).

arise in a highly developed society that is out of touch with its origins and misunderstands the way that billions of people continue to relate to their environments. While environmental history shows us the ubiquity of human interaction with the land, the new ecology emphasizes the tumultuous and even catastrophic natural history of the earth. The greatest extinction episodes in the history of life preceded the evolution of humans. Nature, independent of humans, is often out of balance and equilibrium.

A third influence is the tendency to see environmental risks as inevitably increasing. The problem for environmentalists is not to reduce risk, for that appears to be out of the question, but to manage and distribute risk in an acceptable way.[4] The air will be polluted—the question is how polluted, in what respects, where, and who will suffer the costs. Most non-human life will take even more of a beating in this century than it did in the last one. Since we can't prevent these negative environmental changes, the challenge is how to manage them so that they will be less unacceptable than otherwise would be the case.

3. WILD AND CAPTIVE

One distinction that the NEs are tempted to collapse is that between wild and captive animals. The distinction is often overdrawn in the first place and will become even more blurred in the future. It has been argued that cheetahs who live in the wild passed through an evolutionary tunnel that probably had nothing to do with people. This reduced their genetic diversity to such an extent that, from the point of view of population genetics, they are similar in many respects to populations of captive animals. In the future, NEs argue, the distinction between wild and captive animals will collapse even further as parks and preserves increasingly come to resemble zoos and zoos increasingly come to resemble parks and preserves.

What will drive this pressure towards the further blurring of wild and captive animals are concerns about species survival. For many species, either bringing them into zoos or managing populations in their natural habitats are the only hopes for their survival. The very idea that these animals could be left alone with some "hands-off" management policy is regarded as a dangerous delusion. People are involved in changing global land-use patterns, destroying ozone, and even changing climate. Almost no form of life is unaffected by human action.[5] Animals living under these new global conditions

---

[4] See Beck (1992).   [5] See McKibben (1989).

are not wild in the CE sense of the term, despite the "born-free" mythology that is reinforced by television nature shows. Moreover, management of captive animals is getting better all the time. Sometimes it is even argued that intensive management practices can preserve more of the "wild" traits of some populations than less aggressive policies. On this view freedom and captivity are no longer mutually exclusive.

3. THE DESCRIPTIVE AND THE NORMATIVE

The NE critique of various dualisms in environmental philosophy is not just an intellectual exercise. Various specific policy prescriptions are supposed to follow from this critique: for example, that we should aim for optimal (rather than zero) pollution; wilderness should be intensively managed; wildlife must "pay its own way". Once we see that pressure on wild populations will only increase, that extinction is the only practical alternative to intensive management and captive breeding, and that the difference between wild and captive animals is overstated anyway, then we should give up our opposition to zoos and our sentimental attachments to individual animals and embrace high-tech, intensive management schemes directed towards preserving species. Zoos should be turned loose to bring in more animals from the wild. Captive breeding should be accelerated even if this means "euthanizing" zoo animals who are not part of such programmes.

But slow down. While this story is attractive to many people, its conclusions require further argument. CEs need not give up their substantive views simply because some old distinctions have been called into question. Even if it is true that we are in an age in which distinctions are disappearing, nothing much normative immediately follows from this. Maybe the NEs are right, and wild and captive animals aren't as different from each other as many of us might think. If so, we've learned something. But further argument is needed to show that we should act in some way or another.

4. DUALISMS AGAIN

It might be objected that I have reintroduced one of the dualisms that NEs would reject—the distinction between the descriptive and the normative. It is worth asking how thoroughgoing the NE critique of dualisms is. Indeed, some might argue that rather than rejecting dualisms NEs have assimilated one side of various distinctions to the other. Rather than rejecting the very distinction between wild and captive animals it could be argued that NEs want to treat all animals as captive animals. But even if that is an excessively harsh charge, the distinction between the descriptive and the normative is worth hanging on to. Excepting perhaps certain forms of supervenient naturalism, all moral theories hold that reasonable people can agree about the facts yet disagree about the values.[6]

However, the main point I want to make is that if the NE case against dualisms is successful it should lead us to understand the distinctions that the CEs make in a different way, but it should not lead us to reject these distinctions altogether. In the light of the NE critique we should view such dualisms as expressing pragmatic distinctions, perhaps useful for certain purposes but not for others, matters of degree rather than metaphysical differences of kind, in most cases with important human perceptual dimensions. No case has been made for supposing that such distinctions are unintelligible, pointless, or useless. It would be just as rash and unmotivated to give up these distinctions in the face of the NE critique as it would be to conclude that there is no distinction between the bald and the hirsute on the grounds that even the bald have a little hair and even the hirsute have some bald spots (however small).

We can see how the CE dualisms can be reconstructed by considering the case of wilderness. For the sake of argument suppose that the CEs define wilderness as natural areas that are radically distinct from humans and the effects of their actions. Now let's suppose, as NEs have argued, that there are no such areas—that sometime during human history all areas have been affected by human action, that even now climate change, ozone depletion, and jet contrails are everywhere. What should we conclude from this critique?

What we should not conclude is that wilderness does not exist, and therefore we should abolish the Wilderness Act and disband the wilderness system. What we should conclude instead is that the distinction between wilderness and non-wilderness is a matter of degree. That a particular way of drawing the distinction between wilderness and non-wilderness fails does not show that there is no point in drawing such a distinction or that we fail to pick out something that is important to us when we talk about wilderness.

Consider a case in point. In reflecting on his childhood, John Ruskin remarks that "the pure childish love of nature . . . in myself . . . has always been quite exclusively confined to wild, that is to say, wholly natural places, and especially to scenery animated by streams, or by the sea. The sense of the freedom, spontaneous unpolluted power of nature was essential in it" (Clark 1991: 22). Suppose that an NE points out to Ruskin that what he thought had

---

[6] For discussion of supervenient naturalism see Brink (1989).

been a "wholly natural place" had been inhabited by neolithic hunters. Does this mean that Ruskin had failed to refer when using these words, or that his experience of the "pure childish love of nature" was in some sense ungrounded, to be extinguished in so far as he is fully rational? Of course not. All that is important (holding some other factors fixed) for securing reference or grounding the experience is being able to draw a significant distinction between what is natural and what is not. This distinction need not reflect an essential difference in kind that is part of the fabric of the world. What is important for Ruskin and for us is that there is a distinction in experience or conception.

What does this mean for the distinction between the wild and captive? Even if this distinction is a matter of degree rather than kind, it can still be significant. Even if it is a human distinction that is conventional to some extent, it may still properly play an important role in our moral thinking. Whatever moral force this distinction may have is not blunted by the NE critique.

5. THE RETURN OF THE NORMATIVE

What I have been suggesting is that the NE critique may teach us something about distinctions and how they work, but that it has no immediate implication about what our policies should be. Questions such as whether we should try to preserve areas of the earth that are as free of human influence as possible, and if so what priority these attempts should have, are not answered by pointing out that there are no parts of the earth that are entirely free of the consequences of human action. Nor does it follow from the fact (if it is one) that the distinction between wild and captive animals is a fuzzy pragmatic one, that we are justified in depriving some animals of freedom in order to preserve their genetic material. Although the NE critique of CE may lead us to understand these questions in a somewhat different way, there is little reason to think that we should change our answers to them.

The winding road leads back to the moral considerations involved in keeping animals in captivity. In Essays 11 and 12 I have discussed these considerations in detail. What I have argued is that there is a moral presumption against keeping animals in captivity, and although zoos do provide benefits in the areas of entertainment, research, education, and preservation, they are not significant enough to overcome this presumption. Moreover, I have argued that the idea that by keeping animals in captivity zoos can preserve wild nature is a cruel hoax. If we continue to keep animals in captivity, we should conform to the highest standards of treatment and respect; there should be no question of killing some animals in order to make room·for others who would also be unjustly confined. This is the least that morality demands. These conclusions, contrary to what some may think, do not turn on any particular analysis of wild and captive. For those who want to reject these conclusions there is no substitute for doing the hard work of confronting the moral arguments that I have given.

14

Animal Liberation is an Environmental Ethic

In an influential essay first published in 1980, J. Baird Callicott argued that animal liberation and environmental ethics are distinct and inconsistent perspectives.[1] Callicott had harsh words both for animals and animal liberationists. He referred to domestic animals as "living artifacts" and claimed that it is "incoherent" to speak of their natural behaviour (1980/1989: 30). He wrote that it is a "logical impossibility" to liberate domestic animals and that "the value commitments of the humane movement seem at bottom to betray a world-denying or rather a life-loathing philosophy" (p. 31). All of this is in distinction to Aldo Leopold's "land ethic" which, according to Callicott, is holistic: "[It] locates ultimate value in the biotic community and assigns differential moral value to the constitutive individuals relatively to that standard" (p. 58). "Some bacteria, for example, may be of greater value to the health or economy of nature than dogs, and thus command more respect" (p. 39). From the perspective of the land ethic, "inanimate entities such as oceans and lakes, mountains, forests, and wetlands are assigned a greater value than individual animals" (p. 58). While Callicott grants that a variety of environmental ethics may exist, he suggests that "the extent to which an ethical system resembles Leopold's land ethic might be used . . . as a criterion to measure the extent to which it is or is not of the environmental sort" (pp. 30–1). Animal liberation

This essay began life as a lecture to the Gruppo di Studio "Scienza & Etica" at the Politecnico di Milano in Italy. Subsequent versions were presented in the Faculty of Philosophy at Monash University in Australia, to an environmental ethics seminar in Oxford, and to an environmental ethics conference in London. I have benefited from the probing questions and comments of many people, especially Paola Cavalieri, Roger Crisp, Lori Gruen, Alan Holland, Steve Kramer, and Rae Langton.

[1] 1980/1989. Callicott expresses some misgivings about this essay in the introduction to his 1989 and in a new preface to the original paper published in Robert Elliot's (1995) collection.

fails to satisfy this criterion since, according to Callicott, animal liberation and conventional anthropocentric ethics "have much more in common with one another than either has with environmental or land ethics" (p. 57).[2]

The idea that environmental ethics and animal liberation are conceptually distinct, and that animal liberation has more in common with conventional morality than with environmental ethics, would come as a surprise to many people concerned about the human domination of nature. For one thing, environmentalists and animal liberationists have many of the same enemies: those who dump poisons into the air and water, drive whales to extinction, or clear rainforests to create pastures for cattle, to name just a few. Moreover, however one traces the history of the environmental movement, it is clear that it comes out of a tradition that expresses strong concern for animal suffering and autonomy. Certainly both the modern environmental and animal liberation movements spring from the same sources in the post-Word War II period: a disgust with the sacrifice of everything else to the construction of military machines, the creation of a culture which views humans and other animals as replaceable commodities, and the prevailing faith in the ability of science to solve all of our problems. It is no coincidence that, in the United States at least, both of these movements developed during the same period. Peter Singer's first article on animal liberation (1973) appeared less than three years after the first Earth Day. Even today people who identify themselves as environmentalists are likely to be as concerned about spotted owls as old growth forests and to think that vegetarianism is a good idea. Many people are members of both environmental and animal liberation organizations and feel no tension between these commitments.

This is not to say that there are no differences between environmentalists and animal liberationists.[3] Such differences exist, but so do deep divisions among environmentalists and among animal liberationists. My thesis is that the divisions within each of these groups are just as deep and profound as the differences between them. Leopold's land ethic is one environmental ethic on offer, but so is animal liberation. The superiority of one to the other must be demonstrated by argument, not by appeal to paradigm cases or established by definitional fiat.

I begin by briefly tracing the history of the split between environmental ethics and animal liberation, go on to sketch a theory of value that I think is

[2] For Leopold's land ethic see Leopold (1949).

[3] The Norwegian government has appealed to theoretical differences between environmental ethics and animal liberation in its attempt to reconcile its reputation as an environmental leader with its flouting of the international consensus against whaling.

implicit in animal liberation, and explain how this theory is consistent with strong environmental commitments. I conclude with some observations about problems that remain.

1. ORIGINS

I have already mentioned Callicott's role in setting environmental ethics against animal liberation. However, he does not deserve all the blame. In order to see why we must recover some recent history.

The origins of the contemporary environmental movement were deeply entangled in the counter-culture of the 1960s. Generally in the counter-culture there was a feeling that sex was good, drugs were liberating, opposing the government was a moral obligation, and that new values were needed to vindicate, sustain, and encourage this shift in outlook and behaviour. In 1967 (during the "Summer of Love" in San Francisco's Haight-Ashbury), the UCLA historian Lynn White Jr. published an essay in which he argued that the dominant tendencies in the Judaeo-Christian tradition were the real source of our environmental problems. Only by overthrowing these traditions and embracing the suppressed insights of other traditions could we come to live peaceably with nature.

This view gained philosophical expression in a 1973 paper by Richard Routley. Routley produced a series of cases about which he thought we have moral intuitions that cannot be accounted for by traditional ethics. Routley asked us to consider a "last man" whose final act is to destroy such natural objects as mountains and salt marshes. Although these natural objects would not be appreciated by conscious beings even if they were not destroyed, Routley thought that it would still be wrong for the "last man" to destroy them. These intuitions were widely shared, and many environmental philosophers thought that they could only be explained by supposing that non-sentient nature has mind-independent value.[4]

Throughout the 1970s there was a great deal of discussion about whether a new environment ethic was needed, possible, or defensible. In a widely discussed 1981 paper Tom Regan clearly distinguished what he called an "environmental ethic" from a "management ethic". In order to be an environmental ethic, according to Regan, a theory must hold that there are non-conscious

---

[4] The intuition that it would be wrong for the last man to destroy non-sentient natural features can also be explained by concerns about character or by appeal to transworld evaluations. For the first strategy see Hill (1983); for the second strategy see Elliot (1985). Routley himself adopted a version of the second strategy.

beings that have "moral standing". Passmore had argued in his 1974 book that such an ethic was not required to explain our duties concerning nature, but in a 1973 paper Naess had already begun the attempt to develop a new ethic that he called Deep Ecology.[5]

At the time Callicott was writing his 1980/1989 essay the very possibility of an environmental ethic was up for grabs. Animal liberationist views, on the other hand, were already well-developed and comparatively well-established. Peter Singer's *Animal Liberation* (1975/2001) and Stephen Clark's *The Moral Status of Animals* were in print, and Bernard Rollin's *Animal Rights and Human Morality* was about to go to press. *Animals, Men and Morals*, the influential anthology edited by Stanley Godlovitch, Rosalind Godlovitch, and John Harris had appeared in 1972, and the first edition of *Animal Rights and Human Obligations*, edited by Regan and Singer, appeared in 1976. By 1980 the philosophical literature already included contributions by such philosophers as Thomas Auxter, Cora Diamond, Joel Feinberg, Colin McGinn, Mary Midgley, Timothy Sprigge, and Donald VanDeVeer, in addition to those mentioned above. Callicott hoped to gain a hearing for a new environmental ethic by rejecting as inadequate and denouncing as conceptually conservative both what he calls "ethical humanism" and "humane moralism". Ethical theory should become a "triangular affair", with the land ethic as the third player.

Callicott is correct in pointing out the close affinities between animal liberationist ethics and traditional ethics. There are utilitarian, Kantian, libertarian, Aristotelian, and communitarian animal liberationists. Animal liberationists typically accept the projects of traditional Western ethics, then go on to argue that in their applications they have arbitrarily and inconsistently excluded non-human animals. Part of the explanation for the comparative conceptual conservatism of animal liberationist philosophers is that, for the most part, they have been educated in the mainstream traditions of Anglo-American philosophy, while environmental ethicists often have been educated outside the mainstream and are influenced by continental philosophers, "process" philosophers, or theologians. The split between environmental ethics and animal liberation is as much cultural and sociological as philosophical.[6]

Despite the weakness of the argument and the caricaturing of animal lib-

---

[5] Other important early publications directed towards developing a new environmental ethic include Stone (1974) and Rolston III (1975).

[6] Obviously in part this is an empirical claim that would require systematic investigation to establish fully. I believe that it is true based on my general knowledge of the development of the field.

erationist views, Callicott's 1980 article was remarkably influential within the environmental ethics community.[7] Some of Callicott's themes were echoed by Mark Sagoff in an influential 1984 paper.[8] Sagoff charged that if animal liberationists had their way they would institute such anti-environmentalist policies as contraceptively eliminating wild animals so that fewer would suffer and die, converting wilderness areas into farms where animals could be well taken care of, and adopting starving deer as pets. Sagoff concludes that "[a] humanitarian ethic—an appreciation not of nature, but of the welfare of animals—will not help us to understand or to justify an environmental ethic".[9]

By the early 1980s it seemed clear that environmental ethics and animal liberation were conceptually distinct. To be an environmental ethicist one had to embrace new values. One had to believe that some non-sentient entities have inherent value; that these entities include such collectives as species, ecosystems, and the community of the land; and that value is mind-independent in the following respect: even if there were no conscious beings, aspects of nature would still be inherently valuable. What remained to be seen was whether any plausible ethic satisfied these conditions.

2. CANONICAL ENVIRONMENTAL ETHICS

Once it became clear what was required for membership in the club of environmental ethicists, most animal liberationists did not want to join. Some began to fling Callicott's rhetoric back in his direction. In 1983 Tom Regan wrote that

The implications of [Leopold's maxim] include the clear prospect that the individual may be sacrificed for the greater biotic good . . . It is difficult to see how the notion of rights of the individual could find a home within a view that . . . might be fairly dubbed "environmental fascism" . . . Environmental fascism and the rights view are like oil and water: they don't mix.[10]

Almost immediately some environmental philosophers abandoned one or more of the conditions that had been thought to be definitive of an environmental ethic. By 1986 Callicott himself had given up his belief in the mind-

---

[7] As Edward Johnson (1981) points out in his neglected but definitive refutation, Callicott seems to think that all animal liberationists are hedonistic utilitarians; he neglects to distinguish pain being evil from its being evil all things considered; and his claims about the ecological consequences of widespread vegetarianism are downright preposterous.

[8] Sagoff (1984/1993).

[9] ibid. 92. However, it is important to note that Sagoff explicitly states that he is not advocating environmentalism in this article (p. 87).

[10] Regan (1983: 361–2).

independence of value and had adopted a value theory that he attributed to Hume and Darwin.[11] Collectives such as species, ecosystems, and the land have inherent value, according to Callicott, but the existence of valuers is a necessary condition for their having value.

Holmes Rolston III emerged as the most prominent spokesperson for the old-time religion. He vigorously attacked Callicott for having departed from the true path and having abandoned the idea that "nature is of value in itself" (1992). The philosophy that Rolston has developed satisfies all of the conditions for an environmental ethic: value is mind-independent and exists at several different levels including those of "higher" animals, organisms, species, and ecosystems (1988). Although Rolston has an environmental ethic by anyone's standards, it has not commanded widespread assent. As it has become clearer in his work what mind-independent values would have to be like, there have been few who have been willing to follow him. When the normative implications of his views have been made explicit—that, for example, we should sometimes let animals suffer when we could easily intervene, that on many occasions we should prefer the lives of plants to those of animals, that we have a positive duty not to be vegetarian—few have been willing to embrace his philosophy.

During the 1980s the new environmental ethic that Routley wanted was, to some extent, developed. The problem was that not many philosophers found it plausible. In recent years environmental philosophers have begun to return to more conventional views in value theory. But this makes one wonder what happened to the titanic struggle between environmental ethics and animal liberation which some seem to think continues unabated.

3. TOGETHER AGAIN?

Callicott has expressed regret for the rhetoric of his 1980 essay and, by his own lights anyway, attempted a reconciliation between animal liberation and environmental ethics. In an essay published in the late 1980s Callicott wrote that "[a]nimal liberation and environmental ethics may thus be united under a common theoretical umbrella" (1989: 59), but in the same article he wrote that there is nothing wrong with slaughtering "meat animals" for food so long as

---

[11] "In my own papers, going back to 1979, I have also affirmed the importance of the value question in environmental ethics and early on endorsed the postulate of nature's objective, intrinsic value . . . After thinking very hard, during the mid-1980s, about the ontology of value finally I came reluctantly to the conclusion that intrinsic value cannot exist objectively" (Callicott 1992a: 131–2). For further discussion of Callicott's value theory, see Norton (1995a); Callicott (1996); and Lee (1996).

this is not in violation "of a kind of evolved and unspoken social contract between man and beast" (p. 56) and claimed that animal liberationist philosophers must favour protecting "innocent vegetarian animals from their carnivorous predators" (p. 57). When his 1980 essay was reprinted in his 1989 book, Callicott wrote that "this is the one [of all the essays reprinted] that I would most like to revise (censor) for this publication" (p. 6). When the same essay was reprinted in a 1995 collection Callicott wrote that "I now think that we do in fact have duties and obligations . . . to domestic animals", and that "a vegetarian diet is indicated by the land ethic". However he also says, puzzlingly enough, that "the land ethic leaves our traditional human morality quite intact and pre-emptive".[12]

I suspect that what is going on in part is that Calliott senses that, since he is no longer a canonical environmental ethicist, the differences between his views and those of animal liberationists cannot be as philosophically deep as they once appeared. Yet the revolutionary idea, rooted in the culture of the 1960s, that what we need is a new environmental ethic is one that dies hard. In the next section I will show how an animal liberationist ethic, rooted in traditional views of value and obligation, can take non-sentient nature seriously. A deep green ethic does not require strange views about value.

4. ANIMAL LIBERATION AND THE VALUE OF NATURE

In my view any plausible ethic must address concerns about both animals and the environment. (Indeed, I think that it is an embarrassment to philosophy that those who are most influential within the discipline typically ignore these issues or treat them as marginal.) Some issues that directly concern animals are obviously of great environmental import as well. The production and consumption of beef may well be the most important of them.[13] The addiction to beef that is characteristic of people in the industrialized countries is not only a moral atrocity for animals but also causes health problems for consumers, reduces grain supplies for the poor, precipitates social divisions in developing countries, contributes to climate change, leads to the conversion of forests to pasture lands, is a causal factor in overgrazing, and is implicated in the destruction of native plants and animals. If there is one issue on which animal liberationists and environmentalists should speak with a single voice it is on

---

[12] These quotations are from Callicott's new preface to "Animal Liberation: A Triangular Affair", in Elliot (1995: 29–30).

[13] The case for this has been very convincingly argued by Jeremy Rifkin (1992).

this issue. To his credit Callicott appears to have recognized this, but many environmental philosophers have not.

In addition to there being clear issues on which animal liberationists and environmentalists should agree, it is also important to remember that non-human animals, like humans, live in environments. One reason to oppose the destruction of wilderness and the poisoning of nature is that these actions harm both human and non-human animals. I believe that one can go quite far towards protecting the environment solely on the basis of concern for animals.

Finally, and most importantly, environmental ethicists have no monopoly on valuing such collectives as species, ecosystems, and the community of the land. It has only seemed that they do because parties to the dispute have not attended to the proper distinctions.

One relevant distinction, noted by Callicott in different language, is between the source and content of values.[14] We can be sentientist with respect to the source of values, yet non-sentientist with respect to their content. Were there no sentient beings there would be no values but it doesn't follow from this that only sentient beings are valuable.[15]

The second important distinction is between primary and derivative value. Creatures who can suffer, take pleasure in their experiences, and whose lives go better or worse from their own point of view are of primary value. Failure to value them involves failures of objectivity or impartiality in our reasoning or sentiments.

Suppose that I recognize that I matter morally in virtue of instantiating some particular property, but I withhold the judgement that some other creature matters morally although I recognize that this other creature also instantiates this property. On the face of it, I hold inconsistent beliefs, though they can be made consistent by conceptual gerrymandering. Just as I can appear to assert P & ~P but limit the interpretation of P to "then or there" and ~P to "now or here", so I can say that a particular property is morally relevant only if it is instantiated in me or my close relatives. However, such consistency is not worth having since it rests on an absurd view of how morally relevant properties function. Indeed, it seems to strip them of their significance. Contrary to what has been granted, what makes me morally significant in this case

---

[14] John O'Neill (1993, ch. 2) also makes a similar distinction.

[15] Here we border on some important issues in philosophy of mind that cannot be discussed here. For present purposes I assume that sentience and consciousness determine the same class, and that there is something that it is like to be a "merely conscious" (as well as self-conscious) entity, although a "merely conscious" entity cannot reflect on what it is like to be itself. I say a little more about these matters in Jamieson (1983b). See also various papers collected in Bekoff and Jamieson (1996b).

is not instantiating the property under consideration but rather instantiating the property of being me or my kin. Similar points apply with respect to the sentiments. If I fail to value a creature who instantiates a property in virtue of which I matter morally, then the reach and power of my sentiments are in some way defective. Whether it is reason or sentiment that is involved, in both cases I look out into the world and see creatures who instantiate properties that bestow moral value, yet I deny moral value to those who are not me or biologically close to me. It is natural to say about these cases that I lack objectivity or impartiality. Sidgwick would have chided me for failing to take the point of view of the universe.

Non-sentient entities are not of primary value because they do not have a perspective from which their lives go better or worse. Ultimately the value of non-sentient entities rests on how they fit into the lives of sentient beings. But although non-sentient entities are not of primary value, their value can be very great and urgent. In some cases their value may even trump the value of sentient entities. The distinction between primary and derivative value is not a distinction in degree of value, but rather in the ways different entities can be valuable.

A third distinction is that between intrinsic and non-intrinsic value. Before explaining how I use this distinction, I want to be clear about how I do not use it. G. E. Moore (1922) inaugurated a tradition in which some entities were supposed to be of value because of properties intrinsic to themselves, while other entities were of value because of properties that were extrinsic to them (i.e. relational properties). At first glance it might be thought that this is the same distinction as that between primary and derivative value. What underwrites the value of a sentient creature is that its life can go better or worse, and these properties may be thought to be intrinsic to the creature. But whether a creature's life goes well or ill depends on its relation to the world. These value-relevant, world-relating properties are not intrinsic in Moore's sense. A further reason for avoiding Moore's distinction is that it invites conflating the source and content of values. One and the same property may appear intrinsic under one description and extrinsic under another. For example, the properties that make a creature internally goal-directed may appear intrinsic, but when these properties are described as value-conferring they may appear extrinsic because they require the existence of sentient beings in order to be of value. Various responses can be made to these concerns, but I think that enough has been said to show at least that Moore's distinction is troublingly difficult to make out.

The distinction that I think is useful is that between intrinsically and non-intrinsically valuing something. I speak of "intrinsically valuing" rather than "intrinsic value" because it makes clear that the intended distinction is in the structure of valuing rather than in the sorts of things that are valued.[16] We intrinsically value something when we value it for its own sake. Making the distinction in this way also makes clear that one and the same entity can be valued both intrinsically and non-intrinsically at different times, in different contexts, by different valuers, or even by the same valuer at the same time. For example, I can intrinsically value Sean (i.e. value her for her own sake) yet non-intrinsically value her as an efficient mail-delivering device (i.e. for how she conduces to my ends).

Collecting these distinctions we can entertain the possibility that the content of our values may include our intrinsically valuing an entity that is of derivative value, and that this valuing may be urgent and intense, even trumping something of primary value. The obvious candidates for satisfying this description are works of art. Many of us would say that the greatest works of art are very valuable indeed. We value them intrinsically, yet ultimately an account of their value devolves into understandings about their relations to people (e.g. artists, audiences, potential audiences, those who know of their existence, etc.).

During World War II Churchill evacuated art from London to the contryside in order to protect it from the blitz. Resources devoted to this evacuation could have been allocated to life-saving. Although he may not have represented the decision in this way, Churchill made the judgement that evacuating the art was more important than saving some number of human lives. I don't know whether he was correct in his specific calculation, but he might well have been. Quantity of life is not the only thing that matters; quality of life matters too, and it is to this concern that Churchill's judgement was responsive.

A similar point could be made concerning the destruction of parts of the old city of Dubrovnik by Serbian gunners. I believe that over the course of human history the destruction of the old city would be a greater crime than some measure of death and destruction wrought upon the people of Dubrovnik. Indeed, I believe that some of the people of Dubrovnik share this view. This particular judgement need not be shared, however, in order to accept the basic point that I am making.

Non-sentient features of the environment are of derivative value, but they can be of extreme value and can be valued intrinsically. There are geological

---

[16] This of course is not to deny that some things are better candidates for intrinsically valuing than others. For further discussion see Jamieson (1994).

features of the Dolomites that are profoundly important to preserve. Rivers and forests can have the same degree of importance. Indeed, there may be features of the Italian natural environment that are as important to preserve as the city of Venice.

The main point I am making here is that many people have traditional evaluational outlooks yet value works of art intrinsically and intensely. There is no great puzzle about how they can both intrinsically value persons and works of art. Similarly, animal liberationists can value nature intrinsically and intensely, even though they believe that non-sentient nature is of derivative value. Because what is of derivative value can be valued intensely and intrinsically, animal liberationists can join environmental ethicists in fighting for the preservation of wild rivers and wilderness areas. Indeed, rightly understood, they can even agree with environmental ethicists that these natural features are valuable for their own sakes.

But at this point an objection may arise. The most that I have shown is that non-sentient entities can be intrinsically valued. I have not shown that they ought to be intrinsically valued. Canonical environmentalists can give a reason for intrinsically valuing non-sentient nature that animal liberationists cannot: aspects of non-sentient nature are valuable independently of any conscious being.

The objection is correct in that environmental ethicists who believe in mind-independent value can appeal to normative high ground that is not available to those philosophers who do not believe in mind-independent value. However, it should be noted that even if the value of non-sentient nature were mind-independent, it would not immediately follow that non-sentient nature should be valued intrinsically or that its value would be of greater urgency than that of other entities. But putting that point aside, the fundamental problem with this attempt to seize the normative heights is that they are a mirage. There is no mind-independent value, but none is required in order for nature to be valued intrinsically. Still, having said this, some account needs to be given of how my kind of environmental philosopher moves from the claim that wilderness can be intrinsically valued to the claim that wilderness ought to be intrinsically valued.

First, we should see that this question plunges us into the familiar if difficult problem of how first-order value claims can be defended and justified.[17] In order to give an account of this, very close attention would have to be paid to our everyday moral practices and our strategies of defence, offence,

---

[17] I have discussed the relation between moral practice and moral theorizing in Jamieson (1991a). See also Weston (1985).

justification, and capitulation. I doubt that very much of general interest can be said about this. But as a first approximation, we might say that in order to see how environmentalist claims are justified, we should look at the practices of persuasion that environmentalists employ. Consider an example.

Many people think of deserts as horrible places that are not worth protecting. I disagree. I value deserts intrinsically and think you should too. How do I proceed? One thing I might do is take you camping with me. We might see the desert's nocturnal inhabitants, the plants that have adapted to these conditions, the shifting colours of the landscape as the day wears on, and the rising of the moon on stark features of the desert. Together we might experience the feel of the desert wind, hear the silence of the desert, and sense its solitude. You may become interested in how it is that this place was formed, what sustains it, how its plants and animals make a living. As you learn more about the desert, you may come to see it differently and to value it more. This may lead you to spend more time in the desert, seeing it in different seasons, watching the spring with its incredible array of flowers turn to the haunting stillness of summer. You might start reading some desert literature, from the monastic fathers of the church to Edward Abbey. Your appreciation would continue to grow.

But there is no guarantee that things will go this way. You may return from your time in the desert hot, dirty, hungry for a burger, thirsty for a beer, and ready to volunteer your services to the US Army Corps of Engineers (whose *raison d'être* seems to be to flood as much of the earth's surface as possible). Similarly, some people see Venice as a dysfunctional collection of dirty old buildings, find Kant boring and wrong, and hear Mahler as both excessively romantic and annoyingly dissonant. More experience only makes matters worse.

If someone fails to appreciate the desert, Venice, or Mahler, they need not have made any logical error. Our evaluative responses are not uniquely determined by our constitution or the world. This fact provokes anxiety in some philosophers. They fear that unless value is mind-independent, anything goes. Experience machines are as good as experience, Disney-desert is the same as the real thing, and the Spice Girls and Mahler are colleagues in the same business (one strikingly more successful than the other). Those who suffer this anxiety confuse a requirement for value with how value is constituted. Value is mind-dependent, but it is things in the world that are valuable or not. The fact that we draw attention to features of objects in our evaluative discourse is the common property of all theories of value.

These anxious philosophers also fail to appreciate how powerful psychological and cultural mechanisms can be in constituting objectivity. Culture, history, tradition, knowledge, and convention mediate our constitutions and the world. Culture, together with our constitutions and the world, determines our evaluative practices. Since the world and our constitutions alone are not sufficient for determining them, common values should be seen in part as cultural achievements rather than simply as true reports about the nature of things or expressions of what we are essentially. Evaluative practices are in the domain of negotiation and collective construction, as well as reflection and recognition. But the fact that these practices are in part constructed does not mean that they cannot be rigid and compelling. We can be brought to appreciate Venice, Mahler, or the desert by collectively and interactively educating our sensibilities, tastes, and judgements, but such change often involves a deep reorientation of how we see the world. When I try to get you to appreciate the desert I direct your attention to objects in your visual field, but I am trying to change your way of seeing and thinking and your whole outlook towards nature. I am also trying to change our relationship from one of difference to one of solidarity. Similarly, when advocates of the enterprise society point to missed opportunities for profit and competitiveness, they are trying to educate our sensibilities as well as referring us to economic facts. Their descriptions of how economies work are to a great extent stories about the social world they want to construct.

What I have argued in this section is that animal liberationists can hold many of the same normative views as environmental ethicists. This is because many of our most important issues involve serious threats to both humans and animals as well as to the non-sentient environment; because animal liberationists can value nature as a home for sentient beings; and because animal liberationists can embrace environmental values as intensely as environmental ethicists, though they see them as derivative rather than primary values. What animal liberationists cannot do is claim the moral high ground of the mind-independent value of nature which, since the early days of the movement environmental ethicists have attempted to secure. But, as I have argued, this moral high ground is not there to be claimed anyway. Those who are deep green should not despair because some of our environmental values are to a great extent socially constructed. Constructivism is a story about how our practices come to be, not about how real, rigid, or compelling they are.

Still, many will think that this is a flabby ethic that leans too far in the direction of subjectivism, relativism, constructivism, or some other postmodern heresy. One way of making their point is to return to the distinction between primary and derivative value. Imagine two people: Robin, who thinks that trees are of primary value, and Ted, who denies that humans or gorillas are included in this class. What kind of a mistake are Robin and Ted making? If

I say they are making a conceptual mistake then I will be dismissing some very influential views as non-starters; if I say they are making a normative mistake then my view of what has primary and derivative value will turn out to be just as subjective as my view that deserts are valuable, and therefore just as vulnerable to other people's lack of responsiveness to my concerns.

I want to reiterate that first-order value judgements can be both rigid and compelling, even though to some extent they are relative and socially constructed. But having said this, I want to reject the idea that Robin and Ted are making a logical or grammatical error. Robin, Ted, and I have a real normative dispute about how to determine what is of primary value. At the same time this dispute has a different feel to it than first-order normative disputes (e.g. the dispute about whether or not to value the desert). We can bring out this difference by saying as a first approximation that someone who fails to value deserts lacks sensitivity while someone who fails to value people or gorillas lacks objectivity. Although in both cases the dispute involves how we see ourselves in relation to the world, to a great extent different considerations are relevant in each case. Because questions about primary values are at the centre of how we take the world, abstract principles (e.g. those that concern objectivity and impartiality) are most relevant to settling these disputes. Differences about whether or not to value deserts, on the other hand, turn on a panoply of considerations, some of which I have already discussed.[18]

In this section I have argued that there is a great deal of theoretical convergence between animal liberationists and environmental ethicists. There is also a strong case for convergence at the practical and political level. The environmental movement has numbers and wealth while the animal liberation movement has personal commitment. Both environmental and animal issues figure in the choices people make in their daily lives, but they are so glaringly obvious in the case of animals that they cannot be evaded. Anyone who eats or dresses makes ethical choices that affect animals. Refraining from eating meat makes one part of a social movement: rather than being an abstainer, one is characterized positively as "a vegetarian". While other consumer choices also have profound environmental consequences, somehow they are less visible than the choice of whether to eat meat. This is part of the reason why self-identified environmentalists are often less motivated to save energy, reduce consumption, or refrain from purchasing toxic substances than animal

---

[18] There is much more to say about these questions than I can say here. However, it may help to locate my views if I invoke the Quinian image of the web of belief in which what is at the centre of the web is defended in different ways from what is at the periphery, not because such beliefs enjoy some special epistemological status, but because of the density of their connections to other beliefs.

liberationists are to seek out vegetarian alternatives.[19] Not only is animal liberation an environmental ethic, but animal liberation can also help to empower the environmental movement.

5. REMAINING CONUNDRUMS AND COMPLEXITIES

Where Callicott saw a "triangular affair" and Sagoff saw "divorce", I see the potential for Hollywood romance. It might be objected that my rosy view only survives because I have not dealt in detail with specific issues that divide animal liberationists and environmental ethicists. For example, there are many cases in which environmentalists may favour "culling" (a polite term for "killing") some animals for the good of a population. In other cases environmentalists may favour eliminating a population of common animals in order to preserve a rare plant. Hovering in the background is the image of "hunt saboteurs", trying to stop not only fox hunting but also the fox's hunting.

These difficult issues cannot be resolved here.[20] For present purposes, what is important to see is that while animal liberationists and environmentalists may have different tendencies, the turf doesn't divide quite so neatly as some may think. Consider one example.

Gary Varner (1995), who writes as an animal liberationist, has defended what he calls "therapeutic hunting" in some circumstances. He defines "therapeutic hunting" as "hunting motivated by and designed to secure the aggregate welfare of the target species and/or the integrity of its ecosystem" (ibid. 257). Varner goes on to argue that animal liberationists can support this kind of hunting and that this is the only kind of hunting that environmentalists are compelled to support. What might have appeared as a clear difference between the two groups turns out to be more complex.

In addition to such "convergence" arguments, it is important to recognize the diversity of views that exists within both the environmental and animal liberation movements. Differences between animal liberationists are obvious and on the table. At a practical level animal liberation groups are notorious for their sectarianism. At a philosophical level Tom Regan has spent much of the last fifteen years distinguishing his view from that of Peter Singer's, and I have already mentioned other diverse animal liberationist voices. In recent years the same kinds of divisions have broken out among environmental philosophers, with the rhetoric between Callicott and Rolston (and more

---

[19] These and related issues are discussed in two reports to the United States Environmental Protection Agency (Jamieson and VanderWerf 1993, 1995).

[20] For my approach to some of these conflicts see Essay 12, and Jamieson (1995a).

recently Callicott and Norton) increasingly resembling that between Singer and Regan. Generally within the community of environmental philosophers there are disagreements about the nature and value of wilderness, the importance of biodiversity, and approaches to controlling population. At a practical level there are disagreements about the very goals of the movement. Some would say that preservation of nature's diversity is the ultimate goal; others would counter that it is the preservation of evolutionary processes that matters. Sometimes people assert both without appreciating that they can come into conflict.[21]

There are many practical issues on which neither animal liberationists nor environmentalists are of one mind. For example, South African, American, and German scientists working for the South African National Parks Board, with support from the Humane Society of the United States, are currently testing contraceptives on elephants in Kruger National Park as an alternative to "culling". The Worldwide Fund for Nature is divided about the project, with its local branch opposing it.[22]

Part of the reason for the divisions within both the environmental and animal liberation movements is that contemporary Western cultures have little by way of positive images of how to relate to animals and nature. Most of us know what is bad—wiping out songbird populations, polluting water ways, causing cats to suffer, contributing to smog, and so on. But when asked to provide a positive vision many people turn to the past, to their conception of what life is like for indigenous peoples, or what it is to be "natural". None of this will do. So long as we have a paucity of positive visions, different views, theories, and philosophies will compete for attention, with no obvious way of resolving some of the most profound disagreements.

These are early days for those who are sensitive to the interests of nature and animals. We are in the midst of a transition from a culture which sees nature as material for exploitation, to one which asserts the importance of living in harmony with nature. It will take a long time to understand exactly what are the terms of the debate. What is important to recognize now is that animal liberationists and environmental ethicists are on the same side in this transition. Animal liberation is not the only environmental ethic, but neither is it some alien ideology. Rather, as I have argued, animal liberation is an environmental ethic and should be welcomed back into the family.

[21] To some degree differences among environmentalists have been obscured by the rise of "managerialist" forms of environmentalism which are favoured by many scientists and are highly visible in the media. For a critique, see Jamieson (1990). For alternative forms of environmentalism, see Sachs (1993).

[22] "Villagers slam 'Pill for Elephants'", *New Scientist*, 9 (1996).

15

Ecosystem Health: Some Preventive Medicine

1. INTRODUCTION

In recent years the language of health and disease has often been employed in discussions of environmental quality. Many people in everyday life find it natural to speak of environments as healthy or diseased. A Southern California mesa, formerly populated by interesting and subtle forms of life, now bulldozed and covered with tract houses and shopping malls, can strike one as the environmental equivalent of a cancer-wracked body. A highly acidic lake or a beetle-infested forest can strike us in the same way.

Recently the idea of ecosystem health has emerged, not as an admittedly loose idea gleaned from ordinary conversation, but as a fledgling technical term to be deployed in the discourse of environmental science. Some ecologists, philosophers, and policy analysts believe that ecosystem health can be defined in a rigorous way and employed as a management goal in environmental policy.[1]

For reasons that I explain in what follows, I am dubious about the utility of 'ecosystem health' as a technical term. This expression may have something to recommend it as part of a rhetorical strategy, but even here I am suspicious. Environmentalists have all too often been trapped by their own rhetoric, and the movement as a whole has suffered from its use of

Earlier versions of this essay were discussed in seminars at the Hastings Center and the University of Colorado and I thank everyone who participated in these events.

[1] See the papers collected in Costanza *et al.* (1992), which emerged from research funded by the US Environmental Protection Agency.

misleading metaphors (e.g. "greenhouse effect", captive animals as "ambassadors of the wild").[2] Language is important, and environmentalists need to be clear about what they are asserting.

2. VALUES AND THE LANGUAGE OF HEALTH

The language of health is value-laden. Unfortunately our common cultural conceptions of value are in many respects quite crude.[3]

We tend to think that reasons, desires, and dispositions must be either subjective or objective. Subjective reasons, desires, and dispositions are thought of as rooted in an individual's idiosyncratic states or preferences, and can be explained primarily by facts about the individual in question. What is subjective is person-specific, and therefore in its domain we should expect a great deal of relativity. On this view there is little reason to suppose that subjective reasons, desires, and dispositions will be either systematic or widely shared. Indeed, we should expect them to be piecemeal, fragmented, and arbitrary. Objective reasons, desires, and dispositions, on the other hand, are rooted in impersonal facts about the way things are. They are largely determined by the world rather than by people, and we can expect such reasons, desires, and dispositions to be systematic, consistent, and widely shared. For the world is what we have in common: it is systematic and consistent, and objective reasons should reflect these features of the world.[4]

If a reason, desire, or disposition must be either subjective or objective, each of us has a lot to gain by portraying our states as objective. For if a reason is viewed as objective, then it is more likely to be persuasive to other people than a reason that is viewed as merely subjective. How the world is matters to people, and if we can see the world reflected in someone's reasons, desires,

---

[2] On the misleading nature of the "greenhouse effect" see Kempton (1991). On the misleading idea of captive animals as "ambassadors of the wild" see Essays 11–13.

[3] Of course some philosophical thinking about value is an exception to this, but regrettably some is not. For some sophisticated value theory in environmental philosophy see O'Neill (1993, ch. 1); and various essays by Robert Elliot, including most recently Elliot (1992).

[4] In a recent essay, J. Baird Callicott writes regarding an earlier draft of this essay that "Jamieson's argument . . . is vitiated by the arbitrary and stipulative meaning he gives to the terms *objective* and *subjective*" (1995: 107). In Callicott's view "all reasons, desires, and dispositions clearly belong to the realm of the subjective, according to standard English usage, because they are states of mind" (107). I find these claims surprising for a number of reasons. I will not argue about ordinary language, though I don't think Callicott's claim about "standard English usage" survives a close reading of the *Oxford English Dictionary*. But more importantly, Callicott's reduction of all desires to the domain of the subjective has the effect of effacing the important distinction between (say) the standing desire of most people for happiness and my occurrent desire for tiramisu. Thomas Nagel (1970) marked this kind of distinction by using the language of objective and subjective reasons, and I am writing in this tradition.

and dispositions, then their states will be of interest to us. If we see someone's reasons, desires, and dispositions as subjective, then they will primarily be of interest only to those of us who care about the person in question. People are less likely to be moved by states that they see as facts about their subjects than by states that they see as primarily about the world.

Our tendency to try to objectify goals and purposes that might otherwise be seen as subjective is an ancient one. The language of health has often been mobilized in these attempts. For example, Plato in *The Republic* assimilates his conception of virtue and vice to health and disease. Aristotle and Aquinas were also interested in the conceptual resources of the language of health.

Often when political disagreement is intense one side will characterize the other as "sick", "diseased", or "mentally ill".[5] Racists and xenophobes often use this language to characterize those they hate. They say that Jews, blacks, or "foreigners" are diseased or defective, not that they hate them. If racists do admit that they hate Jews or blacks, they sometimes say that this is an appropriate response to the objective qualities of those whom they hate. Thus the anti-semite may portray his or her racism, not as irrational, unmotivated, or ungrounded, but rather as a response to the fact that Jews are a diseased, defective, or decaying form of human life.

In recent years the language of health has also been employed in the service of a range of social policy goals. At various times over the last generation it has been common to speak of "urban health", the "sick welfare system", or the "ailing economy". The language of health is inviting in these contexts because how I feel is subjective but whether or not I am healthy appears to be objective. Various scientific procedures and instruments are relevant to assessing my health but not to assessing how I feel. Thus, it appears that determining whether or not the economy is healthy, the welfare system sick, or the health-care system pathological is a matter of objective investigation of the properties of these institutions rather than a matter of assessing our subjective attitudes towards them. Claims about the health of various social institutions appear to be true or false while our attitudes towards these institutions simply are what they are. How we conceptualize the functioning of these institutions has implications about whether the solutions to various problems primarily involve changing social arrangements or changing people's attitudes towards these social arrangements.

Environmentalists have long been concerned to establish their agenda, not

---

[5] For example, in the Soviet Union dissenters were often considered mentally ill and consigned to psychiatric hospitals. During the conflict with the Russian parliament Boris Yeltsin denounced his opponents as "drunkards, dope addicts, and the mentally ill". This is ironic since many of them were his close allies during the failed coup of August 1991.

just as a matter of mere subjective preference-satisfaction, but as a matter of realizing objective goods. This is part of why environmentalists have long been attracted to science. Science is our great cultural legitimator; it warrants some reasons, desires, and dispositions as objective, and dismisses others as subjective. If it can be shown that environmentalist goals are somehow implicit in the deliverances of science, then in our cultural context they will have been shown to be of very great urgency.

In recent years attempts to base environmental goals on science have become increasingly problematical.[6] The search for ecological laws on which to base such goals has proved fruitless. The turn towards ecosystem health is another attempt to objectify our environmental goals by basing them on science, but a softer and in some ways less plausible attempt. Thus far the search for ecological laws has merely been unsuccessful; the search for laws of health seems obviously misguided.

3. PROBLEM ONE: THE DE-OBJECTIFICATION OF HEALTH

The first concern we might have about the language of ecosystem health is suggested by the weakness of generalizations about human health. Because of this weakness the supposed objectivity of human health has a way of slipping away under pressure. Even if the language of ecosystem health were unproblematical in other respects, we might still wonder about the degree to which it would succeed in objectifying environmental concerns. Generalizations about what constitutes, indicates, or contributes to health are surprisingly local and culture-bound. There are numerous examples of what are considered treatable conditions in one Western society (e.g. low blood pressure in Germany) that are considered a sign of health in another (e.g. the United States).[7] Even what is considered normal body temperature varies across societies.

Longevity might seem central to conceptions of health, yet it is obvious that people can live long and unhealthy lives, as well as short and healthy ones. Moreover, despite cultural differences in diagnosis and treatment, longevity is about the same in most industrial societies, though it is far from obvious that most industrial societies are equally healthy.

Any notion of health that plays a central role in constructing the idea of ecosystem health will have to be measurable and permit orderings and

---

[6] The history of various attempts to base environmental goals on ecology is nicely traced by Worster (1990). See also Callicott (1992b), and Shrader-Frechette and McCoy (1994).

[7] See Payer (1988) for discussion of this example, and many others.

comparisons. Yet it seems that many particular beliefs and judgements about health are not rooted in measurable indicators or health outcomes. Attempts to provide quantitative criteria for optimal weight, the degree of fitness, or acceptable levels of serum cholesterol (for example) produce seemingly interminable debates. In many cases, not only are there no widely accepted generalizations about what are "healthy" values for various supposed indicators, but it is even contested whether these indicators are relevant to assessments of health. Even when the importance of various indicators is granted, other problems arise. Clearly longevity, competence to engage in a wide range of activities, and the physical ability to act on one's desires all have some claim to be considered as important to health, yet in particular cases they may support inferences about health that taken together are not consistent. Assessments of health are made even more complicated by the fact that, while how we feel is not the same as how healthy we are, it is surely an aspect of our health; and people's feelings of well-being cannot precisely be measured and compared.

I have been arguing that ascriptions of health and disease are surprisingly local and culturally relative. However, it is an obvious fact that there are clear cases of people who are healthy and unhealthy, and would be considered so on any reasonable account in virtually any society. Michael Jordan is "the very picture of health".[8] A visit to a hospital will turn up many people who are not. What to say about most of us is not nearly so clear, however. My point is not that the concept of human health is entirely "a social construction", but rather that there is reason to believe that to some degree this concept is constructed differently in different cultures. In so far as this is true of human health, notions of ecosystem health may appear to be less objective than their champions would like. The extent to which concepts of health are culturally constructed is the extent to which wrapping environmental goals in this language will fail to objectify them in the way in which environmentalists desire.

4. PROBLEM TWO: METAPHOR AND MOTIVATION

Some who find the concept of ecosystem health useful believe that it is a metaphor; others believe that ecosystems are literally healthy or not.[9] In my opinion this discussion is truncated: metaphor isn't the only kind of

---

[8] For those who are not in the know, Michael Jordan is the greatest basketball player who has ever lived.

[9] Callicott (1992b) asserts that talk of ecosystem health is metaphorical while Rapport (in Costanza et al. 1992) appears to be a literalist.

figurative language, and not all uses of language are either metaphorical or literal. The question of whether or not 'ecosystem health' is a metaphor turns more on views about metaphor than on views about ecosystem health.

However, there is an important question that lurks in the background of this discussion. This question concerns whether ascriptions of health and disease have the same motivational force when ascribed to ecosystems that they have when ascribed to humans or other creatures. In my view these ascriptions are sufficiently different in kind for there to be important differences in motivational power. We have reasons to care about whether humans are healthy or diseased that we do not have with respect to ecosystems.

One of the principal reasons why health is important to us is because it bears on how we feel. By 'feeling' (and its cognates) I don't mean to suggest some narrow notion that refers only to sensations. In the sense in which I am using the term, disease affects our feelings by affecting the way in which we think about our future, our goals, our life-plans, and so on, as well as affecting our sensations and experiences. If we discover that we are diseased yet have no unpleasant sensations, this knowledge about ourselves can affect our attitudes towards the future. It may also invoke concern because the diagnosis of disease may support predictions about how we will feel in the future. In short, to a great extent we are concerned about disease because it causes us to be in states that we dislike. Disease may cause us pain and foreshorten our connection to the future. We are concerned about disease in others because they don't like being sick.

Imagine a case in which someone truly claims not to mind being diseased. Perhaps the person has already lived a fulfilling life, and the disease causes no unpleasant sensations. Or perhaps the person does not mind being sick because he or she has an attitude of tranquil acceptance towards both life and death.[10] In so far as the person doesn't mind being sick, either because there are no symptoms or because the person has an attitude towards the illness that we respect, we are much less motivated to undertake aggressive treatment that might return the person to health. For people like this, their disease is less of a problem for us because it is less of a problem for them.[11]

Ecosystems don't mind being diseased, not because they have reached a state of remarkable tranquillity, but because they are not the sorts of things

[10] I once heard the poet Gary Snyder say that if he gets cancer, he hopes that he will refuse treatment and observe the growth of the cancer as the flowering of another aspect of nature, beautiful and valuable in its own way.

[11] Of course disease can also have "secondary" ill effects relating to costs, lost productivity, and so on. However, this does not bear on the point I am making.

that can mind anything. This is an obvious but important difference between humans and ecosystems. Since ecosystems have no preferences about their states, appreciating their desires does not provide a reason for action.[12]

Since ecosystems themselves do not prefer or disprefer any of the states they are in, this should make us wonder whose preferences are at stake in discussions of ecosystem health. The answer is obvious: the preferences of those who are taking part in the discussion.[13] Because ecosystems lack some of the most important properties that lead us to care about the health of someone, it is far from clear what the language of health adds to simple claims about our likes and dislikes in ecosystems. Many of us dislike clear-cut forests for all sorts of reasons, but nothing much seems to be added to our reasons by saying that the clear-cut causes ecosystems to be unhealthy or diseased. Various considerations can be adduced to back the claim of unhealthiness or disease, but to a great extent these considerations can be taken up in our reasons for disliking clear-cuts.

The important point is this: in the human case there is a difference between my friend being in a state that I dislike and one that she dislikes; but there is no such distinction in the case of an ecosystem. Yet without this distinction it is far from clear that appeals to ecosystem health have the motivational power of other appeals to health. This reflects the fact that the objectivity and motivational power of ascriptions of human health are in part grounded in a person's attitude towards his or her own condition, but this objectifying and motivating ground is unavailable in the case of ecosystem health.

It may be objected that this argument proves too much. Plants do not care about the states they are in, yet we are quite comfortable in applying the language of health and disease to them. This objection illuminates an important point. Part of the discomfort one may feel about the concept of ecosystem health concerns the lack of a subject. When we talk about the health of America we are talking about the health of individual Americans. Anyone who rejects this claim is moving in the direction of metaphor, or has an organicist social ontology that keeps rather alarming company (at best Hegel and traditional conservatives, at worst fascists). Part of the task for an advocate of ecosystem health is to convince us that there is a subject that is unified

---

[12] There are some who claim to appreciate the desires of ecosystems, but those who mean this literally are few and far between, and at any rate they are unlikely to be in the business of formulating environmental policy.

[13] Those who are taking part in the discussion can have more or less expansive preferences. For example, when discussing the fate of a particular ecosystem I may take into account the preferences of creatures who are part of this ecosystem and the preferences of all those who care about it. What I do not take into account are the preferences of the ecosystem itself, since it has none.

enough for such ascriptions to apply. Even if ascriptions of health to plants were entirely unproblematical this would remain a difficult obstacle to overcome.

For present purposes the point isn't whether or not we can speak sensibly of the health of plants. Even if we can so speak, in the absence of the attitudinal dimension of our ascriptions of health to humans and other creatures, the motivating power of such language is weakened. This is evidenced by the fact that, everything else being equal, most people are not as motivated to respond to disease in a plant as they are to disease in an animal or human. Indeed, those who think we should be motivated more strongly to be concerned about plants typically tell stories about how much philodendrons enjoy Bach or how broccoli suffer when they are steamed. If we were convinced of these claims then there might be an attitudinal dimension to ascriptions of health and disease to plants, and we might be as motivated to respond to their needs as we are to those of animals. Absent a demonstration of these claims, we might think that someone who ignores the fact that her house-plants are persistently diseased is lacking in horticultural ethics, but our response is dramatically different to someone who fails to get veterinary treatment for his ailing dog. The case for caring for something that cannot care for anything has to be made in a very different way from the case for caring for those creatures who do care for themselves and others, and this difference is reflected in our motivational structure.[14]

5. PROBLEM THREE: A CONDITION OF OBJECTIFICATION

Thus far I have argued that the language of health when applied to ecosystems typically does not have the motivating power that it has when applied to humans and other creatures, and that even ascriptions of human health may not be as objective as they initially appear. In this section I suggest that our preferences with respect to ecosystems are not good candidates for objectification.

Some of our preferences are more plausibly objectified than others. Preferences for pleasure, happiness, success, security, and so on are among them. While there may be people and cultures which have not had these preferences, they are relatively rare. For the most part, preferences for pleasure, happiness, and so on are invariant across humans and their societies. Preferences which

---

[14] I argue this in detail in Essay 14.

are relatively invariant are good candidates for objectification. For when we objectify a preference we seem to suggest that it reflects some feature of the Nature of Things. If the preference in question is widely shared, this suggestion is unlikely to be resisted.

Our preferences in ecosystems are not good candidates for objectification because they are relatively unstable. Nash and others have documented how American attitudes towards nature have changed over the centuries.[15] From a cross-cultural perspective, it is clear that what is seen as deplorable and perhaps diseased in one culture may be seen in a very different way in another culture. People from moist, green regions such as Europe and New England often find the great deserts of the American West to be ugly, dead, and uninviting. People from the American West often find regions with a surfeit of organic material equally repugnant.

Michael Soulé (1990) has suggested that even our preferences for native versus alien plants is open to revision. Indeed, only a few centuries ago colonists in Australia, New Zealand, and North America engaged in wars against native plants and animals, replacing them with those from home which they found familiar. Although a return to overt, wanton ecological imperialism is not likely in the near future, it is not implausible to suppose that we may come to see our preference for isolated, indigenous ecosystems as anachronistic; and instead come to favour ecosystems that are more cosmopolitan, in much the same way in which many people now prefer multicultural experiences to those which are provincial. A celebration of alien plants and surprising biological juxtapositions may be more in tune with the post-modern world than attempts to protect native species. Indeed, some social constructionists may even see the struggle between native and exotic species as more or less the same conflict as that between world culture and "ethnic cleansing".

6. VALUES RECONSIDERED

Thus far I have been critical of using the language of ecosystem health in attempts to objectify our appreciation of certain kinds of ecosystems. It might be thought that the only alternative to these attempts is to suppose that our preferences for some ecosystems rather than others is arbitrary and subjective. But that would be a mistake. In my opinion, we need to reject the false dichotomy that presupposes that values are either part of the fabric of the world or mere subjective states.

[15] Nash (1967/2001).

Many people here and now value natural objects. Some natural objects are valued intrinsically in the way in which we value artworks; others are valued instrumentally in the way in which we value calories. In both cases our valuing can be quite intense. Moreover, reasons can be given as to why others should value natural objects in the way in which we do. This reason-giving activity does not require the language of health and disease, nor does it require supposing that someone who does not share our values is metaphysically or scientifically ignorant. Rather such a person may be insensitive in various respects, or ignorant of his or her own evaluational outlook or that of the wider culture. Or such a person may simply have another view, one which itself is supported by reasons that carry substantial force.

In my view, objectivity is not given to us by nature; it is something that we achieve through the creation of a common culture and way of life. Objectivity is rooted in the roles that various values play in the evaluational outlook of a community. Many values are in motion, becoming more or less objective or subjective, depending on the shifting roles they play in people's lives. However, not all values are equally good candidates for objectification. Facts about our biology, history, and culture, along with the characteristics of what is valued, bear on the chances of objectification. Ecosystem health for reasons that I have already given is not here and now a good candidate for objectification.

Since writing the preceding words, I have been accused of vulgar relativism and conventionalism. Callicott (1995: 107) writes that: "Among the ancient Greeks, slavery was a way of life, a foundational aspect of a common culture. Hence by Jamieson's account, in that time and place, slavery was good, objectively good." He goes on to suggest that I would defend the caste system in India, the subordination of women in Islamic societies, and the suppression of human rights in China.

As a moral vegetarian, vocal advocate of massive reductions in consumption and population, and a critic of zoos and the scientific research establishment, I find it especially ironic to be cast in the role of apologist for the status quo. In this essay and elsewhere I have emphasized that some values are better than others, though there is no uniquely best set of values and that values tend to be dynamic. Perhaps the most important point to make here is that it simply does not follow from the fact that a value has become objectified in a particular society that it is wrong or irrational to fail to act in accordance with this value or to oppose it. Of course it was right to oppose slavery in the "old south" just as it is now right to oppose factory farming and environmental destruction. Having said this I think that it is important to recognize that the objectification of "bad values" is less common than might be thought—the fact that they are bad militates against their objectification. Indeed, all of the examples that Callicott mentions are of values that were contested and resisted in their own cultural contexts

These remarks may help to clear away some of the confusion, but large issues remain that cannot be settled here. The fundamental question that is at issue is whether someone who holds a version of "subjectivism", "emotivism", "conventionalism", or "irrealism" can have deep green normative values. This is another version of the debate that was occasioned by the rise of emotivism in the second third of the twentieth century. Like Hume, Ayer, Stevenson, and others, I think that the question of how morality is constructed is quite distinct from questions about the content of morality. Apparently Callicott disagrees.

7. CONCLUDING REMARKS

I end by noting two further risks entailed by the vocabulary of ecosystem health. This vocabulary invites "medicalizing" our relationship to nature and also contributes to the "scientistic" outlook that makes it difficult for us to explicitly discuss our conflicts about what we value. These risks are not logically implied by the language of ecosystem health, but they are important because of the way that medical discourse is embedded in Western societies.

In recent years a great deal of concern has been expressed about the medicalization of various forms of human behaviour. When mental illness, crime, or nuclear weapons are seen as pathologies, they are represented in a way that seems to remove them from the domain of dialogue and discussion and put them into the domain of physician-experts. If child abuse is a disease then we need professionals to explain this behaviour and treat the disorder. Ordinary people cannot be expected to understand the phenomenon or perhaps even to recognize it. Similarly, if we represent environmental problems as threats to the health of ecosystems, then it is the role of "ecodocs" to restore them to health. If they fail, then they should be sued for malpractice or incompetence.

Ecodocs are scientists by training, typically ecologists or conservation biologists, and they command a particular expertise and vocabulary. The medicine that they bring to the rescue is scientific medicine. But whatever the case for homeopathy and other alternatives in the area of human medicine, the case for their analogues in the environmental area is very strong. Most of us may think that we can recognize a diseased ecosystem, but there is little agreement about what health consists in or how to bring it about.

Scientism has the effect of driving out the idea of individual responsibility. It is not our fault that some ecosystems have been struck by disease, nor do we have the expertise or responsibility to fix them.[16] This thought, which is invited by the language of ecosystem health, is an entirely wrong way of thinking about environmental problems. Diseased ecosystems are not primarily challenges to the resourcefulness of "ecodocs", but challenges to our way of life.

In my view, the environmental problems that we face are not fundamentally scientific problems.[17] In large part the environmental crisis is a crisis of the human heart. Our problems are not primarily in the oceans, the atmosphere, or the forests, but in our institutions of governance, our systems of value, and our ways of knowing. There are contradictions in the structure of our values, and massive failures to act on those values which we hold dear. We are attracted to some elements of nature, but repulsed by others. We face conundrums and confusions in reconciling our attitudes and behaviour. Together we create tragic outcomes that no one intends. Whatever role there may be for the rhetoric of ecosystem health, it should not be allowed to lead us away from the real patient who needs help: human beings, and the institutions that we have created.

[16] An extreme example of the abdication of responsibility can be found in the words of Texaco's company chairman, Alf DeCrane, who was quoted regarding 16.8 million gallons of oil spilled into the Ecuadorian Amazon that "We didn't spill it. God did" (Knight-Ridder Newspapers, 20 August 1995), as if the oil would have been spilled even had there been no pipeline.

[17] This is a constant theme of mine. See e.g. Essay 18.

16

Values in Nature

1. INTRODUCTION

Some people value nature while others do not. John Muir and Oscar Wilde were contemporaries, yet they expressed very different attitudes towards nature. While Muir (1994: 25) wrote about "the immortal truth and immortal beauty of Nature" and claimed that there is "an ancient mother-love" of wild nature in everyone,[1] Wilde was unfavourably comparing nature to art. Wilde (1989: 970) wrote: "What Art really reveals to us is Nature's lack of design, her curious crudities, her extraordinary monotony, her absolutely unfinished condition . . . Art is our spirited protest, our gallant attempt to teach Nature her proper place."[2]

Even among those who value nature, there are important differences both in the degree and in the way in which they value it. Members of the Sierra Club, historical descendants of Muir, value nature for its restorative and spiritual qualities. They say on their website: "For nearly 100 years, Sierra Club members have shared a vision of humanity living in harmony with the Earth".[3]

Earlier versions of this essay were presented to the International Society for Environmental Ethics meeting in conjunction with the American Philosophical Association (APA) in December 2000; at Bowling Green State University; and at Rutgers University. I thank my APA commentators, Lori Gruen and David Schmidtz, for their generous responses; Katie McShane for extensive comments on an earlier draft; Colin McGinn for a useful suggestion; and "the Davids" (Copp and Soble) for a helpful (if breathless) conversation.

[1] http://www.sierraclub.org/john_muir_exhibit/

[2] It should be noted that this quotation is in the voice of a character, Vivian, who is one party to a dialogue, and that in other places Wilde seems to suggest that he places a high value on nature, for example, when he writes that "[t]he things of nature do not really belong to us; we should leave them to our children, as we have received them" (Keyes 1996: 104). I thank John A. Fisher and J. J. Saulino for these references.

[3] http://www.sierraclub.org/policy/bylaws/goalsandpurposes.asp

Many Minnesotans who are not members of the Sierra Club value nature just as intensely, but their interest is in the recreational possibilities that nature presents. These Minnesotans want to hunt, fish, and snowmobile, not hike, meditate, and birdwatch. They see nature as a playground, not as a cathedral.[4]

One way of marking the difference between these Minnesotans and members of the Sierra Club is to say that while members of the Sierra Club recognize values in nature, these Minnesotans derive value from nature. Some might make this point by saying that members of the Sierra Club value nature "intrinsically", while these Minnesotans value nature "instrumentally". From such rhetorical heights the temptation to commit metaphysics is almost irresistible. Value is theorized as inhering in nature, to be apprehended or perceived by the sensitive and discerning.[5] A bright line is then drawn between these realists and objectivists, and those who do not share such expansive metaphysics, such as projectivists, expressivists, and subjectivists, who instead see values as in some way "gilding and staining" the objects of value "with the colours borrowed from internal sentiment".[6] The clash of cultures begins with this lobbing of labels: deep ecologists, Gaians, and environmental philosophers on one side; economists, traditional philosophers, followers of Middle Eastern religions, and (some) Minnesotans, on the other.

The central claim of this essay is that various metaethical commitments neither disable nor uniquely enable strong commitments to nature.[7] This does not mean that there are no interesting relations between metaethical and normative stances, only that one is not determinative of the other. This thought provides some support for the general view that the heavy-duty philosophizing of the cultural warriors is largely irrelevant to developing, maintaining, and acting on serious green commitments. However, in order to reach this conclusion, we are going to have to do some metaethics ourselves.

I begin by providing a topography of the sources of value, briefly sketching how various views can be seen to be consistent with strong commitments to protect nature. Next I briefly sketch one particular metaethical perspective, defend it from several objections, and tell a story about how it makes

---

[4] See Lanegram (2000).

[5] This view is reminiscent of the intuitionism much in vogue in Oxford and Cambridge during the Edwardian period. Perhaps this is related to the common perception of environmentalists as elitists.

[6] These are Hume's words in reference to taste in the *Enquiry Concerning Human Understanding* (1748/1975: 230).

[7] Various philosophers defend similar views, including Blackburn (1998), and Elliot (1997). So far as I can see, however, my thesis does not commit one to any particular metaphysical or metaethical views, whether Blackburn's quasi-realist programme, Elliot's subjectivism, or any other such view.

intelligible some of our moral practices. Finally, I draw some conclusions and mark the limits of what I have accomplished.

2. THE SOURCES OF VALUE

In this section I characterize three families of views about the sources of value. I begin, however, with some remarks on the idea of value having a source, a captivating image that has come into recent prominence, notably in the writings of Christine M. Korsgaard (1996a, chs. 8 and 9; and 1996b, lecture 4).

First some etymology. The word 'source' was apparently borrowed from Old French, and in its earliest English uses it refers broadly to anything which supports something else. In a paradigm use it refers to a column that supports a tabernacle in a church. By the late fourteenth century the word 'source' was also being used to refer to the fountainhead of a river or stream. It is this sense of 'source' that accounts for the power of this idea in value theory. Korsgaard (1996a: 259) writes that "[g]oodness, as it were, flows into the world from the good will, and there would be none without it". The image of goodness flowing into the world, as if bubbling out of a spring, is indeed a beautiful one, but we should not let the poetry blind us to the fact that the idea of the source of value is multiply ambiguous. In one sense the source of value is that in virtue of which something is valuable; in another sense it is that which causes something to be valuable; and in still another sense it is a necessary condition for something to be valuable. However, so long as we are alert to the danger of equivocation, the ambiguity can be tolerated. In what follows I will think of the source of value (simply and vaguely) as a logical requirement on value. I leave open the question of what exactly is the nature of this logical requirement. Like most philosophers who discuss the source of value, I will work with an intuitive understanding, only being precise enough for immediate purposes. Now, back to the show.[8]

On one view the source of value is individual valuers and their attitudes. Call this view subjectivism and say that on this view all value flows from individuals. On a second view, some values are seen as socially constructed. Call this view conventionalism and say that it holds that value flows from communities, as well as perhaps from individuals. A third view maintains that there is a source of value external to individual valuers and communities. Call this view realism and say that it teaches that some value flows from nature.

---

[8] This paragraph has benefited from correspondence with Sarah Holtman and Valerie Tiberius. For further discussion of the metaphor of 'the source of value' see Rabinowicz and Ronnow-Rasumussen (2000).

Before discussing these views in detail, I want to make three preliminary points.

First, it should be noticed that this taxonomy is in some ways misleading. Individuals are parts of communities, and communities and individuals (as Greens seem never to tire of telling us) are part of nature. Nor is 'realism' a good name for the view that nature is the source of value. For it is not just nature that is real; conventions and attitudes are real too, and conventionalists and subjectivists should not give away this word without a fight. But for present purposes, I will contrast realism with conventionalism and subjectivism.

Secondly, in the literature these terms are variously used to refer to semantic, epistemological, and moral psychological views, as well as metaphysical ones. Although I cannot argue the point here, I believe that substantially the same issues arise in each of these idioms, although perhaps in somewhat different forms.

Finally, subjectivism, as I understand it, is the view that all values are subjective; conventionalism is the view that some values are conventionalist and no values are realist; and realism is the view that some values are realist. Thus, conventionalism can encompass subjectivist values, and realism can encompass both conventionalist and subjectivist values. In what follows, I will be concerned with putative values that distinguish these views rather than those that all views might seek to accommodate in the same way. While there are other ways of taxonomizing this domain, I'm going to do it my way. Now for the main event.

Realism comes in two main forms: naturalism and non-naturalism.

Naturalism is the view that values in nature are instantiated by suitably structured sets of natural properties.[9] Examples of natural properties include extension and mass, and may also include complex or relational properties such as genetic structure, species membership, naturalness, wildness, and so on. It is sets of natural properties that matter since value may require the instantiation of a disjunction or conjunction of properties. This of course does not rule out the possibility that a set of value-instantiating properties may be a singleton. For example, someone could hold that value in nature is instantiated by wildness, and that other properties of nature are irrelevant to nature having value. The idea that the sets of properties in question must be suitably structured allows us to recognize a range of possible relations that value may

[9] Among environmental philosophers, I would count Holmes Rolston III as a naturalist, though his views are not easy to classify; see his 1988. Generally, for naturalism about values see e.g. Boyd (1988) and Railton (1986).

bear to the sets of properties that instantiate it. For example, some may hold that value in nature is identical to wildness, others may hold that in some sense it supervenes on wildness, while still others may hold that value emerges from wildness.[10]

The second form of realism is non-naturalism. Non-naturalism holds that the properties in virtue of which value is instantiated are not natural properties such as extension, mass, and so on, but rather non-natural properties such as the simple, indefinable property of goodness.[11] Of course the complications and variations discussed earlier about exactly how properties may instantiate values (e.g. through identity, supervenience, emergence, or some other relation) obtain here as well.

Whatever else may be true of realism, it is easy to see how it countenances values in nature. Consider the following sentence:

(1) The Brooks Range is valuable.

According to realism, (1) is true in virtue of the Brooks Range instantiating some suitably structured set of natural or non-natural properties. Since properties of the Brooks Range figure centrally in the truth-maker of (1), it is natural to speak of value inhering in the Brooks Range and, thus, this being an instance of values in nature.[12] So, complications aside, realism is clearly congenial to assertions of values in nature. It is the other families of views, conventionalism and subjectivism, that have come under suspicion. Let us examine how subjectivism and conventionalism might treat sentences such as (1).

Consider first subjectivism. One version of subjectivism holds that sentences such as (1) are non-propositional expressions of individual speakers' inner states.[13] Thus, properties exemplified by speakers or by the Brooks Range do not figure in truth-makers for these sentences since such sentences do not have truth conditions. However, a second version of subjectivism holds that sentences such as (1) are true just in case the speaker approves of the Brooks Range.[14] The speaker's approving state with respect to the Brooks Range is central to the truth-maker for such sentences.

---

[10] On the varieties of supervenience see Kim (1984/1993); for the concept of emergence see his 1999.
[11] The classic text here is Moore (1903).
[12] We need to be careful, however, since, depending on one's taste in metaphysics, someone might hold, for example, that the truth-maker for (1) is the fact that the Brooks Range is valuable rather than some property of the Brooks Range. Either way, however, properties instantiated by the Brooks Range are central to the truth-maker for (1) even if they themselves are not the truth-makers.
[13] See Ayer (1952).
[14] See Elliot (1997).

The heart of conventionalism is the view that values are cultural construc-tions.[15] One version of conventionalism is simply a quantified version of the second version of subjectivism discussed above. An example of such a view would hold that sentence (1) is true just in case most speakers in our com-munity approve of the Brooks Range. There are, of course, many versions of conventionalism. Communities may construct values in different ways, and there are more quantifiers than natural numbers. Furthermore, approval is only one of the attitudes that might be thought to underwrite value claims. Other such attitudes may include beliefs that the thing in question is of merit, desires that it be widely appreciated, and so on.

What this brief survey shows is that there are versions of subjectivism and conventionalism that imply that sentences such as (1) have truth-makers. Such views hold, for example, that (1) is true just in case the speaker, or most members of the speaker's community, approve of the Brooks Range. Thus, it would seem that such views countenance values in nature.

However, many realists would object to the claim that subjectivism and con-ventionalism can countenance values in nature. They would agree that, from the perspective of these views, claims such as (1) have truth-makers, but since properties of nature do not centrally figure in these truth-makers, they would deny that such views in fact countenance values in nature.

It is not exactly clear what counts as properties of nature. In the case pre-sented, a subjectivist can plausibly claim that being approved of by the speaker appears to be a property of the Brooks Range, and that this property figures centrally in the truth-maker for (1). The realist may want to deny that such apparent properties are real properties of nature, but the onus is on him to show why. It would be implausible to claim that the relational properties of the Brooks Range do not count as real properties of nature, since such impor-tant properties of the Brooks Range as its wildness, naturalness, uniqueness, fragility, and its being prime grizzly and caribou habitat, are all relational.[16] Indeed, in the eyes of many people, it is precisely in virtue of exemplifying these properties that the Brooks Range is valuable.

The Realist's central mistake, according to this critic, is that he confuses the sources of values with their contents.[17] Subjectivism and conventionalism are

---

[15] For a general discussion of some views that can reasonably be characterized as conventionalist, see (Harman 1977, chs. 8 and 9).

[16] The distinction between relational and non-relational properties is not easy to draw in any case. For some relevant discussion see Lewis, "Extrinsic Properties", and Lewis and Langton, "Defining 'Intrinsic'", both reprinted in Lewis (1999).

[17] This important distinction has been drawn in different ways by different philosophers. See e.g. Essay 14; and Callicott (1989), and O'Neill (2001).

theses about what makes moral utterances true, not theses about the contents of moral utterances.[18] Even if I am the source of the Brooks Range having value, sentence (1) is about the Brooks Range, not about me.[19]

Consider how a subjectivist might try to defend the view that her theory countenances values in nature. She might begin in this way. Suppose that subjectivism is true and that I approve of the Brooks Range. It follows from these premises that (1) is true. The next step in the argument is to show that the truth of (1) is sufficient for supposing that there are values in nature; that is, that it follows from the fact that the Brooks Range is valuable that there are values in nature. On the face of it, this inference appears to be quite plausible. If challenged to provide evidence for the truth of the claim that there are values in nature, it would seem natural to assert sentences such as (1). And, indeed, this move is what we might expect from both subjectivists and realists, despite their metaphysical differences.

A further, more general, argument can be given on behalf of the view that subjectivists can countenance values in nature. Someone can be quite confident of the truth of (1), yet quite agnostic about metaethical matters. She could be confident of her belief that there are values in nature, and that deep green normative commitments naturally flow from these beliefs, yet she might be clueless when it comes to adjudicating disputes between realists and anti-realists. Indeed, she may not know that such disputes exist. Despite her ignorance or agnosticism, her everyday assertions and behaviour may be impeccable. If this story is plausible, then metaethical views (or the lack thereof) are quite detachable from the belief that there are values in nature. If this is so, then there is no inconsistency in the idea of subjectivism countenancing values in nature.[20]

A realist will rightly feel uneasy about this argument. The obvious objection is to inferring the conclusion, that metaethical commitments are detachable from normative commitments, from the case of a person who sees no connection herself between them. After all, she could be wrong. One, two, or three billion people making an inference does not make it valid. What is at issue is a logical, not a psychological, point.

Maybe. However, I submit that most people do not have consistent,

---

[18] A different story would have to be told about metaethical views, such as Ayer's which do not construe moral utterances as truth-apt. It may be possible to give such a story by characterizing an alternative notion that has some important features of truth.

[19] While I believe that this claim is true, I confess that it is not easy to say precisely what sentences are about. See Goodman (1961/1972).

[20] It is easy to see how a conventionalist can tell a story that is analogous to the one that I have told for the subjectivist.

coherent, reflective, metaethical views. In everyday life we commit acts of metaethics when reflective thought, unreflective argument, or the simple pressure of serious disagreement takes us to the brink of a rhetorical abyss. At such moments we employ metaethical strategies in the service of our practical ends. On this view, metaethics should be seen as a form of conversational manoeuvring that is part of our everyday moral practice rather than as some immaculate conception that sits in judgement on our practices.[21]

However, the metaethical project of philosophers, rightly understood, is different from either of these approaches. It is an attempt to make sense of how we use moral language. The fact that in everyday life we go on in metaethical ignorance and apparent confusion, suggests (to me, anyway) that the coherence and functionality of our everyday moral practices do not depend on their being backed by some particular metaethical view.[22] Whether we are realists, subjectivists, or, as I suggest most of us are, metaethical opportunists, we go on arguing about sentences such as (1) in more or less the same way—some of us asserting, some denying, and most of us dodging. This suggests that an attempt to impose metaethical correctness on the understanding of sentences such as (1) is part of a reforming philosophical project, rather than an attempt to appreciate everyday discourse and practice. In other words, it is philosophy run amok.[23]

These remarks may seem especially controversial because they are about normative matters, but consider the question of truth, which is in some ways analogous. Tarski's definition of truth (for example) may be important for many reasons, but not because it dramatically vindicates all those hapless souls who go around saying that various things are true or false, in complete ignorance of Convention T. The philosophical project of defining truth is different from the ordinary practice of ascribing truth and falsity. One does not depend on the other, and this is what I am suggesting with respect to the relations between metaethics and everyday moral practice.

Another source of unease that the realist may have is that the subjectivist may be open to objections to which the realist is immune. In particular, some may be impressed by metaphysical arguments against subjectivism which have no traction against realism. A realist may (grudgingly) be brought to

---

[21]   This is not to say that anything goes. Moral theorizing, which sits between metaethics and downright moralizing, involves appeals to consistency, universalization, total utility, and so on. What I insist is that these activities are all part of everyday moral discourse, and that full-blown theories are philosophical constructions that are (in part) hypostasizations of these activities. I discuss these matters further in Jamieson (1991a).

[22]   Thus I assert a version of what Johnston (1992) calls "minimalism".

[23]   Lest I be misunderstood, I refer the reader to Section 5 of this essay and to Jamieson (1999a).

agree that, in principle, subjectivism can account for our normative responses, but still may insist that the actual patterns of our normative discourse are more plausibly captured by appeal to the sorts of properties that realists valorize, rather than those to which subjectivists appeal. I have some sympathy with this view, as will become clear in the next section. However, it is important to see that, while realism may fare better than subjectivism with respect to some objections, the converse may be true with respect to others.

Common metaphysical intuitions (those of philosophers anyway) may be more difficult for subjectivism to cope with than for realism, but realism has a more difficult time than subjectivism in explaining the connection between motivation and normative commitments. If I approve of something it is easy to see why I am motivated to protect it. It is less easy to see why I should be motivated to protect something because it instantiates a property, and downright difficult to see why I should be motivated to protect something because this motivation is consistent with prevailing social attitudes.

The metaphysical robustness of realism also makes it a tempting target for epistemological objections, to which subjectivism is relatively immune. It is very difficult to see how to resolve disagreements between people who have different views about whether the Brooks Range instantiates some non-natural property, or whether the set of natural properties which it instantiates is suitably structured so as to constitute value. On the other hand, sceptics will not get very far challenging the epistemological basis of my knowledge claims about what I approve of, or my claims about the reigning normative conventions of my community.

What the sceptical arguments bring out is that different metaethical views have different implications about how the case for values in nature would have to be made. Various metaethical stances draw our attention to various features of ourselves, society, and the world. But while these arguments bring out important differences between metaethical views, and may provide some reason for preferring one to another, they do not add up to a demonstration that one view is uniquely enabled or disabled with respect to supporting deep green commitments.

3. METAETHICAL PLURALISM

Thus far we have considered views that are absolute in conception. The versions of realism, conventionalism, and subjectivism that we have discussed are at war. Each denounces the other, without taking on board the considerations adduced by partisans of the other perspectives. Thus, for example, according to the versions of realism that we have discussed, there are some values such that individuals and communities have no role to play in their constitution. A similar exclusivity is also characteristic of the versions of conventionalism and subjectivism that we have considered. While versions of each of these views can account for the truth of sentences such as (1), and thus countenance values in nature, in my opinion none of these absolute conceptions is plausible. An intuitively plausible metaethic, in my opinion, would find a place for elements of all of these families of views. Individual responses may be the ultimate source of all values, but these responses are constrained and guided both by nature and communities, and they occur in particular contexts.

My own version of such a view might be called sensible objectivism. It is a form of objectivism since it founds value on a richer basis than a subject's approval, but it is sensible in that it renounces realism.[24] It is pluralist in that it views values as arising from transactions between individuals, communities, and nature, in particular contexts. It is occasionalist in that the contributions of each element that figures in these transactions may differ across occasions. While it may be possible to write some very general, true, biconditional that links what is valuable to contexts, individuals, communities, and nature, I doubt that it would be very informative. On a particular occasion, say one in which vitamin B12 is the object of value, nature may play an extremely important role. On another occasion, say when a work of conceptual art is the object of value, nature may play almost no role in the transaction. Understanding episodes of valuing is something to be done on the ground, not from the air.

In what follows, I will not say much to develop this view, and even less to argue for it. For present purposes what is important is to show the power of a simple thought: that valuing is a contextualized, constrained, object-directed activity. Once we see that the concept of value is a derivative notion—a hypostasization of contextual, constrained, object-directed, valuing activities—we can better understand and resist the temptations of realism.[25] Perhaps then we will feel free to adopt sensible metaethical views or, better yet, to escape our obsession with metaethical questions altogether.

Valuing is something that people do. On the face of it, this may not sound terribly controversial or interesting, but nevertheless over a broad range of discourse the language of values tends to drive out the language of valuing, and

[24] This expression, 'sensible objectivism', is meant to recall Wiggins's (1998, ch. 5) 'sensible subjectivism', the view that is probably closest to the one I sketch here.
[25] For a different view of the relation between valuing and values see Harman (2000).

this is not merely a matter of substituting harmless terminological equivalents. The move from talk about valuing to the language of values is a move towards greater objectification, which itself reflects an escalation in speakers' concerns about what is at stake in the discourse.

Consider the following trios of sentences:

(2) I like chocolate.
(3) I value chocolate.
(4) Chocolate is valuable.

(5) I like solitude.
(6) I value solitude.
(7) Solitude is valuable.

(8) I like world peace.
(9) I value world peace.
(10) World peace is valuable.

Sentence (2) sounds perfectly natural, while both sentences (3) and (4) sound odd. Chocolate is something that we like or not; it is not the sort of thing that we think of as valuable or even the sort of thing that it seems natural to value. It is more plausible to value solitude, however, so (6) sounds about as natural as (5). (7) is acceptable as well but seems to invite completion: for what purpose is solitude valuable? World peace, on the other hand, is so clearly a good that, while (10) seems natural, (8) is curiously weak. Although there are some who glorify war, the first-person pronoun seems out of place when referring to the value of world peace. Nor does (10) seem to require completion in the way that (7) does. While it seems reasonable to ask what solitude is good for, it seems strange to ask the same question about world peace.

The moral of the story is this. As the stakes become higher, as the object of our desire becomes more important to us, we tend to objectify the desire. We begin by expressing our desires in terms of what we like or prefer; then it becomes a matter of what we value; and finally, it is a question of what is valuable. The payoff of this ascent is clear. If something is valuable, then (*ceteris paribus*) everyone should promote or protect it, but no such implication immediately follows from the fact that I like something.[26]

We also make distinctions among the things that we find valuable. According to some philosophers, some things are only of instrumental value, while other things are of intrinsic value. From here it is easy to begin talking about

---

[26] Of course, it does not follow from something being valuable that we have reason to produce more of it. On this point see Dworkin (1993, ch. 3).

"intrinsic values", and soon we may find ourselves on safari in search of values in nature.[27]

Part of what drives this dynamic is the elusive search for (rhetorically and rationally) commanding heights. Intrinsic values trump mere preferences, so wilderness, if it can be shown to have intrinsic value, wins against logging; and, of course, environmental philosophers, with the heavy artillery of intrinsic value on their side, triumph over economists, who have only the slingshot of preference at their disposal.

A more theoretical explanation for this temptation to objectify appeals to the widespread lack of appreciation of the depth, complexity, and available resources in our evaluational structures. Environmental philosophers have tended to fixate on the distinction between intrinsic and instrumental value. Yet intrinsic versus instrumental is only one of many distinctions in our evaluational repertoire. Indeed, this distinction is itself often unstable and fails to have the import that some would suppose. Think of Paula whom I value for her own sake, and also instrumentally for the efficient way in which she keeps my computer from crashing. Or consider the following complicated story.

Suppose that I buy a painting to cover a hole in the wall. Initially I value the painting instrumentally, but when it is hung on the wall I come to value it intrinsically as well. Indeed, I come to value it so greatly that I hang it on another wall where it can be seen to greater advantage. I no longer care about its role in covering the hole in the wall. I have come to value the painting only intrinsically, not instrumentally. But through time I become tired of the painting. A figure in the background begins to remind me of the wicked stepfather who made my childhood so painful. I find that I no longer value the painting intrinsically. I return it to its previous position. But the image of the wicked stepfather continues to haunt me. The house isn't big enough for the two of us. Like any other soap opera, this saga could continue indefinitely. The point is that our evaluational outlooks are dynamic; they are not boringly stable through time, life, and experience.

As for the idea that what I value intrinsically is always more important to me than what I value instrumentally, suppose that I am on a cliff, hanging by a thread above the boiling waters, thousands of feet below. I value the thread by which I am hanging vastly more than my stamp collection, even though I value my stamp collection intrinsically and the string instrumentally.

---

[27] There are several distinct senses of 'intrinsic value'. The one that I am concerned with here is the one that is roughly equivalent to "end in itself". For more on the varieties of intrinsic value, see O'Neil (2001).

As we have seen, even the supposedly simple distinction between intrinsically and instrumentally valuing turns out to be surprisingly complex, and this is only the beginning of the story. In what follows I will gesture towards a few of the remaining complexities.

Let us begin with a paradigm of instrumentally valuing something: I value the matches in my kitchen because they allow me to light the stove. Now notice how different the following cases of non-intrinsically valuing are from this paradigm of instrumentally valuing. I value the photograph of Grete because it represents Grete, whom I value intrinsically. I value the cheerful bark of the dog next door because it reminds me of Grete's infectious exuberance. I value my lover's smile because it embodies her kindness and generosity. I value each step on the ascent of Mt. Princeton (in the Collegiate Peaks Wilderness Area in Colorado), not instrumentally because it will result in getting me to the summit, but because it is part-constitutive of mountain climbing, an activity which I value intrinsically. These examples only begin to suggest the richness of the relationships that exist in our evaluational structures.[28]

What I have been suggesting is that beginning from the idea of valuing as a contextualized, constrained, object-directed activity, we can understand and make intelligible a wide array of evaluative activities. However, thus far the account that I have given is not only incomplete, but also thin and abstract. I want to try to fatten it up by reminding us of a story, told in Essay 14, about how we may actually come to value an aspect of nature.

Many people think of deserts as horrible places that are not worth protecting. I disagree. I value deserts intrinsically and think you should too. How do I proceed? One thing I might do is take you camping with me. We might see the desert's nocturnal inhabitants, the plants that have adapted to these conditions, the shifting colours of the landscape as the day wears on, and the rising of the moon on the stark features of the desert. Together we might experience the feel of the desert wind, hear the silence of the desert, and sense its solitude. You may become interested in how it is that this place was formed, what sustains it, how its plants and animals make a living. As you learn more about the desert, you may come to see it differently and to value it more. This may lead you to spend more time in the desert, seeing it in different seasons, watching the spring with its incredible array of flowers turn to the haunting stillness of summer. You might start reading some desert literature, from the

---

[28] For further discussion see Carter (2000), and James Harold's University of Minnesota doctoral dissertation, "Value Coherence", 2001. In this section I have benefited from correspondence with Ned Hettinger.

monastic fathers of the church to Edward Abbey. Your appreciation would continue to grow.

But there is no guarantee that things will go this way. You may return from your time in the desert hot, dirty, hungry for a burger, thirsty for a beer, and ready to volunteer your services to the US Army Corps of Engineers (whose *raison d'être* seems to be to flood as much of the earth's surface as possible). Similarly, some people see Venice as a dysfunctional collection of dirty old buildings, find Kant boring and wrong, and hear Mahler as simultaneously excessively romantic and annoyingly dissonant. More experience only makes matters worse.

If someone fails to appreciate the desert, Venice, or Mahler, they need not have made any logical error. Our evaluative responses are not uniquely determined by our constitution or the world. We can be brought to appreciate Venice, Mahler, or the desert by collectively and interactively educating our sensibilities, tastes, and judgements, but such change often involves a deep reorientation of how we see the world. When I try to get you to appreciate the desert I direct your attention to objects in your visual field, but I am trying to change your way of seeing and thinking and your whole outlook towards nature. I am also trying to change our relationship from one of difference to one of solidarity.

Although I have only been able to hint at a fuller story, once we begin to see how far we can go in appreciating and understanding our moral life from the perspective of a metaethical pluralism that takes seriously the idea that valuing is a contextualized, constrained, object-driven activity, I believe (and hope) that the attractions of realism will wane.

4. OBJECTIONS

In this section I will consider three related objections to my central claim that a wide range of metaethical views including realism, conventionalism, and subjectivism can countenance values in nature. I call these the Conceptual Objection, the Phenomenology Objection, and the Urgency Objection. I will discuss them in turn.

According to the Conceptual Objection, I have overlooked the importance of the claim that values are *in* nature. Perhaps I am right in supposing that various subjectivists and conventionalists can supply truth conditions for sentences such as (1); it doesn't follow from this that there are values in nature. What the objector balks at is the inference from (1) to the conclusion that there values in nature.

Here is how the argument might go. Consider the following sentence.

(11) Kelly is in the gym.

When we say that Kelly is in the gym we suppose that Kelly's being in the gym is not dependent on my grasping the fact that Kelly is in the gym. Kelly would still be in the gym whether or not I grasped this fact; or, indeed, whether or not I was around at all. Whether or not Kelly is now pumping iron is completely independent of any thoughts that I (or we) might have about the matter. As with Kelly in the gym, so with values in nature. We may grasp (or fail to grasp) values in nature, but their existence does not depend on our so grasping them, or even on whether we exist. Values that are truly in nature are mind-independent, just as Kelly being in the gym is mind-independent. What this example is supposed to bring out is that only Realism can account for the mind-independence of values in nature. Subjectivism (for example) may be able to recruit truth-makers for (1) and convince us that they can rightly be said to reflect properties of nature, but such properties as "being approved of by the speaker" have no claim to mind-independence. Thus they cannot underwrite the claim that there are values *in* nature.

One might cavil at this in a number of ways. One response is to point out that some things that are in something are mind-independent and some things are not. I suppose it would be trivial to point out that the present king of France was in my dream last night, and that his existence is certainly not mind-independent. It is not trivial, however, to point out that it is at least contestable about what we should say concerning such qualities as colour. That colours are not mind-independent, yet are in objects, appears to be one respectable opinion.[29] Are values in nature like Kelly in the gym or are they like redness in the balloon?

One attempt to answer this question appeals to a thought experiment. In a landmark article, Richard and Val Routley (1980) ask us to consider a series of "last man" cases.[30] In one such case, the last man, knowing that he is the final existing sentient being, acts in such a way as to ensure the destruction, after his own death, of the earth with all its ecosystems and landscapes. Surely, it is said, we would think that something valuable has been destroyed, and this

---

[29] For discussion, see Hardin (1988: 59 ff.) and Byrne and Hilbert (1997).

[30] These cases are related to Moore's (1903: 83–4) thought experiment in which he asks us to imagine, "quite apart from any possible contemplation by human beings", an "exceedingly beautiful" world, and a world "containing everything that is most disgusting to us". Moore thinks it is clear that we would do what we could to produce the beautiful world rather than the disgusting one, and that this shows that Sidgwick (1907/1981: 489 ff.) is wrong when he says that "[n]o one would consider it rational to aim at the production of beauty in external nature, apart from any contemplation of it by human beings".

shows that there are mind-independent values in nature that cannot be taken up by subjectivists and conventionalists. There are many ways of responding to this argument, of which the most fundamental is this: we can share the judgement, that the last man destroys something of value, and still reject the conclusion that the value in question is mind-independent. True enough, after his demise there are no minds in the world of the last man; but the value judgement about that world is made by us, now, in our world. The value that we judge to be lost necessarily stands in relations to us.

Another attempt to answer this question appeals to semantics. On this view, part of what it means for values to be in nature is for them to be mind-independent. The truth of realism and the denial of subjectivism and conventionalism follow on semantic grounds from the claim that there are values in nature. This is an attempt to obtain by definition what thus far the realist has not been able to gain by argument, and I believe that it threatens to trivialize the dispute between green realists and their opponents. Green realists get steamed up about this debate because it is a substantial debate. Many of them think that subjectivism is false and pernicious; this is not the attitude one typically takes towards semantic errors. Moreover, viewing the relation between values in nature and realism as semantic is to beg the question against those who oppose realism. No opponent of realism worth her salt will be fazed by such an argument. Indeed, she might respond that if a commitment to realism is built into the semantics of the expression, 'values in nature', then we should say that there are no values in nature. But who cares? We can still love and value nature intensely, while denying realism.

There are views of semantics and semantic discovery which would preserve many of the elements of supposing that the dispute between realism and anti-realism is a substantial one, but this is a response that I cannot pursue here.[31] Indeed, as I have hinted, I think there is something odd about the entire dispute between realists and their opponents, and the reliance on intuitions that each side mobilizes and treats as authoritative is one of its disagreeable features. My project here can best be seen as an attempt to demote the importance of the dispute, rather than as a defence of realism's opponents. Still, what is important to see is that many green realists are committed not just to the truth of realism, but also to the importance of their doctrine. Winning the argument through fancy semantic footwork threatens to trivialize their own position.

---

[31] For a relevant discussion, see Jackson (1998).

The second objection is the Phenomenology Objection. When we have deep, intense experiences—when we climb the Alaskan glaciers, kayak among the seabirds, walk in the rainforests—we feel ourselves in touch with mind-independent values, according to this objector. Realists honour our experiences while subjectivists and conventionalists demand that we renounce the testimony of our own lives.

The problem with this objection is that it confuses what we experience with a particular explanation of what we experience. When climbing an Alaskan glacier or kayaking among the seabirds we may feel awe, respect, and a panoply of other profound emotions. But mind-independent values do not figure in the content of our experience; rather, they figure in a proposed explanation of our experience. The appeal to mind-independent values may appear to provide a natural explanation of our experience, but it is only one among many possible explanations, and it requires defence. The actual facts of our experience do not uniquely determine this as the best explanation.

Indeed, often what might seem to be the most natural explanation of everyday events and experience is not the best one. Folk physics explains the movement of the sun in terms of its orbit around the earth. Folk medicine (at least in my mother's version) teaches that colds are caused by going outside with wet hair. The best explanations of these everyday occurrences are not the ones that apparently feel most natural. David Lewis (1989: 135–6) gets the point almost right when he says:

[A] theory which acknowledges the contingency [of values] cannot feel quite right. You might say that it is unfaithful to the distinctive phenomenological character of lived evaluative thought. Yet even if it feels not right, it may still be right, or as near right as we can get. It feels not quite right to remember that your friends are big swarms of little particles—it is inadequate to the phenomenology of friendship—but still they are.

Lewis, like the objector, fails to distinguish the phenomenology from common-sense theorizing about its cause, and he is too quick to accept what appears to be a reductive identity claim about the nature of friends. Still, the basic point is right: the correct theory may not be the one that is most appealing to common sense. In the case of values in nature, it appears that common sense may prefer the metaphysically extravagant explanation over one that is more sober and austere. But there is no reason why we should indulge common sense in this way.

The third objection is the Urgency Objection, which has two related dimensions. One dimension suggests that only realist values can account for the urgency of our views about nature. If we come to believe that our values are only thinly grounded in the Nature of Things, we will lose confidence in them. We will no longer be able to move from believing that there are values in nature to serious green commitments. The second dimension, which is often thought to reinforce or even entail the first, conjures up the threat of relativism. Unless value is mind-independent, anything goes. Experience machines are as good as experience, Disney-desert is the same as the real thing, and Madonna and Mahler are colleagues in the same business (one strikingly more successful than the other).

Even if there were sound arguments for such conclusions they would not show that realism is true. The most they would show is that the rejection of realism should be kept as an esoteric doctrine, its teaching confined to the *cognoscenti* and other keepers of the secrets.[32] Foot-soldiers in the green brigades should be protected from this teaching, for fear it would erode their courage in battle.

There is a deeper problem with this objection, however. Those who suffer this anxiety about whether values are mind-independent confuse a require-ment for value with how value is constituted. Value is mind-dependent, but it is things in the world that are valuable or not. The fact that we draw attention to features of objects in our evaluative discourse is the common property of all theories of value.

The anxious philosophers who raise this objection fail to appreciate how powerful psychological and cultural mechanisms can be in constituting objectivity. Culture, history, tradition, knowledge, and convention mediate our constitutions and the world. Culture, together with our constitutions and the world, determines our evaluative practices. Since the world and our constitutions alone are not sufficient for determining them, common values should be seen in part as cultural achievements rather than simply as true reports about the nature of things or expressions of what we are essentially. Evaluative practices are in the domain of negotiation and collective construc-tion as well as reflection and recognition. But the fact that these practices are in part constructed does not mean that they cannot be rigid and compelling.[33]

---

[32] See Sidgwick (1907/1981).

[33] An entirely different approach to the first and third objections would be to treat realist claims as expressions of enthusiasm in everyday moral discourse rather than as sober statements about moral ontology. This is Blackburn's (1998) approach and is also in the spirit of Dworkin (1996) (notwith-standing the fact that they seem to think they are in serious disagreement; see their exchange on the Brown University Electronic Article Review Service
(http://www.brown.edu/Departments/Philosophy/bears/9611blac.html)).

5. CONCLUSIONS

The main conclusion I have tried to establish is that a variety of metaethical views are compatible with a commitment to values in nature. Because the largest shadow in this regard has fallen over subjectivism, much of my attention has been devoted to showing that it too can countenance values in nature. However my preferred view is sensible objectivism—a version of metaethical pluralism that views valuing as a contextualized, constrained, object-directed activity—but I have neither developed nor defended that view in detail. If I have been successful in achieving my main purpose, the result should be the deflating of some of the more ubiquitous metaphysical pretensions of environmental philosophy. Yes, deep ecologists, ecofeminists, process theologians, and postmodern bioregionalists love nature; but so can expressivists, projectivists, and even logical positivists.

The larger moral of these reflections is that philosophy, understood as the appreciation of, and reflection on, our practices, leaves the world alone. It may inform and incline our thoughts and actions, but it cannot determine them. In order to teach us how to live, philosophy needs the world and experience. Different metaethical theories provide different accounts of the roles that a range of considerations about how to live and what we should care about play in structuring and producing moral practice, but it is these fundamental considerations themselves that animate our moral lives and motivate change. The power of the green case is to be found in facts about the human domination of nature and our responses to them, not in dubious metaphysics.

17

The City around Us

1. INTRODUCTION

1.1 *The Way We Are*

It may seem odd to many people that a book devoted to environmental ethics includes an essay on the city. We often speak of the environment as if it is everywhere except where we live. The environment is Yellowstone, Estes Park, Cape Hatteras, and other vacation spots. It is the Amazon River basin, Alaska, East Africa, places that many of us care about preserving even though we will never visit them. Indeed, the very logic of wilderness preservation demands that most of us will never visit these areas. For if a great many of us were to visit, say, the Maroon Bells Wilderness Area in Colorado, it would soon take on the trappings of an urban park. That so many of us are willing to pay to preserve places that we never expect to visit confounds conventional economists and would-be developers. After all, what could the value of these areas consist in if not their extractable resources and their potential for recreational development? It is no wonder that such people have no better explanation for the rise of preservationism than that it is a conspiracy of wealthy "limousine liberals" who are out to deny the rest of us the benefits of economic growth. But this story is one that we cannot pursue in this essay. What is important here is that many of us think of the environment as including "the sea around us", in the words of the American naturalist Rachel Carson, but excluding the city around us, and this is a serious mistake. The environment in which most

I would like to thank Professor Dana Cuff for her many helpful suggestions, not all of which I have been able to follow; and Lori Gruen who has been enormously helpful in assisting with my research. In addition, I am grateful to the Organized Research Fund of the Colorado Commission on Higher Education for the grant that supported this project in its early stages.

of us spend most of our time is the urban environment, and any deep understanding of our relationship to the environment cannot ignore this fact.

Increasing urbanization has been a worldwide trend for several centuries. In 1800 about 2 per cent of the world's population lived in urban areas; by 1900 the figure had doubled to 4 per cent; and by 1976 it was 38 per cent. This trend has been even more dramatic in the United States. In 1800 only 6 per cent of our population lived in cities; by 1900 the figure had increased to 40 per cent; and by 1977, 74 per cent of our population lived in cities.[1] Indeed, depending on how we define the key terms, it is arguable that almost no rural areas remain in the United States. When we think of rural life we often think of our forebears, real or imagined, living their lives almost completely untouched by urban influences. They worked on the land, educated their children at home, made their own household necessities, and joined with neighbours at quilting bees, dances, and hoedowns for recreation. Today almost none of this exists. A drive in the country almost anywhere reveals factories, mines, and warehouses, the accoutrements of the industrial functions associated with cities. Rural people today often commute to industrial jobs, gardening in their spare time. The farm, for the few who still own one, is frequently rented to someone who can afford the enormous capital investment needed to make it profitable. Except for rare exceptions, children are no longer educated at home; they are bussed to consolidated schools where they are taught from the same syllabus prescribed for children in towns and cities. Necessities are purchased on shopping trips to the city, or at the new K-Mart in what used to be the village. Entertainment is mostly television and the latest records from *Billboard*'s "Hot 100". Almost the only remaining rural areas are those that are preserved by the federal government, and even some of these would have to be excepted. Yosemite, for example, is one of California's largest cities from May to September. It even has its own jail! And the amenities available there far exceed those that can be obtained in most small towns. But however we define the key terms, it is clear that the urban environment is pervasive. Cities are central in our lives, and despite this or because of it, we both love them and hate them.

1.2 Views of the City

Americans have always had complicated and ambiguous attitudes towards cities. This is reflected in political rhetoric, literature, films, philosophy, and

---

[1] The international statistics are taken from the Population Reference Bureau (1976). The American statistics are from the Bureau of Census (1971). Recent data confirm these trends. See e.g. various reports available from The Population Institute (www.populationinstitute.org).

even architecture. Some intellectuals have been overtly anti-urban. They have seen the city as decadent and depraved; it could corrupt even the best of people. Others have not been anti-urban in principle, but they have viewed American cities as vastly inferior to those of Europe. According to these thinkers, American cities celebrate crass materialism and vulgar commerce at the expense of community, cultivation, and refinement.

The first important anti-urban tract written in America was Thomas Jefferson's *Notes on the State of Virginia*, composed in 1781. Jefferson (1964: 158) argued that cities were inimical to good government: "The mobs of the great cities add just as much to the support of pure government as sores do to the strength of the human body". In a letter to Benjamin Rush, Jefferson wrote: "I view great cities as pestilential to the morals, the health and the liberties of man".[2] Jefferson thought that everyone should be a farmer; or work in an occupation whose services are needed by farmers, like carpenters, masons, and smiths.

Most of our leading nineteenth-century literary figures shared Jefferson's views. Emerson thought that only farmers create wealth, and that all trade rests on their labours. Emerson (1883: 148) also shared Jefferson's views about the moral superiority of the farmer: "That uncorrupted behavior which we admire in animals and in young children belongs to him [the farmer], to the hunter, the sailor—the man who lives in the presence of Nature. Cities force growth and make men talkative and entertaining, but they make them artificial." Emerson's friend Thoreau (1906: 51) disliked cities and their culture even more: "I wish to speak a word for Nature, for absolute freedom and wildness, as contrasted with a freedom and culture merely civil—to regard man as an inhabitant, or a part and parcel of Nature, rather than a member of society". Melville, Hawthorne, and Poe all depicted the city as a sewer of evil and wickedness. In a story set in the future, Poe (1978) portrays a New York so decimated that archaeologists have trouble reconstructing the lives of its inhabitants. Finally, it is determined that nine-tenths of New York was covered by a series of pagodas devoted to the idols of Wealth and Fashion. Although sometimes Henry James tried to like American cities he ultimately failed, living most of his adult life as an expatriate in England. He hated the uniformity of New York's architecture and the diversity of its language and culture. He could never see the skyscraper-dominated skyline as anything other than a "pincushion in profile".

The views of the philosophers were, as we might expect, more subtle and

---

[2] Ford (1905: 146–7).

complex. Although William James did not share completely the views of his brother Henry, he was concerned about the "hollowness" and "brutality" of the large cities. He, along with John Dewey, advocated a decentralized city in which community is recognized as the prime virtue. James's Harvard colleague, California-born Josiah Royce, was more radical in his views. He lodged three charges against the great cities. First, they were so overwhelmed with large numbers of alienated and unassimilated people that the very fabric of society was stretched to breaking point. Secondly, the centralization of culture bred conformity and intellectual stagnation. And thirdly, the cities encouraged the "spirit of the mob" which is antithetical to the preservation of liberty.

In a characteristic passage Royce (1908b: 77) attacks large circulation newspapers on the grounds that they produce "a monotonously uniform triviality of mind in a large proportion of our city and suburban population". Royce's ideal of democracy was the New England town meeting in which "men . . . take counsel together in small groups, who respect one another's individuality, who meanwhile criticize one another constantly" (ibid. 87). He feared that a highly centralized and urbanized nation would "fall rapidly under the hypnotic influence of a few leaders, of a few fatal phrases" (ibid. 95). But contrary to James and Dewey, Royce did not believe that decentralization within the city was a viable solution to urban problems. Rather, Royce advocated a thoroughgoing decentralization of American society in which cities would simply become less important.

We need . . . a newer and wiser provincialism. I mean the sort of provincialism which makes people want to idealize, to adorn, to ennoble, to educate their own province; to hold sacred its traditions, to honor its worthy dead, to support and to multiply its public possessions. I mean the spirit which shows itself in the multiplying of public libraries, in the laying out of public parks, in the work of local historical associations, in the enterprises of village improvement societies . . . I mean also the present form of that spirit which has originated, endowed, and fostered the colleges and universities of our Western towns, cities and states, and which is so well shown throughout our country in our American pride in local institutions of learning.[3]

The views of the most important distinctively American architect, Frank Lloyd Wright, are especially interesting. Wright was raised in rural Wisconsin and never overcame his initial experiences in Chicago. Throughout his life he saw the city as ugly, brutal, and impersonal. He often drew an analogy between cities and malignant tumours, with the architect having the

---

[3] Royce (1908a: 245–6).

responsibility to "take away all urban stricture and depravity . . . and then—absorb and regenerate the tissue poisoned by cancerous overgrowth" (Wright: 1958: 97). Wright thought that technical innovation would make traditional cities obsolete, and envisioned a utopian city he called Broadacre. Now, with the hindsight of almost four decades, it is depressing to realize that Wright's utopian city is more like the sprawling megalopolis of Los Angeles than the functional and picturesque city of San Francisco.

Although the anti-urban tendencies of American thought are very striking indeed, it would be wrong to exaggerate them. Some Americans, like Walt Whitman, celebrated the city. And undoubtedly anti-urban traditions exist in other societies as well. Still, surveys have indicated that most Americans feel great antipathy for cities, even if they live in them.[4] And since the American experience has been quite different from the European experience, it is not surprising that this should be so. Our ruling mythology teaches that we are descended from people who left the "old world" to escape poverty and oppression. Our forebears came to America to begin anew on land of their own. The cities all too often have been seen as a remnant of the past that our forebears were escaping, as a part of the old world transplanted to the new. Undoubtedly much of this mythology is demonstrably false. But true or false, it is such ideas that have shaped our perceptions of the city.

One effect of our anti-urban tradition is that we have been slow to develop an urban policy. This is especially surprising since almost as long as there have been cities in America there have been those who have thought them to be in crisis. The French observer Alexis de Tocqueville, in his classic *Democracy in America* first published in 1835, wrote:

The lower ranks which inhabit these cities [Philadelphia and New York] constitute a rabble even more formidable than the populace of European towns. They consist of freed blacks, in the first place, who are condemned by the laws and by public opinion to a hereditary state of misery and degradation. They also contain a multitude of Europeans who have been driven to the shores of the New World by their misfortunes or their conduct; and they bring to the United States all our greatest vices without any of those interests which counteract this baneful influence. As inhabitants of a country where they have no civil rights they are ready to turn all the passions which agitate the community to their own advantage; thus, within the last few months serious riots have broken out in Philadelphia and New York.

De Tocqueville went on to warn:

---

[4] Catten *et al.* (1969); and Louis Harris Associates (1978).

The size of certain American cities and especially . . . the nature of their population
. . . [is] a real danger which threatens the future security of the democratic republics
of the New World.[5]

Perhaps de Tocqueville's gloomier predictions have not been realized. Still,
who would deny that cities today face crushing problems, ranging from deterioration of basic services like transportation, education, and public safety to
the problems of poverty, or that the quality of urban life has declined in recent
years and continues to decline? Despite this, it was not until 1978 during
the Carter administration that the federal government formulated an explicit
urban policy.[6] Of course, from the very foundation of the republic there have
been *de facto* urban policies. The decisions made in Washington concerning
housing, health care, and so forth have greatly affected the cities. But all too
often these decisions have been made with little sensitivity as to whether or
not their impacts on urban areas have been coherent and consistent.

Although cities have been studied by economists, political scientists, sociologists, and geographers, and despite the fact that cities are the primary
environment for most of us, fundamental questions about the cities around
us have frequently been overlooked or ignored. Are cities good for us? Should
we try to reform them, abolish them, or preserve them the way they are? How
do cities affect our individual psychologies and our collective political and
social systems? How do they affect our values? What influence do they have
on our sense of justice, and on our efforts to create a better society? Obviously not all these questions can be addressed, much less answered, in this
essay. What I hope to do is to raise some fundamental questions about the
urban environment, and to show that these are not "technical" questions
as conceived by social scientists, but rather fundamental value questions
which go to the very core of what we are and how we live; and that, indeed,
the "technical" questions can only be meaningfully addressed in the context
of widespread discussion and debate concerning these more fundamental
questions.

In Section 2 I try to make clear how I use some basic terms, for example,
'city' and 'urban area', and sketch some future trends in urban development.
In Section 3 I discuss some urban problems and the economist's approach to
them. Section 4 focuses on one problem in some detail: the preservation of
urban landmarks. Finally, in Section 5, I discuss the nature and role of utopian

---

[5] de Tocqueville (1945: 289–90).
[6] See US Department of Housing and Urban Development (1978).

thinking about cities. If, as is certainly the case, we can only scratch the surface of the ideas that are examined in what follows, the hope is that the scratch will start an itch to do more and better thinking in an area as important as it is neglected by recent writing in environmental ethics.

2. DEFINITIONS

2.1 What are Cities?

Before we can come to any systematic understanding of the city around us, we must be clear about what we mean by 'city'. Most of us seem willing to use the term 'city' interchangeably with 'urban area'. If we make a distinction at all it is this one: the city is the city proper; an urban area includes suburbs and other areas touched by the city proper. In the past the distinction between cities and urban areas was much sharper. The term 'city' was formerly reserved for the citizens of a community, while 'urban area' referred to the place which they inhabited. In this sense cities, like nations, can be in exile, and it is this sense in which St Augustine spoke of the community of believers, widely scattered as it is, as "the city of God". These considerations are important because they remind us that any assessment of the quality of life in a city cannot ignore the importance of community. We shall return to this theme in Sections 4.7 and 4.8, but for present purposes I shall follow ordinary usage in speaking of cities both as people and as places.

The main problem in developing an adequate definition of the term 'city' is that a very wide range of things have been called by that name. A very small city in Illinois seems to have little in common with Tokyo or Singapore. The ancient cities of the Middle East could hardly have been more different from Los Angeles. I shall not try to give necessary and sufficient conditions for being a city. Our purposes will be well enough served by sketching three characteristics or "symptoms" which most cities—ancient or modern, Eastern or Western—exhibit to some degree.

When we think of cities most of us think of areas that are very crowded; and indeed, population density is one of the marks of a city. But there is no magic number such that everything which reaches a certain threshold of density is a city and everything which fails to reach this threshold is not. The population density of cities varies greatly. San Francisco is almost seven times as dense as Dallas, and Manhattan is four times as dense as San Francisco. Rural areas in the Far East often have population densities of 2,000 per square mile, while some American cities, for example Jacksonville and Oklahoma

City, have population densities of 600 to 700 people per square mile.[7] This shows that cities are not areas of "absolute" high density; rather they are areas of "relative" high density. What is characteristic of cities is that they are significantly more dense than the regions which surround them. Another feature of cities that comes rapidly to mind is their occupational structure. When we think of cities we think of people who earn their living buying, selling, and trading, rather than farming. And indeed, the second mark of a city is that its inhabitants work mainly in non-agricultural occupations. Finally, the third characteristic of cities is that they are important cultural, religious, economic, and administrative centres for the regions that surround them.

2.2 Future Trends

Cities have changed enormously since the time of the Greeks, and there is no question that they will change enormously in the future. The international trends are clear. World population will continue to increase, and the urban population will increase even more. The social structure of the world will be dominated increasingly by huge urban concentrations like those of Mexico City and Tokyo. And the problems with which we must be concerned as global citizens will increasingly be their problems.

The prospects for the United States, however, are not quite so clear, as a look at our own recent history shows. The process of suburbanization began in a major way during the prosperity of the 1920s. During that decade the suburban population of the seventeen largest cities increased almost 40 per cent, a much higher rate of growth than that of the central cities.[8] The Great Depression and World War II inhibited the tendency towards suburbanization, but encouraged by federal housing and highway programmes, it exploded in the post-World War II period. The census figures tell the story well. The suburban share of the population was 33 per cent in 1950. By 1960 it had increased to 43 per cent, and by 1970 it was 50 per cent. During this period the suburbs gained in population mainly at the expense of rural areas. As a result, the country became increasingly urbanized. Since 1970, however, there have been dramatic shifts. In the last decade more Americans have left the cities than have moved to them. Small towns with populations of less than 2,500 are the fastest growing demographic unit, and many rural areas, particularly those in the sunbelt, have been experiencing unprecedented growth. It is far from clear what, if anything, these trends mean. They may be

---

[7] These statistics are taken from lectures by Professor Jean Gottman of Oxford University in the early 1980s.

[8] See Gimlin (1974: 12).

short-term statistical anomalies with very little significance in the long run. Or they may reflect an important long-term change in environmental preferences. But even if the latter is true, it is still not easy to say precisely what this trend foreshadows about our future.

Some geographers and planners have speculated that we are witnessing a shift from an epoch dominated by cities to an epoch dominated by "urban fields".[9] Until the electronics revolution of the last decade it was necessary for people and businesses to reside in close proximity to each other and to sources of relevant information. These circumstances gave rise to hierarchial cities with a central core devoted to business and administration. But with improved transportation and communication it is no longer necessary for people and business to be located close to each other in space. For this reason the traditional city with its dominant central core is redundant and unnecessary, or so some have argued. The central city can and is being replaced by a decentralized urban field, with no single region dominant over the others. If this hypothesis is correct, the flight from the central cities may not be anti-urban at all; it may be the first step in the creation of a new kind of urban area.

Whatever the future holds for America's cities, it is clear that many people no longer want to live in them, and the number is increasing. In the pages ahead we shall discuss a range of questions about the city and urban problems with a view to putting them in philosophical perspective.

3. URBAN PROBLEMS AND ECONOMIC THEORY

Cities confront us with several different kinds of problems. Some are unique to cities, while others exist in rural areas as well but are exacerbated by the urban environment. Some urban problems are rooted in what it is to be a city. For example, one of the characteristics of a city, as we saw in Section 2.1, is that it is an area of relatively high population density. It is not surprising, then, that cities have very high levels of noise and air pollution. Historically, cities have also been associated with high rates of infectious disease, and even today cities have a great many public health problems, ranging from high rates of cancer and ulcers to high rates of suicide and drug addiction. Cities also have high rates of violent death. In both the United States and Western Europe, the rates of traffic death and violent crime increase as population density increases.[10]

---

[9] See e.g. the essays by Webber (1968), and in Wingo, Jr. (1963).

[10] For discussions of the urban problems mentioned in this paragraph see the following: Harrison and Gibson (1976); Elgin *et al.* (1974); US Department of Housing and Urban Development (1978); and Fischer (1976).

It should be evident to even the casual observer that cities face some unique problems, as well as some very severe instances of some familiar ones. Moreover, urban problems often resist the conventional solutions proposed by economists and policy makers. To see why, we must enter the thicket of their terminology.

3.1 Internalizing Externalities

Economists are happiest with what they call private goods. A private good is something to which some assignable individual, whether corporate or not, has an entitlement. He can sell it, or buy more of it. He can exclude people from using it, or he can charge people for using it at his discretion. Private goods are the capitalist's ideal; he would like everything to be a private good. In our society private goods include my Hawaiian shirts, your copy of *Morality's Progress*, and Ronald Reagan's ranch. Sometimes conflicts arise over how individuals use their private goods. The problem is that individuals do not always bear all of the costs associated with producing or consuming these goods. Consider a trivial but real example.

My neighbour has a wood stove which she uses to heat her house. Since Colorado averages 300 days of sunshine per year, I prefer to dry my laundry on the clothes-line even in winter. But I cannot, for the smoke and soot from my neighbour's chimney invades my property and would soil my laundry if I were to hang it out to dry. From an economist's point of view, my neighbour is getting off cheap. I am bearing part of the cost of her heating with wood. She is "externalizing" these costs to me, in the form of the smoke and soot which fouls my yard. The economist's solution is to "internalize" these "externalities" by requiring my neighbour to install smoke-abatement equipment, or by requiring her to compensate me for giving up my right to dry laundry on my clothes-line in winter. This approach is potentially very powerful, as can be seen from another example which is more serious and just as real.

According to a government study, 2 million asbestos-related cancer deaths will occur in the next thirty-five years due to exposures that have already taken place.[11] This is an average of more than 50,000 deaths per year. Monetary losses from illness caused by asbestos exposure are estimated in the hundreds of millions. These losses are part of the cost of producing and consuming asbestos, yet they are not borne by the companies involved nor their consumers. Rather, these costs are externalized into the bodies of asbestos workers

---

[11] This projection is taken from US Department of Health, Education and Welfare (1980). For a general account of the issues see Epstein (1979).

and into the society as a whole in the form of higher insurance premiums and health-care costs. If these costs were internalized, the price of asbestos would be much higher, reflecting the true cost of producing and consuming this substance, and much less asbestos would be used and many fewer people would die. In this case it is easy to see what is to be gained by some and lost by others by internalizing externalities.

3.2 Some Problems for the Economist

Requiring individuals and corporations to internalize externalities is potentially a powerful approach to many environmental problems. Unfortunately, however, this approach has some problems of its own. First, it is more difficult even in theory to identify externalities than it might at first seem. Consider an example. Some people are very sensitive to the clothes worn by others. They find Hawaiian shirts, or mismatched colours, or white socks with black shoes, offensive and upsetting. Still, I doubt that many people would say that I ought to compensate the sensitive soul who dislikes my clothes. We do not think of the annoyance caused to others by dressing unconventionally as an externality that should be internalized. What is different about this case and that of my neighbour's wood stove is that I have a right to dress as I like but she doesn't have a right to foul my air. This suggests that the identification of externalities rests on some prior conception of how rights are distributed— that is, who has what rights. But the determination of who has what rights is far from settled, not only in practice but also in theory, and anyway, it is a job for a philosopher and not an economist. In short, the economic approach to environmental problems must ultimately rest on some controversial philosophical view about what constitutes a just society.

Another example might make the point clearer. It used to be the case that smokers smoked anywhere with impunity. It was a widespread belief that smokers had the right to fill the air, not just their lungs, with smoke, and if someone else didn't like it, that other person should leave. Nowadays most of us think that non-smokers have a right to clean air, and that those who smoke in public violate the rights of non-smokers. The smoker is now typically viewed as externalizing the costs of smoking into the air of non-smokers, rather than as exercising rights in a legitimate way. This is because our conception of the initial distribution of rights has changed. So long as non-smokers were viewed as lacking a right to clean air, smokers were not viewed as externalizing the costs of smoking as they exhaled. Once non-smokers are viewed as having a right to clean air, however, the picture changes. But who has what rights is not decided by the economist's call for internalizing externalities; instead that call assumes that we have already answered this prior question about the distribution of rights.[12]

A second problem with the economist's approach becomes especially apparent in the city. Almost everything an urban dweller does impinges on others. Noise, conversation, and music are ubiquitous. Hundreds of passers-by cannot fail to note the state of my house. How I dispose of my garbage, how often I use my air conditioner, and when I drive my car, all affect others. How can the economist deal with a situation in which externalities are everywhere? The problem is this. The economist's approach suggests a picture in which the usual situation is one in which if I were to exercise suitable restraint, then my use of my private goods would affect only me. In those few cases when it does affect others, I should be forced to internalize these effects. But this picture does not conform very well to urban life. There, it seems, it is rare when, with suitable restraint, one's use of a private good affects only oneself. I enjoy the taste of my Szechuan eggplant alone, but I share the aroma with my neighbour.

3.3 Public Goods: The Economist's Rejoinder and a Reply

In an effort to deal with these problems and others, economists have developed the notion of a public good. Public goods tend to fall into two categories. First, there are some goods that just do not have the logical characteristics of private goods. Everyone benefits from them, though it is difficult to say how much; and it is difficult or impossible to deny benefits to those who are unwilling to pay. Police and fire protection, and access to the legal system fall into this category. But secondly, there are goods, which although they could be denied to those who are unwilling or unable to pay, we believe everyone is entitled to anyway. Education and health care are in this category. Public goods of both varieties are typically provided by governments and financed by taxes.

The introduction of public goods, necessary though it is, creates new problems that cannot easily be resolved. Consider an example. Although there is considerable dispute over how to define 'clean air', almost no one doubts that clean air is a public good and that Denver's air is dirty. It is also clear that dirty air causes severe health problems and even death. One study has shown that current levels of carbon monoxide in Denver probably cause 100 to 125

---

[12] Those who are inspired by the economic analysis of the law might wish to go so far as to advocate distributing all rights on the basis of economic efficiency. For general background see Posner (1981).

heart attacks per year.[13] These heart attacks are not "acts of God"; they are caused by people driving cars. Of course there is no single driver who causes all of these heart attacks, or perhaps even one of them. And we cannot say with certainty which of the thousands of heart attacks which occur in Denver each year are caused by carbon monoxide. It should also be said that drivers in Denver are not wicked people. They do not drive with the intention of causing their neighbours' heart attacks. Rather, they use their cars for the same reasons we do: in order to get to work, to go shopping, and so forth. The "extra" heart attacks are an unintended, though foreseeable, consequence of their individual actions, taken collectively. It should also be said that undoubtedly some of those who suffer heart attacks themselves drive cars. They are not simply the innocent victims of other people's behaviour. On the other hand it also should be noted that in all likelihood some of the victims do not drive, and many of those who do might well prefer other means of transportation were they available. These considerations are relevant in morally evaluating those who drive in Denver. They might lead us to soften the judgements we might otherwise make. Still, whatever we might say about the character of those individuals who drive, it must be acknowledged that our collective behaviour sometimes seriously harms and perhaps even kills innocent people (e.g. young children). They are wronged even if as individuals we don't wrong them. This should lead us to ask: how should a morally conscientious person respond to this?

Some might argue that we should refrain from driving. They might reason in a way that is reminiscent of the eighteenth-century German philosopher Immanuel Kant: I should only use an automobile if I am willing that everyone should use an automobile. But if everyone were to use an automobile, then some innocent people will be seriously harmed. Since I am unwilling to permit innocent people to be seriously harmed, I should not use my automobile. Although this argument follows a familiar pattern of reasoning, it seems to go wrong here. After all, if only half as many people used cars as do now, perhaps no heart attacks would be caused by air pollution. From the fact that I don't want everyone to drive it doesn't follow that I want no one to drive. But the problem with this response to the argument is that just as I might reason in this way to the conclusion that I have no moral duty not to drive, so might everyone reason to this conclusion. And the

---

[13] These data were made available to me by researchers at the National Center for Atmospheric Research. Although there are very few data in this area which can be regarded as definitive, the concerns of this section, which are fundamentally moral, are not affected by the exact details of the nature and extent of the connections between carbon monoxide and heart attack.

result is that 100 or so innocent people suffer heart attacks as a consequence of our actions.

One way of trying to escape this conclusion is to deny that any innocent people are wronged. It might be suggested that environmental problems, like air pollution, do not by and large result in the deaths of particular individuals who are identifiable in advance. Rather, high levels of air pollution impose additional risk on a large pool of individuals, and only a small number of them suffer heart attacks. What we should do in such situations, it might be argued, is to offer people a deal. Suppose that it would cost automobile owners $500 each to eliminate the risk of heart attack caused by air pollution. By voting, cost-benefit analysis, or some other procedure we could present people with a choice: either take your chances with heart attack and pay nothing, or eliminate the risk of pollution-caused heart attack and pay $500. From this perspective the moral problem seems to vanish. Those who suffer heart attacks caused by air pollution are just the losers in a democratic decision.

But there are a great many problems with this approach. First, those who suffer the heart attacks may not have been those who were willing to take the risk. This is especially important in view of the magnitude of the losses. Ordinarily we think that if the risks of a policy or a decision that is really a gamble are very great, people should be permitted to opt out. Most of us would not object too strenuously if a dollar were deducted from our weekly pay and used to purchase a lottery ticket. It is likely that we would lose a dollar a week this way. But a dollar a week isn't much to lose, and there is always the chance that we may win. But suppose instead that we stood to lose our houses. Suppose that a majority of our neighbours had agreed to wager the entire neighbourhood on the outcome of the Super Bowl. Even though there is a chance that we might win and win very big, we would be indignant at being compelled to risk so much. The air pollution case is like this one in some important respects. Those who lose the air pollution bet lose quite a lot indeed. They forfeit their health and perhaps even their lives. It is wrong for a majority to require everyone to play this high-risk game.

A second and perhaps more fundamental objection to this way out is that the distinction between individual and statistical heart attacks is really bogus. Statistical heart attacks are just individual heart attacks about which we know very little. But we do know this: in both cases the victim has a life with friends, family, relatives, acquaintances, a job, a hobby, a pet, and so forth. Our ignorance concerning which individuals will suffer from air pollution makes no moral difference. But whether or not we can identify in advance the victims of our policies in no way determines whether there are such victims. The moral price is the same in each case.

The preceding discussion has unearthed two characteristic features of environmental problems as they arise in the city around us: (1) they often concern the provision and preservation of public goods, and (2) they often arise because individuals find it rational to behave in a way that is collectively irrational. I have tried to show that it is the very nature of the city to exacerbate such problems. I have also argued that these problems cannot be adequately treated from a purely economic point of view. In the next section I shall discuss a specific urban environmental problem. It involves issues in which the limitations of a purely economic analysis are readily apparent. It is an issue which involves conflicting values. It is the problem of preserving landmarks.

4. PRESERVING LANDMARKS

In the city in which I live there is a movie theatre which was built in 1936. For an entire generation, this ornate, art deco theatre was a home away from home. It was where kids spent Saturday afternoons, where teenagers would go on dates, and where their parents would enjoy an evening out. But in the 1970s the Boulder Theater fell upon hard times. It was no longer profitable to operate this large, downtown building as a movie theatre. In the age of the automobile everyone owned cars. New theatres sprang up in shopping centres which offered cheaper rents. The Boulder Theater became a dilapidated building on a valuable piece of land, a prime candidate for demolition.

The story that I tell is typical. Some version of it has been played out in most cities and towns in America. And it is not just a story about movie theatres. Entire neighbourhoods are "redeveloped" out of existence in order to make way for freeways or office buildings. In the late 1960s in San Francisco, a Japanese neighbourhood was razed so that a Japanese cultural centre, catering mostly to tourists, including those from Japan, could be constructed. The story that I tell, then, is not just the story of one movie theatre in one town in Colorado. It is an example of an issue which is increasingly important in virtually every city in the country.

4.1 Economic Theory and Preservation

Having set the stage, we may now ask: what should be done with the Boulder Theater? For those who draw their policy prescriptions solely from economic considerations the answer is simple: use it in the most economically efficient way possible. Under prevailing conditions this is equivalent to saying that the Boulder Theater should be torn down and the land used as a parking lot. In recent years all across America a great number of landmarks have been replaced by parking lots. Downtown real estate is very expensive. Parking lots produce high revenue with low overheads at almost no risk.

Sometimes preservation can be made commercially successful, however. San Francisco's Ghiradelli Square and Denver's Larimer Square are often cited as examples of economically successful preservations. Many believe that such preservations are and must be the way of the future. James Biddle, former president of the National Trust, has written: "We must show that preservations can be good for business. We can elaborate on aesthetic values, but we need to talk cold, hard cash."[14] Still, some would deny that the models of economically successful preservation cited above are real preservations. Except for the building façades, very little has been preserved in either case. But even if the success of these examples is granted, as I think it should be, it is obvious that preservations cannot always be made commercially successful. For example, a thoroughgoing preservationist wants to preserve historic ethnic communities, however poor and deprived. Most of these areas will never be transformed into handsome tourist attractions.

Those who wish to preserve neighbourhoods, buildings, and other land-marks must, at some point, resolutely face their opponents and say that they reject economic efficiency as the ultimate criterion for social policy. In the current political climate such a declaration sounds shocking when put so boldly. Still, there is ample evidence that most Americans do reject economic efficiency as the sole criterion for social policy. Most Americans are com-mitted to preserving endangered species and cleaning up the air and water even if this means that economic growth will be inhibited.[15] Psychological research has indicated that in experimental situations people are willing to trade increments of efficiency for equality, fairness, and other values.[16] What this means is that most people are irrational from the point of view of the economist. But we ordinary folk should not be too deeply stung by this charge. Economists use the terms 'rational' and 'efficient' in peculiar ways that are tailor-made to fit their favoured theory of rationality. Moreover, we can ask an economist some difficult questions about the importance he attaches to efficiency. That efficiency is a good cannot be doubted by any reasonable person. But some economists and the policy-makers and analysts that are influenced by them would justify all economic and social arrangements in

---

[14] As quoted in Gimlin (1974: 163).   [15] Anthony (1982).
[16] McLelland and Rohrbaugh (1978).

terms of efficiency. What makes efficiency the primary virtue of social policies? The answer cannot be that efficient policies are efficient, for that reply
would lead to a vicious circle. It must be that the economist believes that there
are independent grounds for the primacy of efficiency. It is hard to imagine
what they might be. And against this view, there are arguments that have been
developed over thousands of years for the primacy of justice, respect, equity,
and other moral virtues. We common folk who believe that sometimes efficiency must take a back seat to other values should not be cowed by the epi-
thets of economists.

The gospel of efficiency, then, can be rejected in a principled way by the
preservationist. But this rejection of efficiency does not in itself show that
the Boulder Theater or any other landmark ought to be preserved. That task
requires some positive arguments on behalf of preservation.

4.2 What is a Landmark?

Before considering these arguments we should be clear about what we mean
by 'landmark'. I have been using the term very broadly so that it encompasses
buildings, neighbourhoods, monuments, and so forth. But of course not all
such things are landmarks. The tract house in Southern California in which
I was raised is not a landmark. Nor is the suburb of which it is a part. Another
difficulty is that some definitions of 'landmark' imply that they are now being
preserved or that they ought to be. Some even include the reasons for such
preservation as part of the definition. For example, the *American Heritage
Dictionary of the English Language* defines 'landmark' as "a building or site
having historical significance and marked for preservation by a municipal or
national government" (emphasis added). Since we want to discuss some buildings, neighbourhoods, and so forth that have not been marked for preservation by a government, and since we want to examine a wide range of
arguments for such preservation, and not just historical ones, it is clear that
we must use 'landmark' in a slightly different sense than that specified in the
dictionary. Two points about our use of 'landmark' should be noted particularly. First, we shall count as a landmark anything that is a plausible candidate
for preservation, relying on a stock of common-sense examples for purposes
of discussion. Thus in our sense of 'landmark' it makes sense to say that something is a landmark but it ought to give way to something else. Secondly, we
shall separate the question of whether something is a landmark from the
grounds that might be cited for preserving it. We do not want it to be true by
definition that landmarks must be preserved for historical or cultural reasons.

With these emendations in mind, we can go on to consider some arguments for preservation.

There are at least three kinds of arguments that can be given for preservation. The first kind appeals to characteristics of the landmarks themselves. I shall consider two examples: the Argument from the Rights of Landmarks, and the Argument from Aesthetic Features. A second kind of argument for preservation rests on duties to persons other than ourselves. The Argument from Duties to Future Generations and the Argument from Duties to Past Generations illustrate this kind of argument. A third kind of argument for preservation is rooted in considerations about those who presently exist. The Argument from Cultural Identity and the Argument from Common Wisdom will be my examples.

4.3 The Argument from the Rights of Landmarks

The first kind of argument that we distinguished appeals to characteristics of the landmarks themselves as the grounds for why we should preserve them. The most far-reaching of these arguments is the Argument from the Rights of Landmarks. This argument purports to show that it is wrong to destroy landmarks because they have a right to exist independently of human desires or preferences. This argument strikes some people as ludicrous and others as obvious. But to properly evaluate it, we must view it from the perspective of contemporary theories of rights.

In recent years rights to almost everything have been posited by someone. And almost every class of entity has its champions. Two decades ago most people would have ridiculed the claim that animals have rights. But today advocates of animal rights are an important influence on contemporary thought and action. Also in the last two decades environmentalists have begun to argue that natural objects like rivers and trees have rights as well. Legal theorist Christopher Stone argued that rights could be extended to natural objects on the basis of well-established legal principles. Although Stone remains a minority voice, his arguments were sympathetically received by the late Supreme Court Justice William O. Douglas.[17] Some have tried to carry Stone's argument even further, arguing that artefacts like works of art also have rights.[18] Perhaps it is absurd to ascribe rights to urban landmarks, but if it is, at least it is an absurdity that is in keeping with the tenor of the times.

---

[17] See Stone (1974); and Justice Douglas's dissent in *Mineral King v. Morton* 405 US 727, 742 (1972).
[18] For criticism of this view, see Golding and Golding (1979).

How might one argue that urban landmarks have rights? The first stage of the argument would establish some favourable condition that is sufficient for having rights. A long tradition in both moral and legal philosophy holds that having interests is sufficient for having rights. This condition seems more favourable to the preservationist than the oft-cited alternatives of being autonomous or being a party to a contract. It can be argued on the basis of this "interest principle" that infants and comatose humans have rights. It is also easy to see how rights could be extended to non-human animals on the basis of this principle; just as humans have an interest in a long and pleasant life, so do the other higher animals. But what about artefacts like paintings and buildings? Do they have interests? It is true that we often speak of them as if they do. We might say that we "feel sorry" for the house next door since it has been purchased by an irresponsible owner who does nothing to keep it in repair. Or we might say that it was "a good thing" for the paintings in the National Gallery in London that they were evacuated to the countryside before the German bombing began. But on reflection I think we can see that these are not literal uses of language. When a raccoon is hit by a car, we may or may not be disturbed by it; but it is clearly bad for the raccoon. But if a historical landmark is razed and we are not disturbed by it, either for ourselves or for future or past generations, there seems little sense in saying that it was bad for the landmark that was razed. To put the point another way, if there were no other sentient beings in the universe it would still be a bad thing that an animal suffered and died, but it would not be a bad thing that an earthquake swallowed up the ruins of the Roman Colosseum.

The argument I have presented against supposing that artefacts have rights is mainly intuitive and therefore not overwhelming in its strength. But on the other hand the only argument that I have seen in favour of this view rests on an equivocation, as I have tried to show. That is, it rests on supposing that artefacts have interests in the same sense in which humans and other animals do. Until better arguments are presented, the intuitive considerations that I have given seem strong enough to carry the day.

4.4 The Argument from Aesthetic Features

A second example of an argument which grounds the duty of preservation in characteristics of the landmarks themselves is the Argument from Aesthetic Features. This argument is often cited in everyday discussions of preservation. It gains plausibility from the fact that some of the legislation concerning land-mark preservation directly appeals to the aesthetic features of landmarks as the grounds for their preservation. For example, the criteria of eligibility for being listed in the *National Register of Historic Places* explicitly lists high artistic value as one consideration. This suggests that perhaps landmarks ought to be preserved because they embody valuable aesthetic features.

There are two problems with this argument even if it is viewed in a favourable light. First, this argument fails to provide grounds for preserving many landmarks that many people believe ought to be preserved. Houses in which presidents were born rarely embody valuable aesthetic features. Inner-city neighbourhoods seldom have much in common with works of art. Secondly, rather than motivating preservation, this argument only challenges developers to do better. If our interest in landmarks is an aesthetic one, then no one can complain if we destroy a landmark, so long as we replace it with a structure that is aesthetically more pleasing. Such a policy might lead to an environment which is aesthetically more rewarding but one which many of us would believe had lost something important.

There are two more problems with this argument. First, many philosophers believe that aesthetic judgements are objective, but they have not done a good job of convincing other people of this. As a matter of practice, when aesthetic value is debated in the realm of public policy there is a strong tendency for anyone's opinion to be regarded as the equal of anyone else's. As the proverbial (but possibly false) saying goes, "There is no disputing matters of taste". Many people seem to like the Golden Arches, and find the clean austere look of modern office buildings vastly more pleasant than the aesthetic qualities of crumbling warehouses. Secondly, most people, and certainly most decision-makers, regard aesthetic value to be commensurable with other values. That is, most people would trade an increment of aesthetic value for an increment of some other value, say convenience or economic welfare. Thus someone might admit that an office building from the 1920s is aesthetically superior to the one that has been proposed to replace it, but at the same time prefer the proposed building because of the greater convenience it would afford (e.g. better lighting, better plumbing, better electricity, and so forth). Although the Argument from Aesthetic Features provides some reason for preserving some landmarks, it is only of slight help in establishing a thoroughgoing preservationist position.

4.5 The Argument from Duties to Future Generations

The second category of arguments for preservation appeals to our duties to those who are not now alive. The first example of such an argument that we shall consider is the Argument from Duties to Future Generations. The basic idea is that we deprive members of future generations from experiencing the landmarks that we destroy. The fact that they come after us in time gives us no warrant to deny them these pleasures. Therefore it is wrong for us to destroy landmarks.

Two criticisms of this argument merit our attention. First, it must be recognized that virtually everything we do deeply affects members of future generations. Indeed what we do even affects the identity of who will exist in the future.[19] The slightest change in the remote past would have made it highly unlikely that we would now exist. Look at it this way. A necessary condition for my existing is that I originated in the union of a unique sperm and a unique egg. If my mother had stubbed her toe on the way to bed on the night of my conception, I would not have been conceived. For if a child would have been conceived an instant later it would have originated from a different sperm uniting with the egg. The result might have been someone very much like me, as much like me as my brother is, but still a different person. Once we see the radical contingency of our existence, it is obvious that different policies concerning historical preservation would result in different people being born in the future. If we raze a building instead of preserving it, some construction worker has a job who would not otherwise have one. Instead of staying at home and conceiving a child he is out destroying a building. The child whom he does conceive when he returns home from work, who would not otherwise have existed, marries and has children. Her children would not have existed had she not existed. It is easy to see that after several generations the planet would be populated by people who would not have existed had we adopted a different policy concerning historic preservation. But that is to say that the people who would live in a world with preservation are not the same people who would live in a world without preservation. Those people who do exist in the future cannot complain, then, or so a critic of the Duties to Future Generations Argument might contend, that they are harmed by our razing of landmarks, since if we had not razed our historical landmarks they would not have existed.

On the face of it, this argument undercuts the Argument from Duties to Future Generations. The problem is that this argument, if successful, would seem to show that we have no duties at all to future generations; an implication many would find unacceptable. (As for why, see the discussion of the Doomsday device in section 4.6.) It would take us too far afield to properly evaluate this argument, but whether or not it is sound, there is a second argument that serves to diminish the force of the Argument from Duties to Future Generations, one that does not imply that we have no duties to them.

---

[19] The argument in this paragraph is drawn from Parfit (1984).

I have already argued that preservation is, to a great extent, economically inefficient. If that were not the case we could trust preservation to the free market, since the free market, at least under certain ideal conditions, guarantees efficient outcomes.[20] Whenever we preserve a landmark for future generations which would otherwise be destroyed if the market were permitted to operate freely, we are effectively depriving future generations of some economic advantage. It is one thing for us to say that if we lived in the future we would prefer an increment of preservation to an increment of economic welfare, but how do we know what people who live in the generations after us will prefer? Doubtless they will prefer many of the same things we do—health rather than sickness, for example, and clean water rather than muck. So, assuming that we have some duties to future generations, we can allow that we have the duty not to leave them a world that seriously jeopardizes their health or is devoid of clean water. But our degree of certainty on these matters is not easily transferable to convictions about the preferences of future people for landmark preservation rather than extra increments of economic welfare. Posterity might view our landmarks as symbols of a rapacious and disgusting civilization. They might prefer to begin anew. We simply do not know and, in the nature of the case, we can never know.

It might be objected that I have overstated our uncertainty about the preferences of future generations. We know that we are happy that landmarks have been preserved for us, and therefore, it might be argued, we have good inductive evidence for supposing that future people will be happy if landmarks are preserved for them. It is important to remember, however, that cultural preferences can and do change radically, often in a very short time. One example concerns our preferences with respect to wilderness. The contemporary historian Roderick Nash has documented the radical shift in American perceptions of wilderness over the last three centuries. For the Puritans wilderness was "poor, barren, hideous, boundless, and unknown"; for the contemporary environmentalist it is a source of wisdom which "holds answers to questions man has not yet learned how to ask".[21] Even in the case of urban preservation popular attitudes have changed dramatically in the last decade. In the 1960s urban renewal programmes destroyed large numbers of important buildings in the downtown sections of most American cities. What opposition there was to these programmes came mostly from political conservatives objecting to the role of government in these projects. But nowadays many people, regardless of their views on other issues, see the urban renewal of the 1960s as a great

---

[20] This is a well-known result in general equilibrium theory. See e.g. Samuelson (1976: 634).

[21] These passages are quoted by Nash in his 1967/2001: 37, 259.

national tragedy. Moreover, our lack of knowledge concerning the preferences of future generations is particularly troublesome when coupled with the fact, already noted, that to a great extent preservation is a good that is provided to future generations at the price of some increment of their economic welfare. Perhaps there is a strong inductive case for the urgency of people's preference for preservation, but there is an even stronger case for the urgency of their preference for economic welfare. In the end, then, the Argument from Duties to Future Generations fails to be convincing because of the indeterminacy of the preferences of future generations, even if it is true, as we have allowed, that we have some duties to those who will live after us.

At this point, it might be countered that it doesn't matter what future generations would prefer, what matters is what is good for them; and preservation of landmarks would be good for them. This argument is really a version of two other arguments, the Argument from Cultural Identity and the Argument from Common Wisdom, and it will be taken up when we discuss those arguments (in sections 4.7 and 4.8, respectively).

4.6 The Argument from Duties to Past Generations

The second argument that we shall consider which locates our obligation to preserve landmarks in duties to persons other than ourselves is the Argument from Duties to Past Generations. The basic argument is very simple. When people construct buildings, create neighbourhoods, make public sculptures, and so forth, they do these things with an eye to their creations continuing beyond their deaths. Although there is no explicit intergenerational agreement to preserve the creations of the past, still, we have a duty to respect the preferences and desires of our ancestors.

One objection to this argument should first be put to rest. It might be thought that we do not have duties to the dead because the desires of the dead die with them. Consider an example. My father is on his deathbed. I promise him that I will never sell a family heirloom. As soon as he dies I rush to the antique shop and cash in. Have I violated a promise? No, it might be suggested, it doesn't make sense to think of the promise as existing after the death of my father. If I have an obligation to someone, it must be the case that the person in question exists, and though my father once existed he doesn't exist now. Thus, a necessary condition for having an obligation does not obtain and there can be no obligation.

This line of argument is very tempting. It does seem strange to suppose that interests, desires, preferences, intentions, or hopes survive the deaths of their subjects. But supposing they do not is stranger still. If, for example, a promise dies with the person to whom the promise is made, what could be the point of promising someone that you will take care of his children or protect his art collection? At best such "promises" are exercises in collective self-deception. At worst they are a cruel hoax. But in addition to making nonsense of our commitments to the dying, this view threatens to make nonsense of duties to future generations as well. If a necessary condition for having a duty to someone is that she exists, then surely we can have no duties to future people since they do not exist now any more than do the dead. But if we were now to construct a Doomsday device that would explode in the year 2100, surely it is plain that by our actions here and now we would have wronged future people. These considerations suggest that a "timeless" view of morality might be correct. Just as someone's location in space is not in itself sufficient for removing him from the domain of moral concern, so it is with his location in time. That the dead were once alive and that future people will be alive is enough to make them the proper objects of moral concern.

Although this objection against the Argument from Duties to Past Generations founders, there are other objections which fare better. First, it is often far from clear what the intentions and desires of those who lived in the past were. Not every architect and builder cared whether or not his work lived on after his demise; indeed, some continue to build and design with an eye to planned obsolescence. Moreover, even if without exception all of the geniuses of the past cared about the persistence of their creations, a difficult question would remain concerning how their hopes, wishes, and desires generate duties on our part. This difficult question can be illustrated by the following examples.

Suppose that you are sunbathing by a lake on a fine summer day. Several feet from shore there is a child drowning. Suppose that you could save the child with very little risk or even inconvenience to yourself. Moreover, only you are in a position to save the child; there is no one else around. It seems clear that in this case you have a duty to save the drowning child, even though you never agreed to undertake this duty. Now consider quite a different case. You return home one day to find my bicycle parked on your porch. There is a note saying that I have decided to sell it to you and that you owe me $300. You might justly protest, denying that you owe me this money on the grounds that you never agreed to buy my bike. After all, I cannot impose an obligation on you simply by intending that you acquire it and behaving accordingly.

Which of these cases is most similar to the supposed duty to preserve the creations of the past? It is difficult to say. Like the first case, only we are in a position to save the creations of our ancestors. But unlike the first case, it seems that in order to do this we sometimes would have to be willing to pay quite a price. How important is the interest that our ancestors have in the preservation of their creations? Is it a very deep and serious interest, like the interest in life that the drowning child has? Or is it a relatively frivolous interest, like my interest in selling you my bike? These are difficult questions which cannot easily be answered. It is clear, however, that it is very problematical to suppose that the intentions and desires of those who lived in the past are sufficient to impose on us a duty to preserve their creations.

It is also worth noting that even if these considerations about past generations do generate duties of preservation on our part, it is not clear that they lead to conclusions consistent with our considered judgement about the relative stringency of these duties. Most of us believe that whatever duties we have to past generations become weaker with the passage of time. If we owe anything to past generations at all, we owe more to the last generation than the one which lived in 5000 BCE. I may have a stringent duty to my father not to sell the family jewels, but my duties to my ancestors seventeen generations removed are surely not so stringent. Yet for the preservationist, the urgency of preservation seems to increase with the passage of time. If, then, the duty to preserve is grounded in obligations to past individuals, it would seem that the most stringent duty would be to preserve the most recent landmarks even if this would mean destroying more ancient ones—for example, preserving the Athens Holiday Inn at the price of the deterioration of the Acropolis. There is a counter-argument that one might give, however. It might be suggested that our duty is often to preserve older landmarks at the expense of newer ones because we have duties to more people concerning old landmarks than we do concerning new ones. We owe it to the builders of the Acropolis to preserve it, but we also owe this duty to all who have lived between then and now who have wanted the Acropolis preserved. For this reason the duty to preserve old landmarks is often more stringent than the duty to preserve new ones, even though duties do become less stringent with the passage of time.

These considerations are, so far, inconclusive. I have rejected one plausible objection to the Argument from Duties to Past Generations. In addition I have suggested that it is unclear whether the intentions and desires of our ancestors are sufficient for imposing on us duties to preserve their creations. I then pointed out that even if this argument were successful it might imply that landmarks ought to be preserved in roughly the reverse order of priority than most preservationists would urge. There is one remaining objection to the Argument from Duties to past Generations. It is the one which I believe has the most force.

If it were the case that we have a duty to preserve the creations of our ancestors because of their preferences and desires, then we would have a duty to preserve everything and anything that they wanted us to preserve. If, for whatever reasons, they wanted us to preserve their outhouses and storm cellars, but didn't care at all whether we preserved their paintings and cathedrals, then we would be duty-bound only to preserve these mundane objects. Similarly, if we desired that toxic waste dumps and automobile burial grounds should be our gift to future generations, then those who come after us would have a duty to preserve them. This seems perverse. After all, it is the present generation who must live with the legacy of the past. Perhaps respecting the preferences of our ancestors is a good "first cut" at determining what ought to be preserved. Perhaps it would even be very nice of us to preserve what they want us to preserve. But it cannot be that we have a duty to them to do this. For what ought to be preserved surely turns on the properties of the things in question and their impacts on the lives of those living now. To suppose otherwise is to enslave those now alive to the known tastes and preferences of those who have gone before or to the unknown tastes and preferences of those who will come afterwards.

In short, then, although in principle those who live in the present have duties to the dead, there is no good reason for supposing that we have any specific duty to preserve the creations of the past because we owe it to those who have gone before. The Argument from Duties to Past Generations fails to provide a convincing foundation for preservation.

4.7 The Argument from Cultural Identity

The final category of arguments that I shall consider roots our obligation to preserve landmarks in considerations about people who are now alive. One such argument frequently heard in popular discussion is that preserving landmarks is necessary for preserving our cultural identity. The usually unargued assumption that lies in the background is that preserving our cultural identity is a good thing.

We might begin by asking what it means to have a cultural identity. Perhaps the words of Josiah Royce quoted earlier in this essay (Section 1.1) suggest an answer. People with a cultural identity "idealize", "adorn", and "ennoble" their communities. They educate their children in the history and traditions of their culture. They preserve and protect their language, literature, and native arts. They do what they can to help those who are also members of their culture.

Assuming that this is roughly what it means to have a cultural identity, we may then go on to ask why it is a good thing to have one. This is not an easy question to ask, much less answer, in the contemporary climate. In the 1960s the promotion of cultural identity was widely considered to be an important step in the liberation of America's oppressed minorities. In the 1970s the fascination with cultural identity spread beyond African-Americans, Hispanics, and Native Americans to encompass people of virtually every ethnic and cultural background. Many of our recent novels, films, and television programmes, ranging from *Roots* to *Mean Streets*, assert the importance of cultural identity. Perhaps even the current religious revival can be explained in part by a yearning for a common cultural identity in a pluralistic and fragmented society.

If we seriously ask why cultural identity might be a good thing, two answers suggest themselves. The first focuses on the individual. It might be argued that cultural identity is important for human happiness and welfare. Humans are, after all, cultural animals. When we have no strong cultural background to identify with we tend towards the dysfunctional. We become rootless and unstuck. Though we may survive, we do not flourish. The second answer focuses on the society rather than the individual. A society in which individuals have a cultural identity is one in which people are more likely to cooperate and pursue common goals. A society which is unified in purpose and principle is one which is better for everyone to live in.

The first of these answers involves a difficult empirical claim. Whether or not people with a cultural identity are happier or more functional than those without such an identity is a matter for psychological investigation. It would not be an easy investigation to undertake, however, for such murky notions as "having a cultural identity", "being functional", and "being happy" would have to be made operational—that is, we would have to know what counts as evidence for and against each of these attributions. Since there is reason for despair about the possibility of empirically verifying or falsifying this claim, we might as well do some speculating.

There is some reason to believe that people with a cultural identity might be happier and more functional than those without one. People with a cultural identity have more clearly defined roles. What is expected of them is not in doubt. What is of meaning and significance is given by shared cultural norms. But just as there is reason for supposing that cultural identity is conducive to happiness and being functional, so there is reason for believing that it is not. Societies in which people have a strong sense of cultural identity are often intolerant and repressive. Such societies force individuals into moulds not of their own choosing. It is important to remember that cultural identity, which has the ring of something good, is the near neighbour of chauvinism and jingoism, both of which are clearly evils.

The second answer to our question is that a society in which people have a cultural identity is one in which people are more likely to cooperate and to pursue common goals. Two very different kinds of societies in which people might have a deep sense of cultural identity must be distinguished, however. The first kind is one which is homogeneous, and most people share a common cultural identity. Contemporary Poland, a country with few ethnic minorities in which almost everyone is Roman Catholic in religion, might be an example of this kind of society. The second kind of society is one which is pluralistic. In this kind of society most people have a cultural identity, but there is no common cultural identity which they share. Perhaps the United States is, or once was, an example of this kind of society. It could be argued that Italians, Jews, Blacks, and so forth all have a strong sense of cultural identity, but that their identities are as Italian-Americans, Jewish-Americans, African-Americans, and so forth. It is easy to see why cultural identity in the first kind of society would be conducive to widespread cooperation and the pursuit of common goals. It is difficult to see why this would be so in the second kind of society, however.

Some would surely wish to question the very idea that widespread co-operation and the pursuit of common goals is a good. They would point out that those societies with evil purposes and corrupt goals are all the worse for the unity they exhibit. If there must be a Nationalist Japan or a Nazi Germany better they should be fragmented and disunited. Some would go even further and say that except in extraordinary circumstances it is better for all societies to lack widespread cooperation and the pursuit of common goals. They would say that a good society is one which permits individuals to realize their own projects and life-plans. Since there is a richness and diversity in the projects and life-plans of individuals, a good society would create conditions in which many such projects and plans may thrive. For a society to be unified, co-operative, and in pursuit of common goals implies that it is suppressing, overtly or covertly, the individual goals and projects of its citizens. In this view the role of a society is to enable those within it to flourish. There is no further mission for the society as a whole.

It should be clear that the Argument from Cultural Identity raises some interesting questions that are not easily resolved. The most important of these questions centre on (1) whether cultural identity is a good, (2) if it is, why it is, and (3) how important a good it is. Until we get a more convincing affirmative answer to the first, and compelling answers to the second and third questions, this argument remains unpersuasive.

One further question about this argument is worth asking. We have seen

that the case for supposing that cultural identity is important for human happiness and welfare is inconclusive, and that the case for cultural identity as conducive to cooperation and the pursuit of societal goals is most plausible when
there is a common cultural identity widely shared within the society. What
policy regarding landmark preservation would be advocated by someone who
believed that engendering cooperation and the pursuit of common societal
goals were important goods?

The most general answer is that he would favour a policy of preferring
landmarks associated with the dominant culture over those associated with
minority cultures. Indeed, if he considered cultural uniformity a very great
good, he might advocate the destruction of minority landmarks, since they
contribute to maintaining minority cultures which inhibit social unity. Historical landmarks commemorating national leaders and the major events in
the history of the nation would be a major priority for preservation since, in
this view, they help to define a culture. In the case of the United States, it is
hard to see what else in the way of landmarks serves to define a common
culture. Perhaps it is not entirely silly to suggest that the first McDonald's
hamburger stand in Des Plaines, Illinois, the first casino built in Las Vegas,
and the largest used car lot in Texas would be landmarks worthy of preservation if we were to follow this policy, while the sacred burial grounds of Native
American peoples and the architecture of the Shakers would be allowed to
pass from view.[22]

All of this taken together suggests that the Argument from Cultural
Identity does not support a strong presumption in favour of landmark
preservation.

4.8 The Argument from Common Wisdom

The final argument that I shall consider is the one which I think provides the
most powerful reason for preserving landmarks. But before developing this
argument, we need to take stock of what has already been done.

So far I have argued that we have no duty to past or future people to preserve landmarks. If we ought to preserve them it is because such preservation
is good for us. I have further suggested that preservation is often not eco-

---

[22] Shortly after writing these words the following news item came to my attention. "**Threatened**:
The first McDonald's fastfood restaurant, a sleek drive-in hamburger stand in Des Plaines, Ill., was
opened by Ray Kroc in 1955. Nearly 7,000 McDonald's and 60 billion hamburgers later, the parent corporation says that the seatless facility is too small and outmoded and will be replaced in the spring.
However, McDonald's may move the building to create a museum of fast food. It also may be nom-
inated to the National Register of Historic Places" (*Preservation News*, Feb. 1983: 12).

nomically efficient, that appeals to the aesthetic features of landmarks are insufficient to support much preservation, and that considerations about cultural identity do not provide a clear and unambiguous case for preservation. We must rethink what our policy concerning landmarks should be. In order to do this in a way that results in a sensible landmarks policy, we must develop a sensible urban policy; and in order to do that we must ask again what we want from our cities.

If we ask this question, I think the answer is obvious: we want our cities to provide an environment that is conducive to the good life. There are, of course, many different and competing conceptions of the good life. But most plausible conceptions share the view that the good life consists in qualitative goods as well as quantitative ones. To put the point in a different way, the good life cannot plausibly be defined just in terms of access to flush toilets or police protection; it must consider quality of life considerations as well. Although amenities like flush toilets probably bear on the quality of life for most of us, social, psychological, and emotional factors are at least as important. What I am suggesting is that we value cities not only for the material amenities they provide, but also for the possibilities they present for living a life of high quality, where high quality of life includes but does not exhaust the following: security, community, self-respect, self-esteem, adequate housing, adequate nutrition, adequate health care, opportunities for education, recreation, cultural development, and so forth. The question of whether landmarks should be preserved ought to be answered by reference to the impact of such preservation on the quality of life of those who live among and within them.[23]

The view that I wish to urge is that there is a strong presumption in favour of preserving landmarks because there is reason to believe that they are often part of a physical and cultural ecology which is conducive to the living of high-quality lives. Before trying to say what might follow from this about landmarks policy, it is important to consider what arguments can be given for the view. Like most arguments that concern landmark preservation, they are fragmentary and less conclusive than one might wish. Still, they seem to me to carry considerable weight.

The first argument is really a negative one. As long as there have been cities, most attempts at central planning and redevelopment have only made things worse; and therefore, generally speaking, it is better to let well enough alone. The recent American experience is an instructive example.

---

[23] For more on the concept of quality of life see Jamieson and Sneed (1983).

As we noted in the introduction, as long as there have been cities in America there have been those who have thought them to be in crisis. By the end of World War II many people thought the situation had become intolerable. People and wealth were increasingly moving to the suburbs. The central cities could not compete successfully with suburban shopping centres, and their economic base was declining. The housing stock in the central cities was inferior to that of the suburbs and was rapidly degenerating. In 1949 Congress passed the Housing Act which for the first time guaranteed a "decent home" for every American family. The mechanism was to be an unprecedented partnership between the public and private sectors. The Housing Act provided for the creation of urban renewal authorities empowered to assemble large tracts of urban land by negotiation or condemnation. The authorities would develop land-use plans, and then sell these tracts to private developers who were willing to build in accordance with the plans. In 1954 urban renewal authorities were also granted the power to develop commercial areas as well as housing.

From the beginning urban renewal was plagued by controversy. Political conservatives objected to the cost of the programme, the role of government in planning, and the power of urban renewal authorities to condemn land. Many liberals saw urban renewal as a programme designed to bring middle and upper-class people back to central cities, rather than as a programme designed to improve the lot of the city's working-class inhabitants. Some people saw urban renewal as a mechanism for distributing wealth away from small landowners and business executives to large corporations and developers. Others simply thought the projects were ugly. Although many well-intentioned and compassionate people favoured urban renewal at the outset, the consensus now seems to be that this programme was at best a mistake and at worst a tragedy.[24]

The problem, quite simply, is that, like natural ecosystems, urban networks are very complicated and interdependent; and it is extremely difficult to anticipate all of the consequences of one's actions. Very often urban renewal disrupted and displaced stable neighbourhoods that were old and traditional. It destroyed small businesses and dispersed friends and relatives. Corner drugstores, taverns, churches, social halls, and other places that provided the focus for community life were destroyed. Often people whose homes were demolished were not adequately relocated. And all too often when they were, they ended up in large housing projects designed for efficiency and cost-

[24] See e.g. Abrams (1965); Greer (1965); Anderson (1964); Gans (1968, ch. 18); Frieden (1964); and Kessler and Hartman (1973).

effectiveness, rather than community and security. Although the following passage by the contemporary social critic, Jane Jacobs (1961: 4), is perhaps extreme in its rhetoric, it is largely correct about the effects of urban renewal:

Look what we have built with the first several billions: low-income projects that become worse centers of delinquency, vandalism, and general hopelessness than the slums they were supposed to replace. Middle-income housing projects which are truly marvels of dullness and regimentation, sealed against any buoyancy or vitality of city life. Luxury housing projects that mitigate their inanity . . . with a vapid vulgarity. Cultural centers that are unable to support a good bookstore. Civic centers that are avoided by everyone but bums . . . Expressways that eviscerate great cities. This is not the rebuilding of cities. This is the sacking of cities.

The problem with the urban renewal programme and others like it is not that the planners were ill-intentioned or malevolent. They simply did not know enough to carry out the projects which they had undertaken. As a society, we were quite ignorant about the character of urban life in the early days of the programme. But even if everything were known that could be known, there would still be reason to be sceptical of large-scale redevelopment. Human communities are fragile and sensitive. It is easier to destroy them than to create them. It is as difficult to transplant a traditional inner-city community to a high-rise housing project as it is to transplant an entire biological ecosystem (e.g. the Everglades) to an alien environment (e.g. Montana).

This brings us to our second argument. Some might be tempted to dismiss the story about urban renewal that I have told as a special case. The problem is that the projects were not well done, it might be said, not that they were undertaken. Much has been learned from these failures. We will do better next time, and indeed we are doing better even now. Such optimism is not well-founded. Were we to look at a number of such programmes in a variety of countries, we would see that the fate of urban renewal in the United States is the norm rather than the exception. Large-scale redevelopment typically works only when planners have something in mind other than the maintenance of human communities and the pursuit of a high quality of life. An example is the redesign of Paris after the revolutions of 1848. Napoleon III was disturbed at how the narrow winding streets of Paris made it difficult to suppress urban uprisings with modern armies. He commissioned Haussmann to redesign the city in such a way that would make it difficult for the people ever again to control the city in defiance of the government. Haussmann's design was very successful. It has stood succeeding governments in good stead ever since, most recently in May of 1968. Had Haussmann been commissioned to redesign Paris with a view to enhancing the quality of life of its inhabitants, the failures of other planners are an omen of his chances of success. Like wilfully setting out in pursuit of happiness, the intention seems almost certain to guarantee its own frustration.

It is no accident that most ambitious redevelopment programmes fail. Traditional buildings and neighbourhoods are the results of many small decisions by many ordinary people. Buildings have been constructed with the purpose of their users in mind. And when they have not been, over a long period of time people turn these buildings to their ends. A common wisdom is expressed in vernacular architecture and "unplanned" cities. It is the collective wisdom of several generations. It is not easy for any single individual to grasp and articulate this wisdom. The "planning" that is implicit in these traditional structures is likely to embody more subtle distinctions and make possible more worthwhile connections, like the rugs woven by entire families in Afghanistan and Tibet, than any comparable structures that are invented by a planning firm after a month or year of thought. The traditional structures have, after all, stood the test of time. They have survived as long as they have because, at least to some degree, they are adequate to the purposes of the people who have made them and use them. This is more than we can be sure of when we commission planners to rebuild our cities.

The best reason for preserving landmarks, then, is that they embody the common wisdom of those who have built them, lived in them, worked in them, and played in them. They are likely to permit greater community, liberty, security, and so forth, and to make possible a higher quality of life than anything we might invent. This is not to say that the last word in urban planning ought to be the preservation of what has survived. It is to say that it should be the first word, and a word to which we all too often have been deaf.

I have suggested that there is a presumption that urban landmarks should be preserved because they are part of a pattern of life which is more conducive to a high-quality human existence than anything we are likely to invent to replace them. This perspective suggests that, whenever possible, landmarks should be preserved as part of an urban system and not just as idle curiosities. What is valuable about landmarks is their role in human life, and that can be destroyed as effectively by isolating them as by razing them. For all its publicity and acclaim, the French Quarter of New Orleans, for example, is a heart without a body, a mere shadow of its former self. It is a place to visit; it is not a place to live. If we must choose between preserving a landmark that is part of a viable living system or one that is of greater aesthetic value but is not part of such a system, it may well be best to prefer the former. Landmarks are more than the sum of their own parts; they are also, in part, the sum of their relations to the ways of life around them.

It is well to remember that the considerations that have been given create only a presumption in favour of preservation. There are many other concerns which we have, ranging from distributive justice to environmental protection. These concerns might weigh against preservation in particular cases. A viable, comprehensive policy concerning landmark preservation would have to provide a mechanism for weighting these competing interests. To develop such a policy is beyond the more modest ambitions of the present essay. Even so, one can say that the argument I have given does not give preservationists everything they want. Nevertheless, it gives them as much as they are entitled to; and, I think, it makes the strongest case for preservation that can reasonably be sustained.

In conclusion, it should be recognized that the Argument from Common Wisdom, in addition to making the strongest case for preservation that can reasonably be sustained, also encompasses many of the concerns reflected in the other arguments which we have considered. What more respect can we show for the dead than a deep appreciation for the fundamental structures of human life which they have bequeathed to us? What better gift could we give to the future than cities which are not just liveable in, but also make possible the development of all that is best in human life, taken both individually and collectively? And surely nothing could be a better symbol of our cultural identity than cities which protect diversity but also encourage community. Since we are creatures with an aesthetic sensibility, we can be confident that what permits us to thrive will not deeply transgress our sense of beauty. Finally, although landmarks do not have rights, their contribution to the good life is so basic and pervasive that they should enjoy relative autonomy from the passing whims and fancies of urban design.

5. THE PLACE OF UTOPIAN THINKING

Throughout this essay I have argued that, at least when it comes to urban problems, it is usually better to trust the everyday decisions of ordinary people than the social engineering of the experts. I have argued that the tools of economic analysis, so well-entrenched in the bastions of policy-making, are not always adequate for constructive and creative thinking about urban environmental problems. I have argued in particular that the strongest reason for preserving landmarks is not any of the reasons commonly cited, but rather it is because the common wisdom of generations of builders and users working on a piecemeal basis is likely to result in structures that are more conducive to human flourishing than anything that city planners are likely to come up with in their armchairs or at their drawing tables. These conclusions might suggest that there is no place for "unordinary" people, those with utopian visions about what cities ideally can and should be. But that would be wrong.

Utopian thinking about cities is important for a number of reasons. Before discussing these reasons, however, it is important to understand the character of such thinking. Utopian thinking about cities is a form of social theorizing and social criticism. The idea that there is a connection between the physical structures of communities and their social lives is an ancient one. This idea has been especially influential in the United States. During the nineteenth century, many different sects, including the Shakers, the Mormons, and the True Inspiration Congregations, developed distinctive forms of architecture and community planning that were regarded as specially related to the moral and religious beliefs of the community. Even the communal movement of the 1960s was associated with its own distinctive architecture and planning, most notably the geodesic dome and the "Blueprint for a Communal Environment", a document produced by members of several Berkeley community organizations.[25] Generally speaking, architecture and planning in the twentieth century have been dominated by thinkers with a utopian vision. Some were crackpots like Hitler, tinkering with his models and sketches of a new Berlin while the old one was bombed to pieces by the Allies. Others seem merely fatuous, like Paoli Soleri, who labours on in his attempt to create the utopian city of Arcosanti in the middle of the Arizona desert. But others have been very influential on practising architects and planners, perhaps none more than the French architect Le Corbusier and the English planner Ebenezer Howard.

Le Corbusier's vision in the 1920s, like many of his contemporaries in painting, sculpture, and interior design, was the Modernist one. Existing cities were crowded, confused, insanitary, and irrational. They were to be swept away. We would begin anew building in concrete and steel, exploiting the possibilities for efficiency and standardization created by new technologies. Le Corbusier's vision is revealed most clearly in his plan for the reconstruction of central Paris. Everything was to be destroyed, save only a handful of isolated historic landmarks. The new centre-piece was to be a series of sixty-floor office buildings, each stripped of any ornamental detail, each sited on its own piece of

---

[25]   Published in Roszak (1972).

land. This complex of office buildings was to be serviced by a number of high-speed transportation routes carrying workers to their jobs. Outside the central core was to be a series of apartment buildings, each of the same height, every one the same. Le Corbusier conceived of the city as a "tool for living". The purpose of design and planning was to make these tools as efficient as possible. This could be done by making everything as uniform and geometrically perfect as could be. Le Corbusier also saw the need for interaction with nature. For that reason each building was to be sited on its own patch of green. There is a vision of human life and society in Le Corbusier's utopian dreams. It is the vision of uniformity and efficiency. It is the vision of human life as just another job to be completed. It may not be a vision we like very much, but it is one that has been extremely influential in the twentieth century.

Ebenezer Howard's vision was quite different. He was shocked by the ugliness and blight of the British industrial cities at the turn of the century. He thought nothing could be done with the old cities. The solution was to build new ones that were more adequate to human needs and desires. Howard proposed new cities of about 30,000 situated on approximately 1,000 acres of land, surrounded by a greenbelt of farms and gardens. Beyond the greenbelt were the factories that provided the residents with employment. All the land was to be held in common and rented to its users.

The architecture and planning of Le Corbusier and Howard were rooted in different views about human life and human society. Le Corbusier was inspired by breakthroughs in science and engineering. Problems of planning were, for him, technical problems. A viable aesthetic would follow from the study of efficiency. Howard, on the other hand, was influenced by the tradition of utopian socialism. His mission was to harmonize capital and labour, city and country, factory and farm, in practice and not just in theory.

For all their genius, the influence of Le Corbusier and Howard has not always been salutary. The monuments to Le Corbusier are the cold, faceless skyscrapers that now dominate the downtown sections of most of our cities. Howard's legacy is the sprawling suburbs that surround them.

Still, there is a place for utopian thinking about cities. While our traditional patterns of building, our collective wisdom, often embody diversity and tolerance, they often embody less noble characteristics as well. After all, today's innovation becomes part of what preservationists might seek to preserve and protect tomorrow. Here is an example. Most people today would say that we should "design with nature". It would be best for our streets to follow the natural contours of the land and to respect the prominent features of the natural environment. Yet most American cities were originally laid out according to a grid, regardless of the topography. If a hill or a swamp or a river got in the way, it was filled in, bulldozed, or dynamited. If that was impossible, an uneasy and often unworkable truce was established. Preserving the original plans of most American cities would often mean preserving these attempts to dominate nature rather than to coexist with her. Not everything new is good; but neither is everything old. We must learn from the sins of our ancestors, and not complacently bequeath them to our children. Utopian thinkers, one might say, are the conscience of the ages speaking to us now.

How, practically, are utopian thinkers important? Their visions are important, first of all, because they sometimes result in ideas we can use. Le Corbusier made us acutely aware of the possibilities of new materials. Howard gave us the greenbelt, a concept which has become very important in the plans of many middle-sized communities. We need not buy everything these thinkers are selling in order to find something helpful.

Secondly, utopian thinking is valuable because it forces us to clarify our views about what cities are for and where we want them to go. Consider an example. In the introduction to their book *Communitas*, Percival and Paul Goodman (1960: 4) write:

For thirty years now, our American way of life as a whole has been subjected to sweeping condemnation by thoughtful social and cultural critics . . .

In this book we must add, alas, to the subjects of this cultural criticism the physical plant and the town and the regional plans in which we have been living so unsatisfactorily. We will criticize not merely the foolish shape and power of the cars but the cars themselves, and not merely the cars but the factories where they are made, the highways on which they run, and the plan of livelihood that makes those highways necessary.

This passage should make us think. Do we share the Goodmans' view of the automobile? Or is this just another example of pathological hatred of this symbol of middle-class life? If we disagree with the Goodmans, we should know why. If we agree with them, perhaps their book will extend and deepen our belief.

Finally, utopian thinking is important because it gives us a yardstick by which to measure our progress. It reminds us that we ought not to be satisfied with things as they are. Utopian thinkers remind us of what is possible, and of how far we have to go to make human life even remotely as good as it can be.

In conclusion, however, it is important to remember the major theme of this essay. In the end, the cities around us are the creations of ourselves and of our ancestors. They are the primary environments in which most of us live, and they are one of the most important gifts we will give our children. Although we are often told that urban problems are beyond our competence to control, we must not alienate our power and forfeit our responsibility to those who might mystify us with their techniques. For all too often they twist the problems in order to fit their methods, rather than tailoring their methods to the problems that need to be solved. In its own way, urban life is as fragile as the ecosystems of the oceans and the environment of the California condor. Just as a proper humility is necessary for one who wishes to save a species or an ocean, so it is required for one who wishes to preserve what's best in urban life.

18

Ethics, Public Policy, and Global Warming

There has been speculation about the possibility of anthropogenic global warming since at least the late nineteenth century.[1] At times the prospect of such a warming has been welcomed, for it has been thought that it would increase agricultural productivity and delay the onset of the next ice age.[2] At other times, and more recently, the prospect of global warming has been the stuff of "doomsday narratives", as various writers have focused on the possibility of widespread drought, flood, famine, and the economic and political dislocations that might result from a "greenhouse warming"-induced climate change.[3]

Although high-level meetings have been convened to discuss the greenhouse effect since at least 1963,[4] the emergence of a rough, international consensus about the likelihood and extent of anthropogenic global warming began with a National Academy Report in 1983 (National Academy of Sciences/National Research Council 1983); meetings in Villach, Austria, and Bellagio, Italy, in 1985;[5] and in Toronto, Canada, in 1988.[6] The most recent

This material was discussed with an audience at the 1989 AAAS meetings in New Orleans, at the conference "Global Warming and the Future: Science Policy and Society" at Michigan Technological University, and with the philosophy departments at the University of Redlands and the University of California at Riverside. I have benefited greatly from each of these discussions. Michael H. Glantz commented helpfully on an earlier draft, and Karen Borza contributed to the development of this essay in many ways. I gratefully acknowledge the support of the Ethics and Values Studies Program of the National Science Foundation for making this research possible.

[1] Arrhenius (1896, 1908).
[2] Callendar (1938).
[3] Flavin (1989).
[4] See Conservation Foundation (1963).
[5] World Climate Program (1985).
[6] Conference Statement (1988).

influential statement of the consensus holds that although there are uncertainties, a doubling of atmospheric carbon dioxide from its pre-industrial baseline is likely to lead to a 2.5 degree centigrade increase in the earth's mean surface temperature by the middle of the next century.[7] (Inter estingly, this estimate is within the range predicted by Arrhenius (1896).) This increase is expected to have a profound impact on climate and therefore on plants, animals, and human activities of all kinds. Moreover, there is no reason to suppose that without policy interventions, atmospheric carbon dioxide will stabilize at twice pre-industrial levels. According to the IPCC (1990), we would need immediate 60 per cent reductions in net emissions in order to stabilize at a carbon dioxide doubling by the end of the twenty-first century. Since these reductions are very unlikely to occur, we may well see increases of 4 degrees centigrade by the end of the century.

The emerging consensus about climate change was brought home to the American public on 23 June 1988, a sweltering day in Washington, DC, in the middle of a severe national drought, when James Hansen testified to the US Senate Committee on Energy and Natural Resources that it was 99 per cent probable that global warming had begun. Hansen's testimony was front page news in the New York Times and was extensively covered by other media as well. By the end of the summer of 1988, the greenhouse effect had become an important public issue. According to a June 1989 Gallup poll, 35 per cent of the American public worried "a great deal" about the greenhouse effect, while 28 per cent worried about it "a fair amount" (Gallup Organization 1989).

Beginning in 1989 there was a media "backlash" against the "hawkish" views of Hansen and others.[8] In 1989 the Washington Post (8 February), the Wall Street Journal (10 April), and the New York Times (13 December) all published major articles expressing scepticism about the predictions of global warming or minimizing its potential impacts. These themes were picked up by other media, including such mass circulation periodicals as Reader's Digest (Febru-ary 1990). In its December 1989 issue Forbes published a hard-hitting cover story titled "The Global Warming Panic" and later took out a full-page ad in the New York Times (7 February 1990) congratulating itself for its courage in confronting the "doom-and-gloomers".

The Bush administration seems to have been influenced by this backlash. The April 1990 White House conference on global warming concluded with a ringing call for more research, disappointing several European countries that

---

[7] Intergovernmental Panel on Climate Change (IPCC) (1990).
[8] For the typology of "hawks", "doves", and "owls", see Glantz (1988).

were hoping for concerted action. In July at the Houston Economic Summit, the Bush administration reiterated its position, warning against precipitous action. In a series of meetings in 1991, convened as part of the IPCC process, the American government stood virtually alone in opposing specific targets and timetables for stabilizing carbon dioxide emissions. The Bush administration continually emphasized the scientific uncertainties involved in forecasts of global warming and also expressed concern about the economic impacts of carbon dioxide stabilization policies.

It is a fact that there are a number of different hypotheses about the future development of the global climate and its impact on human and other biological activities; and several of these are dramatically at variance with the consensus. For example, Budyko (1988) and Idso (1989) think that global warming is good for us, and Ephron (1988) argues that the injection of greenhouse gases will trigger a new ice age. Others, influenced by the "Gaia Hypothesis"[9] believe that there are self-regulating planetary mechanisms that may preserve climate stability even in the face of anthropogenic forcings of greenhouse gases.

Although there are some outlying views, most of the differences of opinion within the scientific community are differences of emphasis rather than differences of kind. Rather than highlighting the degree of certainty that attaches to predictions of global warming, as does Schneider (1989), for example, some emphasize the degree of uncertainty that attaches to such predictions.[10]

However, in my view, the most important force driving the backlash is not concerns about the weakness of the science but the realization that slowing global warming or responding to its effects may involve large economic costs and redistributions, as well as radical revisions in lifestyle. Various interest groups argue that they are already doing enough in response to global warming, while some economists have begun to express doubt about whether it is worth trying to prevent substantial warming.[11] What seems to be emerging as the dominant view among economists is that chlorofluorocarbons (CFCs) should be eliminated, but emissions of carbon dioxide or other trace gases should be reduced only slightly if at all.[12]

There are many uncertainties concerning anthropogenic climate change, yet we cannot wait until all the facts are in before we respond. All the facts may never be in. New knowledge may resolve old uncertainties, but it may bring with it new uncertainties. And it is an important dimension of this problem that our insults to the biosphere outrun our ability to understand them. We

[9] See Lovelock (1988).   [10] e.g. Abelson (1990).
[11] *New York Times*, 11 November 1989; White House Council of Economic Advisors (1990).
[12] See Nordhaus (1990); Darmstadter (1991).

may suffer the worst effects of the greenhouse before we can prove to every-one's satisfaction that they will occur.[13]

The most important point I wish to make, however, is that the problem we face is not purely a scientific problem that can be solved by the accumulation of scientific information. Science has alerted us to a problem, but the problem also concerns our values. It is about how we ought to live, and how humans should relate to each other and to the rest of nature. These are problems of ethics and politics as well as problems of science.

In Section 1 I examine what I call the "management" approach to assess-ing the impacts of, and our responses to, climate change. I argue that this approach cannot succeed, for it does not have the resources to answer the most fundamental questions that we face. In Section 2 I explain why the problem of anthropogenic global change is to a great extent an ethical problem, and why our conventional value system is not adequate for addressing it. Finally, I draw some conclusions.

1. WHY MANAGEMENT APPROACHES MUST FAIL

From the perspective of conventional policy studies, the possibility of anthro-pogenic climate change and its attendant consequences are problems to be "managed". Management techniques are mainly drawn from neoclassical economic theory and are directed towards manipulating behaviour by controlling economic incentives through taxes, regulations, and subsidies.

In recent years economic vocabularies and ways of reasoning have domin-ated the discussion of social issues. Participants in the public dialogue have internalized the neoclassical economic perspective to such an extent that its assumptions and biases have become almost invisible. It is only a mild exaggeration to say that in recent years debates over policies have largely become debates over economics.

The Environmental Protection Agency's draft report *Policy Options for Sta-bilizing Global Climate* is a good example. Despite its title, only one of nine chapters is specifically devoted to policy options, and in that chapter only "internalizing the cost of climate change risks" and "regulations and stand-ards" are considered. For many people questions of regulation are not distinct from questions about internalizing costs. According to one influential view, the role of regulations and standards is precisely to internalize costs, thus (to echo a parody of our forefathers) "creating a more perfect market". For people

---

[13] Jamieson (1991c).

with this view, political questions about regulation are really disguised economic questions.[14]

It would be both wrong and foolish to deny the importance of economic information. Such information is important when making policy decisions, for some policies or programmes that would otherwise appear to be attractive may be economically prohibitive. Or in some cases there may be alternative policies that would achieve the same ends and also conserve resources.

However, these days it is common for people to make more grandiose claims on behalf of economics. As philosophers and clergymen have become increasingly modest and reluctant to tell people what to do, economists have become bolder. Some economists or their champions believe not only that economics provides important information for making policy decisions but that it provides the most important information. Some even appear to believe that economics provides the only relevant information. According to this view, when faced with a policy decision, what we need to do is assess the benefits and costs of various alternatives. The alternative that maximizes the benefits less the costs is the one we should prefer. This alternative is "efficient" and choosing it is "rational".

Unfortunately, too often we lose sight of the fact that economic efficiency is only one value, and it may not be the most important one. Consider, for example, the idea of imposing a carbon tax as one policy response to the prospect of global warming.[15] What we think of this proposal may depend to some extent on how it affects other concerns that are important to us. Equity is sometimes mentioned as one other such concern, but most of us have very little idea about what equity means or exactly what role it should play in policy considerations.

One reason for the hegemony of economic analysis and prescriptions is that many people have come to think that neoclassical economics provides the only social theory that accurately represents human motivation. According to the neoclassical paradigm, welfare can be defined in terms of preference-satisfaction, and preferences are defined in terms of choice behaviour. From this, many (illicitly) infer that the perception of self-interest is the only motivator for human beings. This view suggests the following "management technique": if you want people to do something give them a carrot; if you want them to desist, give them a stick.[16]

Many times the claim that people do what they believe is in their interests

[14] For discussion, see Sagoff (1988).

[15] Moomaw (1988/1989).

[16] For the view that self-interest is the "soul of modern economic man", see Myers (1983).

is understood in such a way as to be circular, therefore unfalsifiable and trivial. We know that something is perceived as being in a person's interests because the person pursues it; and if the person pursues it, then we know that the person must perceive it as being in his or her interests. On the other hand if we take it as an empirical claim that people always do what they believe is in their interests, it appears to be false. If we look around the world we see people risking or even sacrificing their own interests in attempts to overthrow oppressive governments or to realize ideals to which they are committed. Each year more people die in wars fighting for some perceived collective good than die in criminal attempts to further their own individual interests. It is implausible to suppose that the behaviour (much less the motivations) of a revolutionary, a radical environmentalist, or a friend or lover can be revealed by a benefit-cost analysis (even one that appeals to the "selfish gene").

It seems plain that people are motivated by a broad range of concerns, including concern for family and friends, and religious, moral, and political ideals. And it seems just as plain that people sometimes sacrifice their own interests for what they regard to be a greater, sometimes impersonal, good. (Increasingly these facts are being appreciated in the social science literature; see e.g. Mansbridge (1990), Opp (1989), and Scitovsky (1976).)

People often act in ways that are contrary to what we might predict on narrowly economic grounds, and moreover, they sometimes believe that it would be wrong or inappropriate even to take economic considerations into account. Many people would say that choosing spouses, lovers, friends, or religious or political commitments on economic grounds is simply wrong. People who behave in this way are often seen as manipulative, not to be trusted, without character or virtue. One way of understanding some environmentalists is to see them as wanting us to think about nature in the way that many of us think of friends and lovers—to see nature not as a resource to be exploited but as a partner with whom to share our lives.

What I have been suggesting in this section is that it is not always rational to make decisions solely on narrowly economic grounds. Although economic efficiency may be a value, there are other values as well, and in many areas of life, values other than economic efficiency should take precedence. I have also suggested that people's motivational patterns are complex and that exploiting people's perceptions of self-interest may not be the only way to move them. This amounts to a general critique of viewing all social issues as management problems to be solved by the application of received economic techniques.

There is a further reason why economic considerations should take a back seat in our thinking about global climate change: there is no way to assess accurately all the possible impacts and to assign economic values to alternative courses of action. A greenhouse warming, if it occurs, will have impacts that are so broad, diverse, and uncertain that conventional economic analysis is practically useless. (Our inability to perform reliably the economic calculations also counts against the "insurance" view favoured by many "hawks", but that is another story.)

Consider first the uncertainty of the potential impacts. Some uncertainties about the global effects of loading the atmosphere with carbon dioxide and other greenhouse gases have already been noted. But even if the consensus is correct that global mean surface temperatures will increase 1.5–4 degrees centigrade sometime in the next century because of a doubling of atmospheric carbon dioxide, there is still great uncertainty about the impact of this warming on regional climate. One thing is certain: the impacts will not be homogeneous. Some areas will become warmer, some will probably become colder, and overall variability is likely to increase. Precipitation patterns will also change, and there is much less confidence in the projections about precipitation than in those about temperature. These uncertainties about the regional effects make estimates of the economic consequences of climate change radically uncertain.

There is also another source of uncertainty regarding these estimates. In general, predicting human behaviour is difficult, as recent events in Central and Eastern Europe have demonstrated. These difficulties are especially acute in the case that we are considering because climate change, if it occurs, will affect a wide range of social, economic, and political activities. Changes in these sectors will affect emissions of "greenhouse gases", which will in turn affect climate, and around we go again.[17] Climate change is itself uncertain, and its human effects are even more radically so. It is for reasons such as these that in general, the area of environment and energy has been full of surprises.

A second reason why the benefits and costs of the impacts of global climate change cannot reliably be assessed concerns the breadth of the impacts. Global climate change will affect all regions of the globe. About many of these regions—those in which most of the world's population live—we know very little. Some of these regions do not even have monetarized economies. It is ludicrous to suppose that we could assess the economic impacts of global climate change when we have such little understanding of the global economy in the first place. (Nordhaus (1990), for example, implausibly extrapolates

---

[17] Jamieson (1990).

the sectorial analysis of the American economy to the world economy for the purposes of his study.)

Finally, consider the diversity of the potential impacts. Global climate change will affect agriculture, fishing, forestry, and tourism. It will affect "unmanaged" ecosystems and patterns of urbanization. International trade and relations will be affected. Some nations and sectors may benefit at the expense of others. There will be complex interactions between these effects. For this reason we cannot reliably aggregate the effects by evaluating each impact and combining them by simple addition. But since the interactions are so complex, we have no idea what the proper mathematical function would be for aggregating them (if the idea of aggregation even makes sense in this context.) It is difficult enough to assess the economic benefits and costs of small-scale, local activities. It is almost unimaginable to suppose that we could aggregate the diverse impacts of global climate change in such a way as to dictate policy responses.

In response to sceptical arguments like the one that I have given, it is sometimes admitted that our present ability to provide reliable economic analyses is limited, but then it is asserted that any analysis is better than none. I think that this is incorrect and that one way to see this is by considering an example.

Imagine a century ago a government doing an economic analysis in order to decide whether to build its national transportation system around the private automobile. No one could have imagined the secondary effects: the attendant roads, the loss of life, the effects on wildlife, on communities; the impact on air quality, noise, travel time, and quality of life. Given our inability reliably to predict and evaluate the effects of even small-scale technology (e.g. the artificial heart),[18] the idea that we could predict the impact of global climate change reliably enough to permit meaningful economic analysis seems fatuous indeed.

When our ignorance is so extreme, it is a leap of faith to say that some analysis is better than none. A bad analysis can be so wrong that it can lead us to do bad things, outrageous things—things that are much worse than what we would have done had we not tried to assess the costs and benefits at all (this may be the wisdom in the old adage that "a little knowledge can be a dangerous thing").

What I have been arguing is that the idea of managing global climate change is a dangerous conceit. The tools of economic evaluation are not up to the task. However, the most fundamental reason why management approaches are

---

[18] See Jamieson (1988a).

doomed to failure is that the questions they can answer are not the ones that are most important and profound. The problems posed by anthropogenic global climate change are ethical as well as economic and scientific. I will explain this claim in the next section.

2. ETHICS AND GLOBAL CHANGE

Since the end of World War II, humans have attained a kind of power that is unprecedented in history. While in the past entire peoples could be destroyed, now all people are vulnerable. While once particular human societies had the power to upset the natural processes that made their lives and cultures possible, now people have the power to alter the fundamental global conditions that permitted human life to evolve and that continue to sustain it. While our species dances with the devil, the rest of nature is held hostage. Even if we step back from the precipice, it will be too late for many or even perhaps most of the plant and animal life with which we share the planet.[19] Even if global climate can be stabilized, the future may be one without wild nature.[20] Humans will live in a humanized world with a few domestic plants and animals that can survive or thrive on their relationships with humans.

The questions that such possibilities pose are fundamental questions of morality. They concern how we ought to live, what kinds of societies we want, and how we should relate to nature and other forms of life. Seen from this perspective, it is not surprising that economics cannot tell us everything we want to know about how we should respond to global warming and global change. Economics may be able to tell us how to reach our goals efficiently, but it cannot tell us what our goals should be or even whether we should be concerned to reach them efficiently.

It is a striking fact about modern intellectual life that we often seek to evade the value dimensions of fundamental social questions. Social scientists tend to eschew explicit talk about values, and this is part of the reason why we have so little understanding of how value change occurs in individuals and societies. Policy professionals are also often reluctant to talk about values. Many think that rational reflection on values and value change is impossible, unnecessary, impractical, or dangerous. Others see it as a professional, political, or bureaucratic threat.[21] Generally, in the political process, value language tends to function as code words for policies and attitudes that cannot be discussed directly.

A system of values, in the sense in which I will use this notion, specifies

---

[19] Borza and Jamieson (1990).   [20] McKibben (1989).   [21] Amy (1984).

permissions, norms, duties, and obligations; it assigns blame, praise, and responsibility; and it provides an account of what is valuable and what is not. A system of values provides a standard for assessing our behaviour and that of others. Perhaps indirectly it also provides a measure of the acceptability of government action and regulation.

Values are more objective than mere preferences.[22] A value has force for a range of people who are similarly situated. A preference may have force only for the individual whose preference it is. Whether or not someone should have a particular value depends on reasons and arguments. We can rationally discuss values, while preferences may be rooted simply in desire, without supporting reasons.

A system of values may govern someone's behaviour without these values being fully explicit. They may figure in people's motivations and in their attempts to justify or criticize their own actions or those of others. Yet it may require a theorist or a therapist to make these values explicit.

In this respect a system of values may be like an iceberg—most of what is important may be submerged and invisible even to the person whose values they are. Because values are often opaque to the person who holds them, there can be inconsistencies and incoherencies in a system of values. Indeed much debate and dialogue about values involves attempts to resolve inconsistencies and incoherencies in one direction or another.

A system of values is generally a cultural construction rather than an individual one. It makes sense to speak of contemporary American values, or those of eighteenth-century England or tenth-century India. Our individual differences tend to occur around the edges of our value system. The vast areas of agreement often seem invisible because they are presupposed or assumed without argument.

I believe that our dominant value system is inadequate and inappropriate for guiding our thinking about global environmental problems, such as those entailed by climate changes caused by human activity. This value system, as it impinges on the environment, can be thought of as a relatively recent construction, coincident with the rise of capitalism and modern science, and expressed in the writings of such philosophers as Francis Bacon, John Locke, and Bernard Mandeville.[23] It evolved in low-population-density and low-technology societies, with seemingly unlimited access to land and other resources. This value system is reflected in attitudes towards population, consumption, technology, and social justice, as well as towards the environment. The feature of this value system which I will discuss is its conception of

---

[22] Andrews and Waits (1978).   [23] See also Hirschman (1977).

responsibility. Our current value system presupposes that harms and their causes are individual, that they can readily be identified, and that they are local in space and time. It is these aspects of our conception of responsibility on which I want to focus.

Consider an example of the sort of case with which our value system deals best. Jones breaks into Smith's house and steals Smith's television set. Jones's intent is clear: she wants Smith's TV set. Smith suffers a clear harm; he is made worse off by having lost the television set. Jones is responsible for Smith's loss, for she was the cause of the harm and no one else was involved.

What we have in this case is a clear, self-contained story about Smith's loss. We know how to identify the harms and how to assign responsibility. We respond to this breech of our norms by punishing Jones in order to prevent her from doing it again and to deter others from such acts, or we require compensation from Jones so that Smith may be restored to his former position.

It is my contention that this paradigm collapses when we try to apply it to global environmental problems, such as those associated with human-induced global climate change. It is for this reason that we are often left feeling confused about how to think about these problems.

There are three important dimensions along which global environmental problems such as those involved with climate change vary from the paradigm: apparently innocent acts can have devastating consequences, causes and harms may be diffuse, and causes and harms may be remote in space and time. (Other important dimensions may concern non-linear causation, threshold effects, and the relative unimportance of political boundaries, but I cannot discuss these here.)[24]

Consider an example. Some projections suggest that one effect of greenhouse warming may be to shift the southern hemisphere cyclone belt to the south. If this occurs the frequency of cyclones in Sydney, Australia, will increase enormously, resulting in great death and destruction. The causes of this death and destruction will be diffuse. There is no one whom we can identify as the cause of destruction in the way in which we can identify Jones as the cause of Smith's loss. Instead of a single cause, millions of people will have made tiny, almost imperceptible causal contributions—by driving cars, cutting trees, using electricity, and so on. They will have made these contributions in the course of their daily lives performing apparently "innocent" acts, without intending to bring about this harm. Moreover,

[24] See Lee (1989).

most of these people will be geographically remote from Sydney, Australia. (Many of them will have no idea where Sydney, Australia, is.) Further, some people who are harmed will be remote in time from those who have harmed them. Sydney may suffer in the twenty-first century in part because of people's behaviour in the nineteenth and twentieth centuries. Many small people doing small things over a long period of time together will cause unimaginable harms.

Despite the fact that serious, clearly identifiable harms will have occurred because of human agency, conventional morality would have trouble finding anyone to blame. For no one intended the bad outcome or brought it about or was even able to foresee it.

Today we face the possibility that the global environment may be destroyed, yet no one will be responsible. This is a new problem. It takes a great many people and a high level of consumption and production to change the earth's climate. It could not have been done in low-density, low-technology societies. Nor could it have been done in societies like ours until recently. London could be polluted by its inhabitants in the eighteenth century, but its reach was limited. Today no part of the planet is safe. Unless we develop new values and conceptions of responsibility, we will have enormous difficulty in motivating people to respond to this problem.

Some may think that discussion about new values is idealistic. Human nature cannot be changed, it is sometimes said. But as anyone who takes anthropology or history seriously knows, our current values are at least in part historically constructed, rooted in the conditions of life in which they developed. What we need are new values that reflect the interconnectedness of life on a dense, high-technology planet.

Others may think that a search for new values is excessively individualistic and that what is needed are collective and institutional solutions. This overlooks the fact that our values permeate our institutions and practices. Reforming our values is part of constructing new moral, political, and legal concepts.

One of the most important benefits of viewing global environmental problems as moral problems is that this brings them into the domain of dialogue, discussion, and participation. Rather than being management problems that governments or experts can solve for us, when seen as ethical problems, they become problems for all of us to address, both as political actors and as everyday moral agents.

In this essay I cannot hope to say what new values are needed or to provide a recipe for how to bring them about. Values are collectively created rather than individually dictated, and the dominance of economic models has meant that the study of values and value change has been neglected.[25] However, I do have one positive suggestion: we should focus more on character and less on calculating probable outcomes. Focusing on outcomes has made us cynical calculators and has institutionalized hypocrisy. We can each reason: since my contribution is small, outcomes are likely to be determined by the behaviour of others. Reasoning in this way we can each justify driving cars while advocating bicycles or using fireplaces while favouring regulations against them. In such a climate we do not condemn or even find it surprising that Congress exempts itself from civil rights laws. Even David Brower, the "archdruid" of the environmental movement, owns two cars, four colour televisions, two video cameras, three video recorders, and a dozen tape recorders, and he justifies this by saying that "it will help him in his work to save the Earth" (*San Diego Union*, 1 April 1990).

Calculating probable outcomes leads to unravelling the patterns of collective behaviour that are needed in order to respond successfully to many of the global environmental problems that we face. When we "economize" our behaviour in the way that is required for calculating, we systematically neglect the subtle and indirect effects of our actions, and for this reason we see individual action as inefficacious. For social change to occur it is important that there be people of integrity and character who act on the basis of principles and ideals.

The content of our principles and ideals is, of course, important. Principles and ideals can be eccentric or even demented. In my opinion, in order to address such problems as global climate change, we need to nurture and give new content to some old virtues such as humility, courage, and moderation and perhaps develop such new virtues as those of simplicity and conservatism. But whatever the best candidates are for twenty-first century virtues, what is important to recognize is the importance and centrality of the virtues in bringing about value change.

3. CONCLUSION

Science has alerted us to the impact of humankind on the planet, each other, and all life. This dramatically confronts us with questions about who we are, our relations to nature, and what we are willing to sacrifice for various possible futures. We should confront this as a fundamental challenge to our values and not treat it as if it were simply another technical problem to be managed.

[25] But see Wolfe (1989); Reich (1988).

Some who seek quick fixes may find this concern with values frustrating. A moral argument will not change the world overnight. Collective moral change is fundamentally cooperative rather than coercive. No one will fall over, mortally wounded, in the face of an argument. Yet if there is to be meaningful change that makes a difference over the long term, it must be both collective and thoroughgoing. Developing a deeper understanding of who we are, as well as how our best conceptions of ourselves can guide change, is the fundamental issue that we face.

Postscript

Since this essay was written more than a decade ago, the evidence has continued to mount that human action is bringing about an extreme and rapid climate change whose consequences could be catastrophic for virtually all forms of life on earth. Yet thus far the responses from the nations of the world have been inadequate. The United States in particular has played an obstructionist role in delaying, weakening, and attempting to sabotage international action.

The authoritative source for information about this problem is *Climate Change 2001*, the Third Assessment Report of the Intergovernmental Panel on Climate Change, published in three volumes by Cambridge University Press. For my most recent thoughts on how to approach this problem see Jamieson (2001*b*).

19

Global Environmental Justice

Philosophers, like generals, tend to fight the last war. While activists and policy-makers are in the trenches fighting the problems of today, intellectuals are typically studying the problems of yesterday.

There are some good reasons for this. It is more difficult to assess and interpret present events than those which are behind us. Time is needed for reflection and to gather reliable information about what has occurred. The desire to understand leads to a style of life that is primarily contemplative and retrospective.

But there are also bad reasons for the relative neglect of contemporary problems. Philosophers typically write about what other philosophers write about, and if no one has written about a problem it is difficult to get anyone to write about it. Philosophy is also a deeply historical subject and for the most part the tradition has either been silent about environmental problems or what it has said is itself part of the problem. Moreover, philosophers have a toolbox of theories, methods, and concepts and like most people they want to work on problems that their tools can help to solve. And as I shall try to show, the results of applying philosophical theories of justice to problems of the global environment are disappointing.

One old philosophical wrangle which appears quaint in the context of today is the debate over whether and why there are duties and obligations that transcend national boundaries. It is easy to see why this was a problem in the past. Famines and other extreme events have occurred throughout history, but in many cases it was not known outside the affected regions that people were dying. Even when it was known and people were willing to help, little could be done to help those in need. When people are not culpably ignorant and they are not in a position to be efficacious there is little point in ascribing

Although I have not been able to take all of them into account, I especially thank Stephen M. Gardiner and James W. Nickel for their comments on an earlier draft of this essay.

duties to them. Today things are very different with respect to information and causal efficacy. We live in an age in which national boundaries are porous with respect to almost everything of importance: people, power, money, and information, to name a few. These help to make obligations possible. If people, power, money, and information are so transnational in their movements, it is hard to believe that duties and obligations are confined by borders.

A turning-point in popular consciousness about transnational duties was the Ethiopian famine of 1978. The fact that people in Africa were dying on a massive scale from the lack of what people in the North have in excess could not be denied. Since then images of dying children have regularly been brought into the living-rooms of the industrialized world. With images so stark and ubiquitous the old tactics of psychological evasion have begun to wither. We can no longer claim ignorance about the conditions of extreme poverty in which more than a billion people live. With the advent of jumbo jets and new technologies it can no longer be maintained that nothing can be done to help those in need who live beyond our national boundaries.

For present purposes I will assume that this old philosophical dispute has been resolved and that there are transnational duties and obligations.[1] I will assume further that it is meaningful to discuss whether some of these duties and obligations are related to ideals of global justice.

I will ignore many complications. I will use the terms 'duty' and 'obligation' more or less interchangeably, and will do the same with the terms 'global' and 'international'. I will be vague about the conditions under which a transnational duty is a duty of justice. I will simply assume that people have transnational duties and that it is an open question whether or not some of these are duties of justice. Some may deny that rich countries have duties of justice to intervene in Bosnia or Somalia (for example), but few people (I hope) would assert that it is meaningless or futile even to discuss whether or not they have such duties.

Our present topic arises because of the juxtaposition of the idea of global justice with that of environmental justice. In recent years the term 'environmental' has been used to modify all sorts of traditional harms and wrongs: racism, elitism, fascism, terrorism, blackmail, and so on. In the domestic American context discussions of environmental justice are typically about the fact that the poor suffer disproportionately from the environmental pollution produced by society at large. Dramatic examples of this include the white

---

[1] Of course there are still those who would deny that there are such duties. For discussion and references see Beitz (1979: 15–27).

working-class neighbourhood in Love Canal, New York, which was built on top of a toxic waste dump; the ongoing problem of uranium tailings negligently disposed of on Indian reservations in New Mexico and Arizona; and the continuing attempts to locate toxic waste dumps in poor black communities in the South.[2] In the international context there are similar examples. Questions about global environmental justice are raised when rich countries export toxic wastes to poor countries, sell pesticides to them that have been banned domestically, or make preservationist demands that would affect their prospects for development.

During the negotiations at the United Nations Conference on Environment and Development in Rio de Janeiro in 1992 the Bush administration grumbled that calls for global environmental justice were just attempts to resurrect the 1970s idea of a new international economic order. Those who advocated the creation of a new international economic order wanted to redistribute wealth and power from North to South.[3] Many people viewed the Bush administration's own international environmental policy as similarly anachronistic—the 1980s idea of Reaganomics writ large. If developing countries would privatize their economies and open their markets, then they would become rich enough to protect their share of the global environment. On this view there is no role for transfers or concessions from the rich countries to the poor.

Taken together, these views suggest that the rhetoric of global environmental justice is just the latest wrapping for the old struggle between the world's rich and poor. If both the Bush administration and its critics are right, the only green that world leaders are interested in is money. The main function of the word 'environmental' in 'global environmental justice' is to signal this year's model of last year's concerns, and perhaps to seduce some unwitting environmentalists into aligning with one side or another.

I believe that there is more than this to the idea of global environmental justice. But once the concept is analysed it does seem to break apart. It does not lend itself naturally to the application of "big-picture" theories of justice of the sort given to us by Rawls (1971) and Nozick (1974). Indeed, in my view, although the idea of global environmental justice has many elements, in the end it leads us away from concerns about justice between nations and towards notions of individual responsibility and of moral obligations that are mediated by various non-governmental forms of association. I will begin by distinguishing several elements of the idea of global environmental justice.

---

[2] For discussion of some of these issues see Bryant and Mohai (1992).
[3] See United Nations General Assembly (1974: 3). For discussion see Beitz (1979: 127–76).

1. GLOBAL ENVIRONMENTAL JUSTICE: EXPANDING THE BENEFICIARIES

Part of what is keyed by the phrase 'global environmental justice' is the idea that we may owe duties of justice to entities that traditionally have been regarded as beyond the pale. These may include wild animals, plants, species, populations, ecosystems, forests, canyons, and so on. On this view global environmental justice involves obligations to the global environment.

I agree that we have such obligations, at least to most animals.[4] The endangerment and extinction of many animals has been a global project in which many people and countries have been involved directly or indirectly. It makes sense to suppose that people and countries owe duties to creatures who have survived or not yet succumbed to our onslaught.

However plausible this may be, this is not what has been foremost in the minds of those who have been most vociferous in promoting the idea of global environmental justice. They believe that global environmental justice centrally concerns relations among humans rather than relations between humans and non-humans. If we want to understand what many people mean by 'global environmental justice' we will have to look elsewhere.

2. GLOBAL ENVIRONMENTAL JUSTICE: A CONDITION ON THE PURSUIT OF JUSTICE

On the previous account the occurrence of the word 'environmental' signalled the expansion of the class of those who are the beneficiaries of justice. On the present account the word 'environmental' refers to a condition on the pursuit of justice.

This element of global environmental justice is an important one but it is probably the least discussed of the three that I will distinguish. Global environmental justice, on this view, is the idea that global justice can only permissibly be pursued in ways that are environment-preserving.

The thought can be explained by an analogy. 'Environmental' can be understood as modifying 'justice' in much the same way as 'sustainable' can be understood as modifying 'development'.[5] On this view, the only permissible paths to development are those which are sustainable. If a pathway is unsustainable, then it fails this condition. While there is a lot of controversy about which

---

[4] See Essays 7–15.
[5] However, it should be noted that the expression 'sustainable development' is itself an ambiguous and difficult one. A good introduction to the literature is Pezzey (1992).

pathways satisfy this condition there are some clear cases of those that do not. For example, an approach to development which involves destroying the natural resource base of a country in order to produce commodities for export would clearly seem to fail this condition and thus be ruled out by the idea of sustainable development. Similarly, an approach to global justice that was not environment-preserving would be ruled out by this conception of global environmental justice. As in the case of sustainable development it is not completely clear what this constraint comes to, but it is easy to imagine some cases in which it might be violated. For example, suppose that a rich country intends to transfer resources to a poor country in an attempt to rectify an existing injustice. But suppose that the poor country plans to use these resources to create a huge hydro-project that will destroy ecosystems, kill many animals, and force many people from their homes. This would appear to violate the canons of global environmental justice, understood in this way.

So, one element of global environmental justice conditions the way justice can permissibly be pursued. In this respect it is like a "side-constraint" on the pursuit of justice.[6] This may be an important element of global environmental justice, but it is not the most important one to those who use this language.

3. GLOBAL ENVIRONMENTAL JUSTICE: DISTRIBUTING THE BENEFITS AND BURDENS OF ENVIRONMENTAL COMMODITIES

Perhaps the most important idea of global environmental justice views the environment as a commodity whose distribution should be governed by principles of justice. Since many aspects of the environment cannot physically be transferred from one country to another, this view is more precisely thought of as advocating the distribution of the benefits and costs of environmental commodities according to principles of justice. It is an open question how environmental commodities are defined, how benefits and costs are assessed, and what theory of justice is appropriate.

Even without further characterization some elements of this view are clear. Those who promote this idea of global environmental justice argue that in the course of becoming rich the countries of the North incurred an environmental debt which they now owe to the countries of the South. The rich countries polluted the air, depleted the ozone, reduced biodiversity, and threatened the stability of the global climate. Indeed many would say that these environmen-

---

[6] For the notion of a "side-constraint" see Nozick (1974).

tal debts are the necessary costs of development and not just its inadvertent by-products. The countries of the North became rich by exploiting the environment. Now that they are rich these same countries place a very high value on environmental protection. Environmental commodities are more precious and vulnerable than ever because of the insults that the environment has already suffered. However, instead of acknowledging their environmental debt and arranging a payment plan, the countries of the North are demanding further sacrifices from the countries of the South. In order to help stabilize the climate Brazil is not supposed to develop Amazonia; India is expected to forgo the benefits of refrigeration rather than release ozone-depleting chemicals into the atmosphere; and Indonesia is supposed to devote some of its scarce land to habitat for the Javan Rhino rather than using it in productive activities for the benefit of its burgeoning human population. From the perspective of the developing world it looks as if those who had the party expect those who didn't to pick up the tab. Indeed, it is even worse than this. The party is still going on in the rich countries of the North. Poor people are expected to forgo necessities while the consumerism of the rich continues to increase.

This picture of global environmental justice seems generally to cohere with our overall picture of global justice. The parties who are the subjects and beneficiaries of the obligations are nations.[7] The case for transfers from the North to the South seems very strong from the perspective of most major theories of justice. A Rawlsian might see the Difference Principle as warranting such transfers; an entitlement theorist might base them on the need to rectify past injustices; a utilitarian may view such transfers as utility-maximizing; and a communitarian might see them as required by the social bonds of the emerging global community. On this conception of global environmental justice, the big-picture theories of justice function as they ordinarily do. The environment is seen as a commodity to be distributed in accordance with principles of justice. In principle, it is not different from money, food, or health care.

However, there are problems with thinking of the environment in this way. The first difficulty, unlikely to move many philosophers, is practical. Even if there were widespread agreement that the rich countries have incurred an environmental debt that they must now begin to repay, it is far from clear what is required. There are questions about the size of the debt, its distribution across various societies, and the pace at which the recession-racked

[7] Beitz (1979) and Pogge (1989) have recently rejected what Beitz calls "the morality of states". I agree with them on this point, but neither addresses questions of the environment, and our positive views regarding duties across national boundaries are quite distinct.

economies of the North should be expected to pay it back. Even if there were agreement about all of this, the required steps would be politically impossible. "Foreign aid", as it is generally called, is unpopular in most countries. While still a senator, former Vice-President Gore advocated a global "Marshall Plan" (Gore 1992: 295–360). It is a testament to the political incompetence of his opponents that he could have been elected after advocating such a thing. (For an analysis of the role of environmental values in the 1992 American presidential election see Jamieson (1992).)

The case for this kind of environmental justice also runs into theoretical problems on close inspection. Northern countries, especially the United States, have been unwilling to transfer resources to poor countries without "conditionality". Conditionality requires beneficiaries to allocate resources in a particular way or to permit donors to play a role in the allocation process. Rich countries argue that without conditionality there is no guarantee that transfer payments will go towards preserving the environment. They point out that the governments of some developing countries assault and imprison their own environmentalists (e.g. Wangari Maathai in Kenya) or wink at those who kill them (e.g. the killers of Chico Mendez in Brazil). Moreover it is not just the rich countries who have abused the environment. Many poor countries have serious environmental problems caused by their own greed, shortsightedness and corruption.

The governments of most poor countries are hostile to conditionality. They see it as infringing their national sovereignty and expressing a lack of respect for their political institutions. Furthermore, poor countries point out that there is nothing conditional about the rich countries' exploitation of the global environment.

This clash between conditionality and sovereignty is part of the explanation for the anthropocentric and nationalist tones of the Declaration of Rio. After twenty years of a developing global environmental consciousness, the Declaration of Rio marked no real advance on the Stockholm Declaration of 1972.[8] The rich countries wanted conditionality and the poor countries wanted money; neither got much of what they wanted. Instead they agreed on a document that declared that there is a "right to development", that "human beings are at the centre of concerns for sustainable development", and that "states have . . . the sovereign right to exploit their own resources pursuant to their own environmental and developmental policies".

I believe that part of what this clash between conditionality and sovereignty

---

[8] Both are reprinted in Gruen and Jamieson (1994).

illustrates is the difficulties involved in treating the environment as a commodity, the benefits and burdens of which can be distributed on a global basis according to principles of justice. While this model may work for some kinds of environmental commodities (e.g. toxic wastes, pesticides, and so on), it will not work for all.[9] Many environmental goods are not transferable or are highly diffuse, or their value is non-compensatable.[10]

Consider the problem of biodiversity loss. One argument that has been made is that the entire world benefits from biodiversity, so countries that have a great deal of biological diversity within their borders should be compensated for their preservation efforts. Additional funds may also be owed to them because of biodiversity reductions caused by other parties. While this is a good idea in theory and probably should be supported even in practice, it bumps into problems of conditionality and sovereignty. The recipient of the compensation may not have the inclination or competence to use the transferred resources to preserve biological diversity. Or the government may simply decide that there are more urgent uses for the resources in eliminating poverty, homelessness and so on. To this donors may reasonably object that the recipients are supposed to be the guardians of a public good in which everyone has an interest; if they fail to discharge their duties the donors have permission to intervene. But recipients may reasonably argue that these payments are in part compensation for the rich countries disadvantaging the poor countries by their past and present plundering of a public good for private gain; the recipients therefore have no obligation to use these resources in the ways which the donors demand. Even if there is agreement in principle about the purpose for which these resources should be used, there may be no way to ensure that they are used efficiently in practice without serious breaches of the national sovereignty of the recipient countries. In so far as these breaches occur, the relationship looks more like one of environmental imperialism than environmental justice. But in so far as interventions do not occur, the global environment may continue to suffer.[11]

It is difficult to take one side or the other in this dispute. I find it

[9] One might reasonably object to this model even in some apparently clear cases. For example, it is not obvious that it is morally permissible to transfer toxic wastes from a rich country to a poor one, even if the benefits of receiving the waste appear to make people better off than they otherwise would be.

[10] Sovereignty intuitions are weak with respect to some other commodities as well as environmental ones. Few people believe that ownership entitles someone to destroy a great work of art. The analogy between artworks and environmental commodities is worth exploring in detail, but I cannot explore it here.

[11] In commenting on an earlier draft of this essay, Stephen M. Gardiner pointed out that the apparent clash between sovereignty and conditionality intuitions could be accounted for by a theory that

implausible to suppose that donors always have permission to impose conditions, or that they never have such permission. It seems to me that some forms of conditionality in some circumstances are justified. This belief is widely enough shared to warrant a brief investigation into its roots.

One reason for such a belief may be that unconditional transfers are not in the interests of the donors. This may be either because of a fear that the recipients will use these resources in ways that are directly counter to the interests of the donors, for example by supporting a military build-up, or because the donors will not obtain as much environmental protection as they desire.

A second reason for such a belief may be that unconditional transfers are not in the interests of the recipients. The thought may be that paternalistic conditionality will help recipients spend these resources more wisely, and thus further their own interests more effectively than would be the case if the transfers were unconditional.

A third source of the belief may be that unconditional government-to-government transfers do not ensure that the resources aid those who are entitled to the aid. This belief may involve a return to the idea that environmental justice involves obligations to non-human entities. The concern may be that recipient governments will not devote the resources to improving the forests and protecting the animal populations which are the real objects of concern. However, a second grounding for this belief involves seeing the citizens and residents of the recipient nations as those who are entitled to the benefits of the transfers. The fear is that the benefits will not "trickle down" from the recipient governments to those who have the entitlements.

It may be that under various conditions all or most of these concerns could be made consistent with the idea that there are duties of justice to engage in government-to-government transfers of environmental benefits and burdens. But taken together they appear to erode the plausibility of this view. In the ordinary case, a person or nation is permitted to be foolish with resources that are theirs as a matter of justice. Similarly they can frustrate the interests of those who owed them the resources, and even distribute them unjustly among their own people, without affecting their national claim to the resources. In my view, the strength and depth of the conditionality intuition in this case counts against the plausibility of the view that the environment is a com-

distinguished duties to rectify past injustices from other duties that we may have. On this view, the countries of the North may have duties unconditionally to transfer resources to the countries of the South in order to compensate them for past injustices associated with industrialization of the North. However, the countries of the South may also have duties not to pursue unsustainable development paths. On this view, the clash between the sovereignty and conditionality intuitions flows from confusing distinct duties rather than from treating the environment as a commodity. I cannot pursue this interesting suggestion here.

modity which can be distributed among governments in accordance with principles of international justice.[12]

A second kind of environmental commodity that is difficult to deal with on the basis of this model is one which is not located within the boundaries of any country. The ozone shield and a stable climate are two such commodities. The share of the benefits associated with these commodities which any country obtains may not be proportional to its contribution to preserving them. In order to protect the ozone layer, the United States, for example, was willing to absorb additional costs (by banning spray cans) years before the Europeans were willing to contribute. Currently the Netherlands appears willing to absorb more costs than other nations in order to promote climate stability. The willingness to absorb these costs may have no clear relation to the amount of harm that a nation suffers from the occurrence of the problem. The costs can be distributed according to some formula that is acknowledged to be just, but the benefits cannot be distributed at all. The benefits will be a function of the particular effects of the maintenance of the climate and the ozone shield in particular regions. Given the complexity and unpredictability of the atmospheric system and its social effects, it makes little sense to treat these goods as producing distributable benefits. (I discuss these matters further in Essay 18 and Jamieson (2001b).) For this reason it would be very difficult to treat these problems according to the model of justice currently under discussion.

A third problem with treating the environment as a commodity, the benefits and costs of which can be distributed in accordance with principles of justice, is that many environmental goods are irreplaceable and irreversible. When species are lost or climate changes, they will never return. Nature's path has been irrevocably affected by the development of Western science and technology. It is hard to conceive what the alternatives might have been, much more how to compensate those whose preferences and ways of life have been frustrated or destroyed.

4.   GLOBAL ENVIRONMENTAL JUSTICE VERSUS A GLOBAL ENVIRONMENTAL ETHICS

Thus far I have been explaining some of the complications that arise with respect to the idea of global environmental justice, and the difficulty in

---

[12] The human rights movement brought the topic of conditionality into play. It is plausible to think of international guarantees of human rights as infringements of national sovereignty. It should be noted that although governments in the developing world typically oppose conditionality, often their citizens do not. See e.g. Glantz (1990: 43–4).

squaring this idea with at least some of our intuitions about global environmental protection. This does not amount to the claim that there is no such thing as global environmental justice or that it ought not to be taken seriously. However, the notion is sufficiently problematic that we should try to examine alternatives that may be available in our moral traditions.

One problem that has haunted this discussion is the question of who the subjects and recipients of the duties are. As I have suggested, often in discussions of international justice it is assumed that it is governments which have duties and that typically they are owed to other governments. The costs and benefits 'trickle down' to the citizens or residents of each country. This assumption is problematic in the case of global environmental justice.

The global environmental movement has brought with it a new pattern of alliances and relationships. The environmental interests of the indigenous peoples of Brazil or the women of Kenya are often violated by their own governments, yet they may make common cause with women, indigenous people, or non-governmental organizations in other countries. Non-governmental organizations, scientists, and grassroots organizations have been profoundly important in affecting the future of the global environment. They have brought issues to light and pressured governments to take action, and often their own projects have been very effective. What this structure of relationships suggests to me is that rather than thinking about the problem of the global environment as one that involves duties of justice that obtain between states, we should instead think of it as one that involves actions and responsibilities among individuals and institutions who are related in a variety of different ways. Scientists may have duties to educate and train people who have little opportunity to develop the relevant skills and expertise on their own. Individuals in Europe or Japan may have duties to contribute to non-governmental organizations in Africa or Asia. Americans may have duties to limit their consumption or even to close down the local timber yard that specializes in tropical woods.

What I am suggesting is not that the various ideas of global environmental justice which I have explored be abandoned, but rather that they be supplemented by a more inclusive ecological picture of duties and obligations—one that sees people all over the world in their roles as producers, consumers, knowledge-users, and so on, connected to each other in complex webs of relationships that are generally not mediated by governments. This picture of the moral world better represents the reality of our time in which people are no longer insulated from each other by space and time. Patterns of international trade, technology, and economic development have bound us into a single community, and our moral thinking needs to change to reflect these new realities.

There is another reason why this model is a good one for thinking about duties that involve the environment. One reason why it is awkward to think of the environment as the object of our concern, a condition on our actions, or a commodity to be distributed, has to do with our peculiar relationship to the environment. While we can model various aspects of our relationship to the environment in these various ways, these models neglect the fact that we are situated in the environment. The environment conditions and affects everything that each of us does. The environment called us into existence and continues to sustain us. In part it constitutes our identities. To view the environment solely as a good to be distributed seriously misconceives our relationship to the earth.

20

Discourse and Moral Responsibility in Biotechnical Communication

We are living in the heart of the biotechnological revolution. Almost every day newspapers publish stories about new techniques and products that some scientist, venture capitalist, or major corporation hopes to develop and bring to market. Already biotechnology has a much larger effect on us than most people realize, particularly in the areas of food and medicine. If there were ever a time for an informed public debate about the uses and deployment of these technologies, it is the present. And yet I think that no such constructive debate is likely to occur. In my opinion, the development path of biotechnology will be determined by other imperatives than those that issue from meaningful public discourse. I shall try to explain why in this essay. The reasons are interesting, not just for understanding the development of biotechnology, but also because they generalize and apply to other complex, new technologies as well. Our kinds of societies are appallingly inept when it comes to rationally planning technological innovations and aligning them with our deepest social values.

Before I begin the discussion in earnest, some terms need to be clarified and some questions need putting aside. First, for present purposes nothing much hangs on exactly how 'technology' and 'biotechnology' are defined, so I will be using these terms in a broad, common-sense way. Secondly, I will primarily be discussing (bio)technological innovations as opposed to the technologies themselves. What I mean by a "technological innovation" is a proposal to implement a particular technology in a particular way. I speak in this way in part because I want to bypass the old debate about whether a technology implies its uses, whether it is neutral between them, or whether some complicated third thing is true of their relation.[1] For present purposes I want to remain agnostic to the greatest extent possible about whether a technology implies the particular use under discussion or whether it is a contingent fact that this is the use being envisioned for this technology at this particular moment. Finally, I will often speak the language of benefits and costs. Again, I will use these terms loosely in an everyday way, intending them to encompass both economic and social benefits and costs, but yet not so expansively as to include everything that can affect a creature's interests.

Let us begin by examining a plausible and influential model of how a proposed technological innovation might be assessed in order to see if it is desirable. We might say that if the expected benefits of some innovation exceed its expected costs, then everything else being equal, it should be implemented. Call this the "benefit-cost test" and the calculation that is needed to implement it the "benefit-cost calculation".

The restriction on the benefit cost test signalled by the words 'everything else being equal' is an important one, for the expected benefits of an innovation may exceed its expected costs yet still not be acceptable. The innovation may, for example, involve the violation of some fundamental rights. That an innovation violates rights is generally held to be the sort of consideration that may trump benefit-cost considerations. A classic example of such a case in many people's view is the following one drawn from discussions of the criminal justice system. It may be that the innovation of allowing the authorities to torture suspects would produce benefits that exceed the costs, since some guilty parties who are now acquitted would be convicted and some potential criminals would be deterred from committing crimes by the knowledge that they might face torture if arrested. But even if permitting torture would produce an excess of benefits over costs, it should still be barred, so it is argued, since the use of torture would seriously violate the rights of the accused. Similarly, a beneficial technological innovation may so deeply violate rights to privacy, property, or life that many would judge that it should not be implemented.

Already we can see the central role of information in enabling us to implement the benefit-cost test. Information is critical both in determining whether a rights-violation has occurred and in performing the benefit-cost calculation. Informed consent, which in some vague way must be founded on reliable information, can transform what otherwise would be a rights-violating action

---

[1] In the American debate over gun control the neutralist view is encapsulated in the slogan, "Guns don't kill people, people kill people".

into a permissible one. For example, cutting someone's flesh normally violates their rights but if the person in question consents to an operation, then making the incision is permissible (notice the shift in language, a topic to which I shall return).[2]

When it comes to performing the benefit-cost calculation I think that it is pretty obvious that for almost any complex technological innovation, we are quite unable to do it in a plausible way. We simply do not know how to supply the numbers for assessing proposals to genetically modify food, clone humans, or develop weed-resistant crops (for example). Our inability to perform the benefit-cost calculation is what leads many people to say that the question of whether to implement new technologies is essentially a problem of rational choice under conditions of uncertainty. Those who oppose implementing these technologies then go on to invoke a precautionary principle. If we can't demonstrate in a convincing way that a proposed technological innovation passes the benefit-cost test, then it should not be deployed. But those who favour new technologies argue that since in many cases the benefits can be fairly clearly identified, they should not be forgone on the basis of some imagined or hypothetical costs. Their view is that under conditions of uncertainty we should let economic actors do their thing and develop and deploy new technologies as they see fit. Both sides agree that questions about developing and deploying new technologies are essentially questions about managing uncertainty.

I disagree. The problem of whether to develop a new technology is often a question of ignorance rather than uncertainty. To put the point bluntly, we don't know enough about the consequences of deploying many of these technologies to be uncertain about them.

In order to understand the substance and significance of my claim we need to appreciate the distinction between uncertainty and ignorance, and to distinguish both from fallibility.[3] Fallibility refers to the fact that we could be wrong about virtually any sentence to which we give our assent, from the most homely (e.g. 'I know how old I am') to the most exotic (e.g. 'I know how old the universe is'). But from the fact that we could be wrong about something it does not follow that we are uncertain or ignorant of it. Even though I could be wrong about my age it is not true to say that I am uncertain of my age or ignorant about it.

---

[2] Though what I have to say in what follows bears on the question of informed consent I will not explicitly discuss this matter further.

[3] In this section I draw on two of my previously published papers: Jamieson (1996a, 1996b). I have also been influenced by Wynne (1992), although he draws these distinctions in a somewhat different way.

Uncertainty arises from ignoring fallibility. In order to be uncertain about something we must "blackbox" all sorts of background beliefs or treat them as unquestioned truths even though they could turn out to be false. Consider the following simple example which brings out the difference between uncertainty and fallibility.

Suppose that I discuss selling my bike to a friend. In this context, there is no uncertainty about whether I own the bike. We both take it as given that this is the case. Of course, it may be that due to fraud or forgetfulness I do not own the bike. But in our discussion, these possibilities are not on the table, and so there is no uncertainty about whether I own the bike even though it could turn out that I do not. Now imagine a situation in which we are highly suspicious of each other; it is well-known that I was once convicted of running a bike theft ring, or I suffer from amnesia. When the context is changed in one of these ways, the problem of uncertainty may arise. My friend may demand proof that I really own the bike before she will continue the discussion with me. What this homely example shows is that while we can always be wrong about (most) things, uncertainty requires particular contexts and social conditions. Indeed, this very example has important implications for uncertainty about risk. Uncertainty disappears or is minimized when we trust the institution, person, or data set that is being interrogated. It is magnified or accentuated when there is mistrust, whether founded on fraud or other failings.[4]

Uncertainty is a highly structured epistemological state that presupposes a lot of knowledge about a domain. Ignorance, on the other hand, prevails when our knowledge is so weak with respect to a domain that we are unable to "blackbox" enough elements for uncertainty to emerge. My claim is that when it comes to performing the benefit-cost calculation concerning many technological innovations, we are ignorant rather than uncertain. Not only can we not do the sums, but we don't know with any precision what sorts of things we would have to know in order to do them.

An obvious objection to my claim would be to say that it undervalues the present state of the science with respect to many proposed technologies, and under-appreciates the velocity with which scientific knowledge is increasing. It may be admitted that, while it is true that the benefit-cost calculations cannot now be precisely performed for many technological innovations, nevertheless they can be partially performed, and our ability to do the calculations is improving all the time. The problems that we face are thus problems of uncertainty rather than ignorance, and science is moving quickly to resolve many of the most important uncertainties.

---

[4] For further discussion, see Slovic (1993).

This reply rests on a misunderstanding about what sort of thing uncertainty is and how it gets constructed. Uncertainty is produced not just by narrow scientific mechanisms but also by broad cultural processes. The "blackboxing" that is required to construct uncertainty is a social process that relies on negotiation and accommodation among many interested parties, not just scientists. The materials from which uncertainties are constructed include a substratum of well-established societal conventions, shared purposes, common contexts, and collective knowledge. Assertions of uncertainty about technological innovations play a broad social role as well as a scientific one. They are part of what brings order to our world. Assertions of uncertainty imply both that there are some certainties in the domain under discussion, and that there is a path from one to the other. Claims of uncertainty reflect and establish epistemological order and are part of a process of moving towards closure. Narrow scientific facts alone are insufficient for establishing (or disestablishing) uncertainties. And when it comes to many large-scale technological innovations, we are not far enough along the road to closure for salient uncertainties to mark the way.

However, the most important problem with the reply we are considering is that it assumes that it is scientific information that is most important in making the risk-management problem more tractable. But while scientific information would be important to performing the benefit-cost calculation, it is information about the actual human use and social deployment of the technologies in question that matters most. The benefit-cost calculation for technological innovations depends on who will control them, who has access to them, how they will impact on the global (mal)distribution of wealth, how they will affect human health, how they will affect animal welfare, and on their ecological consequences. Indeed, even the purely biological effects of bio-engineering agricultural products (for example) depend importantly on how these products are actually used by farmers in the field. For any particular technological innovation we are quite ignorant about most of this, in part because the actual benefits and costs of the innovation will depend on decisions that people make subsequent to the initial decision to deploy the technology.[5] What humans will do in the future is not just unknown in the way that facts about the surface of Venus are unknown, but it is indeterminate. Thus, when a technological innovation is assessed *ex ante* there are not yet any facts to be discovered about how humans will use the technology. There are

[5] This is an important and under-appreciated point that bedevils social forecasting. For my first attempt to argue this, see Jamieson (1988*b*). For an unjustly ignored earlier discussion of this point, see Schumacher (1973: part IV, ch. 1).

only more or less reliable predictions that can have the strange effect of falsifying themselves.

Consider an example. Suppose that it is a hot summer day and I am planning to go to the beach. I hear on the radio that hundreds of thousands of people are expected to jam the roads on the way to the sea. I decide to go anyway. To my surprise, the roads are as clear as if it were a rainy, winter day. What happened is that, having heard the radio prediction, many people decided to stay at home. When we predict human behaviour, for example, that hundreds of thousands of people will jam the roads to the beach on a hot summer day, we are not only predicting something that is not yet determinate, but the very act of issuing the prediction can change the behaviour. It is as if the very act of predicting rain could affect the probability of rain occurring. Indeed, often part of the point of issuing predictions is to try to prevent what is being predicted from coming about. Opponents of various technological innovations predict that they will have terrifying consequences as part of a campaign to prevent their implementation.

Of course, we should not make too much of this point. When the behaviour is simple and the population is large or when the population is very small and well-known to us, we can sometimes successfully predict human behaviour. Still the reflexivity of human decision-making makes predicting human behaviour qualitatively different from predicting future states of simple physical systems.[6] While the reflexive nature of agency is important, the case for our ignorance about the effects of many technological innovations does not rest only upon it. Even if humans behaved more like particles than people, we would still be ignorant about the impacts of many of these innovations simply because of the complexity of the social world into which they are injected.

Let us take stock of where we are. I began by sketching a plausible model for how to justify biotechnological interventions. On this model, in order for innovations to be justified they must pass the benefit-cost test. I then argued that for most complex biotechnological innovations we are quite ignorant about how to do the calculation on which the test relies. This is because of the inherent complexity of the impacts of many technological innovations, and because exactly what impacts they have will depend on human agency. Thus far my discussion has been quite abstract, but I will now show how these considerations bear on an actual case of biotechnological innovation.

---

[6] It should be noted, however, that there are some philosophers who hold that indeterminism generally prevails in the physical world. For discussion see Dupré (1993). For more on prediction, see also Jamieson (1999*b*).

Monsanto is one of the world's largest biotechnology companies and a leader in the production of genetically engineered seeds. It has produced seeds for many crops, including canola and corn, that are both herbicide- and pest-resistant. These seeds are expensive to develop and market, and Monsanto requires the farmers who purchase them to sign an agreement promising not to plant the seeds that their crops produce. These agreements are difficult to enforce, especially since Monsanto does business all over the world. The US Department of Agriculture, in conjunction with a Mississippi seed company called Delta and Pine Land, developed and patented a technology that would enable a company to market seeds that would produce crops whose seeds would then be sterile. The technology involves inserting genes into a commercial crop plant that results in the plant producing toxins that will kill its seeds late in its growth cycle. Another gene is then inserted that suppresses the activities of the former genes until the seed is immersed in tetracyclene. When the seed is sold it is immersed and the suppressor gene is deactivated. When the commercial seed is planted it produces the bountiful harvest that is promised but late in the plant's cycle the toxin is released and the new seeds are killed. If the farmer wants to have the same harvest next year he must buy new seeds. Shortly after this technology was developed Monsanto bought Delta and Pine Land for more than one billion dollars, so Delta and Pine is now a subsidiary of Monsanto. At the last count the US Department of Agriculture and Delta and Pine Land had applied for patents on this technology in almost 90 countries.

Opponents of this technological innovation call it "the terminator gene". They argue that this technology will give Monsanto a virtual monopoly on the world's agriculture, and that developing country farmers who are not able to purchase designer seeds will be effectively eliminated from the market. They also argue that there is a substantial risk that the terminator genes will spread throughout nature. Professor Martha Crouch, a biologist at the University of Indiana, has published a series of papers sketching how this might be possible.[7] Opponents of the terminator technology also have more fundamental objections. According to Jeremy Rifkin, "From a social perspective, it's pathological. This is a question of who controls the seeds of life."[8] Protesters in India have set fire to company test fields and the US Department of Agriculture is being sued for violating its mandate to help American farmers.

Monsanto argues that it needs this technology in order to protect its investment in herbicide- and pest-resistant seeds. The agreements that farmers sign

[7] These are available on the web at http://www.bio.indiana.edu/people/terminator.html
[8] As quoted in *Time*, 1 February 1999: 42.

are difficult to enforce and patent protection is weak in many countries. In effect the terminator technology would become a biological enforcer of the company's property rights. Monsanto also argues that this technology is in the interests of developing world farmers since the new seeds will increase their harvests so dramatically that they will be able to buy them even though they are more expensive. As Delta and Pine Land vice-president Harry Collins states: "It will help them become more production-oriented rather than remaining subsistence farmers".[9] Monsanto, along with most plant geneticists who have discussed this matter, discount the possibility of the genes spreading. Indeed the US Department of Agriculture has stated that there appear to be no environmental risks to this technology.

Much more can be said about this technological innovation, but I think it should be clear by now that we are quite incapable of mapping this dispute on to the benefit-cost test. It is clear that this technology would substantially benefit Monsanto, but beyond that its benefits are only speculative. There are a lot of potential costs to implementing this technology but it is unclear how to identify their extent and probability. Some may also see this technology as engaging the "other things being equal" clause in the benefit-cost test because they see Monsanto's potential control over the world's food supply as violating human rights or because they see the whole idea of the terminator gene as morally repugnant or against nature.

I have claimed that with many complex technological innovations we are unable to implement the benefit-cost test *ex ante*, but it is also true in many cases that we cannot perform the test even after the technology has been implemented. Consider nuclear technology with which we have now lived for more than half a century. Did the use of nuclear weapons save lives by bringing World War II to a rapid end? Did nuclear deterrence prevent a third world war from breaking out in the last half of the twentieth century? Will a form of nuclear power be developed that is cheap and safe? These are the kinds of questions that we would have to be able to answer in order to apply the benefit-cost test. I submit that even in the case of a technology that we have lived with for so long we are still quite ignorant about how to apply the benefit-cost test. Nuclear technology, like all complex technological innovations, has simply become part of the fabric of our lives rather than an object of our evaluation.

This brings us to the question of how responsible parties should conduct themselves in discourse about biotechnological innovation. The temptation is

---

[9] As quoted in *Time*, 1 February 1999: 45.

to say something simple and grand (perhaps in the spirit of Habermas). We should speak the truth, we should be sincere, we should be relevant, and so on. But these simple injunctions are open to flexible interpretations.[10] Opponents of Monsanto say they are greedy; the company represents itself as a normal, profit-making entity. These descriptions have profoundly different resonances. Someone may say, signalling agreement, that "many scientists believe" something; others, indicating disagreement, may say that "some scientists believe" it. Who is speaking the truth? In an earlier example I pointed out how the language often follows an evaluation rather than merely characterizing a state of affairs that is open to evaluation. The distinction between cutting someone's flesh and making an incision is morally freighted, as is the difference between terminating a pregnancy and killing a baby. Even overlooking the problem of flexible interpretation, a case can also be made for supposing that we should not always abide by simple rules of truth-telling, sincerity, and so on. Suppose the other parties to the discourse do not conform to them. Suppose that they are vastly more powerful than you. Suppose that without some dramatic intervention they will carry the day and the consequences for the world will be very bad indeed.

The problem of responsible communication becomes even more difficult because of the diverse sites in which discussion of technological innovation occurs. We communicate in peer-reviewed journals, technical reports, lectures and seminars, radio and television, the popular press, through the internet and email, by conversation and gossip. The conventions that govern these different discourses are quite diverse. What would count as a lie in a peer-reviewed journal might be a useful simplification in a television sound-bite.

Another problem for responsible discourse, paradoxically enough, is the sheer volume of information that is available. A few hundred years ago it was possible for someone to have read everything important that had ever been written. In 1472 the library of Queen's College Cambridge contained 199 books. When Thomas Jefferson sold his library to the US Government in the early nineteenth century, providing the nucleus of the Library of Congress, his collection consisted of about 6,000 volumes.[11] Now about 20,000 newly published items arrive at the Library of Congress each day. About 50,000 books are published each year in America alone, and about 400,000 journals are published worldwide. These statistics don't even begin to consider the

---

[10] Americans have recently had a public tutorial on the flexibility of interpretation, especially in regard to words such as 'perjury', 'lying', 'intentional deception', and 'being incomplete about the truth'.

[11] This and subsequent information in this paragraph comes from an interview with James Billington, the Librarian of Congress, in the *International Herald Tribune* for 16 March 1999.

volume of information available on radio, television, and the worldwide web. Oddly enough, a strong case can be made for supposing that as the world has become increasingly information rich, many people have become less knowledgeable about what is important for living a good life and being an informed citizen.[12]

My conclusion, then, is that no constructive public debate is likely materially to affect the trajectory of biotechnological innovation. We are too ignorant of the consequences of these innovations to meaningfully evaluate them according to the benefit-cost test, and we are too awash in words to impose a disciplined discourse about them. Still this is not entirely a counsel of despair. Although there may be no model that will allow the systematic evaluation of technological innovations, we do know something about the changes they will bring and the world into which they are being inserted. In my opinion, social control is increasingly being asserted by large institutions that are corporate in structure, rationalist in outlook, and global in sweep. This tendency is being reproduced in the media whose role it is to reflect on the world and society. Currently, the internet is often a guerrilla voice for those engaging in critical reflection, and it is interesting that most of the opposition to the terminator gene has been generated on the internet while the mainstream press has been much more complacent about this innovation.[13] But there are many people in the world whose job it is to figure out how to bring the internet under commercial control, and they are succeeding by degrees. Whatever potential benefits biotechnological innovation may have, when launched into our current social environment its likely effect will be to magnify the trends that already prevail. If I am right, it will contribute to global inequality, cultural uniformity, and environmental risk. Whether one applauds or deplores these trends is a matter of one's core values. It is a matter of tactics as to how one engages with them. Perhaps, like most large-scale historical forces, these trends will only reverse when they have defeated themselves, but there is pleasure, significance, and even meaning in aligning oneself with the values one believes in, even if they are not likely to prevail in the foreseeable future.

Addendum

I thank Ray Spier (2000) for his thoughtful response to my "Discourse and Moral Responsibility in Biotechnical Communication", and for providing me

---

[12] For an interesting rumination on similar themes, see McKibben (1993).
[13] A good place to begin tracking opposition to the terminator gene is http://www.rafi.org/usda.html, the website of the Rural Advancement Foundation International.

with this opportunity to respond and to assess changes in the landscape that have occurred since my original essay was written.

Spier and I begin from the same basic framework. But Spier is optimistic about the consequences of the widespread use of biotechnology while I am sceptical. In order to understand this difference between us it is helpful to recover my purpose in writing the original article.

My focus in that essay was not on the full range of applications of bio-technology but on their use in cereal production. As a resident of Southern Minnesota I live in a pleasant, wooded community that is an island in a sea of fields devoted to the production of corn and soybeans. Last summer [1999], one-third to one-half of these fields were planted in GMO crops.

What was most striking to me was the "disconnect" between abstract, theoretical discussions of biotechnology in high-brow magazines and quality newspapers, and what was actually happening in the American Midwest. While the debate was gearing up, facts were being established on the ground by seed companies, farmers, elevator operators, and marketers. Their decisions to promote and plant GMO crops were not made on the basis of a global assessment of the risks and benefits of GMO crops, but because they stood to benefit from this agricultural innovation. The operative principle that guided decision-making was (to put it simplistically): "What's good for Monsanto is good for the world". This set me wondering about why disinterested ethical reflection seemed so inefficacious in this case, and what this might mean for the entire project of scientific and engineering ethics. The remainder of this essay reports my current thinking about these issues.

In my opinion, GMO agriculture will live or die by the market; discourse about ethics or the social control of technology will figure primarily as it affects the consumer acceptability of GMO foods or the share prices of the companies involved. This reflects both the power of the market and the weak-ness of ethical discourse in developed societies.

Ethical discourse is weak in developed societies for a number of different kinds of reasons. First, and most obviously, the playing field is not level. Market forces and economic interests are unbelievably powerful in contem-porary societies. This is so obvious as to hardly require comment. Secondly, technology seems to trigger many of the same reactions in people as religion, regardless of the exact form of the technological innovation. Cornucopians will see it as producing manna from heaven and more besides: it will heal the sick as well as feed the hungry. On the other hand, Cassandras will see the new technology as destroying the delicate fabric of social life and inevitably leading to catastrophic accident. These psycho-metaphysical stances are so ubiquitous that reasoned reflection on the risks and benefits of new technologies is often difficult in public fora. Thirdly, contemporary developed societies have not invested in establishing communities of reflection that could play a central role in directing technological development. Such communities are inherently interdisciplinary, and establishing them requires large investments in human capital, maintained over decades. A good model here is the establishment of the American space science community in the wake of the successful launch of the Soviet satellite, Sputnik, in 1957. It was more than a decade before this investment really began to bear fruit, and its most important effects were not felt until much later. By contrast consider the ELSI (Ethical, Legal, and Societal Implications) programme associated with the Human Genome Program. It is (rightly) considered revolutionary that about 5 per cent of the budget of a hard science programme should be invested in studies assessing the ethical and legal consequences of the technologies whose development will be enabled by the scientific research. But 5 per cent of the budget is a pathetic amount to spend if the goal is to create a first-rate community that can effectively assess the social and ethical dimensions of developing technologies. We would still be trying to leave Earth orbit if a similar approach had been taken to the space programme. Finally, it must be said that much of the work that is produced by the small, underfunded, and often demoralized community that studies the human dimensions of technology is not very impressive. Some of the reasons for this are implicit in what I have already said.

In my opinion the trajectory of the development of agricultural biotechnology is more likely to be affected by the market than by reflective ethical discussion. There are both advantages and disadvantages to this, most of which have been discussed at length in other contexts. The obvious advantage is that markets are extremely responsive; generally people get what they want. But some caveats are in order. 'People' here refers to those with hard currency, wants may be informed or uninformed, and the principle of aggregation is "one dollar (or pound or euro), one vote". Even more disturbing is the fact that the market that increasingly determines technological innovation is not the consumer market but the stock market. The stock market is an even worse institution for making these decisions than the consumer market because it is more insulated from broad-based revealed preferences, and is therefore even less egalitarian and more vulnerable to speculation.

Where does this leave the issue of agricultural biotechnology? In my opinion these technologies entail risks without providing solutions to the social problems with which we should be centrally concerned. In my part of America there is (always) talk of a "farm crisis". A little analysis shows that the major causes of the crisis are low commodity prices caused by overproduction, and the increasing share of agricultural income taken by increasingly powerful transnational corporations. Even if the newest and best products from these firms succeed in increasing production and lowering costs it will only exacerbate these problems. Spokesmen for the biotechnology companies often talk about the role their products will play in eliminating famine and malnutrition. But since the ground-breaking work of Nobel Prize-winning economist Amartya Sen in the 1970s, it has been clear that famine and malnutrition are largely caused by shortages of food entitlements (e.g. money) rather than by shortages of food. Any excess production that results from the widespread use of agricultural biotechnology will pit the spending power of the poor who want grain for direct consumption, against that of the growing global middle class who want grain for animal feed so that they can eat more meat. The results of this auction are obvious, as are the effects on global ecology, animal welfare, and human health. Moreover, the widespread use of agricultural biotechnology will continue to empower the handful of transnational corporations that control agricultural inputs at the expense of most farmers, consumers, and even governments. In addition to these problems, I am also concerned about the direct ecological effects of the widespread use of GMO products, since the science in this area is in its very early stages while it is very clear that markets tend to externalize or understate ecological risks. Agricultural biotechnology may be a solution to some problem somebody faces, but it is not a solution to the serious problems of food security and environmental quality that face the global community.

What this exchange between me and Spier shows is that even those of us who agree about the most fundamental features of life (e.g. materialism, consequentialism, etc.) can still disagree about the policies that should flow from these commitments. I am sceptical about the benefits of agricultural biotechnology; he apparently is not. But the deeper issue with which we should both be concerned is the apparent inability of ethical discourse to affect this debate, except indirectly through its impact on stock prices and consumer behaviour. If I am right about this, the disempowerment of ethical discourse in the face of rapid technological change is a very serious problem indeed. Sometimes in my darker moments I wonder whether we should tell our brightest and most highly motivated students who want to change the world that they should become investment bankers rather than scientists or philosophers.

21

Sustainability and Beyond

1. INTRODUCTION

During the decade of the 1980s the phrase "sustainable development" migrated from an obscure report produced by the International Union for the Conservation of Nature and Natural Resources in 1980, through several popular "green" books, to become the central organizing concept of the Brundtland Commission report. Convened by the General Assembly of the United Nations and known officially as the World Commission on Environment and Development, the Brundtland Commission identified sustainable development as the criterion against which human changes of the environment should be assessed, and defined it as development that "meets the needs of the present without compromising the ability of future generations to meet their own needs" (The World Commission on Environment and Development 1987: 43). By joining the words 'sustainable' and 'development', the Commission sought to reconcile the demands of the environment with concerns about global poverty. Ramphal (1992: 143), who served on the Brundtland Commission, has recently written that "the great achievement of the sustainable development concept is that it broke with the old conservationist approach to natural resources and its tendency to place Earth's other species above peoples". While those who were most concerned with poverty could emphasize the word

Earlier versions of this material were presented as a Matchette Lecture to the North American Society for Social Philosophy, and to the Federal Lands Sustainability Project of the University of Colorado Natural Resources Law Center. It was also discussed by the University of Colorado's Environmental Ethics Reading Group. I thank the members of these audiences, the staff of the Center, and Dr Richard Wahl and Dr Joseph Weissmahr for their helpful comments on earlier drafts.

'development' in the Brundtland formulation, environmentalists could just as well emphasize the word 'sustainable'.

The balance between fruitful ambiguity and outright contradiction is a delicate one, and ultimately the idea of sustainable development could not bear the weight of competing interpretations.[1] Over the last decade "sustainable development" has given way to the idea of sustainability. While on the surface this may appear to be a victory for environmentalists, it reflects a number of distinct concerns, including the colonization of the sustainable development discourse by economists, the lack of interest in development in the already developed countries, and the growing awareness that sustainable development should be directed towards building societal capabilities rather than towards development as an end in itself. But while sustainability is almost universally considered to be a good thing (there are few who would defend unsustainability), the tensions implicated in "sustainable development" are increasingly recapitulated in the various conceptions of sustainability. These ambiguities go back to the earliest English uses of "sustain" and its cognates. One family of meanings is related to the idea of sustenance; a concern with needs is a natural extension of this notion. A second family of meanings centres on maintaining something in existence, and leads naturally to a focus on preservation. The former pushes in the direction of "meeting the needs of the present" while the latter leans towards concern for the interests of the future.

In this essay I discuss both the limitations and possible uses of the sustainability discourse. I begin by canvassing various conceptions of sustainability and sketching some difficulties with the notions that have been introduced. Next some possible uses of the idea of sustainability are identified. I go on to discuss these in the context of disputes over public lands in the United States. Finally, I say why we must go beyond sustainability if we are to address successfully the present disorder regarding the human relationship to nature.

2. THE MEANING AND IMPORTANCE OF SUSTAINABILITY

Many questions can be asked about sustainability. Two of the most important are: what exactly is sustainability and how important is it to achieve sustainability? While the answers to these questions overlap, they shall be discussed in turn.

---

[1] Redclift (1987).

2.1 What is Sustainability?

Most people's thoughts about the meaning of sustainability are probably simple and grand: sustainability is about human survivability and the avoidance of ecological disaster. The professional discourse, on the other hand, is complex and technical. What both discourses share is an anthropocentric outlook. It is human survivability and well-being that ultimately matter; nature enters the picture only as a means. (Exceptions to this are "biocentrists", and those who take the interests of animals seriously.)[2]

At least two distinct conceptions of sustainability have been developed. Strong sustainability (SS) asserts that it is "natural capital" that should be sustained while weak sustainability (WS) is centred on well-being.[3] Both conceptions of sustainability have their problems.

WS, which is more likely to be embraced by conventional economists than SS, can be characterized as a state in which "well-being does not decline through time".[4] Here are three problems with the idea of WS.

First, WS makes no essential reference to environmental goods. Clear-cutting forests and driving species to extinction would pass the WS test, so long as human well-being does not decline as a result. In principle, human well-being would not decline so long as other goods that are substitutable for forests and species could be purchased with the money that these policies would produce.

Secondly, there is little reason to object to declines in well-being so long as they are on the optimal path (however optimality is defined). Most of us would prefer a path that involved greater well-being to a path that involved lesser well-being, even if the former path included a period of decline while the latter path did not. This is an abstract version of the common-sense belief that sometimes we would choose to accept a setback (e.g. an operation) in order to produce a result that is better overall (e.g. becoming cancer-free) than the alternatives.[5]

Finally, some would object to characterizing sustainability in terms of welfare rather than resources. For example, Daly writes that "the welfare of future generations is beyond our control and fundamentally none of our business . . . our obligation therefore is not to guarantee their welfare but their capacity to produce, in the form of a minimum level of natural capital" (Daly 1995). The idea is that a generation has a great deal of control over the

---

[2] See Taylor (1986) and Singer (1975/2001).
[3] Beckerman (1994, 1995); Turner et al. (1995); Holland (1996).
[4] Pearce (1993).   [5] Heyes and Liston-Heyes (1995).

resources that it bequeaths to its successors, but little control over their welfare. There is the further objection that it is at least possible that future generations would have the highest welfare levels if we were to exploit nature to the greatest possible extent and invest the economic benefits in ever more convincing virtual reality machines. Whatever may be said on behalf of such a proposal, it would not satisfy any reasonable understanding of sustainability, though it would pass the WS test.

SS is more in the spirit of environmentalism than WS, but it too faces difficulties.

First, since SS is defined in terms of the maintenance of the stock of natural capital, natural capital must be defined and distinguished from human-produced capital. Berkes and Folke (1994: 129) characterize natural capital in the following way:

Natural capital consists of three major components: (1) nonrenewable resources, such as oil and minerals, that are extracted from ecosystems; (2) renewable resources, such as fish, wood, and drinking water that are produced and maintained by the processes and functions of ecosystems; and (3) environmental services such as maintenance of the quality of the atmosphere, climate, operation of the hydrological cycle including flood controls and drinking water supply, waste assimilation, recycling of nutrients, generation of soils, pollination of crops, provision of food from the sea, and the maintenance of a vast genetic library.

What is most striking about this characterization is the degree to which human interests and activity are implicated in the examples of natural capital that are provided. Non-renewable resources are only natural capital if they are "extracted from ecosystems". (It's not clear whether it is the kind of thing that must be extracted or the very material itself if something is to count as natural capital.) Renewable resources such as "wood", "drinking-water", and the "quality of the atmosphere" are not given to us by brute nature. Nature produces trees; humans act on trees in such a way so as to be able to use their wood. What makes water drinking-water is that it is fit for humans to drink. Similarly, atmospheric changes are only deteriorations in the quality of the atmosphere relative to human uses of the atmosphere. The fundamental problem with the idea of natural capital is that the very idea of capital implicitly involves the idea of human transformation and use; thus it is quite difficult to distinguish natural from human-produced capital.

Secondly, some account must be given of what exactly it means to maintain natural capital. Read in the strongest way, any reduction in the stock of Earth's natural resources would violate SS. Read in the weakest way, natural capital would be maintained so long as there were no reduction in the kinds of things that exist, even if the stocks of each kind were radically reduced. Daly reads this requirement as permitting reductions in stock so long as the benefits produced by such reductions are invested in "a real rather than a merely financial substitute—e.g. a capital set-aside from petroleum depletion should be invested in new energy supplies, including improvements in energy efficiency, but not in, say, law schools, medical research, or McDonald's Hamburger franchises" (Daly 1995: 51).

An analogy may help to clarify the point. If I sell part of my stamp collection and use the proceeds to buy more stamps, then it seems plausible to say that my stamp collection is maintained through these transactions. If, on the other hand, I sell part of my stamp collection and use the money to go on a tour of Michelin-starred restaurants, then my stamp collection has not been maintained. Daly's point is that using the benefits of petroleum depletion to invest in new energy supplies is a way of maintaining our energy endowment, while investing in law schools is not. The reason for this is that natural and human-produced capital are complements, not substitutes; therefore human-produced capital of the sort that investing in law schools would provide, cannot be a substitute for the loss of natural capital entailed by petroleum depletion.

Daly gives three arguments for the complementarity of natural and human-produced capital.

The first argument rests on pointing out that the existence of human-produced capital presupposes natural capital, but the existence of natural capital does not presuppose human-produced capital. Even if this claim is true, it establishes very little, for this claim is consistent with supposing that vast amounts of human-produced capital require only tiny amounts of natural capital. We could accept the presupposition and still hold that substitutability is generally the rule.

The second argument rests on viewing human-produced capital as the agent for the transformation of natural capital into products. It is difficult to understand fully this claim since it is misleading to ascribe agency to capital. However, the basic idea appears to be that production requires both natural and human-produced capital. This claim seems just false (except in the most trivial sense) for intellectual property, services, and some other commodities. However even if this argument establishes complementarity over some domain, it is not clear how important this result is without some further account of how invariant are the ratios of natural to human-produced capital. A high degree of variance would indicate a large range of substitutability.

Finally, Daly argues that if human-produced and natural capital were substitutable, then people would not have bothered to accumulate human-produced capital. Since they have bothered to accumulate human-produced capital, substitutability must fail. The fundamental error here is in assuming that natural capital and human-produced capital must either be substitutable or complementary, but cannot be both. As Beckerman points out, commodities may be complements in some respects and substitutes in others. For example, we may regard wood and plastic as complementary—preferring to use wood for some purposes and plastic for others—yet treat them as substitutes in our market behaviour (Beckerman 1995).

To the extent that the distinction can be made at all, the plain fact is that we often treat natural and human-made capital as substitutes. For example, in recent years we have substituted synthetic materials for natural ones across a wide range of uses, and various energy conservation programmes involve substituting behaviour change for resource consumption. Indeed, in Daly's own example it is plausible to suppose that investing in law schools could be a substitute for investing in new energy sources. Since many of the barriers to energy efficiency are institutional, investing in law schools (or other forms of human capital) may do as much to preserve our energy endowment as investing in new energy sources.

Thus far Daly's anti-substitutability claim has been treated as if it were straightforwardly descriptive. But perhaps he is making a normative rather than descriptive claim. His point may be that we ought not to treat natural and human-produced capital as substitutable—not that we do not. But we may ask why we should accept this restriction on substitution if well-being would be improved by violating it, for example, by using the benefits of petroleum depletion for law schools or medical research rather than for energy conservation. The reply may be that while violating this restriction may be a good thing to do, it would not be sustainable, and the attempt here is to give an analysis of sustainability. One response to this reply would be to say so much the worse for sustainability. If concern for sustainability does not lead us to do what is best (or at least better), then it is hard to see why we should make it decisive in our decision-making.

In addition to these questions about what should be sustained, the idea of sustainability also raises questions of scale.[6] No one expects humans or other forms of life to last forever. Indeed, evolutionary theory implies that they will not. Given that "forever" is not a reasonable answer to the question of how long we should try to sustain something, we need some way of thinking about the temporal goal of sustainability. Our resource management policies would

---

[6] Worster (1993).

be very different if sustainability were thought of in terms of millennia rather than decades. Similar questions arise with respect to geographical scale. Should people attempt to maintain natural capital in their bioregions, their states, their countries, their continents, their planet, or in their solar system? These may sound like silly or "academic" questions, but they arise in real debates about (for example) whether a population or species can be reduced or eliminated in one area so long as it is increased or preserved in another. Focusing on national or subnational sustainability can also lead to very different policies regarding trade than focusing on global sustainability.

2.2 How Important Is It to Achieve Sustainability?

As important as sustainability is to many people now, it is hard to believe that it has always been an important goal. Indeed, it is interesting to imagine what response people in diverse cultures at earlier times would have had to the idea of sustainability. While various cultures have been more or less "biophilic"[7] and attitudes towards nature have been many and varied, I doubt that the idea of sustainability would generally have resonated with people outside our immediate cultural context. For most of human history nature has been too large and overwhelming for people to worry about sustaining it. Moreover, whatever sustaining is to be done has been someone else's job in most cultures. God or providence have generally been regarded as the sustainers of both humans and nature. In the twentieth century we have lost confidence in the idea that the world is self-sustaining or under divine protection. At the same time we see that the threat to nature comes primarily from ourselves. Ironically, since there are no other applicants for the job, we who are nature's greatest enemy have appointed ourselves as its saviour. In my opinion, the idea of sustainability is a distinctly modern notion, closely tied to the schizophrenia of modern life that simultaneously persecutes nature while trying to protect it (Essay 12).

The importance of sustainability is not beyond question. Holland (1995) has pointed out that the value of some goods, ranging from disposable nappies to sunsets, is partly constituted by their transitory nature. Any attempt to sustain them would be silly or self-defeating. But perhaps we should go further and embrace the lessons of the new ecology—that turmoil and change is the way of nature.[8] From this perspective everything is disposable or transient, not just nappies and sunsets. On this view, our resistance to change is more psychological than logical. Just as humans fear and avoid death, so they resist environmental change. Tranquil people and societies, more attuned to the

---

[7] Wilson (1984).   [8] Botkin (1990).

ways of nature, would perhaps be accepting of both death and environmental change.

The concern for sustainability may be a distinctively modern one and it may not be appropriate to sustain everything we value. Still, in general, we value sustainability, although people disagree about its scope and importance. Over the human population there is a range of attitudes about the importance of sustainability. Most people probably believe that some things should be sustained at all costs, others got rid of as soon as possible, and that most things fall somewhere in between. What category things end up in depends in part on people's attitudes towards them. Many people think that the human species should be sustained at all costs, as well as human communities and cultures, even ones that are economically inefficient or exploitative. On the other hand, most people probably think that HIV should be driven to extinction as soon as possible. Various snail darters fall somewhere in between, with different people assigning very different weights to the importance of sustaining them.[9]

What is important to recognize is that even if it is generally accepted that sustainability is a good thing, the question of how good a thing cannot be avoided. Sustainability must sometimes be traded off against other goods, including the welfare of our poor contemporaries. This is the trade-off that the Brundtland Commission wanted to avoid, but it is inescapable.

Summarizing this section we can say that the concept of sustainability is deeply contested, perhaps even confused. People disagree about what it is and how seriously we should regard it. Disagreements about sustainability reflect not only different interests, but also different ideals and values. These involve disagreements about the range of proper human relationships to nature, how decisions should be made, and whose voices should prevail. However, despite the contested nature of sustainability, this idea may have its uses.

3. THE USES OF SUSTAINABILITY

It is quite common for parties in environmental disputes to seek the normative high ground. One way of trying to do this is to define a technical term,

---

[9] Here reference is made to a small fish, the discovery of which put the brakes on the half-built, multi-billion-dollar Tellico Dam. There were many reasons not to build the dam, but the fact that it was (temporarily) halted by a "trash" fish led to amending the Endangered Species Act and setting the stage for future assaults on the Act. For discussion, see Wheeler and McDonald (1986).

and then implement the hypothetical imperative suggested by it. For example, some environmentalists have attempted to define a technical notion of ecosystem health, suggesting that environmental policy should follow by implication.[10] If successful, they wrongly bypass the ethical and political disputes that are at the heart of environmental questions. If they fail, they provide another, generally more confused forum in which the ethical and political conflicts are reproduced.[11]

Despite these reservations, it is important for people who disagree to practise a common discourse and, to some extent anyway, have a common conceptual framework. Because of the very breadth of the notion of sustainability and its popular appeal, this language has the potential to structure discourse between people who have quite different values and epistemologies. At this stage anyway, no one owns the sustainability discourse in the way in which ecologists own the discourse of ecosystem health. If parties to a dispute can agree that sustainability matters, then arguments will turn on the meaning of sustainability and how various policies contribute to its realization. There will be room for a great deal of disagreement, but the parties will at least be using the same words even if they assign them different meanings. Some progress will have been made if they can agree on the importance and centrality of sustainability, even if they disagree about what sustainability is and how it can be realized. This may seem like a small achievement, but often parties to various disputes do not even share a common vocabulary, much less a common conceptual framework.

As a negative example, consider the current dispute in America over the death penalty. The small band of abolitionists speaks of the death penalty's lack of deterrence, while those in favour of the death penalty speak of the need for retribution. They disagree not just about the death penalty, but also about what considerations are relevant in deciding whether or not to support it. Not only are their beliefs distinct but their vocabularies are disjoint.

Although the sustainability discourse has some potential usefulness, at the level of abstract, philosophical discussion it is unlikely to have much traction. As we have seen, even the technical definitions of sustainability are excessively abstract and in at least some cases fail to be sufficiently sensitive to environmental concerns. The language of sustainability is likely to be most powerful when used in highly contextualized concrete cases, and when it is employed negatively. These suggestions will be discussed in turn.

People may have no idea what sustainability means in general, yet have

---

[10] Costanza *et al.* (1992).   [11] Essay 15.

definite ideas about what it would be like for Boulder, Colorado, Rocky Mountain National Park, or the Northern Rockies region to be sustainable. Focusing on specific questions not only provides content to various abstract conceptions of sustainability, but also helps make clear the trade-offs between sustainability and other goods. If, for example, sustainability for Colorado's Front Range means that no one can have a lawn because water transfers from other watersheds are not allowed, then some people may decide that sustainability is not such a good idea after all and that it should take a back seat to other values. While some people may think that moving from vague agreement to precise disagreement is a step in the wrong direction, I disagree. I believe that some progress will have been made if people understand the choices and trade-offs they face and confront them directly, even if they disagree (at least initially) about how to respond.

In many specific contexts the language of sustainability can be made more useful by focusing on what is unsustainable rather than on a positive definition of sustainability. Often people who would initially disagree about what sustainability is can agree about when something is unsustainable. Ranchers and environmentalists (for example) may agree that eroded, denuded land is unsustainable, even if they disagree about what it would be like for the land to be sustainable. People may have different ultimate goals, yet be able to work together in preventing practices which they agree are clearly unsustainable. Moreover, once they have found some common ground about what is unsustainable, they may be able to go on to agree about the causes of these unsustainable practices. This, in turn, may bring some agreement about what policies should be adopted and what should be avoided.

If one is correct in thinking that the language of sustainability is most likely to be useful when employed negatively in highly contextualized situations, then ironically the discourse of sustainability is least likely to be useful at the level for which it was originally intended. At the global level there is too little by way of shared beliefs and values to provide enough content to ideas of sustainability to make them effective. Since talk about global sustainability is far removed from concrete cases and situations, meaningful discourse is unlikely to occur. Too many ground-level beliefs and presuppositions drop out at the global level to make progress, and perhaps even mutual intelligibility, possible. The forms of unsustainability and the causal linkages involved are too diverse to command much by way of common responses.

If what has been said is correct, the language of sustainability is more likely to be useful in small communities facing specific problems. However, despite my scepticism, there is a desperate need for human thought and language to become as integrated as the problems we face. While these problems are global, the interests and understandings of humankind are fractured and fragmented. One can hope that the sustainability discourse which has become so ubiquitous may have some role to play in contributing to this integration.

4. SUSTAINABILITY AND THE PUBLIC LANDS

It is an obvious fact that there is a great deal of conflict about the use and control of public lands. Although the sustainability discourse may have some role to play in managing these conflicts, we should not think that it alone can resolve them. Nor should we think that conflicts about the public lands are necessarily caused by how these lands are managed.

There is a great deal of anger, alienation, and insecurity in American society, and this often finds expression in issues that have little to do with the sources of these feelings. If it is true that the causes of conflict over the public lands are wider than these issues themselves, then we should not expect policy change in this area to end the conflict. Another reason we should be modest about the possibility of progress in this area is that the issues are highly politicized; and diverse, often conflicting, interests, preferences, and values are at stake. While progress can be made on such issues, it requires time, goodwill, respectful dialogue, and a sense of community, all of which are in short supply. The idea of sustainability has its uses, but it cannot perform miracles.

It should come as no surprise that debates about the uses and control of public lands are so heated and polarized when there is so much disagreement about how to use private land. A look around Boulder, or any comparable town in the West, shows that there are quite different views about appropriate land-use. Some people use their yards as car parks or storage. Others put in gravel or concrete in order to reduce maintenance. Some xeriscape,[12] while others grow lawns and flowers that are characteristic of the eastern United States. Still others let "nature take its course". People with lawns are often afraid that their yard will be contaminated by weeds or unwanted native plants from the neighbour's yard. The xeriscaper may hate the smells coming from her neighbour's compost pile. Parking a car in a yard is illegal in Boulder. Some neighbourhoods have restrictive covenants against replacing lawns with rocks. When we move to the question of development, conflicts increase. Many people would reject the idea that their neighbours have a right to build additional living units on their property or to open a commercial establishment. Imagine how people

---

[12] This useful word, from the Greek 'xeros' meaning "dry" and the English word 'landscape', was coined by the Denver Water Board in 1981 to refer to landscaping with dryland plants.

would respond to their neighbours turning their land into gravel pits. Zoning restrictions typically separate commercial and residential uses, and specify variable densities in different neighbourhoods. These restrictions are often quite inconsistent, arbitrary, and in many cases involve bad planning; yet to a great extent they are often quite representative of people's attitudes.

In the case of private lands, most people believe that owners' decisions should carry a great deal of weight in determining land-use. In the case of public lands, the very idea of public ownership is contested. Not only do people have different desires about how these lands should be used, but there is little agreement about how conflicts should be resolved.

Many people in the American West believe that there should be a pyramid of authority in which those who live close to the land or use it for extractive purposes should have the loudest voice in determining how public lands are used. Indeed, many of these people are opposed to the whole idea of public land. They believe that, morally speaking, they own these lands but that the federal government has usurped their title to them. Environmentalists and many people who live in the rest of the country reject the pyramid view of whose will should be dominant. They believe that everyone owns the public lands, and that they should be managed in ways that are maximally consistent with a broad range of interests and desires. When the discussion of public lands policy is stuck on whose voices should count in management decisions, the question of sustainability barely arises.[13]

Another factor that tends to push the discussion of sustainability into the background is another view prevalent in many western communities that traditional uses of the public lands should take precedence over non-traditional ones (e.g. recreation). Thus there is a great deal of support for the idea that grazing, mining, and other extractive uses should have priority because they are the "senior" uses of the land.[14] This idea often goes with a romantic view of both western history and contemporary realities. Whether justified or not, this view also tends to undercut discussions of sustainability by defending traditional uses because they are traditional, even if they ultimately lead to what everyone would regard as the degradation of the land.

Reflecting on these conflicts shows how important the sustainability

[13] It is difficult to see exactly what the argument is for the pyramid view. It is not generally held that those who benefit from government programmes should have the loudest voice in determining how they are run. Indeed, when it comes to welfare recipients, the prevailing view seems to be quite the opposite.

[14] It is interesting that these appeals to the importance of place and history typically begin with the settlement of these lands by white immigrants; the much more ancient Native-American claims and uses are hardly discussed outside a narrow legal context.

discourse can be in setting public lands policy. As suggested in the previous section, it can structure the conversation and supply common vocabulary. It can be especially useful when the focus is on what is unsustainable in a specific case. But the sustainability discourse can also help move the conflict away from questions about who should make decisions towards questions about how we want the land to be used. Even though sustainability is not the all-purpose solvent for our environmental problems that many have wanted it to be, it can help to structure and clarify the choices and trade-offs that we face.

5. ENVISIONING SUSTAINABILITY

It has been argued that the sustainability discourse may have some role to play at the present moment in thinking about environmental policy. However, there are serious limits on what can be accomplished in this discourse. Because of its open-endedness, the language of sustainability can draw diverse parties into the conversation. But since we can always ask what should be sustained, for what period, in what region; and even why sustainability is good, and if it is good, how good it is; the discourse of sustainability as it is practised is not likely to bring us to closure with respect to important, long-term issues. Ultimately, the concept of sustainability cannot supply the motivation to act. As Beckerman writes, "a definition of whether any particular development path is technically sustainable does not, by itself, carry any special moral force. The definition of a straight line does not imply that there is any particular moral virtue in always walking in straight lines" (Beckerman 1994).

The most important limitation on the sustainability discourse is that, like any other concept, it directs our attention towards some concerns and away from others. Sustainability, as it is employed in most of its guises, is primarily an economistic and anthropocentric notion. The moral reorientation that is required, which involves new relationships between humans as well as with other animals and the rest of nature, is unlikely to be affected by developing ever more precise understandings of sustainability. We need a discourse that permits deeper discussion of aesthetic, spiritual, religious, cultural, political, and moral values.

In his critique of the way the idea of sustainable development has been deployed in the wake of the Brundtland Commission report, Kothari (1994) has distinguished two notions of sustainable development. One notion is a technical, scientific notion. The other is an ethical notion. According to Kothari, the technical, scientific notion of sustainable development does not get to the heart of the environmental crisis. For that we need a new notion of sustainable development, which he describes in the following way:

The shift to sustainable development is primarily an ethical shift. It is not a techno-logical fix, nor a matter of new financial investment. It is a shift in values such that nature is valued in itself and for its life support functions, not merely for how it can be converted into resources and commodities to feed the engine of economic growth. Respect for nature's diversity, and the responsibility to conserve that diversity, define sustainable development as an ethical ideal. Out of an ethics of respect for nature's diversity flows a respect for the diversity of cultures and livelihoods, the basis not only of sustainability, but also of justice and equity. The ecological crisis is in large part a matter of treating nature's diversity as dispensable, a process that has gone hand in hand with the view that a large portion of the human species is dispensable as well. To reverse the ecological decline we require an ethical shift that treats all life as indis-pensable. (Kothari 1994: 237)

In my view the language of sustainability is not well-suited to carrying the concerns that Kothari has articulated. But whether or not one agrees with Kothari's language and sentiments, I believe that the present disorder regard-ing the human relationship to nature will not be successfully addressed until we have developed a richer set of positive visions. These visions must go beyond the bloodless futures of scientific forecasters, the technological futures of cornucopians, and the single focus futures of those who are interested only in rainforests, women, or American family incomes. What is needed are simple and compelling stories that show us how to participate practically in creating the future in our daily lives, and how to engage in ongoing dialogue with others about how our everyday actions help to produce global realities. Articulating these visions is not the job of academics alone, but also requires the efforts of writers, artists, and people from all walks of life. There is much to be learned from those who live close to nature, and the inheritors of traditions that have been largely subordinated. But until we come to terms with the importance of producing a positive vision, the best we can hope for is that we can successfully muddle through. In these times, the challenge of muddling through is an important one, and should not be taken lightly. But a stop along the way should not be mistaken for the end of the journey.

22

Afterward: Child of the Sixties

It is presumptuous for a philosopher to write an autobiography. What a philosopher has to offer is coherent claims and cogent arguments, and these have little to do with personal circumstances. For claims and arguments, except perhaps those involving words such as 'he', 'she', 'here', and 'now', are neutral with respect to person, place, and time.

Sometimes that is what I believe. But despite this, I often find myself turning first to the "notes on contributors" sections of books and journals. However, when I do this a certain ambivalence sometimes bubbles to the surface. On the one hand I often feel frustrated when I can find nothing about Jane Doe's background, education, and professional position. How I read her article on contemporary contractarian theory depends in part on whether she was a student of Rawls or Gauthier, or has a degree in law or economics. On the other hand I find it in bad taste, and sometimes even infuriating, to read that Doe is a triathlete whose hobbies include growing orchids and racing formula one cars. Who cares?

Still, some of the most interesting and important autobiographies have been written by a diverse group of philosophers which includes Augustine, Rousseau, and Russell. Not only are these autobiographies good literature, they are also important to the interpretation and defence of their authors' philosophical positions. Mill's autobiography, for example, poignantly makes the case against the liveability of Benthamite utilitarianism. Quine's recital of the history of his bodily movements gives us a glimmer of what it is like to live as a behaviourist.

Somewhere in these ruminations may lurk a defence of philosophers' auto-biographies. However, such a defence would do little to justify the present excursus into the story of my life. Hume's autobiography is important because he was the greatest of eighteenth-century philosophers. I cannot even claim without fear of contradiction to be the greatest philosopher to have emerged from my working-class neighbourhood in San Diego, California. Why, then, these autobiographical reflections?

There are three reasons. First, I have a vague feeling that there is something dishonest about the abstractness of most philosophical writing. Anyone who dares to tell people what they ought to do or think, whether Immanuel Kant, Margaret Thatcher, or I, should be willing to give his or her name, address, and telephone number. Secondly, as someone who came of age in the 1960s, and lived the life of a "professional philosopher" in the 1970s and 1980s, my story may be illuminating for someone who is interested in how the practice of philosophy in America has changed and developed over that period. Finally, some may find my story edifying. It is a narrative of moral and intellectual change and, I hope, progress.

I was born in 1947 in Iowa, a state in the heart of the American Midwest. This region is predominantly agricultural, and Iowa is especially famous for the quality of the meat that it produces. I was born in Sioux City, and later moved to Waterloo. My father worked in a bakery, but many of the neigh-bourhood "dads" worked in the "packing houses" (as they were euphemis-tically called). I remember the terrible smells that often wafted over our neighbourhood, and even then it seemed odd to me that the men who worked in the packing houses did not talk about their jobs. But as a child I did not associate the smells with blood, nor did it occur to me that what these men did for a living was to kill animals,

Every summer we used to visit relatives in California and, finally, when I was about 12, we moved to San Diego. We were part of the massive post-World War II migrations that "rationalized" the American labour market. Unlike most Europeans, Americans migrate to jobs rather than waiting for jobs to come to them. Perhaps this is part of what it is to be a nation of immigrants.

When I was 14 I was enrolled in the Academy of California Concordia College, a Lutheran boarding school located in Oakland, in the San Francisco Bay area, about 500 miles from where my parents lived in San Diego. Both of my parents had been forced to drop out of high school due to various unfor-tunate circumstances, and while our family had great respect for education we had no tradition of learning for its own sake. In my early teenage years I conceived strong religious convictions and my education, which involved enormous sacrifice on the part of my parents, was justified on the grounds that I was preparing for the ministry.

While at Concordia I absorbed two major influences. The first was the moralism of the Lutheran tradition, which borders on self-righteousness (and in my case often crossed that border). The second was the generally anti-establishment, counter-cultural attitudes characteristic of the San Francisco Bay area in the early 1960s. These influences found natural expression in my participation in the black civil rights and anti-Vietnam War movements.

Despite my political involvements, I was somewhat distanced from the culture of political activism by my serious intellectual interests and a lingering concern with spiritual and religious issues. These were manifest in the usual adolescent ways: a love of Romantic poetry, sporadic explorations in non-Western religious traditions, and a fascination with psychedelic drugs.

The education that I received at Concordia was more European than American. Greek, Latin, German, history, and religion were required subjects, while science and mathematics were not taken very seriously. I sometimes think that most of my real education occurred at Concordia. It is a credit to the school rather than to me that by the time that I was 18 I had read some Platonic dialogues in Greek, Romantic poetry in German, and mastered more of the literary "canon" than most of those who graduate in humanistic subjects from very good American colleges. Although in many ways I was well-educated, I was not very well prepared for an American university. I knew too much about some subjects and too little about others; and in general, I was a social misfit. I was interested in political activism, but political activists didn't study Greek; and people who studied Greek did not have shoulder-length hair and spend their weekends at "human be-ins". Having by now given up the idea of becoming a minister, and having no interest in any other career possibility, I had no idea what to study. I knocked around various colleges and began various majors including classics, English, history, and sociology. In the autumn of 1967 I wound up in an ethics class at San Francisco State University. This was to profoundly affect my life.

My professor was Anita Silvers. In current American jargon she is "disabled", but really she is one of the most powerful people I have ever known. I took her course in order to find out what it meant to say that the Vietnam War was immoral. Although I didn't get the answer to this question, I did get hooked on philosophy.

By 1968 San Francisco State was largely closed by student and faculty strikes, and California Governor Ronald Reagan's response to these events had turned the campus into a virtual war zone. In addition to numerous beatings and gassings, nearly 1,000 students and faculty were arrested on a single day for the crime of being on campus! I left for Birkbeck College, London, to study with Anita's teacher, Ruby Meager.

When I returned from London I was certain that I wanted to leave

California, live in the country, and do graduate work in philosophy, specializing in ethics and aesthetics. I decided to go to the University of North Carolina at Chapel Hill in order to study with Paul Ziff and W. D. Falk.

Shortly after arriving at Chapel Hill I discovered that graduate students who wanted to be taken seriously did not work on ethics and aesthetics. These subjects were regarded as appropriate only for people who were incapable of doing serious analytic philosophy (generally females). I bowed to my environment and worked mainly in philosophy of science, philosophy of mind, and philosophy of language and linguistics, although I continued to do some work in ethics and aesthetics.

In 1974 I began work on a thesis in philosophy of language, and this is when I began to learn about animals. Paul Ziff, my supervisor, insisted that in order to understand human language it was necessary to understand other animal communication systems. So 1974–5 was devoted to reading Tinbergen, Lorenz, and other classical ethologists. When my thesis was submitted in 1976 there was scarcely a footnote to this literature, but I had gained a lively interest in, and an amateur knowledge of, ethology.

My first job was at North Carolina State University in Raleigh. My new colleague, Tom Regan, had just completed an essay entitled "The Moral Basis of Vegetarianism". This essay had been accepted by the *Canadian Journal of Philosophy*, but had not yet been published. I was bowled over by Tom's paper.

At the time that I first read this paper, I was less invested in animal exploitation than many people. I had grown up on friendly terms with various dogs, fish, birds, and rodents, and during my years in North Carolina I lived with a dog, Ludwig, who was my best friend. I had been vegetarian since 1972, mainly for health reasons, but also to avoid offending my (then) girlfriend. Still I found the ideas in Tom's paper outlandish. It seemed wild to suppose that one could give rigorous, analytically sound arguments that imply that much of what people do is grossly immoral. Yet after some weeks of resistance and struggle, I admitted that Tom was largely right. We became comrades.

From 1975 to 1980 Tom and I were close friends, colleagues, and collaborators. During that time we wrote two papers together, but my debt to him is much greater than even this would indicate. We ate together, drank together, and had intense philosophical discussions that would go on into the night. For me it was a second philosophical education. After 1980 our lives and work began to diverge, but those shared experiences of the late 1970s remain vivid in my memory.

After spending two years at the State University of New York at Fredonia, in 1980 I moved to the University of Colorado, Boulder. Although I have continued to identify with the community of animal liberationist philosophers, my work has increasingly moved in the direction of environmental philosophy, philosophy of science, and moral theory.

There are a number of reasons for this. First, in recent years a number of talented philosophers have written books on the philosophy of animal liberation. In my view this body of work has clearly shown that our treatment of non-human animals is indefensible from the perspective of almost any moral theory. The only even remotely plausible way of evading this result, it seems to me, is by adopting certain views about what morality is and what methods we should employ in our normative theorizing. For this reason (among others) I have become interested in what moral theories are and why anyone might want to have one.

My research in environmental philosophy stems from the idea that our concern about animals should be part of a larger concern about how humans should live in relation to non-human nature. At one time this concern might have seemed marginal, but it is increasingly clear that unless we get our act together life on this planet may not be possible for either human or non-human animals. I have become increasingly interested in the nature of science and its relation to values because it seems to me that, at this point in human history, science may well be the most important engine of social change. If life on this planet is to have a future, science must be brought under moral and political control. For this reason I believe that the critique of science is among the most urgent of tasks.

In some ways I have quite a lot in common with scientists. Despite my poor high school education in science, I have always been interested in scientific subjects, and as a child, I was something of a maths/science prodigy. My class origins are also closer to those of many scientists than they are to philosophers and other humanists. At least in the English-speaking world, scientists typically have more humble origins than philosophers. Finally, scientists, like philosophers, are trained intellectuals who claim to value open debate and the disinterested search for truth. In the light of all this common ground, it has often seemed peculiar to me that over the last fifteen years I have been involved in many acrimonious debates with scientists. What has seemed especially strange to me is that many scientists seem utterly unable to grasp abstract arguments, or go completely beserk on the subject of animal rights. When animal liberation is discussed, scientific rationality, detachment, and objectivity all too often go right out of the window.

In 1985 I met Marc Bekoff, who has since become a close friend and collaborator. Marc had been a student at Cornell Medical School, but dropped out when he could no longer stomach killing cats. He went on to Washington University in St Louis, where he completed a Ph.D. in animal behaviour under the supervision of Michael W. Fox. In collaboration with Marc I became involved in the education of biologists, for several years jointly teaching an advanced seminar on philosophical issues concerning animal behaviour.

While it is difficult to effect change in the scientific community, I am cautiously optimistic. Part of what Marc and I try to do is to affirm some of the basic motivations that lead people to science in the first place—a desire for knowledge and an affection for nature. We also try to show how the present system of organizing science can contribute to the betrayal of these motivations and the scientific values that are associated with them. The hierarchical patronage system that has evolved enforces conservatism and conformity rather than encouraging creativity and critical thinking. While the current generation that dominates the scientific establishment may well be hopeless, many students are aware of changes in cultural attitudes regarding science, and understand that if they are to have careers that will be sustainable over the next half-century, they will have to develop different projects and methods than those of their teachers.

The work that Marc and I do in philosophy of biology may seem excessively incremental or moderate to some people. But I think that the period in which we find ourselves, at least in the United States, is one in which pluralism and diversity within the movement are strengths. There is room for both "moderation" and certain kinds of "extremism". A wide range of opportunities for change were created in the 1980s, and as many of these should be exploited as possible. There is no contradiction in a movement that engages in civil disobedience and public demonstrations, and also attempts to change scientific practice "from within". Nor is there any contradiction in a single individual both advocating the closure of a laboratory, and also trying to educate those who run it.

We need to bring to our activities a long-term perspective. The animal liberation movement is committed to changes that are world-historical in scale, that will take centuries to effect and to consolidate. We are actors in a drama that is much larger than ourselves, and we will be long gone before our most profound goals are realized. The realization of this fact does not make our day-to-day frustrations, much less the unnecessary suffering of a single animal whether human or non-human, any more acceptable. However, such a long-term perspective may help us to see that although eliminating animal suffering is an urgent and demanding obligation, it is one that we are more likely to successfully discharge in a spirit of compassion, understanding, and humility than in a spirit of dogmatism and vindictiveness.

Martin Luther King led the most successful movement for social change that occurred in America in my lifetime. He taught that conflict should not always be avoided, for sometimes it can be creative. But he also taught that reconciliation is the necessary complement of conflict. We would do well to learn from Martin.

REFERENCES

Abbot, P. (1978). "Philosophers and the Abortion Question". *Political Theory*, 6/3: 313–35.

Abelson, P. (1990). "Uncertainties about Global Warming". *Science*, 247: 1529.

Abrams, C. (1965). *The City is the Frontier*. New York: Harper and Row.

Akins, K. (1990). "Science and Our Inner Lives: Birds of Prey, Bats, and the Common Featherless Bi-ped". In Bekoff and Jamieson (1990), vol. i: 414–27.

Alberts, B., and K. Shine (1994). "Scientists and the Integrity of Research". *Science*, 266: 1660–1.

Allen, C. (1999). "Animal Concepts Revisited". *Erkenntnis*, 51: 537–44.

——and M. Bekoff (1997). *Species of Mind*. Cambridge, Mass.: MIT Press.

American Society of Mammalogists (1987). "Acceptable Field Methods in Mammalogy: Preliminary Guidelines Approved by the American Society of Mammalogists". *Journal of Mammalogy*, 68/4, suppl.: 1–18.

Amy, D. R. (1984). "Why Policy Analysis and Ethics are Incompatible". *Journal of Policy Analysis and Management*, 3: 573–91.

Anderson, M. (1964). *The Federal Bulldozer*. Cambridge, Mass.: MIT Press.

Andrews, R., and M. J. Waits (1978). *Environmental Values in Public Decisions: A Research Agenda*. Ann Arbor: University of Michigan, School of Natural Resources.

Anscombe, G. E. M. (1958/1968). "Modern Moral Philosophy". In J. Thomson and G. Dworkin, *Ethics*. New York: Harper and Row: 186–210.

Anthony, R. (1982). "Polls, Pollution and Politics". *Environment*, 24/4: 14–20, 33–4.

Arnold, D. (1995). "Hume on the Moral Difference between Humans and Other Animals". *History of Philosophy Quarterly*, 12/3: 303–16.

Arrhenius, S. (1896). "On the Influence of Carbonic Acid in the Air Upon the Temperature of the Ground". *Philosophical Magazine*, 41: 237–76.

——(1908). *Worlds in the Making*. New York: Harper & Brothers.

Austin, J. L. (1962). *Sense and Sensibilia*. New York: Oxford University Press.

——(1970). "Other Minds". In J. O. Urmson and G. J. Warnock, *Philosophical Papers*. New York: Oxford University Press: 76–116.

Ayer, A. J. (1952). *Language, Truth and Logic*. New York: Dover.

Baier, A. (1983). "Knowing Our Place in the Animal World". In Miller and Williams (1983): 61–77.

——(1991). *A Progress of Sentiments: Reflections on Hume's Treatise*. Cambridge, Mass.: Harvard University Press.

Baron-Cohen, S. (1989). "Are Autistic Children Behaviourists? An Examination of

Their Mental–Physical and Appearance–Reality Distinctions". *Journal of Autism and Developmental Disorders*, 19: 579–600.

BARON-COHEN, S. (1991). "Precursors to a Theory of Mind: Understanding Attention in Others". In A. Whiten, *Natural Theories of Mind: Evolution, Development and Simulation of Everyday Mindreading*. Oxford: Basil Blackwell: 233–51.

—— (1995). *Mindblindness: An Essay on Autism and the Theory of Mind*. Cambridge, Mass.: MIT Press.

—— H. TAGER-FLUSBER, and D. COHEN, eds. (1993). *Understanding Other Minds: Perspectives From Autism*. New York: Oxford University Press.

BATESON, P. (1968). "Ethological Methods of Observing Behavior". In L. Weiskrantz, *Analysis of Behavioral Change*. New York: Harper and Row: 389–99.

—— (1983). *Mate Choice*. New York: Cambridge University Press.

BATTEN, P. (1976). *Living Trophies*. New York: Thomas Y. Crowell Co.

BECK, B. (1982). "Chimpocentrism: Bias in Cognitive Ethology". *Journal of Human Evolution*, 2: 3–17.

—— (1995). "Reintroduction, Zoos, Conservation, and Animal Welfare". In Norton *et al.* (1995): 155–63.

BECK, L. W., ed. (1963). *Kant on History*. Indianapolis: Library of the Liberal Arts.

BECK, U. (1992). *Risk Society*. London: Sage Publications.

BECKERMAN, W. (1994). "'Sustainable Development': Is it a Useful Concept?" *Environmental Values*, 3: 191–209.

—— (1995). "How Would You Like Your 'Sustainability', Sir? Weak or Strong? A Reply to my Critics". *Environmental Values*, 4: 169–79.

BEITZ, C. R. (1979). *Political Theory and International Relations*. Princeton: Princeton University Press.

BEKOFF, M. (1975). "The Communication of Play Intention: Are Play Signals Functional?" *Semiotica*, 15: 231–9.

—— (1977). "Social Communication in Canids: Evidence for the Evolution of a Sterotyped Mammalian Display". *Science*, 197: 1097–9.

—— (1993a). "Review of Griffin". *Ethology*, 95: 166–70.

—— (1993b). "Experimentally Induced Infanticide: The Removal of Birds and its Ramifications". *Auk*, 110: 404–6.

—— (1994a). "Cognitive Ethology and the Treatment of Nonhuman Animals: How Matters of Mind Inform Matters of Welfare". *Animal Welfare*, 3: 75–96.

—— (1994b). "Should Scientists Bond with the Animals Whom They Use? Why Not?" *International Journal of Psychology*, 7: 78–86.

—— (1995a). "Cognitive Ethology and the Explanation of Nonhuman Animal Behavior". In H. Roitblat and J. A. Meyer, *Comparative Approaches to Cognitive Science*. Cambridge, Mass.: MIT Press: 119–49.

—— (1995b). "Naturalizing and Individualizing Animal Well-Being and Animal Minds: An Ethologist's Naivete Exposed?" In A. Rowan, *Wildlife Conservation, Zoos, and Animal Protection: Examining the Issues*. Medford, Mass.: Tufts: 63–115.

——, ed. (2000). *The Smile of a Dolphin: Remarkable Accounts of Animal Emotions*. New York: Discovery Books.

——and C. ALLEN (1992). "Intentional Icons: Towards an Evolutionary Cognitive Ethology". *Ethology*, 91: 1–16.

————(1996). "Cognitive Ethology: Slayers, Skeptics, and Proponents". In R. Mitchell, N. Thompson, and L. Miles, *Anthropomorphism, Anecdotes, and Animals: The Emperor's New Clothes?* Albany, NY: SUNY Press: 313–34.

——and J. BYERS, eds. (1998). *Animal Play: Evolutionary, Comparative, and Ecological Perspectives.* New York: Cambridge University Press.

——L. GRUEN, S. E. TOWNSEND, and B. E. ROLLIN (1992). "Animals in Science: Some Areas Revisited". *Animal Behavior*, 44: 473–84.

——and D. JAMIESON, eds. (1990). *Interpretation and Explanation in the Study of Animal Behavior*, vol. i: *Interpretation, Intentionality, and Communication*, vol ii: *Explanation, Evolution, and Adaptation.* Boulder, Colo.: Westview Press.

————(1991). "Reflective Ethology, Applied Philosophy, and the Moral Status of Animals". In P. Bateson and P. Klopfer, *Perspectives in Ethology 9: Human Understanding and Animal Awareness.* New York: Plenum Press: 1–47.

————(1996*a*). "Ethics and the Study of Carnivores: Doing Science While Respecting Animals". In J. L. Gittleman, *Carnivore Behavior, Ecology, and Evolution*, vol. ii. Ithaca, NY: Cornell University Press: II.

————eds. (1996*b*). *Readings in Animal Cognition.* Cambridge, Mass.: MIT Press.

——A. SCOTT, and D. C. CONNER (1989). "Ecological Analyses of Nesting Success in Evening Grosbeaks". *Oecologia*, 81: 67–74.

——and M. C. WELLS (1986). "Social Ecology and Behavior of Coyotes". *Advances in the Study of Behavior*, 16: 251–338.

BENNETT, W. (1980). "Getting Ethics". *Commentary*, 70: 62–5.

BENTHAM, J. (1789/1989). "The Principles of Moral and Legislation". In T. Regan and P. Singer, *Animal Rights and Human Obligations.* Englewood Cliffs, NJ: Prentice-Hall: 25–6.

BERKES, F., and C. FOLKE (1994). "Investing in Cultural Capital for Sustainable Use of Natural Capital". In A. Jansson, M. Hammer, C. Folke, and R. Costanza, *Investing in Natural Capital.* Washington: Island Press: 128–49.

BERTREAUX, D., R. DUHAMEL, and J.-M. BERGERON (1994). "Can Radio Collars Affect Dominance Relationships in Microtus?" *Canadian Journal of Zoology*, 72: 785–9.

BLACKBURN, S. (1994). *The Oxford Dictionary of Philosophy.* New York: Oxford University Press.

——(1998). *Ruling Passions.* New York: Oxford University Press.

——(2001). *Being Good.* Oxford: Oxford University Press.

BOAKES, R. (1984). *From Darwin to Behaviorism: Psychology and the Minds of Animals.* New York: Cambridge University Press.

BOEHM, C. (1999). *Hierarchy in the Forest.* Cambridge, Mass.: Harvard University Press.

BORZA, K., and D. JAMIESON (1990). *Global Change and Biodiversity Loss: Some Impediments to Response.* Boulder, Colo.: Center for Space and Geosciences Policy, University of Colorado.

BOSTOCK, S. (1993). *Zoos and Animal Rights.* London: Routledge.

BOTKIN, D. B. (1990). *Discordant Harmonies: A New Ecology for the Twenty-First Century*. New York: Oxford University Press.

BOWD, A. (1980). "Ethical Reservations about Psychological Research with Animals". *The Psychological Record*, 30/2: 201–10.

BOYD, R. (1988). "How to be a Moral Realist". In McCord (1988): 181–228.

BRADFORD, P., and H. BLOOM (1992). *Ota Benga: The Pygmy in the Zoo*. New York: St Martin's Press.

BRANDT, R. (1975). "A Moral Principle about Killing". In M. Kohl, *Beneficent Euthanasia*. Buffalo: Prometheus Books: 106–14.

BRINK, D. (1989). *Moral Realism and the Foundations of Ethics*. Cambridge: Cambridge University Press.

BRINTON, C. (1959/1990). *A History of Western Morals*. New York: Paragon House.

BROAD, C. D. (1959). *Five Types of Ethical Theory*. Paterson, NJ: Littlefield, Adams.

BRODY, B. (1975). *Abortion and the Sanctity of Life: A Philosophical View*. Cambridge, Mass.: MIT Press.

BROOM, D. M. (2000). "The Evolution of Pain". *Flemish Veterinary Journal*, 70: 17–21.

BRYANT, B., and P. MOHAI, eds. (1992). *Race and the Incidence of Environmental Hazards*. Boulder, Colo.: Westview Press.

BUDYKO, M. I. (1988). "Anthropogenic Climate Change". Hamburg, Federal Republic of Germany, World Congress on Climate and Development.

BULGER, R. E., E. HEITMAN, and S. J. REISLER, eds. (1993). *The Ethical Dimensions of the Biological Sciences*. New York: Cambridge University Press.

BUREAU OF CENSUS (1971). *Census of Population 1970*. Washington: US Government Printing Office.

BURGE, T. (1992). "Philosophy of Language and Mind: 1950–1990". *The Philosophical Review*, 101: 13–51.

BURLEY, N., G. KRANTZBERG, and P. RADMAN (1982). "Influence of Color-Banding on the Conspecific Preferences of Zebra Finches". *Animal Behavior*, 30: 444–55.

BURY, J. B. (1920/1932). *The Idea of Progress: An Inquiry into its Origin and Growth*. New York: The Macmillan Company.

BYRNE, A., and D. R. HILBERT, eds. (1997). *Readings on Color*. Cambridge, Mass.: MIT Press.

BYRNE, R. (1991). "Review of D. Cheney and R. Seyfarth, *How Monkeys See the World*". *The Sciences*: 142–7.

——and A. WHITEN, eds. (1988). *Machiavellian Intelligence: Social Expertise and the Evolution of Intellect in Monkeys, Apes and Humans*. Oxford: Clarendon Press.

CAIRNS, J. (1978). *Cancer: Science and Society*. San Francisco: W. H. Freeman and Co.

CALLENDAR, G. S. (1938). "The Artificial Production of Carbon Dioxide and its Influence on Temperature". *Quarterly Journal of the Royal Meteorological Society*, 64: 223–40.

CALLICOTT, J. B. (1980/1989). "Animal Liberation: A Triangular Affair". In Callicott (1989): 15–38.

—— (1989). *In Defense of the Land Ethic: Essays in Environmental Philosophy*. Albany, NY: SUNY Press.

—— (1992*a*). "Rolston on Intrinsic Value: A Deconstruction". *Environmental Ethics*, 14/2: 129–43.

(1992*b*). "Aldo Leopold's Metaphor". In Costanza *et al.* (1992): 42–56.

—— (1995). "A Review of Some Problems with the Concept of Ecosystem Health". *Ecosystem Health*, 2/1: 101–12.

—— (1996). "On Norton and the Failure of Monistic Inherentism". *Environmental Ethics*, 18/2: 219–21.

CARRUTHERS, P. (1989). "Brute Experience". *Journal of Philosophy*, 86: 258–69.

CARTER, A. (2000). "Humean Nature". *Environmental Values*, 9/1: 3–36.

CATTEN, W. R., J. C. HERDEE, and T. W. STEINBURN (1969). *Urbanism and the Natural Environment: An Attitude Study*. Seattle, Institute for Sociological Research, University of Washington.

CAVALIERI, P., and P. SINGER, eds. (1993). *The Great Ape Project: Equality beyond Humanity*. London: Fourth Estate.

CHENEY, D., and R. SEYFARTH (1990). *How Monkeys See the World: Inside the Mind of Another Species*. Chicago: University of Chicago Press.

CHISZAR, D., J. B. MURPHY, and W. ILIFF (1990). "For Zoos". *Psychological Record*, 40: 3–13.

CHOMSKY, N. (1959). "Review of B. F. Skinner's *Verbal Behavior*". *Language*, 35: 16–58.

CHURCHLAND, P. M. (1981). "Eliminative Materialism and the Propositional Attitudes". *Journal of Philosophy*, 78: 67–90.

—— (1992). "Perceptual Plasticity and Theoretical Neutrality: A Reply to Jerry Fodor". In P. Churchland, *A Neurocomputational Perspective: The Nature of Mind and the Structure of Science*. Cambridge, Mass.: MIT Press: 255–79.

CHURCHLAND, P. S. (1986). *Neurophilosophy*. Cambridge, Mass.: MIT Press.

CLARK, K., ed. (1991). *Ruskin Today: Selected Writings*. New York: Penguin Books.

CLUTTON-BROCK, J. (1992). "How the Beasts Were Tamed". *New Scientist*, 15 (Feb.): 41–3.

COHEN, C. (1977). "When May Research Be Stopped?" *New England Journal of Medicine*, 296: 1203–10.

—— (1978). "Restriction of Research with Recombinant DNA: The Dangers of Inquiry and the Burden of Proof". *Southern California Law Review*, 51: 1083–113.

COLWELL, R. K. (1989). "Natural and Unnatural History: Biological Diversity and Genetic Engineering". In W. R. Shea and B. Sitter, *Scientists and Their Responsibilities*. Canton, Mass.: Watson Pub. International: 1–40.

CONFERENCE STATEMENT (1988). "The Changing Atmosphere: Implications for Global Security". Toronto, Canada.

CONSERVATION FOUNDATION (1963). *Implications of Rising Carbon Dioxide Content of the Atmosphere*. New York.

CONWAY, W. (1990). "Miniparks and Megazoos: From Protecting Ecosystems to Saving Species". Thomas Hall Lecture. Washington University, St Louis.

—— (1995). "Zoo Conservation and Ethical Paradoxes". In Norton *et al.* (1995): 1–9.

COOK, J. (1969). "Human Beings". In P. Winch, *Studies in the Philosophy of Wittgenstein*. London: Routledge & Kegan Paul: 117–51.

COSTANZA, R., B. G. NORTON, and B. D. HASKELL, eds. (1992). *Ecosystem Health: New Goals for Environmental Management*. Washington: Island Press.

COULSTON, F. (1980). "Benefits and Risks Involved in the Development of Modern Pharmaceutical Products". Unpublished paper. Bonn and Luxembourg.

——and D. SERRONE (1969). "The Comparative Approach to the Role of Nonhuman Primates in Evaluation of Drug Toxicity in Man: A Review". *Annals of the New York Academy of Sciences*, 162: 681–704.

CRANE, T. (1992). "The Nonconceptual Content of Experience". In T. Crane, *The Contents of Experience*. Cambridge: Cambridge University Press: 136–57.

CRISP, R. (1990/1996). 'Evolution and Psychological Unity'. In Bekoff and Jamieson (1996b): 309–21.

CUMMINS, D., and C. ALLEN, eds. (1998). *The Evolution of Mind*. New York: Oxford University Press.

DALY, H. (1995). "On Wilfred Beckerman's Critique of Sustainable Development". *Environmental Values*, 4: 49–55.

DARMSTADTER, J. (1991). *The Economic Cost of CO_2 Mitigation: A Review of Estimates for Selected World Regions*. Washington: Resources for the Future.

DARWIN, C. (1859/1958). *The Origin of Species*. New York: Penguin.

——(1871). *The Descent of Man, and Selection in Relation to Sex*. London: Murray.

——(1896). *The Variation of Animals and Plants under Domestication*. New York: Appleton.

DAVIDSON, D. (1984). "Thought and Talk". In D. Davidson, *Truth and Interpretation*. Oxford: Oxford University Press: 155–70.

——(1986). "A Nice Derangement of Epitaphs". In E. LePore, *Truth and Interpretation: Perspectives on the Philosophy of Donald Davidson*. New York: Basil Blackwell: 459–76.

——(1999). "The Emergence of Thought". *Erkenntnis*, 51: 7–17.

DAVIS, H., and D. BALFOUR, eds. (1992). *The Inevitable Bond: Examining Scientist–Animal Interaction*. New York: Cambridge University Press.

DAVIS, L. S. (1991). "Penguin Weighting Game". *Natural History* (Jan.), 46–54.

DAVIS, M. (2001). *Late Victorian Holocausts: El Niño and the Making of the Third World*. London: Verso.

DAVIS, N. (1991). "Contemporary Deontology". In Singer (1991): 205–18.

——and D. JAMIESON (1987). "Ross on the Possibility of Moral Theory". *Journal of Value Inquiry*. 21: 225–34.

DAWKINS, M. (1986). *Unraveling Animal Behavior*. Essex, England: Longman Group.

——(1993). *Through Our Eyes Only? The Search for Animal Consciousness*. San Francisco: W. H. Freeman.

——and L. M. GOSLING, eds. (1992). *Ethics in Research on Animal Behavior. Readings from Animal Behavior*. London: Academic Press.

——T. HALLIDAY, and R. DAWKINS, eds. (1991). *The Tinbergen Legacy*. London: Chapman and Hall.

DAWKINS, R. (1976/1989). *The Selfish Gene.* New York: Oxford University Press.

—— (1986). *The Blind Watchmaker.* New York: Norton.

—— (1993). "Gaps in the Mind". In Cavalieri and Singer (1993): 80–7.

DE LAS CASAS, B. (1974). *The Devastation of the Indies.* Baltimore: Johns Hopkins University Press.

DE TOCQUEVILLE, A. (1945). *Democracy in America,* vol. i. New York: Alfred A. Knopf.

DEGRAZIA, D. (1996). *Taking Animals Seriously: Mental Life and Moral Status.* New York: Cambridge University Press.

DENNETT, D. (1969). *Content and Consciousness.* London: Routledge & Kegan Paul.

—— (1987). *The Intentional Stance.* Cambridge, Mass.: MIT Press.

—— (1996). *Kinds of Minds.* New York: Basic Books.

DEVORET, R. (1979). "Bacterial Tests for Potential Carcinogens". *Scientific American,* 241/2: 40–9.

DEWEY, J. (1910). *The Influence of Darwinism on Philosophy and Other Essays in Contemporary Thought.* New York: Henry Holt & Co.

DEWSBURY, D. (1992). "On the Problems Studied in Ethology, Comparative Psychology, and Animal Behavior". *Ethology,* 92: 89–107.

DINER, J. (1979). *Physical and Mental Suffering of Experimental Animals.* Washington: Animal Welfare Institute.

DRETSKE, F. (1969). *Seeing and Knowing.* London: Routledge & Kegan Paul.

DUPRÉ, J. (1993). *The Disorder of Things: The Metaphysical Foundations of the Disunity of Science.* Cambridge, Mass.: Harvard University Press.

—— (1996). "The Mental Life of Nonhuman Animals". In Bekoff and Jamieson (1996b): 323–36.

DWORKIN, R. (1993). *Life's Dominion: An Argument About Abortion, Euthanasia, and Individual Freedom.* New York: Knopf.

—— (1996). "Objectivity and Truth: You'd Better Believe It". *Philosophy and Public Affairs,* 25/2: 87–139.

EHRENFELD, D. (1991). "The Management of Diversity". In F. Borman and S. Kellert, *Ecology, Economics, Ethics: The Broken Circle.* New Haven: Yale University Press: 26–39.

EHRLICH, P., and A. EHRLICH (1981). *Extinction: The Causes and Consequences of the Disappearance of Species.* New York: Random House.

EISEMANN, C. H., W. K. JORGENSEN, D. J. MERRITT, M. J. RICE, B. W. CRIBB, P. D. WEBB, and M. P. ZALUCKI (1984). "Do Insects Feel Pain—A Biological View". *Experienta,* 40: 164–7.

EISNER, T., and S. CAMAZINE (1983). "Spider Leg Autotomy Induced by Prey Venom Injection: An Adaptive Response to 'Pain?' ". *Proceedings of the National Academy of Science,* 80: 3382–5.

EKIRCH, A. A., JR. (1944). *The Idea of Progress in America. 1815–1860.* New York: Columbia University Press.

ELGIN, D., T. THOMAS, T. LOGOTHETTI, and S. COX (1974). *City Size and Quality of Life.* Stanford, Calif.: Stanford Research Institute.

ELLIOT, R. (1985). "Metaethics and Environmental Ethics". *Metaphilosophy,* 16: 103–17.

ELLIOT, R. (1992). "Intrinsic Value, Environmental Obligation and Naturalness". *The Monist*, 75/3: 138–60.

——ed. (1995). *Environmental Ethics*. Oxford: Oxford University Press.

——(1997). *Faking Nature: The Ethics of Environmental Restoration*. London: Routledge.

EMERSON, R. W. (1883). *Society and Solitude*. Boston: Houghton, Mifflin, and Company.

EMLEN, S. T., N. J. DEMONG, and D. J. EMLEN (1989). "Experimental Induction of Infanticide in Female Wattled Jacanas". *Auk*, 106: 1–7.

EPHRON, L. (1988). *The End: The Imminent Ice Age and How We Can Stop It*. Berkeley: Celestial Arts.

EPSTEIN, S. S. (1979). *The Politics of Cancer*. Garden City, NY: Anchor Press/ Doubleday.

ERESHEFSKY, M., ed. (1992). *The Units of Evolution: Essays on the Nature of Species*. Cambridge, Mass.: MIT Press.

EVANS, G. (1982). *The Varieties of Reference*. Oxford: Clarendon Press.

FEYERABEND, P. (1975). *Against Method*. London: New Left Books.

FIORITO, G. (1986). "Is There 'Pain' in Invertebrates?" *Behavioral Processes*, 12: 383–8.

FISCHER, C. S. (1976). *The Urban Experience*. New York: Harcourt Brace Jovanovich.

FISHER, J. A. (1990/1996). "The Myth of Anthropomorphism". In Bekoff and Jamieson (1996*b*): 13–16.

FLACK, J. C., and F. DE WAAL (2000). "'Any Animal Whatever': Darwinian Building Blocks of Morality in Monkeys and Apes". *Journal of Consciousness Studies*, 7/1–2: 1–29.

FLAVIN, C. (1989). *Slowing Global Warming: A Worldwide Strategy*. Washington: Worldwatch Institute.

FODOR, J. (1968). *Psychological Explanation*. New York: Random House.

——(1981). "Special Sciences". In J. Fodor, *Representations: Philosophical Essays on the Foundations of Cognitive Science*. Cambridge, Mass.: MIT Press, 127–46.

FOLLESDAL, D. (1994). "Husserl's Notion of Intentionality". In J. Macnamara and G. Reyes, *The Logical Foundations of Cognition*. New York: Oxford University Press: 296–308.

FORD, P., ed. (1905). *Works of Thomas Jefferson*, vol. iv. New York: G. P. Putnam's.

FREY, R. G. (1980). *Interests and Rights: The Case against Animals*. Oxford: Clarendon Press.

FRIEDEN, B. J. (1964). *The Future of Old Neighborhoods*. Cambridge, Mass.: MIT Press.

GALEF, B. (1990/1996). "Tradition in Animals: Field Observation and Laboratory Analyses". In Bekoff and Jamieson (1996*b*), 91–105.

GALES, R., C. WILLIAMS, and D. RITZ (1990). "Foraging Behaviour of the Little Penguin, *Eudyptula Minor*: Initial Results and Assessments of Instrument Effect". *Journal of the Zoological Society of London*, 220: 61–85.

GALLUP, G. (1977). "Self-Recognition in Primates". *American Psychologist*, 32: 329–38.

GALLUP ORGANIZATION (1989). *Concern about the Environment*. Washington: Gallup Organization.

GANS, H. J. (1968). *People and Plans.* New York: Basic Books.

GAVAGHAN, H. (1992). "Animal Experiments the American Way". *New Scientist,* 16 (May): 32–6.

GEIST, V. (1992). "Endangered Species and the Law". *Nature,* 357: 274–6.

GIBBARD, A. (1990). *Wise Choices, Apt Feelings.* Oxford. Oxford University Press.

GIMLIN, H., ed. (1974). *Editorial Research Reports on the Future of the City.* Washington: Congressional Quarterly, Inc.

GLANTZ, M. (1988). "Politics and the Air around Us: International Policy Action on Atmospheric Pollution by Trace Gases". In M. Glantz, *Societal Responses to Regional Climate Change: Forecasting by Analogy.* Boulder, Colo.: Westview: 41–72.

——(1990). "On Assessing Winners and Losers in the Context of Global Warming", workshop report, 18–21 June 1990, St Julians, Malta. Boulder, Colo.: National Center for Atmospheric Research Environmental and Societal Impacts Group.

GLOVER, J. (1999/2000). *Humanity: A Moral History of the Twentieth Century.* New Haven: Yale University Press.

GOLANI, I. (1992). "A Mobility Gradient in the Organization of Vertebrate Movement". *The Behavioral and Brain Sciences,* 15: 249–308.

GOLDING, M., and N. GOLDING (1979). "Why Preserve Landmarks? A Preliminary Inquiry". In K. E. Goodpaster and K. M. Sayre, *Ethics and Problems of the 21st Century.* Notre Dame, Ind.: University of Notre Dame Press: 175–99.

GOODMAN, N. (1961/1972). "About". In N. Goodman, *Problems and Projects.* Indianapolis: The Bobbs-Merrill Company: 246–72.

——(1968). *The Languages of Art.* Indianapolis: Bobbs-Merrill Company, Inc.

——(1970/1972). "Seven Structures on Similarity". In N. Goodman, *Problems and Projects.* Indianapolis: The Bobbs-Merrill Company: 437–46.

GOODMAN, P., and P. GOODMAN (1960). *Communitas.* New York: Vintage Books.

GORE, A. (1992). *Earth in the Balance: Ecology and the Human Spirit.* Boston: Houghton Mifflin.

GRANDIN, T. (1995). *Thinking in Pictures: And Other Reports From My Life with Autism.* New York: Doubleday.

GREER, S. A. (1965). *Urban Renewal and American Cities.* Indianapolis: Bobbs-Merrill.

GRIFFIN, D. (1976/1981). *The Question of Animal Awareness: Evolutionary Continuity of Mental Experience.* New York: The Rockefeller University Press.

——(1978). "Prospects for a Cognitive Ethology". *The Behavioral and Brain Sciences,* 4/5: 27–38.

——ed. (1982). *Animal Mind–Human Mind.* New York: Springer-Verlag.

——(1984). *Animal Thinking.* Cambridge, Mass.: Harvard University Press.

——(1991). "Progress Towards Cognitive Ethology". In Ristau (1991): 3–17.

——(1992). *Animal Minds.* Chicago: University of Chicago Press.

GRINER, L. (1983). *Pathology of Zoo Animals.* San Diego: Zoological Society of San Diego.

GRUEN, L. (1990/1996). "Gendered Knowledge? Examining Influences on Scientific and Ethological Inquiries". In Bekoff and Jamieson (1996*b*): 17–27.

GRUEN, L., and D. JAMIESON, eds. (1994). *Reflecting on Nature: Readings in Environmental Philosophy*. New York: Oxford University Press.

GUTZWILLER, K. J., R. T. WIEDENMANN, K. L. CLEMENTS, and S. H. ANDERSON (1994). "Effects of Human Intrusion on Song Occurrence and Singing Consistency in Subalpine Birds". *Auk*, 111: 28–37.

HAILMAN, J. (1978). "Review of Griffin". *Auk*, 95: 614–15.

HAMILTON, W. D. (1964). "The Genetical Evolution of Social Behavior I and II". *Journal of Theoretical Biology*, 7: 1–16, 17–52.

HANKE, L. (1959). *Aristotle and the American Indians: A Study in Race and Prejudice in the Modern World*. Bloomington, Ind.: Indiana University Press.

HANSON, N. R. (1958). *Patterns of Discovery*. Cambridge: Cambridge University Press.

HARDCASTLE, V. (1999). *The Myth of Pain*. Cambridge, Mass.: MIT Press.

HARDIN, C. L. (1988). *Color for Philosophers: Unweaving the Rainbow*. Indianapolis, Ind.: Hackett Publishing Company.

HARE, R. M. (1976). "Ethical Theory and Utilitarianism". In H. D. Lewis, *Contemporary British Philosophy*. London: Allen and Unwin: 23–38.

—— (1982). *Moral Thinking*. New York: Oxford University Press.

HARGROVE, E., ed. (1992). *The Animal Rights, Environmental Ethics Debate: The Environmental Perspective*. Albany, NY: SUNY Press.

HARMAN, G. (1977). *The Nature of Morality: An Introduction to Ethics*. New York: Oxford University Press.

—— (2000). "Desired Desires". *Explaining Value and Other Essays in Moral Philosophy*. Oxford: Oxford University Press: 117–35.

HARRISON, G., and J. GIBSON, eds. (1976). *Man in Urban Environments*. Oxford: Oxford University Press.

HEDIGER, H. (1964). *Wild Animals in Captivity*. New York: Dover.

HENSON, P., and T. A. GRANT (1991). "The Effects of Human Disturbance on Trumpeter Swan Breeding Behavior". *Wildlife Society Bulletin*, 19: 248–57.

HERMAN, B. (1993). *The Practice of Moral Judgement*. Cambridge, Mass.: Harvard University Press.

HERMAN, L., and P. MORREL-SAMUELS (1990/1996). "Knowledge Acquisition and Asymmetry between Language Comprehension and Production: Dolphins and Apes as General Models for Animals". In Bekoff and Jamieson (1996b): 289–306.

HETTINGER, E. C. (1989). "The Responsible Use of Animals in Research". *Between the Species*, 5: 123–31.

HETTINGER, N. (1994). "Valuing Predation in Rolston's Environmental Ethics: Bambi Lovers versus Tree Huggers". *Environmental Ethics*, 16: 3–20.

HEYES, A., and C. LISTON-HEYES (1995). "Sustainable Resource Use: The Search for Meaning". *Energy Policy*, 23/1: 1–3.

HILDEBRAND, G. H. (1949). *The Idea of Progress: A Collection of Readings, selected by Frederick J. Teggert*. Berkeley: University of California Press.

HILL, T., JR. (1983). "Ideals of Human Excellence and Preserving Natural Environments". *Environmental Ethics*, 5: 211–24.

HIRSCHMAN, A. (1977). *The Passions and the Interests*. Princeton: Princeton University Press.

HOBSON, P. (1990). "Concerning Knowledge of Mental States". *British Journal of Medical Psychology*, 63: 199–213.

HOLLAND, A. (1995). "The Use and Abuse of Ecological Concepts in Environmental Ethics". *Biodiversity and Conservation*, 4: 812–26.

——(1996). "Substitutability: Or, Why Strong Sustainability is Weak and Absurdly Strong Sustainability is not Absurd". In J. Foster, *Environmental Economics: A Critique of Orthodox Policy*. London: Routledge: 119–34.

HOLTON, G., and R. MORISON, eds. (1978). *Limits of Scientific Inquiry*. New York: W. W. Norton and Co.

HORGAN, J. (1996). *The End of Science: Facing the Limits of Knowledge in the Twilight of the Scientific Age*. Reading: Addison-Wesley Publishing.

HORNSBY, J. (1986). "Physicalist Thinking and Conceptions of Behaviour". In P. Pettit and J. McDowell, *Subject, Thought and Context*. Oxford: Oxford University Press: 95–115.

HUBEL, D. (1979). "The Brain". *Scientific American*, 241/3: 44–53.

HUME, D. (1738/1888). *A Treatise of Human Nature*. Oxford: Clarendon Press.

——(1748/1975). *Enquiry Concerning Human Understanding*. Oxford: Clarendon Press.

HUMPHREY, N. K. (1977). "Review of Donald R. Griffin, *The Question of Animal Minds*". *Animal Behavior*, 25/2: 521–2.

HUNTINGFORD, F. A. (1984). "Some Ethical Issues Raised by Studies of Predation and Aggression". *Animal Behavior*, 32: 210–15.

HURKA, T. (1993). *Perfectionism*. Oxford: Oxford University Press.

HUTCHINS, M., B. DRESSER, and C. WEMMER (1995). "Ethical Considerations in Zoo and Aquarium Research". In Norton *et al.* (1995): 253–79.

——and C. WEMMER (1991). "Response: In Defense of Captive Breeding". *Endangered Species Update*, 8: 5–6.

HUXLEY, J. (1942). *Evolution: The Modern Synthesis*. New York: Harper.

IDSO, S. B. (1989). *Carbon Dioxide and Global Change: The Earth in Transition*. Tempe, Ariz.: IBR Press.

INTERGOVERNMENTAL PANEL ON CLIMATE CHANGE (1990). *Policymaker's Summary: Working Group III*. Geneva: World Meteorological Association and United Nations Environment Programme.

JACKSON, D., and S. STICH, eds. (1979). *The Recombinant DNA Debate*. Englewood Cliffs, NJ: Prentice-Hall.

JACKSON, F. (1998). *From Metaphysics to Ethics: A Defense of Conceptual Analysis*. Oxford: Oxford University Press.

JACOBS, J. (1961). *The Death and Life of Great American Cities*. New York: Vintage Books.

JAMIESON, D. (1983a). "Animal Rights and Human Morality". *Ethics and Animals*, 4: 13–18.

——(1983b). "Killing Persons and Other Beings". In Miller and Williams (1983): 135–46.

JAMIESON, D. (1988a). "The Artificial Heart: Reevaluating the Investment". In D. Mathieu, *Organ Substitution Technology*. Boulder. Colo.: Westview: 277–96.

—— (1988b). "Grappling for a Glimpse of the Future". In M. Glantz, *Societal Responses to Regional Climatic Change*. Boulder, Colo.: Westview Press: 73–93.

—— (1990). "Managing the Future: Public Policy, Scientific Uncertainty, and Global Warming". In D. Scherer, *Upstream/Downstream: Essays in Environmental Ethics*. Philadelphia: Temple University Press: 67–89.

—— (1991a). "Method and Moral Theory". In Singer (1991): 476–87.

—— (1991b). "The Poverty of Postmodernist Theory". *University of Colorado Law Review*, 62: 577–95.

—— (1991c). "The Epistemology of Climate Change: Some Morals for Managers". *Society and Natural Resources*, 4: 319–29.

—— (1992). "From Baghdad to Rio: Reflections on Environmental Values and Behavior". unpublished paper.

—— (1993). "Ethics and Animals: A Brief Review". *Journal of Agricultural & Environmental Ethics*, 6 (special suppl. 1): 15–20.

—— (1994). "Ziff on Shooting an Elephant". In D. Jamieson, *Language, Mind, and Art: Essays in Appreciation and Analysis, in Honor of Paul Ziff*. Dordrecht: Kluwer: 121–9.

—— (1995a). "Wildlife Conservation and Individual Animal Welfare". In Norton *et al.* (1995): 69–73.

—— (1995b). "What Society Will Expect from the Future Research Community". *Science and Engineering Ethics*, 1: 73–80.

—— (1996a). "Scientific Uncertainty: How do we Know When to Communicate Research Findings to the Public?" *The Science of the Total Environment*, 184 (May): 103–7.

—— (1996b). "Scientific Uncertainty and the Political Process". *The Annals of The American Academy of Political and Social Science*, 545 (May): 35–43.

—— (1999a). "Singer and the Practical Ethics Movement". In D. Jamieson, *Singer and His Critics*. Oxford: Basil Blackwell: 1–17.

—— (1999b). "Prediction in Society". In D. Sarewitz, R. A. Pielke Jr., and R. Byerly Jr, *Prediction: Decision-Making and the Future of Nature*. Washington: Island Press: 315–25.

—— ed. (2001a). *A Companion to Environmental Philosophy*. Oxford: Blackwell Publishers.

—— (2001b). "Climate Change and Global Environmental Justice". In P. Edwards and C. Miller, *Changing the Atmosphere: Expert Knowledge and Global Environmental Governance*. Cambridge, Mass.: MIT Press: 287–307.

—— (forthcoming a). "Consequentialism". In D. Gobaisi (ed.), *The Encyclopedia of Life Support Systems*. Published by EOLSS for UNESCO.

—— (forthcoming b). "Is There Progress in Morality?" *Utilitas*.

—— and M. BEKOFF (1992). "Carruthers on Nonconscious Experience". *Analysis*, 52/1: 23–7.

—— and T. REGAN (1985). "Whales are not Cetacean Resources". In M. W. Fox and L.

Mackely, *Advances in Animal Welfare Science, 1984*. The Hague: Martinus Nijhoff: 101–11.

——and J. SNEED (1983). "What is Quality of Life?" Boulder, Colo.: Center for the Study of Values and Social Policy, University of Colorado.

——and K. VANDERWERF (1993) "Cultural Barriers to Behavior Change: General Recommendations and Resources for State Pollution Prevention Programs, A Report to US EPA". Boulder, Colo.: Center for Values and Social Policy, University of Colorado.

————(1995). "Preventing Pollution: Perspectives on Cultural Barriers and Facilitators, A Report to US EPA". Boulder, Colo.: Center for Values and Social Policy, University of Colorado.

JEFFERSON, T. (1964), *Notes on the State of Virginia*. New York: Harper and Row.

JENNINGS, H. S. (1906). *Behavior of Lower Organisms*. New York: Columbia University Press.

JOHNSON, E. (1981). "Animal Liberation versus the Land Ethic". *Environmental Ethics*, 3/3: 265–73.

JOHNSON, L. E. (1991). *A Morally Deep World: An Essay on Moral Significance and Environmental Ethics*. New York: Cambridge University Press.

JOHNSTON, M. (1992). "Reasons and Reductionism". *The Philosophical Review*, 101/3: 589–618.

——(1993). "Objectivity Refigured: Pragmatism without Verificationism". In J. Haldane and C. Wright, *Reality, Representation, and Projection*. New York: Oxford University Press.

KANT, I. (1795/1963). "Perpetual Peace". In Beck (1963): 85–135.

——(1798/1963). "An Old Question Raised Again: Is the Human Race Constantly Progressing?" In Beck (1963): 137–54.

——(1930/1980). *Lectures on Ethics*, trans. L. Infield. Indianapolis: Hackett Publishing Co.

KEELEY, L. H. (1996). *War before Civilisation*. New York: Oxford University Press.

KEMPTON, W. (1991). "Public Understanding of Global Warming". *Society and Natural Resources*, 4: 331–45.

KENNEDY, J. S. (1992). *The New Anthropomorphism*. Cambridge: Cambridge University Press.

KENNEY, S. P., and R. L. KNIGHT (1992). "Flight Distances of Black-Billed Magpies in Different Regimes of Human Density and Persecution". *The Condor*, 94: 545–7.

KESSLER, R., and C. HARTMAN (1973). "The Illusion and the Reality of Urban Renewal: A Case Study of San Francisco's Yerba Buena Center". *Land Economics*, 49/4: 440–53.

KEYES, R., ed. (1996). *The Wit & Wisdom of Oscar Wilde*. New York: HarperCollins.

KIM, J. (1984/1993). "Concepts of Supervenience". In J. Kim, *Supervenience and Mind: Selected Philosophical Essays*. Cambridge: Cambridge University Press: 53–78.

——(1999). "Making Sense of Emergence". *Philosophical Studies*, 95/1–2: 3–36.

KINKEL, L. L. (1989). "Lasting Effects of Wing Tags on Ring-Billed Gulls". *Auk*, 106: 619–24.

KIRKWOOD, J. K., A. W. SAINSBURY, and P. M. BENNETT (1994). "The Welfare of Free-Living Animals: Methods of Assessment". *Animal Welfare*, 3: 257–73.

KORSGAARD, C. M. (1996a). *Creating the Kingdom of Ends*. Cambridge: Cambridge University Press.

—— (1996b). *The Sources of Normativity*. New York: Cambridge University Press.

KORTLANDT, A. (1954). "Cosmologie der Dieren Een Nieuw Veld van Onderzoek". *Overdruk ait Vakblad noor Biologen, Vier-en-Dertigste*, 1: 1–14.

KOTHARI, R. (1994). "Environment, Technology, and Ethics". In Gruen and Jamieson, (1994): 228–37.

KRECH III, S. (1999). *The Ecological Indian: Myth and History*. New York: W. W. Norton & Co.

KREEGER, R. J., P. J. WHITE, U. S. SEAL, and J. R. TESTER (1990). "Pathological Responses of Red Foxes to Foothold Traps". *Journal of Wildlife Management*, 54: 147–60.

KUHN, T. (1970). *The Structure of Scientific Revolutions*. Chicago: University of Chicago Press.

LAFOLLETTE, H. (1980). "Licensing Parents". *Philosophy and Public Affairs*, 9: 182–97.

LANEGRAM, D. A. (2000). "Minnesota: Nature's Playground". *Daedalus*, 129/3: 81–100.

LASCH, C. (1991). *The True and Only Heaven: Progress and its Critics*. New York: W. W. Norton and Company.

LAUDAN, L. (1977). *Progress and Its Problems*. Berkeley: University of California Press.

LAURENSON, M. K., and T. M. CARO (1994). "Monitoring the Effects of Non-Trivial Handling in Free-Living Cheetahs". *Animal Behavior*, 3: 547–57.

LEAHY, M. (1991). *Against Liberation: Putting Animals in Perspective*. New York: Routledge.

LEE, K. (1989). *Social Philosophy and Ecological Scarcity*. New York: Routledge.

—— (1996). "The Source and Locus of Intrinsic Value". *Environmental Ethics*, 18/3: 297–309.

LEOPOLD, A. (1949). *A Sand County Almanac*. Oxford: Oxford University Press.

LESLIE, A. (1990). "Pretence, Autism and the Basis of 'Theory of Mind'". *Psychologist*, 3: 120–3.

LEVINE, R. (1978). *Pharmacology: Drug Actions and Reactions*. New York: Little, Brown.

LEWIS, C. S. (1947). *The Abolition of Man*. New York: Macmillan.

—— (1971). "Vivisection". In W. Hooper, *Undeceptions*. London: Geoffrey Blass.

LEWIS, D. (1989). "Dispositional Theories of Value". *Proceedings of the Aristotelian Society*, suppl. vol. 63: 113–37.

—— (1999). *Papers in Metaphysics and Epistemology*. New York: Cambridge University Press.

LILLA, M. (1981). "Ethos, 'Ethics', and Public Service". *Public Interest*, 63: 3–17.

LINEBAUGH, P., and M. REDIKER (2001). *The Many-Headed Hydra: Sailors, Slaves, Commoners, and the Hidden History of the Revolutionary Atlantic*. Boston: Beacon Press.

LONG, D. (1964). "The Philosophical Concept of the Human Body". *Philosophical Review*, 73/3: 321–37.

Loosli, R. (1967). "Duplicate Testing and Reproducibility". In R. Regamey, W. Hennessen, D. Ikic, and J. Ungar, *International Symposium on Laboratory Animals*. Basel: S. Karger: 117–23.

Lorenz, K. (1988/1991). *Here Am I—Where Are You? The Behavior of the Greylag Goose.* New York: Harcourt, Brace, Jovanovich.

Louis Harris Associates (1978). *A Survey of Citizen Views and Concerns about Urban Life*. Washington: Department of Housing and Urban Development.

Lovelock, J. E. (1988). *The Ages of Gaia: A Biography of Our Living Earth*. New York: Norton.

Ludwig, D., R. Hilborn, and C. Walters (1993). "Uncertainty, Resource Exploitation, and Conservation: Lessons from History". *Science*, 260: 17.

Ludwig, E. G. (1981). "People at Zoos: A Sociological Approach". *International Journal for the Study of Animal Problems*, 2/6: 310–16.

Luntley, M. (1988). *Language, Logic and Experience*. LaSalle, Ill.: Open Court.

McCord, G., ed. (1988). *Essays on Moral Realism*. Ithaca, NY: Cornell University Press.

McDowell, J. (1983). "Criteria, Defeasibility, and Knowledge". *Proceedings of the British Academy*, 68: 455–79.

McGiffin, H., and N. Brownley, eds. (1980). *Animals in Education: The Use of Animals in High School Biology Classes and Science Fairs*. Washington: Institute for the Study of Animal Problems.

McIntyre, J., ed. (1974). *Mind in the Waters*. New York: Charles Scribner's Sons.

McKenzie, A. A. (1989). "Humane Modification of Steel Foothold Traps". *South African Journal of Wildlife Research*, 19: 53–6.

McKibben, B. (1989). *The End of Nature*. New York: Random House.

—— (1993). *The Age of Missing Information*. New York: Plume.

—— (1998). *Maybe One: A Personal and Environmental Argument for Single Child Families*. New York: Simon and Schuster.

Mackie, J. L. (1977). *Ethics: Inventing Right and Wrong*. Harmondsworth: Penguin Books.

McLelland, G., and J. Rohrbaugh (1978). "Who Accepts the Pareto Axiom? The Role of Utility and Equity in Arbitration Decisions". *Behavioral Science*, 23: 446–56.

Magalhaes, H., ed. (1974). *Environmental Variables in Animal Experimentation*. New Jersey: Associated University Presses, Inc.

Major, R. E. (1990). "The Effect of Human Observers on the Intensity of Nest Predation". *Ibis*, 132: 608–12.

Mansbridge, J., ed. (1990). *Beyond Self Interest*. Chicago: University of Chicago Press.

Marr, D. (1982). *Vision*. San Francisco: Freeman.

Martin, C. (1978). *Keepers of the Game: Indian–Animal Relationships and the Fur Trade*. Berkeley: University of California Press.

Mason, W. (1986). "Behavior Implies Cognition". In W. Bechtel, *Integrating Scientific Disciplines*. Boston: Kluwer: 297–307.

Matthews, G. (1978). "Animals and the Unity of Psychology". *Philosophy*, 53: 437–54.

May, R. (1990). "Taxonomy as Destiny". *Nature*, 347: 129–30.

MAYO, D. (1983). "Against a Scientific Justification of Animal Experiments". In Miller, and Williams (1983): 339–59.

MAYR, E. (1991). *One Long Argument: Charles Darwin and the Genesis of Modern Evolutionary Thought*. Cambridge, Mass.: Harvard University Press.

MERLEAU-PONTY, M. (1962). *Phenomenology of Perception*. London: Routledge & Kegan Paul.

MILL, J. S. (1863/1993). *Utilitarianism, On Liberty, Considerations on Representative Government*. London: J. M. Dent.

——(1865/1884). *An Examination of Sir William Hamilton's Philosophy*. New York: Henry Holt.

MILLAR, A. (1996). "The Idea of Experience". *Proceedings of the Aristotelian Society*, 96: 75–90.

MILLER, H., and W. WILLIAMS (1983). *Ethics and Animals*. Clifton, NJ: Humana Press.

MITCHELL, R. (1990). "A Theory of Play". In Bekoff and Jamieson (1990), vol. i: 197–227.

——and N. THOMPSON, eds. (1986). *Deception: Perspectives on Human and Nonhuman Deceit*. Albany, NY: SUNY Press.

MONTALI, R., and M. BUSH (1982). "A Search for Animal Models at Zoos". *ILAR News*, 26/1 (Fall).

MONTGOMERY, S. (1991). *Walking with the Great Apes*. Boston: Houghton Mifflin Company.

MOODY-ADAMS, M. M. (1997). *Fieldwork in Familiar Places: Morality, Culture, and Philosophy*. Cambridge, Mass.: Harvard University Press.

——(1999). "The Idea of Moral Progress". *Metaphilosophy*, 30/3: 168–85.

MOOMAW, W. R. (1988/1989). "Near-Term Congressional Options for Responding to Global Climate Change". In D. E. Abrahamson, *The Challenge of Global Warming*. Washington: Island: 305–26.

MOORE, G. E. (1903). *Principia Ethica*. Cambridge: Cambridge University Press.

——(1922). "The Concept of Intrinsic Value". In G. E. Moore, *Philosophical Studies*. London: Routledge & Kegan Paul.

MORGAN, L. (1894). *Introduction to Comparative Psychology*. London: Scott.

MOSS, T. (1984). "Modern Politics of Laboratory Animal Use". *Science, Technology, and Human Values*, 9: 51–6.

MUIR, J. (1994). "Anthropocentrism and Predation". In Gruen and Jamieson (1994): 23–5.

MYERS, M. L. (1983). *The Soul of Modern Economic Man*. Chicago: University of Chicago Press.

NAESS, A. (1973). "The Shallow and the Deep, Long-Range Ecology Movements". *Inquiry*, 16/1: 95–100.

NAGEL, T. (1970). *The Possibility of Altruism*. New York: Oxford University Press.

——(1974). "What is it Like to be a Bat?" *Philosophical Review*, 83: 435–50.

——(1979). *Mortal Questions*. New York: Cambridge University Press.

——(1986). *The View From Nowhere*. New York: Oxford University Press.

NASH, R. (1967/2001). *Wilderness and the American Mind*. New Haven: Yale University Press.

NATIONAL ACADEMY OF SCIENCES/NATIONAL RESEARCH COUNCIL (1983). *Changing Climate*. Washington: National Academy Press.

NISBET, R. (1980). *History of the Idea of Progress*. New York: Basic Books.

NOBLE, C. (1982). "Ethics and Experts". *Hastings Center Report*, 12/3: 7–15.

NORDHAUS, W. (1990). "To Slow or not to Slow. The Economics of the Greenhouse Effect". New Orleans: American Association for the Advancement of Science.

NORRIS, K., ed. (1966). *Whales, Dolphins and Porpoises*. Berkeley: University of California Press.

NORTON, B. G. (1995a). "Why I am Not a Nonanthropocentrist: Callicott and the Failure of Monistic Inherentism". *Environmental Ethics*, 17/4: 341–58.

——(1995b). "Caring for Nature: A Broader Look at Animal Stewardship". In Norton et al. (1995): 102–21.

——M. HUTCHINS, E. F. STEVENS, and T. L. MAPLE, eds. (1995). *Ethics on the Ark: Zoos, Animal Welfare, and Wildlife Conservation*. Washington: Smithsonian Institution Press.

NOZICK, R. (1974). *Anarchy, State and Utopia*. New York: Basic Books.

——(2001). *Invariances: The Structure of the Objective World*. Cambridge, Mass.: Harvard University Press.

O'BRIEN, S. J., and E. MAYR (1991). "Bureaucratic Mischief: Recognizing Endangered Species and Subspecies". *Science*, 251: 1187–8.

OLSEN, G. H., S. B. LINHART, R. A. HOLMES, G. J. DASH, and C. B. MALE (1986). "Injuries to Coyotes Caught in Padded and Unpadded Steel Foothold Traps". *Wildlife Society Bulletin*, 14: 219–23.

——R. G. LINSCOMBE, V. L. WRIGHT, and R. A. HOLMES (1988). "Reducing Injuries to Terrestrial Furbearers by Using Padded Foothold Traps". *Wildlife Society Bulletin*, 16: 303–7.

O'NEILL, J. (1993). *Ecology, Policy and Politics: Human Well-Being and the Natural World*. London: Routledge.

——(2001). "Meta-ethics". In Jamieson (2001a): 163–76.

O'NEILL, O. (1991). "Kantian Ethics". In Singer (1991): 175–85.

OPP, K.-D. (1989). *The Rationality of Political Protest*. Boulder, Colo.: Westview.

PÄÄBO, S. (2001). "The Human Genome and Our View of Ourselves". *Science*, 291: 1219–20.

PAPINEAU, D. (1993). *Philosophical Naturalism*. Oxford: Blackwell.

PARFIT, D. (1984). *Reasons and Persons*. Oxford: Oxford University Press.

PASSMORE, J. (1974). *Man's Responsibility For Nature: Ecological Problems and Western Traditions*. New York: Scribner's.

PAULY, P. (1987). *Controlling Life: Jacques Loeb and the Engineering Ideal in Biology*. Berkeley: University of California Press.

PAYER, L. (1988). *Medicine and Culture*. New York: Penguin Books.

PEARCE, D. (1993). *Economic Value and the Natural World*. London: Earthscan.

PENCE, G. (1991). "Virtue Theory". In Singer (1991): 249–58.

PETERSON, D. (1989). *The Deluge and the Ark: A Journey in Primate Worlds*. Boston: Houghton Mifflin.

PETTIT, P. (1991). "Consequentialism". In Singer (1991): 230–40.

PEZZEY, J. (1992). "Sustainability: An Interdisciplinary Guide". *Environmental Values*, 1: 321–62.

PHILIPS, M., and S. AUSTAD (1990/1996). "Animal Communication and Social Evolution". In Bekoff and Jamieson (1996b): 257–67.

PIETZ, P. J., G. L. KRAPU, R. J. GREENWOOD, and J. T. LOKEMOEN (1993). "Effects of Harness Transmitters on Behavior and Reproduction of Wild Mallard". *Journal of Wildlife Management*, 57: 696–703.

POE, E. A. (1978). "Mellonta Tauta". In T. Mabbott, *Collected Works of Edgar Allan Poe*, vol. iii. Cambridge, Mass.: Harvard University Press.

POGGE, T. W. (1989). *Realizing Rawls*. Ithaca, NY: Cornell University Press.

POPULATION REFERENCE BUREAU (1976). *1976 World Population Data Sheet*. Washington.

POSNER, R. A. (1981). *The Economics of Justice*. Cambridge, Mass.: Harvard University Press.

PURTON, A. (1978). "Ethological Categories of Behavior and Some Consequences of their Conflation". *Animal Behavior*, 26: 653–70.

PUTNAM, H. (1960/1975). "Minds and Machines". In H. Putnam, *Mind, Language and Reality, Philosophical Papers*, vol. ii. New York: Cambridge University Press: 362–85.

QUINE, W. O. (1951/1961). "Two Dogmas of Empiricism". In Quine (1961): 20–46.

—— (1960/1975). *Word and Object*. Cambridge, Mass.: MIT Press.

—— (1961). *From a Logical Point of View*. New York: Harper.

RABINOWICZ, W., and T. RÖNNOW-RASMUSSEN (2000). "A Distinction in Value: Intrinsic and for its Own Sake". *Proceedings of the Aristotelian Society*, New Series, 100: 33–51.

RABINOWITZ, A. (1986). *Jaguar, Struggle and Triumph in the Jungles of Belize*. New York: Arbor.

RACHELS, J. (1976/1989). "Do Animals Have a Right to Liberty?" In T. Regan and P. Singer, *Animal Rights and Human Obligations*. Englewood Cliffs, NJ: Prentice-Hall: 122–31.

—— (1990). *Created from Animals: The Moral Implications of Darwinism*. New York: Oxford University Press.

RADNER, D., and M. RADNER (1989). *Animal Consciousness*. Buffalo: Prometheus Books.

RAILTON, P. (1986). "Moral Realism". *Philosophical Review*, 95: 163–207.

RALLS, K., K. BRUGGER, and J. BALLOU (1979). "Inbreeding and Juvenile Mortality in Small Populations of Ungulates". *Science*, 206: 1101–3.

RAMPHAL, S. (1992). *Our Country, The Planet: Forging a Partnership for Survival*. Washington: Island Press.

RAUDZENS, G., ed. (2001). *Technology, Disease and Colonial Conquests, Sixteenth to Eighteenth Centuries*. Boston: Brill.

RAWLS, J. (1971). *A Theory of Justice*. Cambridge, Mass.: Harvard University Press.

REDCLIFT, M. (1987). *Sustainable Development: Exploring the Contradictions*. London: Methuen.

REGAN, T. (1975). "The Moral Basis of Vegetarianism". *Canadian Journal of Philosophy*: 5: 181–214.

—— (1980). "Cruelty, Kindness and Unnecessary Suffering". *Philosophy*, 55/214.

—— (1981). "The Nature and Possibility of an Environmental Ethic". *Environmental Ethics, 3: 19–34.*

—— (1983). *The Case for Animal Rights*. Berkeley: University of California Press.

REICH, R., ed. (1988). *The Power of Public Ideas*. Cambridge, Mass.: Harvard University Press.

RICHARDS, J., ed. (1978). *Recombinant DNA: Science, Ethics and Politics*. New York: Academic Press.

RICHARDS, R. (1987). *Darwin and the Emergence of Evolutionary Theories of Mind and Behavior*. Chicago: University of Chicago Press.

RIFKIN, J. (1992). *Beyond Beef*. New York: Penguin Books.

RISTAU, C., ed. (1991). *Cognitive Ethology: The Minds of Other Animals*. Hillsdale, NJ: Erlbaum.

RODD, R. (1990). *Biology, Ethics, and Animals*. Oxford: Oxford University Press.

ROJAS, M. (1992). "The Species Problem and Conservation: What are we Protecting?" *Conservation Biology*, 6: 170–8.

ROLLIN, B. (1981). *Animal Rights and Human Morality*. Buffalo: Prometheus Books.

—— (1989). *The Unheeded Cry: Animal Consciousness, Animal Pain and Science*. New York: Oxford University Press.

ROLSTON III, H. (1975). "Is There an Ecological Ethic?" *Ethics*, 85/1: 93–109.

—— (1982). "Are Values in Nature Subjective or Objective?" *Environmental Ethics*, 4: 125–51.

—— (1988). *Environmental Ethics, Duties to and Values in the Natural World*. Philadelphia: Temple University Press.

—— (1992). "The Wilderness Idea Affirmed". *The Environmental Professional*, 13/4: 370–7.

RORTY, R. (1993/1998). "Human Rights, Rationality, and Sentimentality". In R. Rorty, *Truth and Progress: Philosophical Papers*, vol. iii. New York: Cambridge University Press: 167–85.

—— (1994/1998). "Feminism and Pragmatism". In R. Rorty, *Truth and Progress: Philosophical Papers*, vol. iii. New York: Cambridge University Press: 202–27.

ROSENFIELD, L. (1968). *From Animal Machine to Beast Machine*. New York: Octagon Books.

ROSENTHAL, D., ed. (1991). *The Nature of Mind*. New York: Oxford University Press.

ROSENTHAL, S., and R. MILLICAN (1954). "The Role of Fluids, Electrolytes and Plasma Proteins in Experimental Traumatic Shock and Hemorrhage". *Pharmacological Reviews*, 6: 489–520.

ROSENZWEIG, M. (1990). "Do Animals Choose Habitats?" In Bekoff and Jamieson (1996b: 185–99).

ROSS, M. (1978). "The Ethics of Animal Experimentation: Control in Practice". *Australian Psychologist*, 13: 375 ff.

ROSZAK, T., ed. (1972). *Sources*. New York: Harper and Row.

ROUTLEY, R. (1973). *Is There a Need for a New, an Environmental Ethics?* Proceedings of the XV World Congress of Philosophy, Varna, Bulgaria.

—— and V. ROUTLEY (1980). "Human Chauvinism and Environmental Ethics". In D. Mannison, M. McRobbie, and R. Routley, *Environmental Philosophy*. Canberra: Australian National University: 96–189.

ROWAN, A. (1980). *Alternatives to Laboratory Animals: Definition and Discussion*. Washington: The Institute for the Study of Animal Problems.

—— (1984). *Of Mice, Models, and Men*. Albany, NY: SUNY Press.

ROYCE, J. (1908a). *The Philosophy of Loyalty*. New York: Macmillan Company.

—— (1908b). *Race Questions, Provincialism and Other American Problems*. New York: Macmillan Company.

RUSE, M. (1991). "The Significance of Evolution". In Singer (1991): 500–10.

RUSSELL, B. (1921). *The Analysis of Mind*. London: Unwin, Human Limited.

RYDER, R. (1975). *Victims of Science*. London: Davis-Poynter.

SACHS, W., ed. (1993). *Global Ecology: A New Arena of Political Conflict*. London: Zed Books.

SACKS, O. W. (1995). *An Anthropologist on Mars: Seven Paradoxical Tales*. New York: Knopf.

SAGOFF, M. (1984/1993). "Animal Liberation and Environmental Ethics: Bad Marriage, Quick Divorce". In Zimmerman *et al.* (1993): 84–94.

—— (1988). *The Economy of the Earth*. New York: Cambridge University Press.

SALEM, D. J., and A. ROWAN, eds. (2001). *The State of the Animals 2001*. Washington: Humane Society of the United States.

SAMUELSON, P. A. (1976). *Economics*. New York: McGraw-Hill Book Company.

SAVAGE-RUMBAUGH, S., and K. BRAKKE (1990). "Animal Language: Methodological and Interpretive Issues". In Bekoff and Jamieson (1996b): 269–88.

SCANLON, T. (1982). "Contractualism and Utilitarianism". In Sen and Williams (1982): 103–28.

SCHALLER, G. B. (1993). *The Last Panda*. Chicago: University of Chicago Press.

SCHELER, M. (1954). *The Nature of Sympathy*. London: Routledge & Kegan Paul.

SCHNEIDER, S. H. (1989). *Global Warming: Are We Entering the Greenhouse Century?* San Francisco: Sierra Club Books.

SCHUMACHER, E. F. (1973). *Small is Beautiful: Economics as if People Mattered*. New York: Harper Perennial.

SCITOVSKY, T. (1976). *The Joyless Economy: An Inquiry into Human Satisfaction and Consumer Dissatisfaction*. New York: Oxford University Press.

SEARLE, J. (1983). *Intentionality: An Essay in the Philosophy of Mind*. New York: Cambridge University Press.

—— (1992). *The Rediscovery of the Mind*. Cambridge, Mass.: MIT Press.

—— (1994). "Animal Minds". In P. French, T. Uehling, and H. Wettstein, *Midwest Studies in Philosophy*, vol. xix: *Philosophical Naturalism*. Notre Dame, Ind.: University of Notre Dame Press: 206–19.

SEN, A., and B. WILLIAMS, eds. (1982). *Utilitarianism and Beyond*. Cambridge: Cambridge University Press.

SHOEMAKER, S. (1975). "The Problem of Other Minds". In J. Feinberg, *Reason and Responsibility*. Encino, Calif.: Dickenson Publishing Co.: 213–29.

——(1994). "Self-Knowledge and 'Inner Sense'". *Philosophy and Phenomenological Research*, 54/2: 249–314.

SHRADER-FRECHETTE, K. S., and E. D. MCCOY (1994). *Method in Ecology: Strategies for Conservation*. New York: Cambridge University Press.

SIDGWICK, H. (1907/1981). *The Methods of Ethics*, 7th edn. Indianapolis: Hackett Publishing Co.

SILVERMAN, S. (1994). "Process and Detection in Fraud and Deceit". *Ethics and Behavior*, 4: 219–29.

SINGER, P. (1972a). "Famine, Affluence and Morality". *Philosophy and Public Affairs*, 1/3: 229–43.

——(1972b). "Moral Experts". *Analysis*, 32: 115–17.

——(1973). "Animal Liberation". *New York Review of Books* (5 Apr.).

——(1974). "Philosophers Are Back on the Job". *New York Times Magazine* (7 July).

——(1975/2001). *Animal Liberation*. New York: Ecco Press Books.

——(1979/1993). *Practical Ethics*. Cambridge: Cambridge University Press.

——(1981). *The Expanding Circle: Ethics and Sociobiology*. New York: The New American Library.

——ed. (1985). *In Defense of Animals*. Oxford: Basil Blackwell.

——ed. (1991). *A Companion to Ethics*. Oxford: Basil Blackwell.

——(1998). *Ethics into Action: Henry Spira and the Animal Rights Movement*. Lantham, Md.: Rowman and Littlefield.

SKINNER, B. F. (1953). *Science and Human Behavior*. New York: The Macmillan Company.

SLOVIC, P. (1993). "Perceived Risk, Trust, and Democracy". *Risk Analysis*, 13/6: 65–82.

SMALL, R. J., and L. B. KEITH (1992). "An Experimental Study of Red Fox Predation on Arctic and Snowshoe Hares". *Canadian Journal of Zoology*, 70: 1614–21.

SMITH, K. (1998). "Storytelling, Sympathy and Moral Judgement in American Abolitionism". *The Journal of Political Philosophy*, 6/4: 356–77.

SMITH, M. (1991). "Realism". In Singer (1991): 399–410.

SMITH, W. (1990/1996). "Communication and Expectations: A Social Process and the Cognitive Operations it Depends upon and Influences". In Bekoff and Jamieson (1996b): 234–53.

——(1991). "Animal Communication and the Study of Cognition". In Ristau (1991): 209–30.

SMYTH, D. H. (1978). *Alternatives to Animal Experiments*. London: Scholar Press.

SOBER, E., and D. S. WILSON (1998). *Unto Others: The Evolution and Psychology of Unselfish Behavior*. Cambridge, Mass.: Harvard University Press.

SORABJI, R. (1993). *Animal Minds and Human Morals*. Ithaca, NY: Cornell University Press.

SOULÉ, M. E. (1990). "The Onslaught of Alien Species, and Other Challenges in the Coming Decades". *Conservation Biology*, 4: 233–9.

SPIER, R. (2000). "A Response to Jamieson's 'Discourse and Moral Responsibility in Biotechnical Communication'". *Science and Engineering Ethic*, 6/2 (Apr.): 279–85.

——ed. (2001). *Science and Technology Ethics*. New York: Routledge.

STANNARD, D. (1992). *American Holocaust*. New York: Oxford University Press.

STONE, C. (1974). *Should Trees Have Standing?* Los Altos, Calif.: William Kaufman.

STRAWSON, P. F. (1985). *Skepticism and Naturalism: Some Varieties*. New York: Columbia University Press.

SWAZEY, J. P., M. S. ANDERSON, and K. S. LOUIS (1993). "Ethical Problems in Academic Research". *American Scientist*, 81: 542–53.

TAYLOR, P. (1986). *Respect for Nature: A Theory of Environmental Ethics*. Princeton: Princeton University Press.

TEMKIN, L. (1993). *Inequality*. New York: Oxford University Press.

THOMAS, K. (1983). *Man and the Natural World: A History of the Modern Sensibility*. New York: Pantheon Books.

THOREAU, H. D. (1906). *The Writings of H. D. Thoreau*, vol. ix. Boston: Houghton, Mifflin, and Company.

TINBERGEN, N. (1951). *The Study of Instinct*. Oxford: Oxford University Press.

——(1963). "On Aims and Methods of Ethology". *Zeitschrift fur Tierpsychologie*, 20: 410–29.

TOOLEY, M. (1973). "A Defense of Abortion and Infanticide". In J. Feinberg, *The Problem of Abortion*. Belmont, Calif.: Wadsworth: 51–91.

TRAVAINI, A., F. PALOMARES, and M. DELIBES (1993). "The Effects of Capture and Recapture on Space Use in Large Grey Mongooses". *South African Journal of Wildlife Research*, 23: 95–7.

TUAN, Y.-F. (1989). *Morality and Imagination: Paradoxes of Progress*. Madison: The University of Wisconsin Press.

TURNER, R. K., P. DOKTOR, and N. ADGER (1995). "Sea-Level Rise and Coastal Wetlands in the UK: Mitigation Strategies for Sustainable Management". In A. Jansson, M. Hammer, C. Folkc, and R. Costanza, *Investing in Natural Capital*. Washington: Island Press: 266–90.

UNITED NATIONS GENERAL ASSEMBLY (1974). *Declaration on the Establishment of a New International Economic Order*. New York: Official Records: Sixth Special Session.

US DEPARTMENT OF HEALTH, EDUCATION AND WELFARE (1980). *Asbestos Exposure*. Washington: National Cancer Institute.

US DEPARTMENT OF HOUSING AND URBAN DEVELOPMENT (1978). *The President's National Urban Policy Report*. Washington: US Government Printing Office.

VANE-WRIGHT, R., C. HUMPHRIES, and P. WILLIAMS (1991). "What to Protect? Systematics and the Agony of Choice". *Biological Conservation*, 55: 235–54.

VARNER, G. (1995). "Can Animal Rights Activists be Environmentalists?" In C. Pierce and D. VanDeVeer, *People, Penguins, and Plastic Trees*. Belmont, Calif.: Wadsworth: 254–73.

——and M. MONROE (1990). "Ethical Perspectives on Captive Breeding: Is it for the Birds?" *Endangered Species Update*, 8: 27–9.

VISSCHER, M. (1982). "Review of Rollin". *New England Journal of Medicine*, 306: 1303–4.

WARNOCK, G. J. (1971). *The Object of Morality*. New York: Methuen.

WATSON, J. B. (1930). *Behaviorism*. Chicago: The University of Chicago Press.

WATSON, J. D. (1968). *The Double Helix*. New York: Atheneum.

WEBBER, M. M. (1968). "The Post-City Age". *Daedalus*: 1091–110.

WEIL, M., and R. SCALA (1971). "A Study of Intra- and Interlaboratory Variability in the Results of Rabbit Eye and Skin Irritation Tests". *Toxicology and Applied Pharmacology*, 19: 276–360.

WERNER, H. (1948). *Comparative Psychology of Mental Development*. Chicago: Follett.

WERTHEIMER, R. (1971). "Understanding the Abortion Argument". *Philosophy and Public Affairs*, 1/1: 67–95.

WESTON, A. (1985). "Beyond Intrinsic Value: Pragmatism in Environmental Ethics". *Environmental Ethics*, 7: 321–39.

WHEELER, W. B., and M. J. McDONALD (1986). *TVA and the Tellico Dam, 1936–1979: A Bureaucratic Crisis in Post-Industrial America*. Knoxville, Tenn.: University of Tennessee Press.

WHITE, L., JR. (1967). "The Historical Roots of Our Ecological Crisis". *Science*, 155: 1203–7.

WHITE, R. J. (1971). "Antivivisection: The Reluctant Hydra". In T. Regan and P. Singer, *Animal Rights and Human Obligations*. Englewood Cliffs, NJ: Prentice-Hall: 163–9.

WHITE HOUSE COUNCIL OF ECONOMIC ADVISORS (1990). *The Economic Report of the President*. Washington: Executive Office of the President, Publication Services.

WHITT, L. A., M. ROBERTS, W. NORMAN, and V. GRIEVES (2001). "Indigenous Perspectives". In Jamieson (2001a): 3–20.

WIGGINS, D. (1998). *Needs, Values, Truth: Essays in the Philosophy of Value*. Oxford: Oxford University Press.

WIGGLESWORTH, V. B. (1980). "Do Insects Feel Pain?" *Antenna*, 4: 8–9.

WILDE, O. (1989). "The Decay of Lying: An Observation". *The Complete Works of Oscar Wilde*. New York: HarperCollins.

WILLIAMS, B. (1972). *Morality: An Introduction to Ethics*. New York: Harper & Row.

—— (1993). *Shame and Necessity*. Berkeley: University of California Press.

WILLIAMS, D. (1992). *Nobody Nowhere: The Extraordinary Autobiography of an Autistic*. New York: Avon Books.

WILSON, E. O. (1975). *Sociobiology: The New Synthesis*. Cambridge, Mass.: Harvard University Press.

—— (1984). *Biophilia*. Cambridge, Mass.: Harvard University Press.

WILSON, M. D. (1995/1999). "Animal Ideas". In M. D. Wilson, *Ideas and Mechanism: Essays on Early Modern Philosophy*. Princeton: Princeton University Press: 495–512.

WILSON, R. P., B. CULIK, R. DANFIELD, and D. ADELUNG (1991). "People in Antarctica— How Much do Adelie Penguins *Pygoscelis Adeliae* Care?" *Polar Biology*, 11: 363–70.

WINGO, L., JR., ed. (1963). *Cities and Space*. Baltimore: Johns Hopkins Press.

WITTGENSTEIN, L. (1970). *Zettel*. Berkeley: University of California Press.

—— (1980). *Remarks on the Philosophy of Psychology*. Oxford: Basil Blackwell.

WOLFE, A. (1989). *Whose Keeper? Social Science and Moral Obligation*. Berkeley: University of California Press.

—— (1991). "Up from Humanism". *American Prospect*, 2/4: 112–25.

WORLD CLIMATE PROGRAM (1985). "Report of the International Conference on the Assessment of the Role of Carbon Dioxide and of Other Greenhouse Gases in Climate Variations and Associated Impacts, Villach, Austria, 9–15 Oct. 1985". Geneva: World Meteorological Organization.

THE WORLD COMMISSION ON ENVIRONMENT and DEVELOPMENT (1987). *Our Common Future*. New York: Oxford University Press.

WORSTER, D. (1990). "The Ecology of Order and Chaos". *Environmental Review*, 14: 1–18.

—— (1993). "The Shaky Ground of Sustainability". In Sachs (1993): 132–45.

WRIGHT, F. L. (1958). *The Living City*. New York: Bramhall House.

WULFF, K., ed. (1979). *Regulation of Scientific Inquiry: Social Concerns with Research*. American Association for the Advancement of Science Selected Symposium no. 37. Boulder, Colo.: Westview Press.

WYNNE, B. (1992). "Uncertainty and Environmental Learning: Reconceiving Science and Policy in the Preventive Paradigm". *Global Environmental Change*, 2: 111–27.

YOERG, S. I. (1991). "Ecological Frames of Mind: The Role of Cognition in Behavioral Ecology". *Quarterly Review of Biology*, 66: 287–301.

ZIFF, P. (1960). *Semantic Analysis*. Ithaca, NY: Cornell University Press.

—— (1966). "The Simplicity of Other Minds". In P. Ziff, *Philosophic Turnings*. Ithaca, NY: Cornell University Press: 168–80.

—— (1970). *Understanding Understanding*. Ithaca, NY: Cornell University Press.

ZIMMERMAN, M. E., J. CALLICOTT, G. SESSIONS, K. J. WARREN, and J. CLARK, eds. (1993). *Environmental Philosophy: From Animal Rights to Radical Ecology*. Englewood-Cliffs, NJ: Prentice-Hall.

INDEX